# Deyohahá:ge:

# Indigenous Imaginings

Building on the important critical interventions of the Indigenous Studies Series under Deanna Reder's editorial tenure, Indigenous Imaginings publishes compelling interdisciplinary scholarship that takes seriously the visionary and grounded work of Indigenous thinkers, artists, and activists, centred in ethical engagement with Indigenous worldviews, sovereignties, philosophical frameworks, legal orders, and politics. We seek projects that expand and unsettle the boundaries of discipline, form, and method in the humanities and social sciences, with a particular emphasis on the literary and expressive arts. Books in the series challenge us to think in deeper and more complex ways about Indigenous peoples' intellectual, artistic, and cultural productions, histories, politics, and lived relations (both human and other-than-human), and to help us envision vibrant Indigenous futures beyond the settler colonial imaginary.

SERIES EDITOR
Daniel Heath Justice (Cherokee Nation / ᏣᎳᎩ ᎠᏰᎵ)
Canada Research Chair in Indigenous Literature and Expressive Culture
University of British Columbia

# Deyohahá:ge:

## Sharing the River of Life

DANIEL COLEMAN, KI'EN DEBICKI,
AND BONNIE M. FREEMAN, *editors*

This book has been published with the help of a grant from the Federation for the Humanities and Social Sciences, through the Awards to Scholarly Publications Program, using funds provided by the Social Sciences and Humanities Research Council of Canada. Wilfrid Laurier University Press acknowledges the support of the Canada Council for the Arts for our publishing program. We acknowledge the financial support of the Government of Canada through the Canada Book Fund for our publishing activities. Funding provided by the Government of Ontario and the Ontario Arts Council. This work was supported by the Research Support Fund.

LIBRARY AND ARCHIVES CANADA CATALOGUING IN PUBLICATION

Title: Deyohahá:ge: : sharing the river of life / Daniel Coleman, Ki'en Debicki, and Bonnie M. Freeman, editors.
Names: Coleman, Daniel, 1961– editor. | Debicki, Ki'en, editor. | Freeman, Bonnie M. (Bonnie Marie), 1962– editor.
Description: Series statement: Indigenous imaginings | Includes bibliographical references and index.
Identifiers: Canadiana (print) 2024036533X | Canadiana (ebook) 20240365550 | ISBN 9781771126472 (softcover) | ISBN 9781771126489 (EPUB) | ISBN 9781771126496 (PDF)
Subjects: LCSH: United States—Ethnic relations. | LCSH: Canada—Ethnic relations. | LCSH: Wampum belts—United States. | LCSH: Wampum belts—Canada. | LCSH: Reconciliation. | CSH: First Nations—Treaties.
Classification: LCC E77.2 .D49 2025 | DDC 305.897/071—dc23

Cover and interior design by Lara Minja, Lime Design.
Front cover image: #TAG mural project.

© 2025 Wilfrid Laurier University Press
Waterloo, Ontario, Canada
www.wlupress.wlu.ca

Every reasonable effort has been made to acquire permission for copyrighted material used in this text, and to acknowledge all such indebtedness accurately. Any errors and omissions called to the publisher's attention will be corrected in future printings.

No part of this publication may be reproduced, stored in a retrieval system, or transmitted, in any form or by any means, without the prior written consent of the publisher or a licence from the Canadian Copyright Licensing Agency (Access Copyright). For an Access Copyright licence, visit http://www.accesscopyright.ca or call toll-free to 1-800-893-5777.

Wilfrid Laurier University Press is located on the Haldimand Tract, part of the traditional territories of the Haudenosaunee, Anishnaabe, and Neutral Peoples. This land is part of the Dish with One Spoon Treaty between the Haudenosaunee and Anishnaabe Peoples and symbolizes the agreement to share, to protect our resources, and not to engage in conflict. We are grateful to the Indigenous Peoples who continue to care for and remain interconnected with this land. Through the work we publish in partnership with our authors, we seek to honour our local and larger community relationships, and to engage with the diversity of collective knowledge integral to responsible scholarly and cultural exchange.

# Contents

A Note on the Cover   xi

*Ohèn:ton Karihwatéhkwen:*
The Words That Come Before All Else   xiii
*Ki'en Debicki*

Acknowledgements, Greetings, and Thanks   xix

Introduction   3
*Daniel Coleman, Ki'en Debicki, and Bonnie M. Freeman*

# 1   Original Instructions

**CHAPTER ONE**
Gä•sweñta' Reflections   29
*Oren Lyons*

**CHAPTER TWO**
Where the Roots Touch: tsi niyothahinen ne Tehontatenentshonteronhtáhkwa   35
*Amber Meadow Adams*

**CHAPTER THREE**
*Wunnáumwash*: Wampum Justice   52
*Kelsey Leonard*

**CHAPTER FOUR**
The Chain, Naturally Understood   67
*Kayanesenh Paul Williams*

# 2 Learning from the River

**CHAPTER FIVE**
Guswenta Space: An Invitation to Dialogue   109
*David Newhouse*

**CHAPTER SIX**
Navigating the Two Row in the Academy   121
*Vanessa Watts*

**CHAPTER SEVEN**
Two Rows of Reconciliation   136
*Rick Hill*

**CHAPTER EIGHT**
Below Decks in the Covenant: Blackness in the Two Row Tradition   150
*Phanuel Antwi*

**CHAPTER NINE**
Towards Peace: Living in the Three White Rows of the Two Row   167
*Sara General*

## 3  Living on the River

**CHAPTER TEN**
The Pen Pal Project: Bridging the Divide with
the Teachings of the Two Row Wampum Treaty   189
*Suzie Miller and Scot Cooper*

**CHAPTER ELEVEN**
*Deyohahage Gihe gowa'hneh*: Living the
Two Row Wampum, on the Grand River   206
*Ellie Joseph and Jay Bailey*

**CHAPTER TWELVE**
The Deep and Rippling Consciousness of Water:
Youth Experiences of Transition with the Two Row
on the Grand River Paddle   221
*Bonnie M. Freeman and Trish van Katwyk*

Contributors   241

Glossary   247
*Taylor Leeal Gibson*

Notes   265

Bibliography   285

Index   297

# A Note on the Cover

*Adapted from* https://tagsix.net/blog/2018/7/10/what-is-tag

#TAG is an Indigenous-led research project infused with the spiritual power of dreamtime, includes elements of prophecy (the Eagle and the Condor), and follows a path of practice that the Spirit World or Ancestors governed. For some of our team, TAG was an experiment in faith and consent, learning to navigate the world according to Indigenous ways of knowing. We, the research team and the Youth Advisory Council, agreed to be the human vehicles bound by the Ancestral contract and used by the spiritual dimension of the Universe to manifest a message for humanity.

This was Indigenous research in practice, learning to trust ourselves, each other, and the unknown for direction and guidance. TAG was guided by the following questions: How do youth understand Indigenous identities in the context of Traditional Knowledge and arts-based practices? Does the cross-cultural Indigenous exchange of knowledge promote community health and/or assist in reconciliation? Do young people benefit from learning about Indigenous cultures from Indigenous Peoples?

The project involved young people (ages fourteen to twenty-four) from Six Nations and the Brantford area—half of the participants identified as Indigenous, while the other half identified as settlers or non-Indigenous people. Under our Youth Advisory Council's leadership, twenty-two young people participated in three days of workshops on Six Nations.

Over the three days, the youth participated in ceremonies, socials, dancing, art, and storytelling about Haudenosaunee, Métis, and Mapuche cultures, histories, and identities. During this period of experiential learning, the youth were encouraged to doodle and draw pictures and images that represented what they saw and heard. At the end of the workshops, the Alapinta muralists collected the youth's drawings and integrated their ideas into the two sister public art murals that were painted in Six Nations and Brantford in the proceeding three weeks.

The mural in Brantford featured the Two Row Wampum and the Claus Wampum Belt. It reminded us of the relationships and promises that Indigenous and non-Indigenous people had made, and it encouraged non-Indigenous people to be accountable to treaties and responsibilities—to uphold promises and to protect the land and water.

On October 1, 2016, we launched the murals with a community event in Six Nations where we feasted, played games, gave thanks, listened to DJs Shub and Krystal Riverz spin awesome beats, and felt gratitude for all the relationships we had built.

The #TAG final report (https://drive.google.com/file/d/1a6QH7k2DTApYgtAbJ-WqSFvBfjQYELUU/view) describes the second of these murals, the one featured on the cover of this book, as follows:

> This mural tells the story of the relationships between Indigenous and Non-Indigenous people as they travel down the river of life together. It includes the wampum treaties and tells the story of how we can respectfully move into the future together. It is a reminder of our obligations and responsibilities to one another.

# Ohèn:ton Karihwaténhkwen

## The Words That Come Before All Else

*Ki'en Debicki*

———

These past years, especially from 2020 to 2022, have been a period of incredible difficulty for the human world. For many, if not for most, it has been a time of fear, suffering, and isolation. Our minds and bodies have been laid out on the ground, and because visiting has become dangerous in the wake of COVID-19 with its requirements of quarantine and social distancing, we have not had each other to help us up off the floor, to remind us that there is still light in the world, and to wash away our tears. Yet, Haudenosaunee Knowledge, as it so often does, offers us insight into the pandemic.

Atsi'tsya'ka:yon, Sky Woman, saw her world ended and reborn. Alone in a new reality, she reached out and made a community with the nonhuman beings of what we now know as Earth. She made communion with muskrats, turtles, geese, and seeds. This was not her first time dealing with aloneness. *The Myth of the Earthgrasper*, a version of our creation recorded by Sotsisowah (John Mohawk), speaks of a practice called "downfending." As a girl in the Sky World, Atsi'tsya'ka:yon was separated from her people, from human community, to allow for a period of growth—both spiritual and physical—to occur in a protected environment. Her maturation unfolded on her own terms without coercion or the confusion of "shoulds." Her isolation also protected others from the power of her feminine divine, presumably until her own ability to impact the world became known to her. When she alit upon turtle's back, that feminine divine found its calling, and she rebirthed a world.

Well, friends, we have all collectively experienced downfending for the past two years. As we reach what is hopefully the end of the worst of the pandemic, let us turn our minds and our capacities to rebirth and to a connection with each other that will imagine into being a new world. Instructions on how to begin again have been left by ancestors like Atsi'tsya'ka:yon. First, renew relationships with nonhuman beings. Second, humbly ask for help. Third, honour those who offer themselves and their gifts in the process of creation. Fourth, plant the seeds of future generations.

The book in your hands is an effort to follow the tracks of those who have come before us, to follow original instructions. So, let us begin in the right way.

*Taiethinonhwera:ton ne onkwe'shon:'a. E'tho kati neniohtonhake ne onkwa'nikon:ra.*

We greet the human beings, all those people who are part of our lives, seen and unseen, who share their gifts for the good of all.

*Taiethinonhwera:ton ne iethi'nihstenha tsiohwentsia:te. E'tho kati neniohtonhake ne onkwa'nikon:ra.*

We greet with loving kindness, our Earth Mother, she who provides for all our needs and gives us a home, a ground, in the endless expanse of space.

*Taiethinonhwera:ton ne iothonton:ni. Kano:ta ne:'e konwatikowa:nen. E'tho kati neniohtonhake ne onkwa'nikon:ra.*

To the grass people, the plant nation, we give greetings and respect. You who are made of sunshine and dew and cradle our feet as we walk about the earth: we love you.

*Taiethinonhwera:ton ne wahianiiontha. Niiohontehsha ne:'e konwatikowa:nen. E'tho kati neniohtonhake ne onkwa'nikon:ra.*

To the hanging fruits, the berries and tree foods, we thank you. Sky Woman brought heart-berries from the spirit world and their medicine sustains us.

## OHÈN:TON KARIHWATÉHKWEN

*Taiethinonhwera:ton ne kahrharonnion. Ohwahtha ne:'e konwatikowa:nen. E'tho kati neniohtonhake ne onkwa'nikon:ra.*

To the tree nation, we send such love. You give us breath, shade, food, beauty, and health. You give us the paper upon which this book is printed. Maple is the leader, the first to wake in Spring; a practiced rebirther.

*Taiethinonhwera:ton ne kontirio. Oskenon:ton ne:'e konwatikowa:nen. E'tho kati neniohtonhake ne onkwa'nikon:ra.*

To the game animals, our elder kin, who have always shown us how to live well in this place, thank you. You give of yourselves so that we may live, may we never take you for granted.

*Taiethinonhwera:ton ne kahnekaronnion. Kaniatarake:ron ne:'e konwatikowa:nen. E'tho kati neniohtonhake ne onkwa'nikon:ra.*

To the waters everywhere, the lakes are the leaders. Let us give thanks to Kanyatarí:io, Lake Ontario, our life sustainer.

*Taiethinonhwera:ton ne tionhehkwen. O:nenhste, ohsahe:ta tahnon onon'onsera ne:'e konwatikowa:nen. E'tho kati neniohtonhake ne onkwa'nikon:ra.*

We give love and respect to our sustenance, the foods that keep us here. The three sisters lead us, ask us to remember how to live together.

*Taiethinonhwera:ton ne teiowerawenrie. E'tho kati neniohtonhake ne onkwa'nikon:ra.*

To the winds, the four directions, we thank you for the air we breathe, for clearing away pollution, for bringing new weather and change.

*Taiethinonhwera:ton ne iethisotho:kon ratiwe:ras. E'tho kati neniohtonhake ne onkwa'nikon:ra.*

To the thunderers who keep the dangers in the ground, we give love and respect. Thank you for keeping us humble, for keeping us safe. You remind us of the power of our inner spark.

*Tatshitewatenonhwera:ton ne etshitewahtsi:'a entiehke:ne karahkwa. E'tho kati neniohtonhake ne onkwa'nikon:ra.*

Elder Brother Sun, you give us light, colour, heat, vision, hope— such beauty. Without you nothing would grow, nothing would live. Every morning you follow your duty and remind us that we too must remember our original instructions.

*Taiethinonhwera:ton ne iethihsotha ahsonthennehkha wenhni:tare. E'tho kati neniohtonhake ne onkwa'nikon:ra.*

Our dear grandmother moon, thank you for regulating the waters, for watching over those of us who create new life. Your shine shows us the way through darkness and your beautiful face tells us we need not be perfect.

*Taiethinonhwera:ton ne iotsistohkwaronnion. E'tho kati neniohtonhake ne onkwa'nikon:ra.*

Star nation, thank you for connecting us, for giving us direction, and intergenerational knowledge. You remind us to grasp the knowledge of where we come from with both hands, and to look into the future and the past as we live our lives.

*Tatshitewatenonhwera:ton ne Skaniatari:io. E'tho kati neniohtonhake ne onkwa'nikon:ra.*

Handsome Lake, thank you for your part in restoring our practice of giving thanks. We know your journey was not easy, but you have given us much to reflect on about how our personal choices effect our spirits and our minds.

| | |
|---|---|
| *Taiethinonhwera:ton ne ratironhia'kehro:non teionkhiia:taton. E'tho kati neniohtonhake ne onkwa'nikon:ra.* | Guardians, thank you for watching over us, for being such good ancestors. May we take up your modeling and also be good ancestors for future generations. |
| *Tatshitewatenonhwera:ton ne Shonkwaia'tishon. E'tho kati neniohtonhake ne onkwa'nikon:ra.* | To the one who made our bodies, sculpted us from clay, and breathed our spirits to life, thank you. Your creations are so beautiful, this world has so much to offer, and you have placed our feet upon its soil. May we relearn to be kind humans in your original image. |
| | And that is how our minds are to be. |

# Acknowledgements, Greetings, and Thanks

We editors of this collection of essays would like to thank all the contributors to this book who offered their knowledge, experience, and wisdom to this project. We have learned so much from each of you! We also send our greetings and thanks to all those who envisioned and then brought Deyohahá:ge: Indigenous Knowledge Centre into its flourishing state at Six Nations Polytechnic, from the Indigenous Knowledge Guardians who set its original mandate to the visionary leaders at Six Nations Polytechnic (SNP) who continue to oversee its daily operations. We are grateful to have received funding to generate this book from the Social Sciences and Research Council of Canada (SSHRC) Connections grant program, which, because of the lockdowns during the COVID-19 pandemic, allowed us to redirect their funding support from the conference we originally proposed to producing this book as well as the *Deyohahá:ge: Indigenous Knowledge Centre 10th Anniversary* film. Many of the people mentioned above, who participated in founding Deyohahá:ge: or who continue to facilitate its operations, are featured in the film, which you can see at https://www.youtube.com/watch?v=EF05-RFNVTU. We also wish to thank Sophie Goellnicht and Susie O'Brien of McMaster's Department of English and Cultural Studies for their administrative support for this project. We are grateful to Deanna Reder and Siobhan McMenemy who initially welcomed our proposal for this book to the Indigenous Studies series at Wilfrid Laurier University press, and to Daniel Heath Justice, who joined the team as senior editor of the new Indigenous Imaginings series when our manuscript arrived at the press. Daniel's enthusiastic support for this project kept us grounded through the vagaries of the publishing process. We are grateful to the anonymous readers whose evaluations of this book and its contributions were so affirming and helpful in refining the final version. We thank Murray Tong, editor at WLUP, who listened alertly and who made sure the content and format of the book aligned with its overall intent.

DANIEL COLEMAN would like to thank Ki'en and Bonnie for their friendship and the chance to work on this project together; our contributors for sharing their knowledge and experience in this book in such thoughtful and powerful ways; the Two Row Research Partnership group (its members are named in our Introduction) for many years of learning together; Rick Hill and Rick Monture for getting me thinking about the Covenant Chain-Two Row Wampum, and Amber Meadow Adams, later on, for continuing to deepen my understanding; as well as Rick Hill, Rebecca Jamieson, and Sara General at Six Nations Polytechnic for creating the conditions for *Deyohahá:ge:* to do its work, and Tanis Hill, Heather Bomberry, Taylor Gibson, Derek Sandy, Stevie Jonathan, and many others for making it the flourishing Indigenous Knowledge Centre and meeting place that it is. I would also like to thank my friends and colleagues in the Department of English and Cultural Studies at McMaster for always supporting my efforts to learn about Haudenosaunee wampum's rich history and relevance. I am deeply grateful for my good fortune in knowing and loving Wendy Coleman and being known and loved by her. I offer my greetings and thanks to the many beings that make up the biome at the Head of Lake Ontario. They have suffered so much and still generate beauty and life each day. May it always be so.

KI'EN DEBICKI: Gratitude to my co-editors whose previous experience, wisdom, and vision were teachers to me during the entire process of putting this manuscript together. Huge thanks to our contributors who bravely committed to a writing project during COVID-19 and followed through! Thanks also to our contributors for their willingness to work with a bunch of academics and to allow this publication to go through the peer-review process (without which I would personally be in a precarious situation within the university). Thank you to Norma General and Rick Hill for first talking to me about my identity struggles through the teachings of the Two Row. I offer deep love and gratitude to Eugenia Zuroski, who is a colleague, mentor, interlocuter, co-conspirator, and beloved friend. I could not have got through this pandemic or this transition without you. All my love to Wren, the best human and a constant light in darkness. Finally, nyawen to the waters everywhere, especially to Kanyatarí:io (Lake Ontario), your love allows my life; I give it back, and give it back, and give it back.

BONNIE M. FREEMAN: I would like to extend my wholeheartedness and gratitude to both Daniel and Ki'en for their friendship and work on this book. I would like to extend my gratitude to all the authors who have contributed to this book. Each of these authors has deeply thought, lived, and demonstrated the philosophy and principles of the Two Row Kaswentha in these chapters. This book represents a small portion of the many who are living the principles of the Kaswentha, so it is important for me to also acknowledge and thank our Six Nations Knowledge Carriers (current and those that have passed), community members, students, and faculty who have been and continue to be involved with Six Nations Polytechnic Deyohahá:ge: and the Two Row Research Partnership group. These meetings have provided an opportunity for me to continue to learn and be inspired by the Kaswentha and our Onkwehonwe:neha. The knowledge, presentations, and thoughtful conversations presented by Rick Hill, Taylor Gibson, Rick Monture, Daniel Coleman, Tanis Hill, Sara General, Heather Bomberry, Derek Sandy, and the many students and community members during these meetings have greatly contributed to my lifelong learning of the Kaswentha. This has truly inspired my work in discovering how we can live our ancient knowledge in our current lifestyles. I would also like to thank Trish van Katwyk for trusting me and stepping into a canoe to paddle the Grand River with me. Our paddling journey has taught us so much about working together, relationships, and learning the language of the land and water, as well as the importance of slowing ourselves down to the flow of the water so that we were open to engaging in what we needed to learn. I would also like to acknowledge Ellie Joseph and Jay Bailey, cofounders of the Two Row on the Grand Paddle (2015 to present), for their continued friendship and dedication in carrying forward this cultural learning adventure and striving to build and continue the peace, respect, and friendship between our Six Nations community and non-Indigenous communities that want to learn more about the Haudenosaunee. I would also like to acknowledge and thank Hickory Edwards for his leadership and organization, as well as our Haudenosaunee leaders and all that participated in the 2013 Two Row Wampum Renewal Campaign Paddle, Onondaga Nation to the Hudson River and the United Nations in New York City. Your efforts have sparked a resurgence in our people's understanding and ability to live the principles of the Kaswentha—Nya:weh!

# Deyohahá:ge:

# Introduction

*Daniel Coleman, Ki'en Debicki, and Bonnie M. Freeman*

———

This book brings Grand River minds together to consider how those who walk on different paths can share the river of life far into the future. That's why it is entitled *Deyohahá:ge:* (Cayuga language for "two roads or paths") and *Sharing the River of Life*. It is a timely book. More than at any time in history, people across Turtle Island and around the globe are asking how to repair the damaged relationships humans have with the natural world and with the Indigenous Peoples who developed ways of living that respect and nurture the animals, plants, humans, and other beings that inhabited the earth around them. This book, authored by Six Nations people and their neighbours, reflects on the founding treaty agreement made between incoming Europeans and Indigenous North Americans, commonly known as the Covenant Chain or Two Row Wampum agreement, as a guide for building healthy relations for the future. Essentially, the chapters in this book help readers see how far-reaching the Haudenosaunee philosophy of peace-making conveyed in what Oren Lyons calls the "grandfather of the treaties" is to the problems we face today: how to build just and peaceful relations between Indigenous and non-Indigenous people after years of American and Canadian colonial oppression; how people who live "between the rows" of Western and Indigenous ways of doing things can reconcile themselves within that charged spiritual and ethical intercultural space; how institutions such as courts, schools, churches, or universities might "decolonize" their practices and assumptions; how new generations might reconnect with the wisdom conveyed in the wampum tradition in practical, everyday ways.[1] How, even in these late days challenged by a hyper-consumptive economy, climate change, dysfunctional institutions, global pandemics, and systemic injustice, "we" (Indigenous, settlers, and more recently arrived newcomers) might seek what the seventeenth-century formulators of the Covenant Chain-Two Row Wampum agreement called *ka'nikonhriyo'tshera't* (trust), *kentèn:ron* (friendship), and *skén:nen* (peace).

This book and its title came from a meeting held in 2007 at Six Nations Polytechnic (SNP) in Ohsweken. It's important that we tell readers about the community that gave us the shape and initiative to produce this book. At this meeting, Elders Lottie Skye, Ima Johnson, and Hubert Skye; SNP leaders Linda Staats and Rebecca Jamieson; Haudenosaunee professors Bonnie Freeman, Karen Hill, Dawn Martin-Hill, and Rick Monture; and non-Indigenous professors Will Coleman and Daniel Coleman (same last name, but not relatives) met to discuss a vision for a new Indigenous Knowledge Centre. The idea was for the two institutions, McMaster University and SNP, to cooperate on establishing a new research hub on Six Nations territory that would collect Indigenous Knowledge sources—particularly Haudenosaunee history, language, and culture—for the benefit of future generations. Given universities' long-running practice of expropriating and distorting Indigenous Knowledges, the Centre would be Indigenous-led on Indigenous land for the benefit of Indigenous Peoples. The idea was that knowledge that benefits Indigenous Peoples in the first instance would be of benefit to their settler-colonial neighbours in the second. The knowledge of the ancestors would show us how to be good ancestors for future generations.

When we asked Lottie, Ima, and Hubert for their thoughts about how to conceive this jointly sponsored, Haudenosaunee-led centre, they conferred with one another for some time, then turned to us, and said: "You should call it *Deyohahá:ge:*, the two roads, the two paths. You will need to bring together the best of Haudenosaunee and the best of Western thought to build the knowledge that future generations need." They were alluding to the Covenant Chain-Two Row Wampum's way of conceiving relationships that goes back in Haudenosaunee thinking to the beginning of Creation, when the twins who created the world that we now inhabit showed, right from the onset, such different priorities, such different ways of being, such different paths for living. At that first meeting, the

0.1 Deyohahá:ge:'s logo, designed by Rick Hill

Elders posed the question at the heart of this book: how we might understand the Covenant Chain Two Row relationship, not just in colonial and treaty history, but today. After all the betrayals, the failures to live in good relation, and the broken trust between Indigenous Peoples and settler-colonial Canadians and Americans, how might we today follow our distinctive paths and still find a healthy way—within our own minds and hearts, let alone within our political relations, not to mention with our increasingly threatened Mother, the Earth—to share the river of life?

We three editors got to know one another and many of the Six Nations-based writers who contributed the chapters of this book by meeting to discuss the question the Elders had posed. With staff at the newly formed

*Deyohahá:ge*: IKC, such as Rick Hill, Tanis Hill, Sara General, and Heather Bomberry, we formed a discussion group that we called the Two Row Research Partnership, and we met once a month at SNP to talk about the Covenant Chain-Two Row treaty relationship. All three of us editors are professors at McMaster University: Daniel in English and Cultural Studies, is of British-Scandinavian ancestry; Ki'en, cross-appointed in Indigenous Studies and English and Cultural Studies, is Wolf Clan *Kanien'kehá:ka* (Mohawk); Bonnie, cross-appointed in the School of Social Work and Indigenous Studies, is Algonquin and *Kanien'kehá:ka*, and lives at Six Nations. We knew one another from work, but we got to know one another by meeting monthly to talk about the Covenant Chain-Two Row treaty relationship—how it evolved; how it was encoded in wampum; how different generations of Haudenosaunee *Rotiyaneshon* (Chiefs) and *Yakoyaneshon* (Clan Mothers) understood it; how surrounding Indigenous Peoples such as Anishinaabe or Algonquins interpreted it; how British, Dutch, French, Canadian, and American negotiators took it up and used it. All in an effort to understand the Elders' suggestion that the two roads or paths might lead us to healthy and good ways to share the river of life.

Each generation, it seems, undergoes circumstances that make it urgent to "polish the wampum," meaning to wipe off the dust and grime of neglect and disrepair. The *Yakoyaneshon* and *Rotiyaneshon* who originally formulated the rules of engagement foresaw that treaty relationships would only thrive if their "signatories" met regularly to refresh their memories and renew them. For us in our time, a host of urgencies—armed conflict at what have come to be known as the land reclamations at Douglas Creeks Estates (2006) and Land Back Lane (2019); the ongoing revelations of the extent of the genocidal violence of the Indian Residential School (IRS) system; the repeated disappearances of Indigenous women, girls, and 2SLGBTQIA+ people as a continuation of that genocide; the extinction of traditional languages; the enormous gaps in education, poverty, health, incarceration rates, and clean water supply; the ever-increasing rates of police lethality against Black and Indigenous kin; plus the industrial destruction of earth, air, and water—all these and more have intensified our desire to investigate ways to rebuild our relationships, to wipe off the dust of strategic indifference and enforced forgetting, in order to generate the original Covenant Chain-Two Row values of trust, friendship, and peace for our times. The track record of simply imposing Euro-Canadian and Euro-American ideas about how to build these things is not good. We, therefore, felt the importance of following the Elders' advice to consult the Haudenosaunee model of linked arms and two paths to see what guidance it has for us to share a good way of life on a healthy river.

Our monthly meetings helped us get to know each other. They introduced us to the thinking and writing of others in the Grand River community who had been thinking about these things longer than we have. As we shared what we were learning, consulted with the Knowledge Guardians SNP had identified and honoured for their knowledge of Haudenosaunee languages and traditions, talked with language teachers and reserve-based thinkers, and gathered oral and written resources, we felt a growing responsibility to join Deyohahá:ge:'s larger project of finding permanent ways to record and share these elements of Haudenosaunee wisdom and knowledge. So we three editors applied for funding from SSHRC to host a gathering of knowledgeable people at Six Nations (there are many more people to consult than we could gather in one room!) to talk about the Covenant Chain-Two Row Wampum treaty relationship, both its history and its relevance for the future. Our idea was that we would then collect either video or written records of what they said for publication or posting on the web.

We'd already received the funding when the COVID-19 virus swept through our communities and shut down public gatherings. It was a difficult time. SNP and McMaster both had to scramble to offer classes online, while both communities lost Elders to the pandemic. In a time when we were conscious of trying to restore the knowledge of Elders, the disease was targeting Elders. For Indigenous communities, in particular, where fluent language speakers are few, these losses were especially devastating. Our Two Row Research Partnership group had to move to meeting online—making us feel the distance poignantly as members of our community struggled with grief. But adapt we must. We canceled our conference plans and instead sponsored a video documentary that asked the founders in individual interviews to reflect on the formation and accomplishments of Deyohahá:ge: from the perspective of its tenth anniversary.[2] We are now following up the video with this book that brings together essays on the Covenant Chain–Two Row treaty relationship by people who are on or near the Six Nations Reserve. Of course, unless we want to create an encyclopedia, the format of a book limits the number of chapters we can publish and keep the book to a reasonable size. There are so many other people who have important knowledge to share on this topic. This book is only a small sampling of what people in the Grand River region have to say about the Covenant Chain–Two Row treaty tradition. Indeed, Grand River-based people have a lot to share about this tradition, and readers can find another recent book on the Two Row Wampum called *Ǫ da gaho dẹ:s: Reflecting on Our Journeys*[3] that presents Haudenosaunee, Anishinaabe, and Canadian settler participants' reflections arising from teaching circles on Two Row principles led by Gae Ho Hwako (Norma Jacobs), Elder in residence at Wilfrid Laurier University. We are pleased to follow in that book's footsteps by bringing together a further range of Grand River Haudenosaunee thinkers' and writers' understanding of this tradition's set of guidelines for how to build *ka'nikonhriyo'tshera't* (trust), *kentèn:ron* (friendship), and *skén:nen* (peace).[4]

## A NOTE ON LANGUAGE

This book gathers the minds of several Haudenosaunee scholars and thinkers from different communities and generations. As such, there is a degree of variation in the Indigenous languages used on these pages. This variation comes not only from the different languages of our Nations— Kanien'kehá, Gayogo̱hó:nǫ', Onödowá'ga:, Onoñda'gegá' Nigaweño'deñ', Onʌjotaʔa:ka, and Skarò·rəʔ—but from dialectic and generational differences as well. Language standardization is a recent effort born of language revitalization programs. Kanien'kehá, for example, did not undergo systemic standardization until the mid-1990s, and dialect differences between certain communities and reserves are still maintained. To honour each individual contributor's relationship with their language (e.g., first language speakers, second language learners, etc.), we editors have not sought to conform the different languages and dialects used within the chapters of this book. To aid in comprehension, we have, where possible, provided translations and notes on words in different dialects or languages that refer to the same concept or treaty. For example,

*Deyohahá:ge:* is Cayuga for two paths, while *Tékeni Teyohà:te* is the Mohawk phrase for the same. Rather than force all language usages to conform, we honour the Covenant Chain-Two Row in this volume by letting differences in language stand. We are also grateful to multilingual Taylor Gibson, Turtle Clan, Cayuga Nation Senior Researcher at Deyohahá:ge: Indigenous Knowledge Centre for creating the glossary of Haudenosaunee and other non-English terms at the back of this book.

## THE COVENANT CHAIN-TWO ROW TREATY TRADITION

We know it's not common to speak of the Covenant Chain-Two Row treaty tradition. People usually speak of these two wampum belts as distinct —the Two Row Wampum or The Covenant Chain of Friendship— even as they also recognize that the two are related, if different, ways of laying out similar principles. Influenced by writers in this volume, we editors have come to understand that the principles of relationship-building referred to in these wampum belts are much older than the arrival of

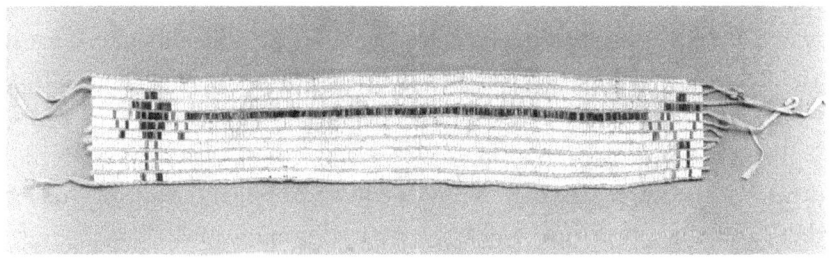

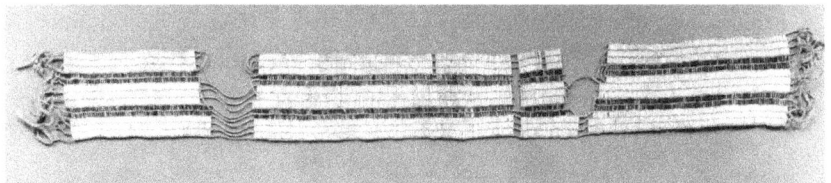

0.2 (*above*) *Tehontatenentshonteronhtáhkwa*, "the thing by which they link arms," a.k.a. the Covenant Chain. (Credit: Rick Hill) • 0.3 (*below*) *Tékeni Teyohà:te*, "two roads or paths," a.k.a. the Two Row Wampum. (Credit: Rick Hill)

Europeans on Turtle Island, so pinning them to the arrival of the Dutch in the early 1600s or to the formalizing of ally relations with the British in the 1660s or with the Anishinaabe and other Indigenous Nations at Niagara in 1764 isolates these moments of transaction from the conceptual and legal ecosystem in which each of these transactions occurred. As Kayanesenh Paul Williams puts it in his contribution to this volume,

> To remove a council from the context of that system, and to inspect it as an independent transaction, a "treaty," fails to recognize the principles of Haudenosaunee law that make councils work: continuity, responsibility, reciprocity, foresight, mutual help, respect, trust, friendship, peace, and a dozen others. The principles are not invented or accepted each time: they are the rules. The individual transaction, viewed out of the context of the entire system that defined and controlled it, loses meaning, effect, and functionality. It is like seeking to understand an animal without considering its habitat or its family, herd or pack: you are left with an isolated specimen.[5]

Our phrase "Covenant Chain-Two Row treaty tradition" tries to name that longer historical flow, the broader system of peace-making within which *Tehontatenentshonteronhtáhkwa* (the thing by which they link arms) and *Tékeni Teyohá:te* operated. As councillor for the Mohawk Nation Council of Chiefs in the recent court decision, *R. v. Montour and White*, Williams, Amber Meadow Adams (also a contributor to this book), and others on the Applicant team convinced Judge Sophie Bourque of Quebec that this longer, historical flow of treaty tradition means that:

> Amidst the turbulence of that era [of French and British competition for Indigenous trade alliances], two civilizations encountered one another and, in response to the challenge that this represented, they devised a distinctive mechanism to favour and govern a mutually beneficial relationship, the Covenant Chain.
>
> Through their entry into and subsequent renewals of the Covenant Chain, the parties intended to establish a lasting relationship characterized by both a military and friendship alliance. This alliance was to

be guided by the principles of Haudenosaunee diplomatic protocol and included a conflict-resolution procedure.

> The Court concludes that the Covenant Chain is a treaty between the Haudenosaunee and the British, as recognized by s. 35(1).[6]

So, to speak of the Covenant Chain-Two Row Wampum as a *treaty tradition* is not meant to freeze it as a transaction limited to a singular past moment or event. We use the term *tradition* to trace that continuous flow from ancient concepts (original instructions) conveyed in Creation stories to the official formulation of the Covenant Chain and Two Row Wampum agreements with the Dutch and British and onwards to contemporary times, including contemporary courtrooms in Canada and the USA.

Amber Meadow Adams traced that millennial flow from Creation to the Quebec court in her expert testimony at *R. vs. Montour and White*. In her chapter in this volume, she demonstrates how the concepts of *Tehontatenentshonteronhtáhkwa* were born from the seeds of new life that Sky Woman brought with her when she fell from Sky World, each seed sending out a tendril and finding an answering sustenance in the soil muskrat had supplied. Embryonic life reaches out for answering life, much like the twins in Atsi'tsya'ka:yon's womb, connecting through the umbilicus to the body of their mother. "Usually spoken of in English as the 'Covenant Chain,'" Adams explains,

> *tehontatenentshonteronhtáhkwa* describes a reaching across the space between *ka'nikòn:ra* [mind, decision, and direction] and *ka'shatstenhsera* [the capacity to bring into being].[7] It describes the connection, mind to mind and arm to arm, that sustaining life requires. These are the pieces of the word: *te-*, a dualic prefix that describes action taken by two together, something double, a simultaneity. *-[h]ontate-*, a form of pronominal prefix that indicates an act of reciprocity, a doubled reflexive that describes mirrored action between two groups…*-nentsh-* is the verb root describing an arm, sometimes the forearm. *-onte*, an infix that acts like a preposition, describes spatial orientation, something attached to the end of something else. The form of the verb ending *-ahkwa* places the verb phrase temporally as something undertaken at a past point and continued into the present moment.[8]

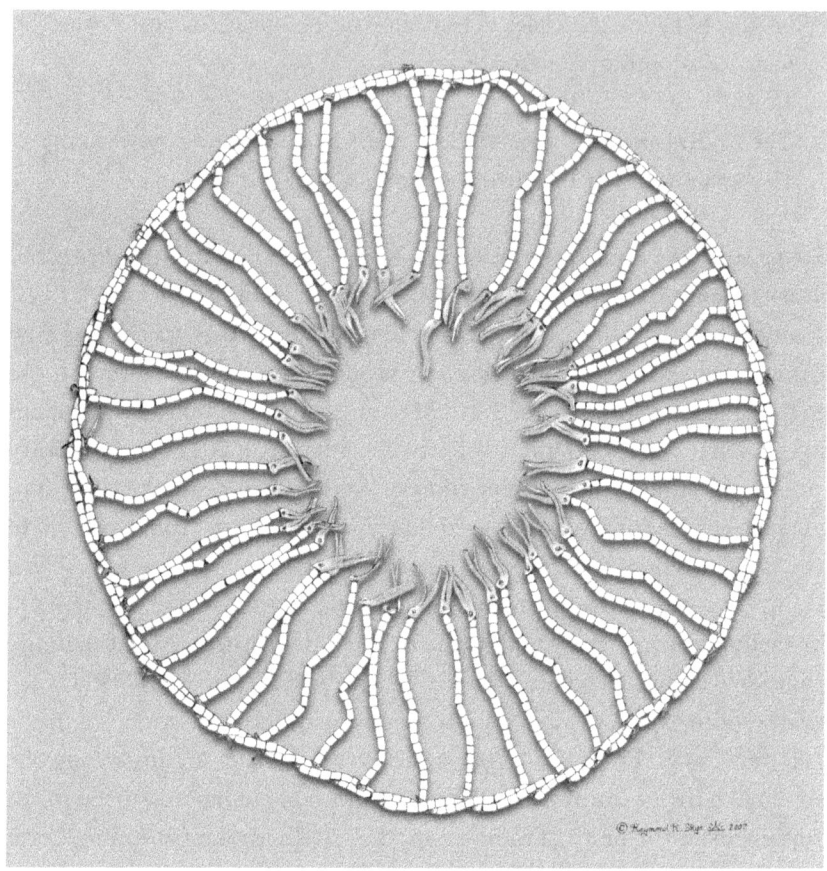

0.4 Circle Wampum, *Teyonnityohkwanhakstha*, "The Thing the People Use on an Ongoing Basis, to Wrap Around Themselves." (Credit: Raymond R. Skye, Tuscarora artist, Six Nations of the Grand River Territory)

"-Ahkwa," the flow from past to present: Adams traces the "ecosystem" of the Covenant Chain idea back through the roots and stems of Haudenosaunee language to the founding epic of Haudenosaunee civilization, the Creation of Turtle Island that was told and retold long before Europeans arrived.

As renowned Tuscarora artist, cultural historian, and lifelong student of wampum Rick Hill, another contributor to this volume, has explained, this powerful image of reaching out to make life, mind to mind and arm to arm, became central to a second important Haudenosaunee epic narrative, the story of the Peacemaker who brought the *Kayanerenkó:wa*, the "Great Law of Peace." The Peacemaker conducted a long journey from one to the next of the five original Nations (the Tuscaroras joined later in the 1720s, making it Six Nations), during which he convinced the leaders in what is today upstate New York to depart from bloodshed and to embrace clear-minded discussion as a way to peace. He then instructed all fifty Chiefs to clasp arms in a circle around the Tree of Peace. "By interlocking their arms," writes Hill, "(meaning that they should be of one mind and treat each other with respect), the Chiefs provided a protective circle within which the people reside."[9] People from all directions of the Earth would be welcome to trace the white roots of peace to the tree at their centre, but they would need to protect the tree with their linked arms. Indeed someday, the Peacemaker predicted, the tree could be weakened, it may even tip over, and the Chiefs' grip on each other's arms would have to be strong enough to hold it up.[10]

In their discussion of the origins of what we might now call the Chain of Linked Arms after its formal depiction in wampum, Adams and Hill do not look to the arrivals of Cartier on the St. Lawrence in 1534 or to those of Champlain and the Dutch in the early 1600s for the "first treaty." They don't cite the beginnings in the formalizations of allyship between the Haudenosaunee and the British once the latter began to consolidate an administration for their dispersed colonies in the mid-seventeenth century. These elaborations took place later, once the Chain of Linked Arms had long been established in Haudenosaunee social and political philosophy.

They also look to Haudenosaunee sources for guidance over what to do when people in relationships part ways. Looking at the relationship of the twins in the Creation story, Adams notes their shared determination to create the world we know, but the difference in their ways of going about it. It's not our purpose here to go deeply into the nuances of the complex relationship between the twin brothers, but just to say that De'haĕⁿ'hiyawă''khoⁿ' (He Grasps the Sky with Both Hands) and O'hā'ă' (Flint), Sky Woman's grandsons, create the Earth we know between them. De'haĕⁿ'hiyawă''khoⁿ' sets out patiently to create a cooperative ecosystem in which humans can thrive, while O'hā'ă', who is always in a hurry, creates plants, animals, and natural features that can cause harm."¹¹ One of the first realizations, then, in this early story about the challenges of linking arms, is the question of what to do when the partners diverge in values, means, or methods. When their differences sharpen so dramatically that they threaten to destroy the relationship and the world they have made, the twin brothers agree to keep separate, with De'haĕⁿ'hiyawă"khoⁿ ruling the daytime and O'hā'ă' active in the night. They share the river of life, but they walk on different paths.

*Tékeni Teyohà:te*, the two separate roads or paths, commonly imagined with reference to the iconography of the Two Row Wampum, emerges, therefore, within the already existing context of *tehontatenentshonteron-htáhkwa*, the protocol for linking arms. It represents a way to rethink or renew strained relationships. By the time the Kanien'keha:ka met the Dutch on the Hudson River, for example, they had seen what firearms could do when Champlain shot several of their relatives in 1609. They had begun to experience the effects of smallpox and tuberculosis. So, they were cautious about the need to walk carefully on separate paths with these newcomers, even as they welcomed them to trade in their homelands.

In Jake Thomas's version of the oral history, we have this interpretation of the two rows in the famous Wampum. The Haudenosaunee said to the Dutch: "I have a canoe and you have a vessel with sails and this is what we shall do. I will put in my canoe my belief and laws. In your vessel you shall put your belief and laws. All my people will be in my canoe, your people in your vessel. We shall put these boats in the water and they shall always be parallel, as long as there is Mother Earth, this will be everlasting."¹² This clarification about how to link arms to peacefully share the river assured the newcomers, who were few in numbers and weak from months of travel, that they would not be overtaken or assimilated into Haudenosaunee ways. They would be allowed to continue in dignity and respect, even as they discussed with the *rotiyaneshon* how to build a long-term relationship as friends and allies. This is the version of the Covenant Chain-Two Row treaty relationship that has become most widely known in our own times.¹³

With the reversal of fortunes over time, where the supertanker of settler colonialism today completely swamps the river, let alone the Haudenosaunee canoe, Indigenous activists have turned to the clear demarcations of the two separate rows to insist on Haudenosaunee sovereignty and to resist the impositions of the settler-colonial state. "One of the two paths signifies the whiteman's laws and beliefs, and the other signifies the laws and beliefs of the Onkwehonweh," Jake Thomas said. "The white background signifies purity, good minds, and peace, and they should not interfere with one another's views."[14] On the basis of the Two Row Wampum, then, Mike Myers, a member of the Haudenosaunee delegation to the Penner Commission in Ottawa in 1983, told the commissioners: "We are not part of Canada. We have never desired to be a part of Canada, and we have no future plans to be part of Canada."[15] And on this basis, writers in this volume, such as Vanessa Watts, Rick Hill, and Sara General, ask what part Indigenous scholars should play in the effort to "decolonize" the university if they are instructed by Two Row thinking not to interfere in the newcomer's vessel. Given the casual brutality inflicted on the twenty-or-so thousand Haudenosaunee living in what is today called Canada by the thirty-some-million Canadian sailors in the settler-colonial supertanker, it's not hard to understand why resistors and activists would repurpose the Two Row Wampum into a separatist flag.

But to fasten too fiercely onto the separation of the two rows can cause harm to the thousands of people who have a foot in each vessel, not to mention impeding the covenant to link arms. "If this happens that my people wish to have their feet in each of the two boats," Thomas's oration warned, "there will be a high wind and the boats will separate and the person that has his feet in each of the boats shall fall between the boats, and there is no living soul who will be able to bring them back to the right way given by the Creator but only one—the Creator himself."[16] On the basis of this statement, Rick Hill has noted that some contemporary Haudenosaunee people have said that Confederacy members who enter the settler-colonial supertanker have forfeited their culture and religion. They are "split-minded" and have lost their birthright.[17] Hill doesn't agree with this interpretation. For one thing, he notes that the statement says the Creator can save people from drowning in the water, but for another, he notes that the space between the rows represents the river of life, made up of "three rows apiece that are said to symbolize peace, friendship, and respect,"[18] not rejection, shunning, or forfeiting.

What might aid look like from Shonkwaia'tishon towards those who "fall" into the waters between the vessels? Might it look like a resurgence of young people straddling lives in multiple places with multiple belongings? People who use the "best of Western and Indigenous thinking" to develop good minds to envision a healthy future? Might it look like an increasing embodied fluidity? Perhaps it is those of us in the in-between helping each other?

What are we to make of the damnation associated with water in interpretations of the Covenant Chain-Two Row that claim those who exist between the rows are in some way lacking, lost, or impure? How, too, can we speak of the so-called damnation of falling off the ship/canoe and into the waters below without speaking of the Middle Passage? As Phanuel Antwi's chapter in this volume demonstrates, there is no doubt that there were enslaved Africans in the holds of the Dutch and British sailing ships of the Covenant Chain-Two Row treaty partners. As he notes, Haudenosaunee people were both forced into and participated in slavery. Any meaningful discussion of reviving and repolishing the Covenant Chain-Two Row to guide our political and sociocultural relationships in the present and future must acknowledge and be accountable to its connection to the wake and the hold of racial capitalism, as he and other Black studies scholars, such as Christina Sharpe, instruct. Water includes Black kin who did not survive the Middle Passage and Asian indentured workers who did not survive the *kala pani,* the "dark waters;" they became ocean. How, then, can we speak of Indigenous kin who exist between worlds as responsible for their own demise in the waters between the vessels? As forsaken? Water is ancestors. Water is life. And there were also those who survived, as Antwi observes, "below decks" within and ever since the covenant was made. Good minds need to consider their places today in the two rows and on the river of life.

Many Onkwehonwe feel they have one foot in each of the two boats—leaving many to question their experience of trying to bridge between their own culture and that of global capitalism. For most, existing in the settler world was not a choice of their own due to residential schools, the sixties scoop, the Indian Act, and other Canadian assimilative and genocidal policies. As a result, many question their Onkwehonwe identities, wondering if they are to blame for the experiences of daily life that necessitate unequal participation in Indigenous and non-Indigenous worlds, or wondering if they are to blame for experiences of daily life that necessitate participation in colonial, capitalist systems that not only harm our own peoples, but our Black kin as well.

Miller and Thomas pose the problem this way: "The Whiteman said, 'What will happen if your people…go into my vessel?' The Onkwehonweh replied, 'If this happens, then they will have to be guided by my canoe.'"[19] As we reflect on the unavoidability of existing in (at least) two worlds, we editors seek to bring compassion, openness, and trust to this matter of being "between the rows." Part of the value of a volume such as this is in the sharing and opening of dialogue and reflection on what the Covenant Chain-Two Row has to teach us about cross- or bi-cultural living. We do not pretend to be authorities on the issue, but welcome, including in the pages of this volume, conversation, differing opinions, and live anecdotal evidence that may continue to evolve our thinking, understanding, and application of historical, ancestral, and current interpretations of the Two Row-Covenant Chain.

Take, for example, Sara General's contribution to this collection in which she describes her disillusionment at a set of federal government-Assembly of First Nations (AFN) talks and how the advice of a Six Nations Haudenosaunee Knowledge Keeper led her to focus on the values and philosophy of the in-between rows of the Two Row. Rather than see this "space" as the river where a person between boats can drown, Sara looks to the white beads' reference to relationship and "the way the space of engagement should feel—peaceful and respectful—whether that engagement is happening with other nations, museums, universities, or family members."[20]

Writers in this volume, Sara General and David Newhouse, pay special attention to these three white rows, which Newhouse calls the "kaswentha space." Like Ellie Joseph and Jay Bailey, who each year sponsor a Two Row Paddle of Haudenosaunee and their neighbours on the shared Grand River, they don't see the white space as blank but as the living ecosystem that binds the two rows together. By placing the Two Row version of the agreement back in the ecosystem of the linked arms, we can see how the three white rows give specific content to the rope, you could say, the Chain of Linked Arms—which make up what David Newhouse calls the "ethical space"—that makes up the *Tehontatenentshonteronhtáhkwa*.

## THE EVOLUTION OF THE TREATY RELATIONSHIP OVER TIME

The protocols of the Covenant Chain-Two Row treaty tradition were repeated in treaty council after treaty council throughout the colonial era.[21] Writers before us have attended to the European records such as the *Jesuit Relations*, which observe in detail the seventeen wampum belts, including the Covenant Chain, brought by Kanyenkéha:ka envoy Kiotsaeton to make peace with the French-Algonquin alliance in 1645.[22] Or to *Onoñda'gegá'* orator Sadakanahtie's 1694 address to Benjamin Fletcher, governor of the colony of New York, reminding the British of how they had extended their friendship of linked arms with the image of a bark rope and, later, an iron chain.[23] But we will give two examples here—one Haudenosaunee and one British—of the ways in which the imagery and language of the Covenant Chain-Two Row tradition were self-consciously presented in treaty discussions between Haudenosaunee *rotiyaneshon* and British colonial authorities as an ongoing, evolving, and elaborating system.

Here is Canesatego addressing the Governor of Maryland as recorded in the Pennsylvania Council Minutes for June 16, 1744, during discussions over the Treaty of Lancaster:

> above one hundred years ago, the Dutch came here in a ship, and brought with them several Goods, such as awls, knives, hatchets, guns and many other particulars, which they gave us, and when we saw what sort of People they were, we were so well pleased with them, that we tied their ship to the Bushes on the Shore; and afterwards, liking them still better the longer they staid with us, and thinking the bushes too slender, we removed the rope, and tied it to the trees; and as the trees were liable to be blown down by high winds, or to decay of themselves, we, from the affection we bore them, again removed the rope, and tied it to a strong and big rock (here the Interpreter said, they mean the Oneida country) and not content with this, for its further security we removed the rope to the big Mountain (here the Interpreter says they mean the Onondago country) and there we tied it very fast, and rowll'd wampum about it; and, to make it still more secure, we stood upon the Wampum, and sat down upon it, to defend it, and to prevent any hurt coming to it, and did our

best endeavours that it might remain uninjured for ever. During all this time the newcomers, the Dutch, acknowledged our right to the lands, and solicited us, from time to time, to grant them parts of our country, and to enter into League and Covenant with us, and become one people with us.

After this the English came into the Country, and as we were told, became one People with the Dutch. About two years after the arrival of the English, an English Governor came to Albany, and finding what great Friendship subsisted between us and the Dutch, he approved it mightily, and desired to make us as strong a League, and to be upon as good terms with us as the Dutch were, with whom he was united, and to become one People with us; And…he found that the Rope which tied the ship to the great Mountain was only fastened with Wampum, which was liable to break and rot, and to perish in a course of years, he therefore told us, he would give us a Silver Chain, which would be much stronger, and would last for ever. This we accepted, and fastened the ship with it, and it has lasted ever since.[24]

Canesatego's speech illustrates very clearly the way in which Haudenosaunee diplomats understood the evolutionary nature of the Covenant Chain-Two Row way of relating. The Haudenosaunee built a trade accord with the Dutch. As the relationship evolved, it moved up the Mohawk River, linking arms with different nations of the Haudenosaunee Longhouse of Nations, who themselves had linked arms with one another into the Confederacy. As the story unfolds, Conesatego demonstrates the process of adaptation as the Dutch ship is anchored to different features on the shore—the bushes, the tall rock from which the Oneidas take their name, and the mountain at Onondaga. With each move, the material by which the arms are linked changes from rope to rope interwoven with wampum and eventually to a silver chain. It is clear that Conesatego understood "treaty" in evolving terms, as Paul Williams indicates in his chapter below:

> If the relationship is like a river of time, the individual transactions are like stones in its path, markers of particular events, and to focus only on them is to miss the whole point. The relationship is not a creature of English, French or Dutch law. It was created by taking the principles that brought the Haudenosaunee nations together in peace, *Kayanerenkó:wa*, and applying them to relations with the newcomers.[25]

As the career of Sir William Johnson, superintendent of Indian Affairs for Britain's northern colonies from 1755 until his death in 1774, shows, these Haudenosaunee principles established the *grundnorm* for treaty-making in the crucial period when Britain was trying to consolidate its administration after the conquest of New France in 1763. Johnson lived on the Mohawk River and married Konwatsi'tsayén:ni Mary (Molly) Brant, a Canajoharie Kanien'kehá:ka and *yakoyaner*. Mary was reputedly a granddaughter of Deyohninhohhakarawenh, "King Hendrick," so in marrying her, Johnson became related directly to social and political power within Haudenosaunee society. He was given the name Warraghyhagey and became fluent in the Mohawk language. Through his powerful family connections, Johnson became fluent in the principles of *Kayanerenhtserakó:wa*. Johnson's many orations of the agreement demonstrate that not only did the British understand the principles of the Covenant Chain-Two Row treaty tradition, but they also officially deployed this tradition themselves, using it to expand their network of Indigenous allies, first to ward off French resistance, and later to try to stem the spread of American revolt. Here is a portion of Johnson's speech to Mohawk leaders when he was newly appointed as superintendent in 1755:

> Behold Brethren these great books, 4 folio volumes of the records of Indian affairs which lay open upon the table before the Colonel. They are records of the many solemn Treaties and the Various Transactions which have passed between your Forefathers and your Bretheren the English, also between many of you here present & us your Brethren now living. You well know and these Books testifie that it is now almost 100 years since your Forefathers & ours became known to each other. That upon our first acquaintance we shook hands & finding that we should be useful to one another entered into a Covenant of Brotherly Love & mutual Friendship. And tho' we were at first only tied together by a Rope, yet lest this Rope should grow rotten & break we tied ourselves together by an Iron Chain. Lest time or accidents might rust & destroy this Chain of Iron, we afterwards made one of Silver, the strength & brightness of which would subject it to no decay. The ends of this Silver Chain we fixed to the Immoveable Mountains, and this in so firm a manner that no Mortal enemy might be able to remove it. All this my Bretheren you know to be

Truth. You know also that this Covenant Chain of Love & Friendship was the Dread & Envy of all your Enemies & ours, that by keeping it bright & unbroken we have never spilt in anger one drop of each other's blood to this day. You well know also that from the beginning to this time we have almost every year, strengthened & brightened this Covenant Chain in the most public & solemn manner. You know that we became as one body, one blood & one people.[26]

Echoing Canesatego and the *rotiyaneshon* before him, Johnson tracks an evolving story of the linked arms that became a rope, then a chain—this time an iron chain, which is improved by being recast in silver. Here, we see that these understandings had been recorded, not just in ropes, chains, or wampum, but also in the treaty council minutes books, which Johnson had reviewed in advance of the meeting with the Mohawks. His speech emphasizes the importance of keeping the chain polished and bright by meeting annually to review the century-old relationship and, ultimately, to be so firmly linked as to be one body, blood, and people.

Johnson, too, understood treaty not as an isolated transaction but as a centuries-long flexible relationship that needed regular review, adaptation, and repolishing. And he also understood it, via the Haudenosaunee *Kayanerenhtserakó:wa*, as non-exclusive. If the rafters of the Longhouse of Peace could be extended to other Nations, such as the Tuscaroras, Johnson would try to extend the Covenant of Linked Arms to others as well.

This is why, at the close of the Seven Years War and the uprising led by Chief Pontiac of the "Western nations" who had been trading partners with the French, Johnson created an adapted version of the Covenant Chain Wampum to formalize his proposal to make peace and link arms with twenty-four First Nations at the Treaty of Niagara in 1764. Noting the belt's use of European numerals, its adaptation of the "lozenge" shape to represent the council fires of different Nations, and a path of white beads between them that extends the familiar image of the linked arms at its centre, Anishinaabe scholar Alan Corbiere, whose ancestors were present at the Treaty of Niagara, observes that Johnson's Covenant Chain, known as the Niagara Belt, "represents a syncretic blend of symbols between two literary traditions."[27] It borrows iconography from earlier Haudenosaunee wampum and adapts practices from European

0.5 Replica of the Niagara Belt commissioned by Nathan Tidridge and made by Ken Maracle (Deer Clan, faith keeper of the Lower Cayuga Longhouse) for the Commemoration of the 250th Anniversary of the Treaty of Niagara ceremony, August 1–2, 2014. Queen at the Council Fire – Canada's Constitutional Monarchy (canadiancrown.com). (Credit: Nathan Tidridge)

literacy, such as reading numbers from left to right. For Corbiere, this syncretism suggests "a tradition akin to British common law, in which the compilation of various rulings on various torts had eventually led to a system of common law based upon precedents that lawyers, judges, and others in the legal profession could consult and debate in order to resolve a dispute or issue, in a manner informed by prior decisions and actions."[28] Johnson's uptake and adaptation of wampum itself had precedents in previous treaty councils, where, for example, the French at Trois-Riviéres had exchanged their own wampum for those presented by Kiotsaeton in 1645.[29] Johnson went on to try to cement Covenant Chain relationships with various Nations, from the Ohio people to the west in 1764 to the Cherokees to the south in 1770 and the Wabanaki Confederacy in the Maritimes in 1766.[30]

This story of how the concept of linking arms to make friendship and peace grew from the Haudenosaunee Creation narrative throughout the Covenant Chain-Two Row treaty tradition shows why Oren Lyons, the Onondaga Chief whose thoughts on the tradition open this volume, calls it the "grandfather of the treaties." The ground rules for how to make good relations—how to make trust, friendship, and peace—have been carried in the flow of this tradition now for thousands of years. It's our hope that this book will help readers see the power and ongoing relevance of this evolving set of protocols for building good relations.

## SHARING THE RIVER

To build or rebuild ways of relating based on trust, friendship, and peace, the Covenant Chain-Two Row treaty also asks us to consider our commitment to nonhuman relations as central to the agreement. The river upon which our vessels sail is alive; so too, the wampum.

In her chapter on wampum justice, Shinnecock environmental studies scholar Kelsey Leonard reminds us that wampum in her people's language is a living being imbued with the power for justice when it is held and used to speak the truth: this is the meaning of the word *wunnáumwash*. "Wunnáumwash," writes Leonard, "is often said after an Indigenous person delivers a speech...in which wampum was always present."[31] Referencing their ability to filter the pollution in our waters, Leonard asks us to follow the model of the quahog by "polishing the truth" in our human and nonhuman relationships so that we might "polish the chain" of covenant between us. Reviewing the meanings of wampum (as we do in this book) is a way of "polishing the truth" and respecting the life of the molluscs. When someone holds kaswentha or wampum in their hands, the beads represent and honour the life of the quahog clam. There is a responsibility to the life of the quahog to tell and honour the truth. Leonard asserts that "we must recognize that the treaty agreements made using wampum were not just made between Indigenous Peoples, settlers, or humans alone but that they were also made with the wampum. We then can understand that the polishing of our covenant is a responsibility to the remembrance of truth that we must uphold not only for ourselves but also for the wampum."[32] That is to say, the agreement one makes when holding the wampum is an agreement that encompasses not just what humans promise to one another but also their promise to the environment, to the truth-telling, clear-water-filtering quahog themselves, whose bodies are central to the agreement.

A significant motivation for the gathering together of the pieces in this collection is to show the ongoing, real-life impact of the Covenant Chain-Two Row. What does the wampum teach us that we can apply to the daily activities of "sharing the river"? David Newhouse, for example, discusses the kaswentha as an "ethical space of engagement" where "mutual respect, mutual responsibility, and reciprocity"—what he calls a "politics of respect"—can operate in a university classroom to emphasize notions of "cooperation, collaboration, and caretaking."[33] By using the kaswentha, Newhouse creates "more than just a dialogic classroom space" but a space for "speaking about Canada itself: a grand experiment in living between the Two Rows and trying to answer what I've come to call the Guswenta Question: How do we live well together?"[34] This question also motivates the community work of Suzie Miller and Scot Cooper in their chapter on the Pen Pal Project, which connected schoolchildren on the Grand River reserve and in the town of Caledonia.

Following the 2007 Douglas Creek land reclamation and occupation, elementary school teacher, Suzie Miller (Mohawk, Wolf Clan) codeveloped the project with Scot Cooper, a settler specialist in children's narrative therapy, in Norfolk and Haldimand counties. The Pen Pal Project sought to "polish the chain" of relationships between youths sharing the ecology of the Grand River. Through embodied practice, photography, art, and letter writing, children from both communities were shown the roots and ongoing relevance of the Covenant Chain-Two Row agreement in sustaining relationships of respect and trust. Miller and Cooper talk about how these initiatives encouraged "cultural creativity" that gathered people together to generate collective documentation that serves not only as an "archive" of the neighbouring communities' collective wisdom and knowledge but also as a testament to shared hopes and preferences for the future.

Another remarkable and practical "application" of Covenant Chain-Two Row principles can be seen in the nine-day Two Row Paddle on the Grand River, organized by co-founders Ellie Joseph (Mohawk, Turtle

Clan) and Jay Bailey (settler). Since 2015, this paddle by canoe and kayak has taken place each summer on the Grand River, departing from Cambridge, Ontario and proceeding through Six Nations to the mouth of Lake Erie at Port Maitland, Ontario. Joseph and Bailey describe how they were inspired by participating in the four-hundred-year-anniversary Honor the Two Row Paddle on the Hudson River from Albany, New York, to the United Nations in New York City. The authors discuss the importance of bringing the philosophy and understanding of the Two Row Wampum to both Indigenous and settler peoples. The voyage down the Grand gives paddlers the literal, physical experience of sharing the river, keeping the canoes and kayaks parallel to each other while respecting each other's space. Joseph and Bailey reflect in their chapter on the paddlers' responses to the experience of ceremony, re-enactment, cultural teachings, and being in Creation on the river each day. They also describe how this initiative has grown to include community involvement and partnerships with Six Nations agencies and groups and how they, as a grassroots initiative, have adapted to continuing the paddle during COVID-19.

In a related chapter, Six Nations community member and Algonquin/Mohawk scholar Bonnie Freeman and her Dutch Canadian colleague Trish van Katwyk share from the SSHRC-funded interviews they conducted with Haudenosaunee and settler youth who participated in the Two Row Paddle project described in Ellie Joseph and Jay Bailey's chapter. The youth discuss the importance of the new insights that emerged from their participation in the paddle, especially what they learned in the context of a caring and cooperative community composed of Indigenous and non-Indigenous paddlers. Freeman and van Katwyk reflect on how the young people's stories suggest a new connection with nature, a feeling of family with other paddlers, empathy, respect, and trust for one another, as well as the capacity to deal with differences. The two scholars highlight the importance of the youths' indication of a new cyclical understanding of time so that historical events became relevant to their ability to engage the inequities of the present and how new feelings of connection to the ecosystem of the river generated a new understanding of the need for cooperation, mutual respect, and land-based reconciliation for both Indigenous Peoples and settlers. If we are going to share the river in the future, we are going to have to build peace, friendship, and respect, not just for each other but for the river itself. In this sense, the youths' experience of the Two Row Paddle allowed them to hold the ancient *wunnáumwash* once again in their hands, to feel the truth-telling of the creatures that live within the water for themselves.

## CONCLUSION

Part of what drew us to the work of putting together this collection was the richness and diversity of insight into ways of relating and living that the Covenant Chain-Two Row offers to those who sit within, alongside, and even across its shared and distinct ways of life. Complexity and nuance abound. We hope the contributions gathered here will affirm, expand, and keep active Haudenosaunee treaty knowledges at all levels of relation: within ourselves, our friendships, our families, our Clans, our Nations, across Nations, and with the more-than-human world. At its core, this is a book that seeks to honour generations of Six Nations thought and practice based in Covenant Chain-Two Row philosophies and practicalities. What you hold in your hands, then, is a call, a call that you can choose how to answer: you could turn away, or you could turn towards. No matter what you decide, however, there's no denying that you, too, are in a vessel on the river of life. Where do you sit? Or do you stand? Who is in the vessel with you? What keeps your vessel seaworthy? How do you keep your balance? Are you paddling or just hitching a ride? Are your arms linked with ours? Are they linked with the others who travel the river of life? Can you see the river? The wake? Are the waters of the river of life well? Healthy?

It is our hope that these writings might polish the strength of our peace, trust, friendship, and respect for one another so that we might extend care across the kaswentha space, between us as embodied individuals, and to the ecology that sustains us all. Nyawen.

# 1
# Original Instructions

CHAPTER ONE

# Gä•sweñta' Reflections

*Oren Lyons*

---

*Excerpts from the writing and speeches of Oren Lyons. This series of statements on the Covenant Chain-Two Row Wampum was assembled and edited by Rick Hill, Dec 16, 2020.*

> *Without the help of the Iroquois, the Dutch settlers would have never survived here. Let's stay together, listen to each other, and find solutions for future generations.*
>
> —DUTCH CONSUL GENERAL ROB DE VOS, 2013[1]

> *We've worked hard to get here. It still is a work in progress. But in spite of everything, the Two Row still prevails. Our allies, our friends, our brothers from across the sea, are here.*
>
> —OREN LYONS, FAITHKEEPER, ONONDAGA NATION ON THE FOUR HUNDREDTH ANNIVERSARY OF THE TWO ROW WAMPUM TREATY, 2013[2]

The Two Row is the oldest and is the grandfather of all subsequent treaties. The words "as long as the sun shines, as long as the waters flow downhill, and as long as the grass grows green" can be found in many treaties after the 1613 treaty. It set a relationship of equity and peace.

We laid down some discussion points at that time. We said [to the Dutch], "You want to trade in our territory, but we see that you're not seeming to go away. So we think that maybe we better talk about relationship. How are we going to deal with one another?" So we set up the Two Row Belt, which just actually says that this is your ship, your people, your ways of life, your governments; our canoe, our people, our way of life, we go down the River of Life, the Guswenta, side-by-side. And we'll be hooked together with the chain, three links: Peace, Friendship, and Forever, for as long as the Sun rises in the east, as long as the rivers run downhill, and as long as the grass grows green.[3]

The field of white represents peace and the river of life. We will go down this river in peace and friendship. You will note the two rows do not come together, they are equal in size, denoting the equality of all life, and one end is not finished, denoting the ongoing relationship into the future.[4]

This is a great humanitarian document because it recognizes equality in spite of the small size of the White colony and ensures safety, peace and friendship forever, and sets the process for all of our ensuing treaties up to this moment.[5]

I think that Two Row Belt was a great observation and a great comment on how we saw life. And the two rows are equal side-by-side going down. The white representing Peace and the River of Life and one row representing the boat and the other a canoe. Held together by these three links we call the Covenant Chain, friendship.[6]

Indian nations' agreements always were inclusive. They encompass not only the human elements of life but all life. So protection of the commons was inherent in all these agreements. The commons are what belong to one and all—the air we breathe, the water we drink, the land we live on. And today, we see the necessity for those protections.

We are told that when this land was being created, our Creator was challenged to a bet by his brother. The subject of their game was: would there be life? And in one throw, supported by all the living forces of the natural world, our Creator won this bet. He won it all for us. We commemorate this each year in part of our Midwinter ceremonies.

This is not just a quaint legend. It is a reminder that, as scientists now agree, life on earth is the result of chance, as well as of intent. Life on earth is a fragile matter. That magnificent gamble could have gone the other way: life could just as easily not have been at all.

A thousand years ago or more, the Great Peace Maker came among our people. He introduced the principles of peace, health, equity, justice, and the power of the good minds, which is to say, to be united in thought, body, and spirit. He brought peace to our warring nations and he raised new leaders, clan mothers, and chiefs, instructing us on our conduct and our responsibilities.

Among those many instructions, one continues to resonate around the world today. He said to us, "When you sit in council for the welfare of the people, think not of yourself, nor of your family, or even your generation. Make your decisions for the seventh generation coming so that they may enjoy what you have here today. If you do this, there will be peace." That is a profound instruction on responsibility that should be the basis for the world's decision-makers today.

We were instructed to create societies based on the principles of Peace, Equity, Justice, and the Power of Good Minds. Our societies are based upon great democratic principles of the authority of the people and equal responsibilities for men and women. This was a great way of life across this Great Turtle Island and freedom with respect was everywhere. In making any law, our chiefs must always consider three things: the effect of their decision on peace; the effect on the natural world; and the effect on seven generations in the future. We believe that all lawmakers should be required to think this way, that all constitutions should contain these rules.

Our leaders were instructed to be men of vision and to make every decision on behalf of the seventh generation to come; to have compassion and love for those generations yet unborn. We were instructed to give thanks for All That Sustains Us.

Thus, we created great ceremonies of Thanksgiving for the life-giving forces of the Natural World, as long as we carried out our ceremonies, life would continue. We were told that "The Seed is the Law." We will continue to plant the seeds of life.

We were instructed to be generous and to share equally with our brothers and sisters so that all may be content. We were instructed to respect and love our Elders, to serve them in their declining years, to cherish one another. We were instructed to love our children, indeed, to love ALL children. We were told that there would come a time when parents would fail this obligation and we could judge the decline of humanity by how we treat our children.

The catastrophes that we have suffered at the hands of our brothers from across the seas has been unremitting and inexcusable. It has crushed our people, and our Nations, down through the centuries. You brought us disease and death, and the idea of Christian dominion over heathens, pagans, and savages. Our lands were declared "vacant" by papal bulls, which created law to justify the pillaging of our land. We were systematically stripped of our resources, religions, and dignity. Indeed, we became resources of labor for goldmines and cane fields. Life for us was unspeakable and cruel.

The nation-states are still colonizers. The issue is land. As long as it's culture and feathers and dancing, it's fine. As soon as you say "land" or "sovereignty," it's different.[7]

The colonizers have to be aware that there are forces larger than human forces. These forces are absolute with no mercy and if you don't learn you're just going to suffer the consequence. The instruction has to come from the leadership and from the people.[8]

Our prophecies tell us that life on earth is in danger of coming to an end. Our instructions tell us that we are to maintain our ceremonies, however few of us there are, and to maintain the spirit of those ceremonies, and the care of the natural world.

We were told that there would come a time when the world would be covered with smoke, and that it would take our elders and our children. It was difficult to comprehend at the time, but now all we have to do is walk outside to experience that statement. We were told that there would come a time when we could not find clean water to wash ourselves, to cook our foods, to make our medicines, and to drink. And there would be disease and great suffering. Today we can see this, and we peer into the future with great apprehension. We were told there would come a time when, tending our gardens, we would pull up our plants and the vines would be empty. Our precious seed would begin to disappear. We were instructed that we would see a time when young men would pace back and forth in front of their chiefs and leaders in defiance and confusion.

I think at the time there was a real option on the part of Europeans to change when they came here. I think at that time if they listened more to our direction and took our teachings a little bit more realistically it might have been a great opportunity to change direction.[9]

So then, what is the message I bring to you today? Is it our common future? It seems to me that we are living in a time of prophecy, a time of definitions and decisions. We are the generation with the responsibilities and the option to choose The Path of Life for the future of our children, or, the life and path which defies the Laws of Regeneration. Even though you and I are in different boats, you in your boat and we in our canoe, we share the same River of Life— what befalls me, befalls you. And downstream, downstream in this River of Life, our children will pay for our selfishness, for our greed, and for our lack of vision. 500 years ago, you came to our pristine lands of great forests, rolling plains, crystal clear lakes and streams and rivers. And we have suffered in your quest for God, Glory, and Gold. But, we have survived. Can we survive another 500 years of "sustainable development?"[10]

The chiefs said that sometime in the future, a big wind would come and blow the two vessels apart. And those standing with one foot in the boat and one in the canoe would fall into the river of life, and no power this side of the creation could save them.[11]

We can still alter our course. It is NOT too late. We still have options. We need the courage to change our values to the regeneration of our families, and all life that surrounds us. Given this opportunity, we can raise ourselves. We must join hands with the rest of Creation and speak of Common Sense, Responsibility, Brotherhood, and PEACE. We must understand that the law is the seed and only as true partners can we survive.

But we also know that all the world faces the same crisis; that every people and every living thing shares the same challenges. And we are here to offer our partnership, our knowledge and our ideas. It is time to move beyond "calls to action" and well-meaning agendas. The forces that are injuring our Mother the Earth are not waiting to create subcommittees, to set dates for meetings, or to set budgets.

Today we have met, we have taken one another's hands, and we have begun to make commitments, reminding ourselves that not only our own future generations depend upon us, but every living thing, relies on us to fulfill our responsibilities. We must learn to use the power of the Good Mind. The end of this legacy we will write with our own conduct.

So that's what we are, we're allies. It's a common fight, a common cause. It's for the future. It's for peace. What could be better? It's a good fight. We should be happy to be in it and happy to be able to make that difference. I believe it's this generation and the next one coming who are going to determine whether we survive.[12]

Dah nay to (Now I am finished).

Oren R. Lyons, Faithkeeper, Turtle Clan, Onondaga Nation Council of Chiefs, Haudenosaunee

CHAPTER TWO

# Where the Roots Touch

## tsi niyothahinen ne Tehontatenentshonteronhtáhkwa

*Amber Meadow Adams*

———

We break from the seed that's held us all for a year's bitter gestation. The seed has names: quarantine, self-isolation, sheltering in place, stay-at-home orders, and, in the brutal rhythm of prisonspeak lockdown. This seed, tsi ne yonkyats, is also called fear. Loss. Grief. Frustration. Boredom. Trauma for some, poverty for many, and denial for those who've twisted and fought their way nowhere out of this darkness. This seed is the hard-walled womb we all share. Cramped, but protective. Pulsing with words, but lonely. Too small for our restless bodies, but life's sustained nowhere else.

Now, a tendril. Vaccine technology germinated, hitching deaths downward. The radicle of another rooting, another birth into a world changed is coming. But the hard shell that's held nearly eight billion of us while we shift and moult into our next bodies has not yet broken, the womb not emptied fast enough. We wait. In this moment of the possible, all potentialities drawn together in the slenderest, nakedest rootlet of that-which-is-not-yet, we see, again, how life hangs from strands like this—the whispered beginning of being.

Let me tell you a story.

Before there was an Earth, before there was light or time, when the space between life and not-life was made of shadows and degrees, a girl they would call Yotsi'tsishon, the perfected flower, became the tendril of a root spilled from a seed cracked. Young, and carrying within her the doubled seed of a daughter, she fell from a world ne èneken, above us, into a long darkness. Absence of light made her sight useless, and the terror of a fall with no horizon, no known end, pulled her mind into strange shapes. It was a darkness deepened with grief for all she'd lost from that world above—mother, husband, family, name. There was also loneliness in that darkness, and hunger yet to come. And, always, gnawing and nuzzling, despair. There aren't many falls like this. Inanna and Orpheus may have walked their way down to the land of shades. Persephone was kidnapped, raped, and queened, always mourning her mother's sunlight. But no one, not even Milton's or Rushdie's Satan, took a fall like this and lived.

What turns this girl's mind from the ease of death, caught and set down on the cold crags of Ranyatenhkó:wa's shell, alone and full of a child she could not hope to keep alive? What moved her to stand and make her own warmth, her own time, by shifting and dancing and defying the void? The storytellers don't say. Hati nahòten, Yotsi'tsishon now finds herself rooted and reaching outward. A cotyledon, the first leaflet that stretches itself like an arm from broken seed, feeling for whatever will feel back. What she finds in the story is the closed mouth and curled claws of Anokyen, the muskrat, from which she coaxes the mud that will become all Earth. From mind to shoulder, mind blunted by fear to fingertips clumsy with cold, she bridges a gap between the will to be alive and the will to make life. These two potentialities reach each other in a lightning's flicker that brings ka'nikòn:ra, decision and direction, into contact with ka'shatstenhsera, the capacity to bring into being. Potentiality becomes action in that flicker, in that touch of fingertip seeking life to fingertip bearing it. They just brush, but it's enough to bring Earth into being.

Here, Tehontatenentshonteronhtáhkwa begins.

Usually spoken of in English as the "Covenant Chain," *tehontatenentshonteronhtáhkwa* describes a reaching across the space between ka'nikòn:ra and ka'shatstenhsera. It describes the connection, mind to mind and arm to arm, that sustaining life requires. These are the pieces of the word:

*te-*, a dualic prefix that describes action taken by two together, something double, a simultaneity. *-[h]ontate-*, a form of pronominal prefix that indicates an act of reciprocity, a doubled reflexive that describes mirrored action between two groups (in this case, the groups are grammatically masculine, but, in this usage, the term is inclusive of human and other beings). *-nentsh-* is the verb root describing an arm, sometimes the forearm. *-onte-*, an infix that acts like a preposition, describes spatial orientation, something attached to the end of something else. The form of the verb ending *-ahkwa* places the verb phrase temporally as something undertaken at a past point and continued into the present moment. A decision made, and made again, and made again and again, seeded from mind to mind through generations of cultivating ka'nikonhriyo'tsera't in a process both frighteningly precarious and unendingly sustainable. The whole verb phrase *tehontatenentshonteronhtahkwa* word-paints two people, or groups of people, or wills of people, with the ends of their arms attached to each other's, past and now, perpetually, in an act of sustained connection. Layers of specific action within a matrix of relationships that translate poorly into *covenant chain*.

A moment to parse that Anglophone knock-off. *Covenant* is an English word with shallow Latin roots. From *convenire*; *con*, together, plus *venire*, the infinitive verb form *to come*, to arrive someplace, physically or metaphorically. Arriving together comes near the meaning of the infix *-[h]ontate-*, the reciprocal reflexive describing action taken together. But *covenant* is a word we can see now, two decades into the twenty-first century, only in the slanted light of the Crown-supervised scholarship that produced it. Finally published in 1611, after two centuries of struggle that left heads on spikes and charred bones to drop from the stake, the King James Bible was created to be the authorized text of the Church of England. Its translators from Ancient Hebrew and Greek into Latin, thence into English (a porous shapeshifter barely a millennium old), charged *covenant* with the solemnity of a promise to God. An agreement not between human beings and Creation but with the one true Creator. Still a commitment made sometime in the past and remaining in force now, the distinction between the English and Haudenosaunee interpretations of who could be invited into such an agreement matured in the half-century between the King James Bible's publication and the

Crown's début in Kanyèn:keh. Spoken each Sunday, in church and at weddings and burials and baptisms, taught and repeated in the outbreaths of drama and verse, proverbs, profanities, and symbolism, the translator's art of the King James Bible forms the verbal universe of the people to whom the Haudenosaunee extended Tehontatenentshonteronhtáhkwa in the seventeenth and eighteenth centuries.

*Chain* entered English—rather, its ancestor, Anglo-Saxon—with the Norman French invasion of 1066. Its Latin root, *catēna*, had circulated in that place six centuries earlier, carried by Roman legions that occupied Indigenous Britain (a mix, by then, of Celt, Welsh, Cornish, Pict, and many other peoples speaking a variety of languages) by making relationships with Indigenous British leaders. *Catēna* in the Latin of the legions referred to a strand of metal, leather, or rope made by interlocking pieces. Its shadow meaning was the shackle, the iron cuffs that bound prisoners and captives, the tether that let the slave move across the yard to work, but no farther. If these earlier chains were made of fibre and fetters, the post-conquest English of Medieval and Early Modern England turned that chain into gold and silver, a symbol of authority, even sovereignty, underwritten by its appearance in the King James Bible (in Genesis 41:42 and Ezekiel 16:11, for example) as a ruler's ornament. To become enchained with gold or silver was to assume the power to enchain another with rope and iron. The tension bundled into seventeenth-century connotations of *chain*, translation of a translation of a translation, was almost certainly obscured by yet another layer of translation into Kanyen'kéha and other Haudenosaunee languages. Even had it not been, the core act of Kayanerenhtserakó:wa, the Haudenosaunee legal and political (and familial, and ecological, and spiritual) system—consensus—builds from commonalities, postponing conflict until the new relationship is solid enough to take some friction. A two-step we're still teaching our Canadian and American treaty partners.

Translations come with interests, whether cynical or just fumbling. It's easy to see how readily a twenty-first-century translator might slide arm into arm, elbows bent, as if they were only the fleshy imitations of metal links—connection, without relationship. *Tehontatenentshonteronhtáhkwa* becomes "their arms make a chain," an interpretational blurring that allows Anglophone scholars (including exclusively Anglophone Indigenous scholars) to dive deep into arguments about the historical context and legal significance of "the Covenant Chain" without slipping awènke, under the surface, to look for the earth from which *chain, covenant, -nentsh-*, or *-onte-* have grown. *-onte-*, the prepositional infix describing something attached to the end of something else, doesn't tell us where the endpoint of *-nentsh-* (the arm, an arm, arms) exists in space. Haudenosaunee grammar is full of four-dimensional maps, its grammar pinning actions onto what Einstein would eventually, with less precision, call "spacetime." The assertion that Indigenous languages are "verb-based" has become a homily, a sermon on the flatness of the European invader languages versus the life and dynamism of the languages they've gnawed down for centuries. What happens when we get precise about the possibilities that one "verb-based" language carries? What happens when we ask, for example, where exactly an arm ends? To begin an answer, we have to go back to the world ne èneken, the world above the sky. Specifically, to the hole someone tore in it.

Yotsi'tsishon (or Katsi'tsakayon, or Awenha'i, depending on the version), the girl who emerges from the seed of that deathless, self-contained place above, wasn't the person who broke it or volunteered to dangle from its edge. Once her husband uprooted Onodja, the great tree that gives all light in that world, Yotsi'tsishon, pushed or kicked or tripped, tries to break her fall by grabbing onto its roots. A reflex—we all put our arms out into empty space, reaching for arms that aren't there. Yotsi'tsishon, in some versions, peels bark and pulp away from the tree's roots, scrapes earth and seeds—of niyohontehsha, the wild strawberry, and oyen'kwahon:we, tobacco—under her fingernails. In the flailing of a survival reaction, Yotsi'tsishon answers the question of what's attached to the end of one's arm first in the story of Creation: soil, bark, seeds, and plant matter in the growing medium of grip sweat. Her arm ends in clenched fingers slicked with yethi'nihstenha tsi yonhwenhtsyàke. With Earth, the last mother she'll ever have that she doesn't have to become herself.

The image of arms ending in Earth repeats from this point in the Creation story through the remaining two-thirds of the narrative. Yotsi'tsishon is caught by the wings of water birds and set down on the back of Ranyahtenhkó:wa, the great Snapping Turtle. It's an emergency stopgap. Ranyahtenhkó:wa's not set up for intensive use and consistent occupation. To stay alive past the current crisis, Yotsi'tsishon needs soil, but it's out of her reach. To lengthen her grasp, she asks for help from the other beings who live in this new-risen and soilless place. Even before Yotsi'tsishon's landing, these other beings—beaver and otter, muskrat and snapping turtle, fish, ducks, geese, and heron—see this stranger falling and gather to decide what she is and what to do. In their council, they extend Yotsi'tsishon's reach for earth, tsi nahò:ten teyakonhwentsyon:ni, even before she knows there's another side of the fire who can help.

Once landed, Yotsi'tsishon and all the other beings sit down to a recognizably constituted Council: she, the human being, on one side; they, the other kinds of beings, on the other. The fire between them on that wet shell burns between minds, the lightning flicker of ka'shatstenhsera meeting ka'nikòn:ra. They discuss, all together, how they will use their ka'shatstenhsera, their energy and strength, and decide that they'll pool it to nurture her life. In decision, in council, is where their minds touch before the ends of their arms do. The slip of mud in Anokyen's paws and mouth is the realization of that across-the-fire agreement and a moment in the story that reverberates with meaning throughout Haudenosaunee law and the treaty relationships that flow from it. By narrating the council between animals that comes before the council between animals and a human, they show us how the act imagined and the act taken twin each other. Each exists discretely, but both require the other—imagination feeding action, and action feeding imagination further—to sustain momentum. Attaching at the ends, arm to arm, need not be, and cannot only be, a physical connection, nor even the metaphorical echo of a physical connection. It is, first, the connection of mutual imagination. And the vehicle of that mutual imagination at this doubled council—one half before Yotsi'tsishon lands, one half after—is talk.

Talk is what left this story for us living today. The talkers not only told the story, they lived out what the story teaches in the way they told it. The fullest versions of the Haudenosaunee story of Creation we have now are the product of speech written down by J.N.B. Hewitt, a scholar from Tuscarora of collaged ancestry and hard-fought education. He handwrote over 160 manuscript pages of Skanyataríːyo John Arthur Gibson's telling of the Creation story in Onoñda'gegá' during visits to Grand River between 1888 and 1890. He also transcribed shorter, though still substantial, versions told by Skanawati John Buck, Sr. (who, while holding the Turtle Clan Onoñda'gegá' Chief's title, also held a Tutelo Chief's title), a version in Kanye'kéha told by Dayodekane Seth Newhouse, and another in Onöndowa:'ga' gawé:no by John Armstrong (whom Hewitt visited in Allegany). Hewitt's work is often called "recording" or "transcribing"; by his own description, the process was much more two-sided. In a letter to Laura Cornelius from 1902, Hewitt reports hearing Skanyatarí:yo speak five or six words and then stopping him so he could write the words down, or ask for repetition or a gloss. An exhausting, frustrating process for both, but something nearer conversation—council—than the image of the passive, invisible scribe-ethnologist cultivated by Hewitt's contemporaries.

Hewitt compounded this mutuality by confirming vocabulary, narrative details, and the substances of whole texts with other people he worked with at Grand River and in other Haudenosaunee communities over a period of decades. The talking that he and Skanyatarí:yo, Skanawati, and many others did across the fire leaves us a written artifact that not only narrates the principles of Tehontatenentshonteronhtáhkwa, but also reifies Tehontatenentshonteronhtáhkwa as the collaboration that produced the texts. At the end of Hewitt's arm was a pencil that touched paper, which in turn became full of Skanyatarí:yo's spoken words. At the end of Skanyatarí:yo's arm, a door opened, a table shared, and the waves of sound and language, knowledge and thought, extended toward the other man. A chain of connection still at far remove from the talking around the fire we used to do to pass this story from mind to mind. Yet even this remove works to reinforce the not-now parts of Tehontatenentshonteronhtáhkwa, the mutual imagining that comes before, with, and after the act agreed—skarihwa't—reminding us that imagination doesn't move only forward in the Haudenosaunee philosoverse, working ka'shatstenhsera into what may be, but can also turntoward the what might have been and the infinite circles of how else it could've gone.

And that tokat non:wa space takes us into the darkest part of the story.

The men who set down these stories tell us almost nothing about what ends of whose arms touch from the time that bit of earth passes between Anokyen's hands and Yotsi'tsishon's. The story sharpens again when

Yotsi'tsishon's daughter meets Turtle Man (or, in some versions, the West Wind) and becomes pregnant with twin boys. In between, Yotsi'tsishon and her daughter form Earth itself. Imagine all the ways their arms ended: fingers folded around the wisps of new soil, knuckles scraping the ridges of Ranyahtenhkó:wa's bare shell, elbows bent and propping them up against new mounds and slopes when they rested, looking up into darkness. The seed and plant matter tucked under Yotsi'tsishon's fingernails, attached to her arms' very ends, must have been scraped or fallen out onto Earth, potential life passed from her arms to yethi'nihstenha's, waiting for sun and warmth and rain to germinate and multiply.

Did they eat? Did they dip their hands into the endless water in which Ranyahtenhkó:wa swims to drink? The storytellers don't say, nor do they tell us whether the two women inoculated and enriched the nearly sterile Earth with the substances of their own bodies, still carrying life from the place ne èneken—their sweat, their blood, their breastmilk, their tears, and their waste. Imagining the moment-to-moment physicality of surviving and creating (a tough double act, even for us who live in a formed Earth) these two women embody brings every reach and pull, grab and push, every form of touch between their bodies and Earth's body to mind. It shows them doing and making and sharing by feel in this unsighted world where touch, even the touch of air rippled by soundwaves that carry their words, is the primary form of communication. They grab hands, lock arms, pinch, pick, brush, and hold.

Yotsi'tsishon, arm crooked, held her daughter when she was an infant the way people still do when infants are given names in longhouse. She does the same after her daughter's death, holding her grandsons with an arm that ends in a sheltering elbow. This darkness, if we use our own tactile sense to probe it, shows us that arms end not according to anatomy, but action.

Most of the actions in this part of the story connect the actors directly to Earth, to each other, or to both at once.

The story refocuses when a stranger, a male being called Turtle Man (or the West Wind, as in John Armstrong's version), meets Yotsi'tsishon's daughter and she becomes pregnant. This, unlike the story's other conception scenes, is a touchless process; he lays two arrows across the girl's belly as she sleeps and then retreats from the story, making only one later appearance. Here, the story shifts gaze onto the twins, Taharonhyawakon and Tawiskaron, whose relationship dominates the last half to third of the story. We are shown this relationship from its very beginnings, when the twins talk to each other in the womb:

> The first voice said to the other, "What will you do after you leave this womb and you are born?"
>
> The second answered, "I will create human beings and they will live together as groups. And I will create everything that human beings will need to live by and the things I create will make these human beings happy to live upon the earth. And what will you do?"
>
> "I will make the attempt to do as you say. It must come to pass that I will have an impact on the earth."[1]

Council again. They identify a problem—what will they do with their lives, their ka'shatstenhsera?—and share each other's imagined actions through talking. They continue to talk until those ni'nikò:nra, two distinct minds, are turned toward an action as one, ska'nikòn:ra. They agree. Ka'nikòn:ra has been applied to ka'shatstenhsera before they act. Now, all that remains is to see how that spoken reach across the gap, mind to mind, will manifest in action, hand to hand.

When the brothers talk in utero, four important things happen at once.

First, though it's unsaid, and we have to imagine what fills this dark space, they are each attached to their mother by an umbilicus. It's hard to imagine a more visceral metaphor for the human connection with yethi'nihstenha tsi yonhwentsyàke, our Mother the Earth, than the umbilical cord that attaches a fetus to its mother. Belly to belly, gut to gut, oxygen and nutrients move through blood from the mother to the child she grows, feeds, protects, and insulates. Akwesasne midwife and teacher Katsi Cook rightly reminds us that the womb is the first environment. Physiologically, it's the microcosm of the macrocosm—Earth, Creation, the cosmos—we enter at birth. Practically, it's very much part of the macrocosm; the food one's mother eats, the water she drinks, the air she breathes, and the hormones and neurotransmitters external stimuli may produce in her all pass through the cord's blood into the developing human. From conception, we deal with the greater Mother, Earth, wrapped in the husk of the smaller human mother whose cord blood first brings us to both. That the story introduces us to the twins here, in utero, rather than after birth, or as half-grown creators, draws a line, again, under the prime relationship in human existence: the one we hold with yethi'nihstenha yonwhentsyakekha. The Haudenosaunee story of Creation says this over and over again, lapping us with waves of signification, but this moment, when we first see these two creators tied cord and cord to their mother (who is likewise tied to her Mother), throws a narrow spotlight on what comes first. Before they talk to each other, before they make any connection as brothers, they're far along into an attachment to ni'nihstenha/yethi'nihstenha—their mother/Mother—that will last, in the womb and out of it, for the length of their lives and beyond, when their bodies return to hers.

Second, they are tied to their mother with separate cords. Both monozygotic (identical) and dizygotic (fraternal or sororal) twin fetuses develop their own umbilici. Even though their mother is shared, each child, no matter how like its twin, grows a biologically unique connection with her. Each of the twins' separate cords makes part of a broad narrative arc that charts difference-in-likeness (and its obverse) through the Creation story as a whole. This tension becomes visible and pointed in the episodes, putting Tawiskaron and Taharonhyawakon stage front. Separate, biologically unique umbilical cords ripen quickly into differences of ni'nikòn:ra; having just agreed on a plan for what comes after birth, they differ on the routes they'll take to that birth:

> When it was time for them to be born, one said to the other, "which of us shall go first?"
>
> ... "You go first," the first voice said. "As for me, I see light here, and I shall exit through this spot."
>
> As the other began to depart, he called back, "Do not do this. If you do, you will kill our mother." Then the first twin was born. In a moment, the second male child emerged from his mother's armpit. As Young Woman gave birth, she died.[2]

Tawiskaron announces he will follow a light he sees—hard to reconcile with the context of the story, as Earth has yet no light source. Even if it did, his mother's arm hanging from her shoulder down her trunk would cover it. Taharonhyawakon warns his brother away from a path that will kill their mother, himself exiting "in the usual way," a path not without risk, but one much more likely to leave their mother living and capable of further creation. The rest of the story offers plenty to mine what might be called the psychology of each brother's relationship with his mother, in all her faces: the person who gives birth to them, the grandmother who steps into that role after her daughter's death, and Earth that is both fleshed and made from the flesh of these mothers. It offers even more on what Western psychology would call the relationship with the self. *Self* remains a specifically Eurocentric, post-Enlightenment construct with no straightforward correspondences in Haudenosaunee languages or conceptual categories. Folded into ka'nikòn:ra, a term that encompasses the twined matrices of behaviour and motivation, conscious and unconscious, knowledge of one's own interiority appears at this point in the story as an ingredient in ka'nikonhriyo'tshera't. A good mind—ka'nikonhrí:yo—knows itself. If the brothers are a type for humanity (or, at least, Haudenosaunee), then the story defines humanity's relationships with yethi'nihstenha as personal, intimate, idiosyncratic, and shaped by that part of the ka'nikòn:ra bundle that looks honestly at how one's desires and reactions grow or fail to grow. Because the prime relationship is all these things, it has to be known and negotiated fresh every time, again and again, for every person who emerges into being.

Third, these brothers use speech to communicate and reconcile the personal, mind-in-mind relationships each develops with yethi'nihstenha, and they use it in specific, deliberate ways. Tawiskaron asks his brother, spontaneously, what will you do once we get out of here? His question, he shows us, is the fruit of his own reflection, of a period of thought he undertakes before speaking, words with himself before all else. His brother Taharonhyawakon offers an answer full-formed, the result of his own period of thought. But this talk doesn't take place in the middle of a crisis—not during their birth, and not right after their emergence into a Mother's womb beyond their mother's, in which they have to deal immediately with the chaos, grief, and multiplied survival pressures of their mother's death. Taharonhyawakon, the long-range thinker, answers questions about what each imagines, wants, and plans before the pressure's on, giving both room to think and gently toss the matter back and forth across the space bright with ka'shatstenhsera. Tawiskaron responds, though vaguely and with an ominous self-centring.

That gap in the story evokes one of the fundamentals of council procedure, which is amplified in the treaty process: nobody demands a response right away, and nobody (at least, nobody familiar with protocol) delivers a response right away. To do the former is to bully the people whose help you need, to "throw ... on their backs," in the words of Shakoyewatha at Niagara in 1792, the very people for whom you carry kentèn:ron, compassion and a duty of care. To do the latter is to make a public show of disrespect, for the matter at hand and for those with whom you're addressing it, and to display your lack of seriousness and solidity as a partner. If Tawiskaron's quicker than he is thoughtful here, it's a feature of ro'nikòn:ra—his mind, his anima—we're shown throughout the story. But his eagerness to enter into his brother's plans also shows ronoronhkwa'tsera't, his love and esteem for his brother underlying a long narrative arc of conflict between them.

Through this conflict, the brothers talk. Half the length of Skanyatarí:yo's version is dialogue. It's only when they stop talking to each other that their conflict becomes physical, even murderous—so violent that it nearly destroys the still-fragile Earth. (In fact, their long period of using talk to prevent and resolve conflict gives Earth time to gather size and maturity, enough, in the end, to recover from the damage they do her; had they fought earlier in the narrative, yethi'nihstenha might not have survived it.) Tempting as it might be for students or scholars who miss its significance to skip all the back-and-forth between the brothers, their constant communication defangs conflict and enables quick repair after its climax. It's a mimetic demonstration of what, in the strange, structured world of the Canadian judicial system, emerges from case law as "procedural treaty rights." We don't expect our Tehontatenentshonteronhtáhkwa treaty partners to work with us just on the what (a thriving, healthy yethi'nihstenha tsi yonhwenstyàke, for example) but also on the how: an open, well-traveled, bi-directional channel of communication in good faith that we don't wait for an Oka or a Caledonia to use. This one short scene in the Creation story offers a single demonstration, among hundreds in Haudenosaunee narrative, of exactly how that works.

Fourth, building on the three before, we're shown that relationships between people on two sides of the fire work *only* where relationships between human beings and yethi'nihstenha tsi yonhwentsyàke work. When Tawiskaron cuts his way out of his mother through rib and armpit, he must also first slice through the umbilical cord that feeds and breathes for him. Though he survives delivery, he begins his life on Earth by, in effect, slitting his own throat. The act, though implied rather than explicit, resonates with many other points in the Creation story that name breath as the defining difference between death and life. The first consequence of his decision to cut his mother's body open to exit it is to end his own access to oxygen through cord blood, and thus likely his own life, though he survives. The second eliminates his own and his brother's supply of nourishment, warmth, and protection; when Tawiskaron kills his mother, he destroys both his and his brother's source of breast milk, body heat, and all an infant's many survival needs a mother can meet. The circle of Tawiskaron's damage widens exponentially, from himself to his closest family, including his grandmother, whose grief drives her to throw his brother Taharonhyawakon into the bush in an act of attempted passive murder. After their mother is buried, Tawiskaron disturbs her body, poking it, then cutting it, finally decapitating it, and so preventing her from returning to life after a ten-day rest in the earth. This damage shapes all Earth; Yotsi'tsishon's daughter had been her co-creator and sole companion, and her death, once made permanent, halves Yotsi'tsishon's capacity, physical and emotional, to grow the only source of sustenance for the three survivors and all other beings emerging, or about to emerge, in that place.

Tawiskaron decides alone on a course of action. He has his own unique connection to his mother that enables the growth of his own ro'nikòn:ra and the ka'shatstenhsera to realize it. Taharonhyawakon, also with his own will and his own capacity, cannot persuade, or prevent, or unmake Tawiskaron's actions, even though they endanger Taharonhyawakon's (and every other being's) life, directly and indirectly, throughout the rest of the story. Though the capacity to create that both ro'nihstenha, his mother, and yethi'nihstenha, our Mother the Earth, carry are greater than those of the twin fetuses, that very capacity creates a Tawiskaron who makes his relationship with ro'nihstenha/yethi'nihstenha one of mutual destruction. One slash jags outward to scar all Earth. His brother, Taharonhyawakon, makes his relationship with the same body, the same yethi'nihstenha, one of mutual creation. Yet: this mutual creation can't be sustained while Tawiskaron destroys. The idea they agree on and the plan they negotiate before birth ties them together, mind to mind and arm to arm. Neither Tawiskaron nor Taharonhyawakon ever unmake that agreement, or replace it with something else, or explicitly break that bond. Neither when they fight, nor when they decide to put a little distance between themselves to better reconcile, do they ever dissolve the project of their brotherhood.

However, when Tawiskaron cuts the cord tying him to ro'nihstenha/yethi'nihstenha, he also cuts the cord tying Taharonhyawakon to yethi'nihstenha, and that has the ultimate effect of cutting the cord between them. What's the point of agreeing to do something with or on Earth, if you've been severed from her? How can you reach another's arm if your own has come unattached from Earth, and you're grasping for a handhold in the void? How do you knife your own cord without knifing your brother's? Yotsi'tsishon's fall dramatizes the viscerally terrifying lifelessness of a cord cut. The two-sidedness of Tehontatenentshonteronhtáhkwa is always, ohèn:ton karihwatéhkwen, the two-sidedness of the connection between human beings and yethi'nihstenha yonhwentsyakekha. We hold Earth first. How we hold her, and how she, in turn, holds us, is the blood that runs through every treaty, every policy, and every law. We can't talk about what they mean and how we use them today without talking about all four quarters of the circle—each brother, or family, or nation, or alliance and the kind of relationship each has grown with yethi'nihstenha, and each of yethi'nihstenha's states of being as they are cut or smoothed, up and breathing or lying in a dead twilight.

In the late half of the seventeenth century, when the Haudenosaunee were bringing the British Crown into the house and offering space across the fire, the part of that relationship matrix that attaches the ends of human arms to Earth didn't have to be articulated fully every time. "The usual ceremonies" is a phrase many European recorders at the treaty councils of the time used to describe what always came first: tsi karhákta, the Wood's Edge, the three bare words, and the renarrating of the history of how the Haudenosaunee extended

Tehontatenentshonteronhtáhkwa to the British Crown and brought them from the edge of things into the heart of the house. Did that mean everyone understood them? Haudenosaunee law governs Haudenosaunee people, at home or in treaty council. It's a way of living with the kind of earth we're set down in, our nationhood. We treated visitors to that land as people who understood their visits to be conditional on following the rules required for living with that kind of earth. Once someone was made family, it became that family's responsibility to make sure the person, or nation, understood and followed those rules. Meanwhile, the Industrial Revolution had begun in England, quickened by the transatlantic slave trade. Europeans would begin pulling resources out and dragging invasives of all kinds in, changing the Haudenosaunee home biome under our feet. Not all at once, and not completely, even now. Enough to break the seed of our world, yethi'nihstenha as we've known her for millennia, and force the rootlets of what we've had to become, and are becoming next, out into another long darkness.

Generations into this process, the fall already begun, we can no longer assume that we or our treaty partners have the means to sustain a Tehontatenentshonteronhtáhkwa relationship with each other, because we can no longer assume either side of this brotherhood still holds yethi'nihstenha by the other arm. If this treaty relationship begins in the cord blood, then that's where we begin its repair. The first place to work on, if the story of the twins is the head of the path Tehontatenentshonteronhtáhkwa makes, is our own relationship with yethi'nihstenha—not as nations, or Haudenosaunee, or humanity before we do it as human beings. Onkwehon:we, each of us ourselves. We have to grieve what we've each lost of her, or never had—paradise paved, birdsong silenced, plastic food and good farmland covered in cardboard mansions, yethi'nihstenha opened for business. We have to acknowledge that this hurts, and hurts us all, profoundly, and specifically, and unequally. It demands courage to sit with the terror of what comes next, and to find again our love and awe for her.

Tawiskaron doesn't get it all wrong. If his brother's the visionary with arms that grab sky, Tawiskaron's the constant pragmatist. Their grandmother, whatever her failures in that role, is his to take care of. They're both always hungry, always scraping, and, like too many of yethi'nihstenha's children, worn by chronic need into lesser ka'shatstenhsera where much is needed to survive the moment. The family expert in scrounging for the today you have to make it through before the tomorrow you've planned for, Tawiskaron would be the first to tell us that life can't wait, that we need to emerge *now* from the splitting seed into what's living beyond it.

We're in the midst of multiple simultaneous crises—within us, between us, and beyond us, all the way to the edges of this lonely island on Ranyahtenhkó:wa's back—that won't wait for any more contemplation, or discussion, or denial. Tawiskaron's right. Any policy, any court win, any right we can prop up, any piece of knowledge we can save and seed, and any part of Tehontatenentshonteronhtáhkwa we can breathe life back into feeds the cord that draws survival for another day from yethi'nihstenha tsi yonhwentsyàke. Arms attached, even in the ugliest grip of structural racism and the suicide pact of ecological stomp-dancing, are still attached; the brothers, even fighting to kill, never let go. A little blood can be squeezed into the cord between us and yethi'nihstenha to keep both sputtering along if we twist hard enough for long enough. But the longer we fight, the more exhausted we become, and the more damage she sustains.

We don't have to do all the hard thinking and grieving, we don't have to know all our fears and rages and refusals by name or go through all possible permutations of fucking up before we can think clearly, talk with each other compassionately, and agree on what we will create together now. We have stories. The people who came before us bundled them carefully and passed them to us, mind to mind, arm to arm, in the hope, I believe, that we'd use them. They've left us maps that are not only specific, but mimetic—even reified—for maintaining and, when needed, repairing the matrix of relationships encoded in Tehontatenentshonteronhtáhkwa. The Haudenosaunee story of Creation is not the only story we still have that shows us how relationships between people and with Earth are not separate domains, but mutual requirements. It's a core principle of what we might call Haudenosaunee environmental law and, because everyone has to practice it in order for it to work, it appears in story after ceremony after song after garden after potful of soup bubbling over the fire tsi niyonkwarihò:ten. That treaties are law is a truth universally acknowledged by both brothers, Haudenosaunee and the Crown. Some of us remember parts of this truth. Some forget all of it. Some put hard work into denying and throwing it away. Like most breakage, these fractures and self-cuttings cause pain. The first medicine for restoring skatne ka'nikòn:ra is remembering the cord, and how not to cut it, that binds us to the body of our mother.

Treaties are stories, too. If Tehontatenentshonteronhtáhkwa is a story about how and why people connect, and Tékeni Teyohà:te (the Two Row) is about what's in the space they cross when connecting, then the Creation story is about why things begin. Obvious, of course, but there's some nuance to where the storytellers put the end of that beginning. Earth never reaches completion. We're left, by the end, in a place that has become almost like the place ne èneken, but isn't quite the climax community of a Carolinian biome like the one within which those telling the story to J.N.B. Hewitt 130 years ago lived. Creation's never finished. Nor are treaties. We carry what we are handed, beginning again, knowing that people get tired, people let go, the path gets weedy, scary things happen, Earth shifts, and we don't always know when the seed will crack and the fragile green arm of new life will reach into another empty place.

Here, now, we kick against a shell grown stuffy and small with waiting. We can't know what the fall will be, or how we'll land, or if we'll meet kindness and council at the bottom. We know only how to begin again—how to sip our mother's blood and so think, how to talk and so act together, how to grasp hands and so live belly to belly with our mother the Earth. We know how to begin, and begin again, and again and again, because that's what Creation is. We've been here before. But, like all firsts, it asks us to brave the long space between broken seed and the place where the mind lands and the roots touch.

CHAPTER THREE

# Wunnáumwash

## Wampum Justice

*Kelsey Leonard*

---

### INTRODUCTION

As a Shinnecock woman, I was born with a natal connection to the sea. Shinnecock means "People of the Stony Shore" in our language, and within that shore lie our ancient Mollusk relatives—the quahog and whelk. These two relatives, when harvested and carved, form what we know today as wampum. These relatives have sustained eastern Indigenous Peoples of Turtle Island for thousands of years. We share the same home where islands meet bays meet ocean in a spiral where there is no beginning or end. Algonkian Peoples[1] have harvested wampum since time immemorial. Women have the spiritual responsibility to care for wampum, and traditionally, they were renowned harvesters and keepers of wampum. So much has shifted since the onset of colonization in relation to how others now come to know wampum. There is a profound disconnect. Many will label wampum as beads or stones, rarely recognizing its origin in the sea. These mischaracterizations lead to the consumption of wampum as money, diplomatic credentials, or art without truly ever understanding the beauty of its spirit.

The settler-colonial obsession with domination over nature has led to the Anthropocene, our current geologic age where humanity bears the responsibility for planetary degradation. Davis and Todd challenge us to reimagine our relationships with one another and the natural world through a process that affords the potential to reclaim Indigenous conceptualizations of justice and dismantle colonial logics. They note that "by dating the Anthropocene to colonialism we can at least begin to address the root of the problem, which is the severing of relations through the brutality of colonialism coupled with an imperial, universal logic."[2] As an extension of this approach, this chapter challenges us to rethink conceptualizations of wampum and justice.

The western world conceptualizes justice in the form of a maiden—"Lady Justice," as she is often called—who holds the scales of "justice" in each hand, personifying a delicate balance of societal morality and truth. Her blindfold represents impartiality and her sword is an ever-present reminder of the "rule of law."[3] However, Indigenous Algonkian conceptualizations of justice do not position an adversarial act of balancing truth, morality, and objectivity; rather, they are braided together. Instead of Lady Justice, we have Wampum Justice. Wampum justice does not try to personify justice but recognizes that wampum itself is living. Wampum justice carries the intergenerational memory of truth over millennia. More than four hundred years after colonists disembarked the Mayflower, wampum still embodies Algonkian justice. For centuries, it was mischaracterized as money[4] and commodified within a system of colonialism and oppression that sought to erase truth and deny justice for Indigenous Peoples. Reclaiming the subject of justice removes the fetishization of humans as solo actors and recognizes the inherent agency of wampum as a node of relationality and lifeforce for truth-keeping in all conduct and covenants. Our recognition of the agency of wampum stems from Indigenous understandings, as Watts highlights, of "agency as being tied to spirit, and spirit exists in all things, then all things possess agency."[5] Wampum has spirit.

An account of wampum justice is required to remedy the mischaracterizations and false assumptions of wampum put forward by settler-colonial scholars and systems of intellectual colonialism through the dispossession and oppression of Indigenous Knowledge systems. This chapter first explores the conceptualization of wampum justice. The chapter then distinguishes between justice and diplomacy and the discursive meanings associated with wampum. It then explores the recognition of wampum as living and imbued with the power for justice when we speak the truth—*wunnáumwash*. Last, the chapter recognizes the practices of harvesting wampum and its connection to spiritual, cultural, and political processes for justice. All together, the chapter aims to show that wampum justice does not equate with punishment, war, or money, but rather with truth. From truth flows peace, love, and friendship—the pillars of Indigenous nationhood.

## FROM BIRTH TO BEADS: LIVING WAMPUM

Wampum has its own life force. It is a source of life so unique that it is worthy of carrying words of peace and friendship across generations. Of all the living beings on this planet that we could have fashioned to carry words of peace and friendship, why is the form we know best, wampum, made from quahog shells?[6] These Mollusk relatives are not easy to harvest or carve into the beads woven into patterned belts embedded with ancestral knowledge. Their selection is purposeful. They have meaning.

Quahogs live in muddy sands along eastern Atlantic shores. They prefer estuarine waters that provide lower salinity levels than the open ocean.[7] Some studies have found that quahogs live between 46 and 106 years.[8] They are also remarkable bivalve filter feeders that take in water and clean approximately one gallon of water per hour.[9] They are often an indicator of healthy waters for humans and other-than-human relations. In recent decades, increased nutrient pollution from wastewater contamination and stormwater run-off have depleted shellfish beds throughout the eastern Atlantic waters that quahogs call home.[10] Ocean acidification also poses severe threats to the well-being and future of quahogs. Griffith and Gobler found that quahogs are less likely to acclimate within a generation to changes in pH levels of coastal habitats with potential additional stressors, including temperature changes, food insecurity, and harmful algae.[11] If quahogs are to exist for future generations, we must fulfill our covenants to the wampum to care for the sea. We cannot continue to take without a commitment to restore. More recently, restoration efforts to protect quahogs include creating hard-clam sanctuaries where they can thrive without the threat of overharvesting.

The quahog cannot be replaced. Quahogs are unique to the estuarine ecosystems of the eastern Atlantic. The deep purple hues of the shell cannot be replicated, although some have tried to use shells without adequate coloring or that are too brittle to be carved. Or worse yet, colonial wampum-makers tried to replace the living relative with glass or plastic beads, thus fueling settler territorialization and usurpation of even wampum bead-making to line the pockets of colonial authorities. Each plastic bead furthers fossil fuel extraction, exacerbating climate change. In turn, climate change advances ocean acidification and environmental pollution, threatening wampum ecosystems. When Indigenous Peoples acquiesce to the severing of relationships between wampum and the sea, they are consumed by the logics of coloniality, mistakenly imagining wampum can be replaced and synthetic replicas created. Instead, we must remember our sacred responsibility as wampum keepers to care for the water and habitats that sustain our Mollusk relatives.

Wampum justice means we polish our promises to the wampum through habitat conservation and restoration. Some Indigenous Nations along the eastern Atlantic coast, such as the Shinnecock Indian Nation, have environmental departments with dedicated staff and programs from hatcheries to estuarine restoration for shellfish protection.[12] In doing so, Indigenous Nations recognize that we have a responsibility to care for wampum across its life cycle from birth to beads. Indigenous scholars continue to theorize about contemporary meanings of relationality, kinship, and connection with wampum.[13] Emerging from this theoretical discourse is the recognition that polishing the Covenant Chain is not about our rights as humans but instead our responsibilities. Words were spoken to the wampum before it was carried and presented to form new covenants. Wampum has agency. Wampum has its own spirit. Wampum is alive. Indigenous agency is derived from our wampum-human connection expressed through ceremony, marriage, food, politics, treaty-making, and more. In every aspect of our lives where truth should be embedded in our hearts and minds, you will find wampum to keep us connected to our Mother—the Earth—to center our purpose and remove ego.

## HARVESTING WAMPUM

The practice of harvesting wampum is complex, involving cultural, spiritual, and political relations and responsibilities. For wampum justice to exist, a set of relations must be practiced, from harvesting to food to carving to diplomacy to nation-building. Indigenous sovereignty is based on the woven nature of these relations coming together in pursuit of truth—*wunnáumwash*. Wampum harvesting also represents a deep spiritual connection among Algonkian Peoples. As Mashpee Wampanoag Tribal citizen and wampum harvester Marcus Hendricks shares, "When I come out onto the water there's a connection to my ancestors. A relationship that goes through my blood into my veins...I was taught really young to take the time to give thanks and say a few prayers to the Creator. We do that anytime we're harvesting anything from Mother Earth."[14] The gathering process connects us to a place of blood memory where we build relationships of gratitude with wampum. The harvesting of quahogs happens at a local scale across eastern coastal Tribal Nations. Harvesters only take what is needed for food and livelihood. Overharvesting of clam beds is expressly prohibited throughout eastern coastal communities, and Tribal members are charged with expelling those who would attempt to do so. Larger, more mature quahogs are harvested with attention to size and thickness. They are more easily harvested at low tides, and traditionally, women would wade into the water to dive and dig for clams. Affectionately known as "clam diggers," an individual's feet are used to dig out the clams, later replaced with the creation of the Shinnecock rake, and then they are gathered into a basket for hauling to shore. All parts of the quahog are used (See Figure 3.1).

Quahogs have delicious meat with rich nutritional value and are a first food for Algonkian Peoples. They are often fashioned into many contemporary Americana delicacies where the Indigenous origin is often erased, such as clam chowder, clam bakes, clam puffs, clam pies, baked clams, etc. However, these dishes still fill Indigenous homes and bellies throughout eastern coastal Indigenous communities. The insatiable settler desire for shellfish is a complicated web of interference with and prohibition of Indigenous Peoples' traditional harvesting practices. Settler-colonial laws attempt to regulate the harvesting of shellfish

3.1 Harvesting of quahogs—a first food—along Shinnecock shores in Long Island, New York. (Credit: Kelsey Leonard)

and overall habitats to the exclusion and burden of Indigenous Peoples. Despite these oppressive regimes, wampum harvesting remains resiliently practiced. After the meat is transformed into edible delicacies, the shells of quahogs are broken and carved into beautiful beads or shapely pieces for incorporation into all aspects of our cultural existence.

Wampum-making is a practice of truth-telling, rendering stories of our communities that last beyond our finite mortality. For centuries, wampum has been stolen from Indigenous Peoples. In removing wampum

3.2 Daniel Hill, Mashpee Wampanoag tribal citizen, carries the new wampum belt. (Credit: Daniel Hill)

and mischaracterizing it as the last remaining remnant of the "vanishing Indian" to be caged in museums, the colonizer usurps its rightful place as a representation of law. According to Jeffrey G. Hewitt, this practice furthers the colonizer's attempts to deny Indigenous sovereignty and sources of law. The distortion results not solely from the violence of extraction and usurpation of our intellectual canon to the confines of colonizer's curiosity cabinets but also from the manufacturing of wampum as "mystic relics" for consumption by the miseducated settler-colonial masses.[15]

Despite these injustices, wampum-making continues to build new stories of truth-telling. A new wampum belt was created in 2020 by more than one hundred Wampanoags and made with five thousand wampum beads harvested from Atlantic waters (see Figure 3.2).

The belt was made to commemorate four hundred years of Indigenous resilience after the Mayflower landing in what is currently known as Plymouth, Massachusetts, in 1620. As was mentioned earlier, so many wampum belts remain missing and stolen, including Metacom's wampum belt, which has not been seen since 1677. In creating this new belt, the Wampanoag Nation hopes that international education about the meaning and importance of wampum as a living source of law and justice might aid in returning the many missing relatives.[16] The first step towards healing is to acknowledge that justice is denied to us as Indigenous Peoples when the truth is stolen.

## WAMPUM JUSTICE

As Indigenous Peoples, our conceptualizations of justice, although vibrant and persistent, have been largely absent from the legal canon and discourse due to the hegemony of coloniality. As MacIntyre underscores, modern conceptions of justice are built on the philosophical thinkers emerging from western traditions.[17] As sovereign Indigenous Nations, we have our own laws, policies, and mechanisms for nurturing ecological balance. Indigenous notions of justice stem from our relationships with and responsibilities to the natural world.[18] Eurocentric notions of justice centre the individual.[19] However, despite this conflict, there is an area of consensus where both philosophical traditions understand justice and truth as intertwined.[20] As Anishinaabekwe scholar Deborah McGregor affirms, "there are other 'peoples' in the world who are deserving of justice or who can dispense justice if balance and interdependence are not respected."[21] Moreover, beyond humans, other relatives including wampum have the spirit and agency to dispense justice. What justice has wampum gifted?

In documenting his engagement with early Algonkian Peoples, Roger Williams wrote in *A Key into the Language of America* that the phrase *wunnáumwash* means "speaks the truth."[22] Later, Trumbull noted that *wunnáumwash* is often said after an Indigenous person delivers a speech.[23] During these speeches, wampum was always present. In this way, the concept of *wunnáumwash* (truth) is integral to understanding the power and connection to wampum common among Algonkian and Indigenous Nations of Turtle Island in realizing justice. Wampum justice advances ethical conduct among all peoples, inclusive of human and more-than-human relations. Our words are our medicine; they should never be wielded to inflict violence or harm. Principles like this are the essence of wampum justice. In this understanding, our speech should mimic our Mollusk relatives. Quahogs filter the pollution in our waters. They take out the bad and return to us water that is healthy to support life. Quahogs are life-givers. They are purifiers and truth-seekers. These processes of life produce truth and help us to conceptualize what justice means in our world—to speak the truth.

Although wampum is birthed from eastern Atlantic waters, it has spiritual, cultural, and political meaning throughout Turtle Island among Algonkian, Anishinaabek, and Hodinöhsö:ni'. Wampum in the Algonkian language is an abbreviated form of the word *wampumpeag*. Similarly, quahog is a shortened version of the complete name *Poquaûhock*. Among the Anishinaabek, wampum is referred to as *miigis* in Anishinaabemowin.[24] The Mohawk refer to wampum beads as *otsi'nehtara'shón:'a*.[25] In these relational practices of naming, we see how wampum, inclusive of beads, strings, and belts, formed the foundation of justice across many Nations.

One wampum belt, the Teioháte (Two Paths/Roads in Mohawk language) Kaswenta (Wampum Belt) or Two Row Wampum, was a treaty made circa 1613 between the Hodinöhsö:ni' and Dutch in what is currently known as New York.[26] The belt constituted terms of relationality between the Hodinöhsö:ni' and settlers that would allow for coexistence and mutual respect.[27] Visually, the belt consists of two lines of deep purple quahog hues separated by rows of white wampum beads. The meaning of the belt has been retold as follows:

> It is on a bed of white wampum, which symbolizes the purity of the agreement. There are two rows of purple, and those two rows have the spirit of our ancestors; those two rows never come together in that belt, and it is easy to see what that means. It means that we have two different paths, two different people. The agreement was made that your road will have your vessel, your people, your politics, your government, your way of life, your religion, your beliefs—they are all in there. The same goes for ours....They said there will be three beads of wampum separating the two, and they will symbolize peace, friendship, and respect.[28]

In addition, the Two Row Wampum is said to embody the following principles handed down from the Kayanerenkó:wa (Great Law of Peace), including Sken:nen (peace), Kasastensera (strength), and Ka'nikonrí:yo

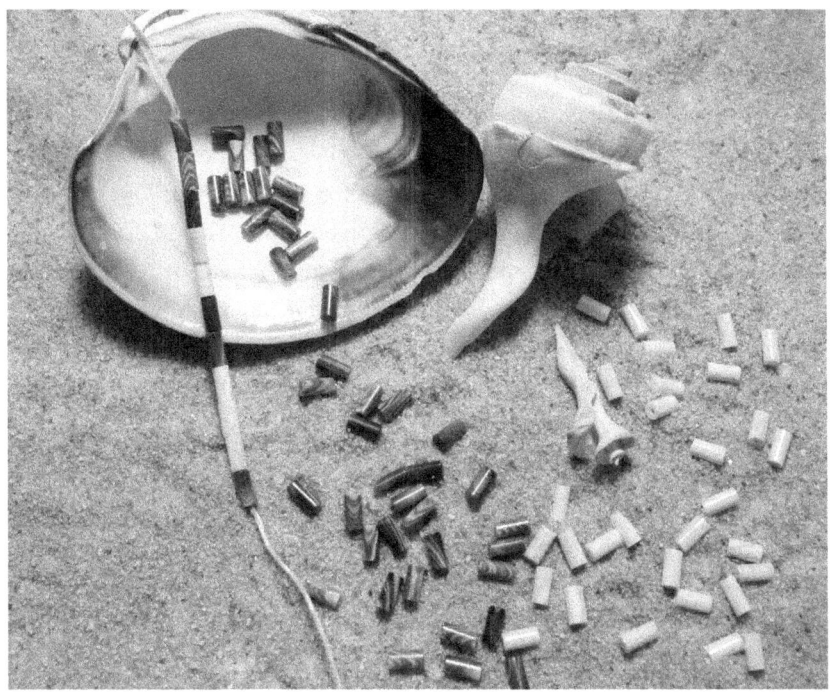

3.2 Quahog and whelk shells with carved wampum beads in purple and white hues strung on sinew. (Credit: Kelsey Leonard)

(good mind).[29] Together, these principles are integral to the realization of justice through truth-telling. The Two Row Wampum is a foundational treaty upon which subsequent treaties between the Hodinöhsö:ni' and settler-colonial nations, such as the U.S. and Canada, are based.[30] The Two Row Wampum recognizes the inherent sovereignty of Indigenous Nations.[31] As Hallenbeck highlights, the woven belt is the physical manifestation of the connection between "water, sovereignty, and law."[32] Indigenous scholars have also noted the unique connection between the Two Row Wampum, earth law, and protection of the natural world.[33] Coleman relays the knowledge of Oneida Faith Keeper Bob Antone that the Two Row Wampum was more than a treaty made between two nations; it also included the Creator.[34] However, there is another party to the treaty—the wampum itself. Using wampum to craft the belts depends on a relationship with the quahog, and there is a responsibility to care for these Mollusk relatives, as well as the Atlantic coastal waters from which they originate, in recognition of our relational reciprocity.

Wampum belts have been interpreted in the literature as records or texts of treaty-making and diplomacy. However, they are more. They are not the treaty text; they are a treaty-maker with spirit, agency, rights, and responsibilities alongside other living beings in the creation of covenants. Historically, it was perceived that wampum keepers breathe life into the wampum when they would deliver speeches. However, it is the opposite. When an orator carries wampum, it filters out all the bad in their mind, heart, or words. That orator embraces the life force of the wampum to speak only the truth. To share a form of medicine that connects across time and space is more than a diplomatic convention. As Hill and Coleman highlight, wampum belts, including the Kaswenta, "were essential elements in Hodinöhsö:ni' treaty-making, which was based on the belief that wampum could capture the words and pledges made in its presence."[35] There is an ancestral connection to wampum and recognition of its power to hold memory. The failure of the settler-colonial state to fulfill its commitments made in wampum agreements is an act of colonial violence. Mohawk legal scholar Beverly Jacobs notes that colonialism and the subsequent repeated violations of the Two Row Wampum have led to the denial of justice for Hodinöhsö:ni'.[36]

We need a renewed commitment to finding a path for our shared future, given the state of the Anthropocene and our potential for planetary collapse. Unfortunately, the insatiable consumption of the natural world through property rights regimes is a daunting obstacle to reconciliation and restoration. Settler-colonial notions of justice stem from a desire for boundary-making and property ownership, while wampum justice centres on the collective shared coexistence of humans and more-than-humans. In this way, treaty-making is a practice of wampum justice that centres on relationality and responsibilities over rights-based frameworks. In the establishment of agreements, we are bound by words and actions whereby our continued commitment to the renewal or "polishing" of our covenants forms the basis of our treaty relationship, and this renewal extends to the wampum. Therefore, diplomacy per se does not achieve justice. Justice must be performed through a sustained commitment to truth.

## DIPLOMACY IS NOT JUSTICE

In the literature, scholars refer to the diplomatic history of wampum but rarely move beyond settler conceptions of diplomacy to advance Algonkian understandings of wampum justice.[37] Diplomacy within western knowledge systems centres around negotiations between nations as embedded within Westphalian logics of settler-colonial relations.[38] The term *wampum diplomacy* emerged from what Carlson notes are the "logics of coloniality" whereby Indigenous concepts and relations are mischaracterized through Eurocentric and anthropocentric lenses that establish false equivalences and hegemonic interpretations of Indigenous existence.[39] Diplomacy is also predicated on disputes and, thereby, the need for diplomatic means of resolution.[40] Corbiere refers to this settler-colonial construction as the duality of wampum and war. The contemporary retelling of humanity's relationship to wampum is often associated with this duality of war or peace overshadowing its true purpose.[41]

In 1949, Wilbur R. Jacobs, a settler scholar, conceptualized wampum's widespread use as a form of "colonial Indian diplomacy."[42] However, Jacobs mischaracterized wampum as a diplomatic tool; in the same way, half a century later, Shell mischaracterized wampum as the original currency or "American money."[43] The false equivalence of wampum to money is a function of colonialism. It is a form of propaganda that furthers the purported integrity of the capitalist economic systems thrust upon Indigenous Peoples and our way of life since contact. It implied our consent to economic structures of imbalance and oppression when none was ever given. Western conceptualizations of wampum weaponized and militarized the species, as evidenced by its misapplied Latin name, *Mercenaria Mercenaria*. This colonial name proliferates the false proselytization of quahogs and wampum as currency or money.[44] Watts underscores how these falsities support the larger colonial machine, stating that "Colonization is not solely an attack on peoples and lands; rather, this attack is accomplished in part through purposeful and ignorant misrepresentations of Indigenous cosmologies."[45] In reclaiming wampum from the settler imaginary of coloniality and domination, we restore ancient pathways for justice.

Jacobs did get something right in his writings on wampum. He said wampum "had certain mystic qualities never fully understood by Europeans."[46] In this statement, Jacobs captures the essence of European misconceptions of wampum and how settlers never fully grasped the life-giving agency and truth-keeping purpose of wampum. "Wampum diplomacy" was theorized based on Eurocentric perceptions of settler-Indigenous negotiations and treaty-making.[47] Rarely has the philosophical understanding from Indigenous Peoples' perspectives been explored or appreciated. In this way, wampum is mischaracterized as a tool of diplomacy whereby there are sides and Westphalian parties engaged in negotiation, but absent are understandings of *wunnáumwash* and the call and response of truth keepers. Wampum justice, in contrast to conceptualizations of wampum diplomacy, centres relationality and accountability to not only humans but to wampum itself, the recognition that wampum is living and has agency. When we position wampum at the forefront of our considerations of what justice should look like, we, in turn, consider the environments that sustain these Mollusk relatives. We, in turn, ask ourselves what the quahogs need to be healthy and thrive.

## CONCLUSION

Wampum justice does not exist to resolve disputes or manage negotiations. It is a way of living that emphasizes truth in all our ways of thinking and doing so that we might be accountable to a collective greater than our individual existence. Wampum, like the truth, does not deteriorate, although it must be stewarded, polished, and renewed. Wampum is more than diplomatic credentials. It is a responsibility to speak the truth—*wunnáumwash*. If we are to go beyond wampum diplomacy to understand the totality of wampum justice, we must recognize that the treaty agreements made using wampum were not just made between Indigenous Peoples, settlers, or humans alone but that they were also made with the wampum. We then can understand that the polishing of our covenant—the remembrance of truth—is a responsibility we must uphold not only for ourselves but also for the wampum.

Wampum is integral to who we were, are, and will be as Algonkian Peoples. However, climate change threatens our coastal shores and bays. Ocean acidification, sea level rise, wetland migration, and other extreme climatic changes pose grave threats to estuarine environments.[48] Our treaty responsibility is not only to one another as Indigenous Peoples and settlers but also to wampum. We all have a responsibility to care for wampum. To polish the covenant not only among humans but with the natural world. To care for ecosystems that support a precious planetary relation, the same places and environments that have sustained Algonkian Peoples for millennia. Wampum justice advances notions that our existence can be in positive relation to the water. In that stewardship, we find a deeper understanding of our original foundation and what true peace and friendship should and can mean. Our coexistence is not solely dependent on our human maintenance of peace but also on our ability to match that balance and harmony with our treatment of the natural world.

Wampum justice is part of a larger universe of Indigenous theoretical understandings of justice, and its indelible legacy across time, place, nations, and peoples of Turtle Island is truly remarkable. Indigenous concepts of justice are diverse.[49] With this in mind, the conceptualization of wampum justice put forward in this chapter is not meant to inscribe monolithic principles of Indigenous justice but instead to reclaim the discourse of wampum from the grasp of the settler imaginary and logics of coloniality. The full exploration of the form and practice of wampum justice is beyond the scope of this chapter. However, my hope is that this conceptual reclamation will allow for deeper conversations among other Indigenous scholars who seek to understand and illuminate the experiences, practices, and relationships of wampum justice.

Wampum justice requires a commitment to truth. Our existence as eastern Indigenous Peoples is tied to the continued existence of wampum, despite centuries of oppression, dispossession, and violence–We Are Still Here. Our relationality is predicated on our ability to connect, love, heal, and find peace in the solace of truth. Wampum justice guides us in living out these moral and ethical commitments. Wampum reminds us of the power of truth in realizing justice. For eastern coastal Peoples and those who wish to share this seascape with us, there is no justice without truth;

there is no justice without wampum. Wampum justice binds us to what it means to be in good relation to each other as humans and all other life on this planet. This chapter set out to reclaim Indigenous conceptualizations of wampum through the lens of wampum justice, simultaneously an ancient practice and contemporary condition for just relationality grounded in truth–*wunnáumwash*.

CHAPTER FOUR

# The Chain, Naturally Understood

*Kayanesenh Paul Williams*

---

The past one hundred years have seen constant tension between the insistence of Indigenous nations on maintaining and fulfilling treaty relationships and the efforts of the governments of Canada and its provinces to minimize the importance and meaning of the treaties. Today's battlegrounds, on the waters of the Bay of Fundy and in court, are over the meaning of specific words in court decisions and in documents nearly three centuries old.[1] By focusing on words and documents, we lose sight of the essence. The treaty relationship is the hinge between nations.[2] It is the key

---

1  In 2020, negotiations on fisheries between Canada and the Wabanaki Nations broke down. Canada had been insisting on "Rights Reconciliation Agreements," in which the Mi'kmaq, Wolastoqiyik, and Peskotomuhkati would defer, for at least ten years, any discussion of the spirit and intent of the treaty relationship concerning fisheries, as well as any movement toward joint management of fisheries, in exchange for commercial fisheries licensed and regulated by Canada. The Supreme Court of Canada's 1999 decision in the *Donald Marshall* case confirmed a "moderate livelihood" fishery, and the lack of definition of those words morphed into defiant boats on the water.
2  Prime Minister Justin Trudeau's mandate letters to cabinet ministers all refer to the importance of the Government of Canada "restoring respectful nation-to-nation relationships" with Indigenous Peoples.

to their coexistence[3] and, in the case of Indigenous nations surrounded by modern nation-states, to their continued existence. The relationship, and the individual transactions that mark its path through history, exist in the legal systems of the nations on either side of the council fire. Yet in court, partly because the cases are populated by Euro-American lawyers, judges, and their governments, and despite admonitions that "the treaties should be interpreted as the Indians would naturally have understood them," it is Euro-American values, laws, and interests that determine the outcomes.

In this paper, I want to explain that the thinking behind the principle that "the treaties should be interpreted as the Indians would naturally have understood them," as articulated by Euro-American courts, is fundamentally flawed. It is flawed, first of all, because it is based on the assumption that the transaction was being made in Euro-American law by vastly unequal parties. *No.* For the first two centuries of the process, the councils[4] were conducted pursuant to Haudenosaunee law, understood and accepted by both sides and governed by principles of equality and reciprocity. It is flawed, secondly, by the underlying idea that a treaty is a document. *No.* A treaty is an agreement. The documents are one kind of evidence of the agreement, and so are the records of the council, in addition to the wampum belts that were exchanged and the recollections of people on both sides. It is flawed, thirdly, and most importantly, by the thinking that a "treaty" is an indi-

---

3 In *Haida Nation v. British Columbia*, 2004 SCC 73 (CanLII), the Supreme Court of Canada said that "treaties serve to reconcile pre-existing Aboriginal sovereignty with assumed Crown sovereignty, and to define Aboriginal rights." If the court had approached the question looking through the lens of Haudenosaunee law, it would have at least said that the treaties define the rights and obligations of the nations on both sides of the fire, not just the rights and not just of one side. We also need to understand that there are at least three distinct definitions of "reconciliation" floating around Canada today: the legal definition seeks to explain how two apparently inconsistent sovereignties can coexist; the moral definition, as explained by the Truth and Reconciliation Commission of Canada, includes compensation, atonement, and restoration for the crimes of the residential school system; and then there is Justice Binnie's statement in *Mitchell v. MNR* 2001 SCC 33 (CanLII) that Aboriginal peoples should reconcile themselves to Canadian sovereignty.
4 Haudenosaunee relationships with Indigenous Nations predate the arrival of Europeans. Their relationships with Europeans emanate from councils with the Dutch, the French, and the British. Canadian courts have not yet considered whether "treaty" (as used in the Indian Act or the Constitution Act 1982) includes agreements between Indigenous Nations.

vidual transaction to be examined in isolation. *No.* In Haudenosaunee—
and Anishinaabe, Wabanaki, and Crown-Imperial—terms, the individual
transactions are part of a relationship. If the relationship is like a river of
time, the individual transactions are like stones in its path, markers of particular events, and to focus only on them is to miss the whole point. The
relationship is not a creature of English, French or Dutch law. It was created
by taking the principles that brought the Haudenosaunee nations together
in peace, *Kayanerenkó:wa*, and applying them to relations with the newcomers. To interpret that relationship "as the Indians would have understood
it" requires knowledge of the legal system that is its ecosystem. Instead,
the courts have relied on their assumption that "the Indians" were illiterate, weak, unsophisticated, and at such a severe disadvantage in the negotiations that they should at least be given the benefit of some doubt in the
interpretation of the all-important written documents.

Let's explode some assumptions, shall we?

Treaties between the Crown and Indigenous nations are different from
the rest of Canadian law. They are barely mentioned in statutes.[5] They are
not created by legislation. They are aspects of the Crown's prerogative
powers, a vestigial area of law most Canadian lawyers and judges barely
know.[6] Canada says they are not the subject matter of international law.

---

5 Section 88 of the Indian Act makes provincial laws subject to the terms of treaties; Section 35(1) of the Constitution Act, *1982* recognizes and affirms "existing" treaty rights. Mention in the Constitution Act makes these rights part of the "supreme law of the land," to which all other laws are subordinate, but treaty and Aboriginal rights can be infringed by federal and provincial laws, provided there is justification in the public interest, a proper process is followed, and the justification is compatible with "reconciliation."

6 The prerogative is, for example, what permits the Government of Canada to create Indian reserves; to recognize "bands," and to extend "Indian status" to people who were omitted. See, e.g., *Ross River Dena First Nation Council Band v. Canada*, 2002 SCC 54 and *Madawasaka Maliseet First Nation v. Canada*, 2017 SCTC 5.

They don't fit easily within the Canadian legal system—half of what happened in treaty-making took place outside it.[7]

In 1990,[8] the Supreme Court of Canada adopted a principle set out by the United States Supreme Court a century earlier: treaties should be interpreted as the Indians would naturally have understood them.

> In construing any treaty between the United States and an Indian tribe, it must always…be borne in mind that the negotiations for the treaty are conducted, on the part of the United States, an enlightened and powerful nation, by representatives skilled in diplomacy, masters of a written language, understanding the modes and forms of creating the various technical estates known to their law, and assisted by an interpreter employed by themselves; that the treaty is drawn up by them and in their own language; that the Indians, on the other hand, are a weak and dependent people, who have no written language and are wholly unfamiliar with all the forms of legal expression, and whose only knowledge of the terms in which the treaty is framed is that imparted to them by the interpreter employed by the United States; and that the treaty must therefore be construed, not according to the technical meaning of its words to learned lawyers, but in the sense in which they would naturally be understood by the Indians.[9]

---

7   Indigenous legal systems are beginning to be recognized as part of "the law of the land" in Canada. See *Pastion v. Dene Tha' First Nation*, 2018 FC 648 (CanLII) and Binnie J.'s comment in *Mitchell v. MNR*, 2001 SCC 33 (CanLII) that the Constitution of Canada has its deepest roots in Canadian soil in the legal systems of Aboriginal peoples. A warning to those who might want to use that statement: he followed it almost immediately with an explanation that, pursuant to a theory of "shared sovereignty," the boat and the canoe of the Two Row Wampum had merged into one ship of state.

8   *R. v. Sioui*, 1990 CanLII 103 (SCC). The issue before the court was whether Wendat men entering a Quebec provincial park could exercise a treaty right to continue to practice their religion by building a ceremonial fire in violation of the park's rules. The transactions the Court found to be "treaties" occurred during the final taking of Montreal and Quebec by the British in 1760.

9   *Jones v. Meecham*, 175 US 1 (1899). The treaty transaction in question in that case involved Minnesota Anishinaabeg in the 1830s. That the Indians would "naturally" understand things a certain way—once one thinks about whether one can "naturally" understand an election, a scientific paper, or really anything, one concludes that the word in this context is either meaningless, or obtuse, or racist. And while the people of the United States might have understood (naturally) the term in a particular way a hundred years ago, for a Canadian court in 1990 to adopt the wording without comment leaves a small eddy of confusion behind the case.

For people for whom "treaty" means the "numbered treaties" that Canada entered into after 1867, and especially those who say they practice "Aboriginal law,"[10] both the principle and many of the reasons[11] the courts gave to support it are welcome.[12] In court, they help level the playing field.[13]

From a Haudenosaunee perspective, though, the principle is right, even if the reasons are very different from the courts' view of law and

10   The Truth and Reconciliation Commission of Canada distinguished between "Aboriginal law," the laws of Canada about Indigenous Peoples, and "Indigenous law," the laws of those peoples themselves. See also *Pastion v. Dene Tha' First Nation*, 2018 FC 648 (CanLII): Indigenous legal systems are part of "the law of the land" in Canada.
11   It is always dangerous to generalize, especially about statements that, while apparently benevolent, pack a wallop of racism. During the years of treaty-making in western Canada, many Indigenous leaders were skilled diplomats, both in their own legal systems and by any objective measure. There are several instances of Indigenous parties having their own interpreters; the treaties were made not because these peoples were "weak and dependent" but because it was easier for Canada to make agreements than wars. On the other hand, the Chiefs were more often than not illiterate; the document was drafted in legal terminology alien to them; contracts are generally interpreted "as against the drafting party," especially where one party is at a legal disadvantage. In Anglo-American contract law, where one party controlled the drafting of a contract, and a court finds ambiguity in the terms, those ambiguities are generally resolved in favour of the other party.
12   In *Sioui*, the Supreme Court explained that "the Indian people are today much better versed in the art of negotiation with public authorities," and twenty years later, *Beckman v. Little Salmon/Carmacks First Nation*, 2010 SCC 53 (CanLII) at para. 12, said that "the increased detail and sophistication of modern treaties represents a quantum leap beyond the pre-Confederation historical treaties…The courts were obliged to resort to general principles (such as the honour of the Crown) to fill the gaps and achieve a fair outcome. Modern comprehensive land claim agreements, on the other hand…" The result is that, despite the huge power differential and dependency involved in "modern" treaties, the fact that the Indigenous parties are "lawyered up" tends to erase any resolution of ambiguities in their favour and reduce the role of the honour of the Crown.
13   Making litigation easier does not make the transactions fair. In *Mikisew Cree First Nation v. Canada (Minister of Canadian Heritage)* 2005 SCC 69 (CanLII), the Supreme Court of Canada noted that "it is not as though the Treaty 8 First Nations did not pay dearly for their entitlement to honourable conduct on the part of the Crown: surrender of the aboriginal interest in an area larger than France is a hefty purchase price." In the latest United States Supreme Court decision on treaty interpretation, *Washington State Department of Licensing v. Cougar Den Inc.* (2019) 586 US, the court explained, "like many such treaties, this one was by all accounts more nearly imposed on the Tribe than a product of its free choice…by any fair measure, it was a bargain-basement deal" in favour of the United States government.

history. Eventually, if they remain unchecked, the courts' reasons will be used to erode the power of Haudenosaunee treaty rights and relations with Canada and the United States.[14]

For a century and a half, between 1645 and 1830, the laws and processes governing relations between Indigenous and colonizing nations were Haudenosaunee. One should interpret the events through the lens of Haudenosaunee law because the people on both sides of the fire understood that legal system and were working effectively within it. "The Indians" were not unsophisticated and overpowered, dependent, and weak peoples in the presence of their conquerors and their conquerors' laws. They were confident, articulate, competent diplomats representing a complex government with real military power, their actions and thinking deeply rooted in their own laws.[15]

Those laws are based on principle rather than detail. Sotsisowah John Mohawk explained: "It is not something written in paragraphs and lines because it doesn't matter whether the letter of the thing is right. The questions that have to be before the people are "What is the thinking? Is the thinking right?"[16]

In the same 1990 decision, the Supreme Court of Canada, for the first time, set out its rules for deciding whether a transaction is a "treaty." A degree of solemnity is required. Mutual engagements must be given. The Crown must be represented by a person the Indians could have believed had authority to bind it. For a legal system like Canada's, which finally recognized and affirmed treaty rights in the amendments to its constitution

---

14 Part of the threat is that the Covenant Chain is put forward as a defence either by self-represented people or by lawyers with little historical knowledge or knowledge of Haudenosaunee law and history. In other words, a string of losing cases creates the momentum of legal precedent: *Mississaugas of Scugog Island v. National Automobile, Aerospace, Transportation and General Workers Union*, 2007 ONCA 814 (CanLII); *M.M.(Re)*, 2013 ABPC 59 (CanLII); *Rice c. R.*, 2016 QCCS 4610 (CanLII), *R. v. Fournier*, 2005 CanLII 24244 (ONSC), *R. v. Dickson*, 2017 ABPC 315 (CanLII).

15 It is necessary to exercise caution with the documentary record—because of the illiteracy of the Indigenous party; because of the technical legal terms often used, with meaning in one culture and not the other; because documents are to be interpreted as against the drafting party (see footnote 11); and because the writers often had their own institutional or personal agendas.

16 Sotsisowah John Mohawk, "The Indian Way is a Thinking Tradition," *Northeast Indian Quarterly* 4, no. 4 (Winter 1987): 13–17.

in 1982, a definition of what constitutes a treaty is a useful tool.[17] In 1981, the Ontario Court of Appeal had expanded some of the thinking by saying that the record of the council from which the treaty document emerged should be considered part of the treaty, and that the conduct of the parties afterward could give the courts guidance as to how they understood it. But the focus remained on the document itself.[18] In the 1990 *Sioui* decision, once the court decided the council met the criteria, it turned to interpreting the written document. That focus on treaties as documents—actually, as "the specific [English] words used in any written memorandum"—continued in the Supreme Court of Canada's next major treaty decision nine years later in the two *Donald Marshall Jr.* cases. The Nova Scotia Court of Appeal had decided that "extrinsic evidence" about the historical context of the transaction ought to be admitted in court only to resolve ambiguities. The Supreme Court decided that, in fairness, it should look at more than just one document:

> The starting point for the analysis of the alleged treaty right must be an examination of the specific words used in any written memorandum of its terms.
>
> The question is whether the underlying negotiations produced a broader agreement between the British and the Mi'kmaq, memorialized only in part by the Treaty of Peace and Friendship, that would protect the appellant's activities…
>
> …even in the context of a treaty document that purports to contain all of the terms, this Court has made clear in recent cases that extrinsic evidence of the historical and cultural context of a treaty may be received even absent any ambiguity on the face of the treaty.

---

17 Earlier Canadian court decisions suggested that a treaty was anything that could be construed by the Indians as "the word of the white man." *R. v. White and Bob*, 1965 CanLII 643 (SCC).
18 *R. v. Taylor and Williams*, 1981 ONCA (CanLII), 236.

> ...where a treaty was concluded verbally and afterwards written up by representatives of the Crown, it would be unconscionable for the Crown to ignore the oral terms while relying on the written terms.
>
> "Generous" rules of interpretation...are dictated by the special difficulties of ascertaining what in fact was agreed to. The Indian parties did not, for all practical purposes, have the opportunity to create their own written record of the negotiations. Certain assumptions are therefore made about the Crown's approach to treaty making (honourable) which the Court acts upon in its approach to treaty interpretation (flexible) as to the existence of a treaty...the completeness of any written record...and the interpretation of treaty terms once found to exist.[19]

From a Haudenosaunee perspective, the Supreme Court of Canada totally missed the point. It perpetuated the view in the laws of Canada and the United States that the key to treaty interpretation is the written document, that treaties are distinct transactions, and that each one is to be viewed as a separate event.

Instead, in Haudenosaunee law, the lens through which "the Indians would have understood it," each meeting after the seminal agreements that established the relationship is a deliberate reaffirmation of an organic, continuous relationship.[20] The relationship is a fundamental concept of a complex, respectable legal system.[21] To remove a council from the context of that system and to inspect it as an independent transaction, a "treaty," fails to recognize the principles of Haudenosaunee law

---

19  *R. v. Donald Marshall (I)*, 1999 SCC at paras. 5, 7, 11, 12, 14.

20  Actually, it is more complicated than that: the relationships do evolve and deepen over time—the Covenant Chain itself evolves from a rope tied to a tree on the shore of the Mohawk River, through an iron chain fastened to a rock, and finally to the silver chain attached to the mountain at Onondaga. But the basic relationship, once the nations became one family, is constant.

21  To lay the groundwork for proving the proposition that the treaties are creatures of Haudenosaunee law, I have written a law textbook setting out the structure and principles of that legal system. See Kayanesenh Paul Williams, *Kayanerenkó:wa: the Great Law of Peace* (Winnipeg: University of Manitoba Press, 2018). While *Kayanerenkó:wa* describes how people and nations are to get along with each other, I consider the Haudenosaunee story of Creation a description of how humans and their societies are to get along with this place—environmental constitutional law.

that make councils work: continuity, responsibility, reciprocity, foresight, mutual help, respect, trust, friendship, peace, and a dozen others. The principles are not invented or accepted each time: they are the rules. The individual transaction, viewed out of the context of the entire system that defined and controlled it, loses meaning, effect, and functionality. It is like seeking to understand an animal without considering its habitat or its family, herd or pack—you are left with an isolated specimen.

Haudenosaunee law is a law of relationships. It is based on the principle of family,[22] of being related. Politically, the longhouse of one extended family is the metaphor for the way *Kayanerenkó:wa*[23] brought the nations out of the dark and bloody times by making everyone, and every nation, into relatives. Environmentally, Haudenosaunee understanding of our place in the universe requires us to greet, thank, and acknowledge every living being as a relative.[24] The meta-narrative of creation teaches us our responsibilities. Legally, once a person or a nation is no longer a stranger

---

22 Alvin Toffler, in *Future Shock* (1970), described how the North American nuclear family is a mobile, convenient economic unit that quickly, and in the service of industry, has substantially replaced the extended family. Ontario's *Child, Youth and Family Services Act* (SO 2017 ch. 14, s. 6) requires that "all services to First Nations, Inuit and Métis children and young persons should be provided in a manner that recognizes their cultures, heritages, traditions, connection to their communities, *and the concept of the extended family*." But this only works where the service providers and the courts that supervise them have enough knowledge and understanding of what they are supposed to "recognize," including what "extended family" means.

23 In this paper and my other writing, I use Grand River Mohawk language and orthography. For ease of reading, but reluctantly, I italicize key Haudenosaunee law-words but not proper names. I use a person's original name first. I name treaties after their dates and locations rather than after the colonial representative.

24 In the first formal Haudenosaunee communication to the United Nations, Sotsisowah John Mohawk wrote: "All of this political activity is set in the roots of an ancient tradition of the spirituality of our peoples. This cosmology places the Haudenosaunee in a balanced, familiar relationship with the Universe and Earth. In our languages, the Earth is our Mother Earth, the Sun our Eldest Brother, the Moon our Grandmother, and so on. It is the belief of our people that all elements of the Natural World were created for the benefit of all living things and that we, as humans, are one of the weakest of the whole Creation since we are totally dependent on the whole Creation for our survival." Sotsisowah John Mohawk, *Basic Call to Consciousness* (Akwesasne Notes, 1977), 2.

but a relative, a web of mutual responsibilities and obligations follows.[25] Linguistically, it is impossible to speak to or about a person or thing without considering one's relation to it or them.

When we speak of the Covenant Chain, the noun-based English language impels us toward the physical symbol of the silver chain, to be held firmly, to be protected from tarnish, and to be repolished frequently. The Haudenosaunee perspective, descriptive and verb-based, uses the metaphor of "it attaches our arms together" to symbolize the ongoing, living family relationship that lies at the foundation of the relations between the Haudenosaunee and other nations.

In the written record of every council in which the Covenant Chain is mentioned, the word "Brothers" appears in the same paragraph. Treaty relations are family relations.[26]

When a Euro-American lawyer or court isolates an event to determine its impact, it replicates the scientific method. Separated from context, the subject can be examined more simply, tested more easily, and defined more effectively. To advance scientific knowledge, this method is brutally efficient. But it has serious flaws. In the laboratory, DDT seemed to be the perfect insecticide. In the real world, its toxic bioaccumulation wiped out not only insects but the birds and fish that depend on them and began to sicken humans.[27] A "treaty" examined out of its legal context—a lawyer will assert, a historian will confirm, a judge will conclude—becomes the answer to "what happened on September 23 and 24, 1664?" The answer may confirm whether specific commitments were made. An isolated event, like an amoeba under the microscope, is easier to scrutinize, test, and conceive. But an ant examined in this way, as an isolate, reveals nothing of its essentially social nature. The conduct of a nation in one

---

25   Does it follow "naturally"? No: that is why it requires reaffirmation, re-minding, and repolishing. It is why we gather for birthdays, anniversaries, and funerals. Being family requires continuous hard work.

26   If there is a seminal moment in the making of *Kayanerenkó:wa,* it is not the culmination of the confrontation between Thadadahoh and everyone else (a "good vs. evil" contest). It is the moment the Peacemaker meets Hayonwatha, the grieving man, and in the words that will lead to the first condolence, that great act of compassion, greets this stranger as "my younger brother." Throughout the making of the law, the Peacemaker extended and initiated relationships.

27   Rachel Carson exposed this in 1962 in *Silent Spring,* first serialized in the *New Yorker.*

transaction depends very much on its prior and future relations with its partners, as well as on its own culture and history.[28]

The 2016–20 first term of the Trump "administration" in the United States were disruptive of alliances and balances precisely because dealings with other nations were treated as purely transactional (as one would expect from a real estate operator who never expected to deal with his clients again).[29] International relations work because they are *relations*. International treaties work because they are part of a web of norms, assumptions, and other relationships that make them viable.

The Haudenosaunee perspective on the long-term mutuality of relations was explained by Tiyanoga Hendrick Peters ("King Hendrick"), a Kanyenkehá:ka leader and speaker:

> What we are now going to say is a matter of great moment, which we desire you to remember as long as the Sun and Moon lasts. We are willing to sell you this large tract of land for your people to live upon, but we desire that this may be considered as part of our Agreement that when we are all dead and gone your Grandchildren may not say to our Grandchildren, that your Forefathers sold the land to our Forefathers, and therefore be gone off them. Let us all be as Brethren as well after as before giving you Deeds for lands. After we have sold our land we in a little time have nothing to show for it; but it is not so with you, your Grandchildren will get something from it as long as the world stands; our Grandchildren will have no advantage from it; they will say we were fools for selling so much land for so small a matter and curse us; therefore let it be a part of the present agreement that we shall treat one another as Brethren to the latest Generation, even after we shall not have left a Foot of land.

---

28 Canadian courts may glean the intention of parties to treaties from their subsequent conduct: *R. v. Taylor and Williams*, 1981 CanLII 1657 (ON CA).
29 The "Great Frauds and Abuses" that the Royal Proclamation of 1763 was aimed at preventing "for the future" were individual transactions in Haudenosaunee lands that threatened the relationship between the Confederacy and the colonies—culminating in the short, sharp war of the summer of that year. Real estate transactionality is not a new problem.

> We know our lands have become more valuable. The white people think we do not know their value. But we are sensible that the land is everlasting, and the few goods we receive for it are soon worn out and gone.[30]

He was not just saying that the Haudenosaunee knew the land that was being sold was more valuable than the compensation the colony was offering. He was explaining that a deal that would otherwise be seen as exploitative was acceptable only because it was part of a relationship: "As long as the Sun and Moon lasts we shall treat one another as Brethren to the latest Generation."

Similarly, Thayendenegea Joseph Brant explained the massive land cession in the 1768 Treaty of Fort Stanwix as part of the brotherly relationship:

> Your people in this country thought themselves confined on account of their numbers with regard to a Scarcity of Land…we considered upon it, and relinquished a great Territory to the King for the use of his Subjects, for a Trifling consideration…as a proof of our sincere Regard towards them…we expected a permanent, Brotherly Love and Amity would be the Consequence, but in vain.[31]

The relationship was meant to endure. There is no divorce between brothers. European observers marveled at the fidelity of Indigenous nations to their commitments, perhaps not realizing the power that a sacred promise implied. In 1747, seeking to convince the British government of the importance of restoring the relationship with the Haudenosaunee,

---

30  Tekarihoken Tiyanoga Hendrick Peters to William Penn, 1754; cited also in Timothy J. Shannon, *Indians and Colonists at the Crossroads of Empire: the Albany Congress of 1754* (NY: Cornell University Press, 2000), 166. See also the Oneida *Royaner* Agwalongdongwas (Good Peter) explaining to the New York commissioners in 1784 that "the land they had now agreed to sell was more out of Friendship than out of a Pecuniary Reward, and that they could not part with any more." In Franklin B. Hough, ed., *Documents Relating to the History of the Colony of New York* (Albany, 1861), 103.

31  Thayendenegea Joseph Brant to Sir Frederick Haldimand, Quebec, May 21, 1783, Public Record Office, Colonial Office Papers, 42, v. 44, pp. 133–35. By the 1780s, the Haudenosaunee had been stung numerous times by the Crown's inconstancy, including by the "Great Frauds and Abuses" in land transactions described by the *Royal Proclamation of 1763*.

Cadwallader Colden cited a century of faithful Haudenosaunee adherence to commitments.[32] In 1836, Lieutenant Governor Bond Head of Upper Canada sought to explain why the Crown could not honourably break the promises it had made at Niagara seventy years before:

> It will be asked, in what way were these our promises made? It is difficult to reply to this question, as it involves the Character of the Indian Race.

> An Indian's word, when it is formally pledged, is one of the strongest moral securities on earth: like the Rainbow, it beams unbroken when all beneath is threatened with annihilation.[33]

The metaphors—as long as the sun and moon last, as long as the grass grows and the waters flow[34]—are used by speakers on both sides of the council fire. The brotherhood is frequently expressed as permanent and perpetual: "The Covenant Chain…may be preserved inviolable and that mutual love and friendship may continue between you and them so long as the Sun and the Moon endures."[35]

In 1783, the Treaty of Paris ended the War of American Independence. Britain ceded land, including the Haudenosaunee heartland, to the United States. The Haudenosaunee treated this as a breach of their fundamental relationship, which their law and their nature prevented them from doing. They complained to Allan MacLean at Niagara:

---

32 Cadwallader Colden, *The History of the Five Indian Nations*, 1927 (NY: Cornell University Press, 2017).

33 *Correspondence Respecting Indians between the Provincial Secretary of State and the Governors of British North America* (Queen's Printer, 1837), 128. Nor are these principles restricted to Haudenosaunee thinking. In 1761, Mi'kmaq Grand Chief Toma Denny told the Governor of Nova Scotia that "as long as the Sun and the Moon shall endure, as long as the earth on which I dwell shall exist in the same state you this day see, so long will I be your friend and ally…" (Nova Scotia Archives I, pp. 699–700, Ms. Doc. V. 37, No. 14, PRO CO 217/18/276).

34 Lord Denning, Britain's most prominent judge, borrowed those words to describe how Canada was bound to fulfill the terms of the treaties and the Royal Proclamation of 1763, in *Her Majesty the Queen ex rel. Indian Association of Alberta v. Secretary of State for the Colonies*, [1981] All E.R.

35 George Clark, Lieutenant Governor of New York, to the Haudenosaunee, June 15, 1742; LAC RG10, V. 820, 2642.

That if it was really true that the English had basely betrayed them by pretending to give up their country to the Americans Without their Consent, or Consulting them, it was an act of Cruelty and injustice that Christians *only* were capable of doing, that the Indians were incapable of acting so to friends[36] and Allies, but that they did believe we had sold & betrayed them.[37]

In contrast, when European nations violated the relationship, they did so as a matter of pragmatic policy and opportunity. Challenged in the House of Lords about whether the Treaty of Paris was a violation of the Crown's commitment to the Haudenosaunee in the 1701 Albany Treaty, Lord Walsingham denied that "forever" really meant "forever":

"But our treaties with them bound us to everlasting protection." This is one of those assertions which always sounds well, and is calculated to amuse the uninformed mind. But what is the meaning of "in perpetuo" in treaties? That they shall endure as long as the parties are able to perform the conditions. This is the meaning of perpetual alliances, and in the present day with America, the Indian nations were not abandoned to their enemies; they were remitted to the care of their neighbours, whose interest it was as much as ours to cultivate friendship with them, and who were certainly the best qualified for softening and humanizing their hearts.[38]

---

36  More than two hundred years ago, "friends" had a wider meaning than today's assumption that it is restricted to social relationships. It included family, friends, allies, and lovers. Another mistake in courtly interpretation of treaties is the assumption that the English of the documents is the English of today.

37  Allan MacLean to Sir Frederick Haldimand, May 18, 1783, LAC Haldimand Papers B 103, pp. 175–82, in Charles Johnston, *The Valley of the Six Nations* (Toronto: Champlain Society, 1964), 37.

38  Barbara Graymont, *The Iroquois in the American Revolution* (Syracuse, NY: Syracuse University Press, 1972). The "neighbours" had recently conducted the genocidal Sullivan-Clinton campaign against the Haudenosaunee. Niagara, where the Chiefs met with MacLean, had become a refugee camp.

Foundational to Haudenosaunee law is the continuity of the family through the generations and, therefore, the continuity of the law. The *Rotiyaneshon*, in making decisions, are to cast their minds to the impact on future generations. The horror of the dark days before the coming of the peace is imprinted so deeply that, to survive, we need the Law of Peace that binds us to be perpetual. The difference in perspectives can be seen in 1960 at a session of the Canadian Joint Parliamentary Committee on Indian Affairs when a delegation from the Six Nations Grand River Territory explained the Covenant Chain:

> Senator Horner: Well, we had hoped the British would last forever, but still there have been many alterations in the form of their governing themselves. Forever is a long time.
>
> Chief Hill: Oh yes, but that is one of the principal traditions, that it is supposed to last.
>
> Senator Horner: In this changing world?[39]

The Haudenosaunee Law of Peace emerged from a dark and bloody time, in which, as Odatsehte Howard Elijah explained in Oneida in 1995, the women and children were made poor by the actions of the young men, the warriors. Achieving peace, and sustaining it, requires not only long-term commitment but also long-term honesty and altruism. The Covenant Chain relationship emerged from that thinking. Sotsisowah John Mohawk explained:

> The Six Nations, the Confederacy, actually was born in an environment of chaos and devised ways to address that kind of environment. But there's a trick. The people who are going to manage that, who are going to lead the way out of that jungle, those people can never lie. They have to be completely honourable, all the time. They can't take sides. They have to be neutral. Peacemakers aren't people with an agenda. They don't

---

39 Parliamentary record of the Joint Parliamentary Committee on Indian Affairs, June 22, 1960.

come to your country to take your forest. They don't come there to kill your buffaloes. They're there to end the violence. That's all. So they have to be completely honourable, completely honest. That's what I think the Six Nations Confederacy had as its thing. The culture that was around the Council was a culture of people who were dedicated to pursuing peace.[40]

We humans are far from perfect. Politicians fail to keep their promises. So do nations. As our world moves away from the sacred and toward the secular, it also recedes from considering the rights of future generations or of the natural world toward short-term opportunism and commodification. United States law enshrines treaty rights but provides that Congress can break treaties if it does so purposefully.[41] Canadian law does the same: even though section 35 of the 1982 Constitution Act lies outside the Charter of Rights and Freedoms (with its built-in limits), the courts have constructed paths to "infringements" of entrenched Aboriginal and

---

40 Sotsisowah John Mohawk, KUNM Public Radio, University of New Mexico, 2005. To be sure, there continued to be warriors. *Kayanerenkó:wa* recognized that as its roots spread, the peace would require protection. When the Haudenosaunee invited another people into the peace, the warriors would sometimes offer an unattractive alternative. But every Haudenosaunee leader has inherited the thinking that to maintain peace, we all have to carry the honesty and integrity of the Peacemaker. That has a counterpart in the laws of Canada and the United States, where "the honour of the Crown infuses every treaty obligation" and "treaties are the supreme law of the land." This kind of relationship only works if there is sufficient sustained honesty to foster the trust that matures into friendship.

41 In *McGirt v. Oklahoma* (2020), the United States Supreme Court held that, for jurisdictional purposes, a large part of Oklahoma is still the Creek reservation because it had been reserved by treaty and not disestablished by Congress. The majority (5–4) of the Court held that "Congress has never withdrawn the promised reservation. As a result, many of the arguments before us today follow a sadly familiar pattern. Yes, promises were made, but the price of keeping them has become too great, so now we should just cast a blind eye. We reject that thinking. If Congress wishes to withdraw its promises, it must say so. Unlawful acts, performed long enough and with sufficient vigor, are never enough to amend the law. To hold otherwise would be to elevate the most brazen and longstanding injustices over the law, both rewarding wrong and failing those in the right." Within three weeks after the decision, the federal government "remedied" the decision by handing jurisdiction over to the state.

treaty rights through justification and compensation.[42] Nothing is truly binding. Nothing is sacred.

And that is the point: these are two very different legal *systems*, each with its own sets of principles, assumptions, and norms. To take a single "treaty" out of the context of the system in which it was made and examine it through the lens of the other system guarantees a failure of understanding.

Euro-American lawyers, judges, and courts will inevitably do this. They can't help it. In 2012, Chief Justice Lance Finch of British Columbia explained that "the *lack* of knowledge of another culture's precepts, meanwhile, is further fraught and exacerbated by the *presence* of one's own, pre-existing cultural tenets":

> The danger in retaining and imposing our ideas of what constitutes "law" according to our training and established habits of mind, is that we may inadvertently give weight only to those elements of an Aboriginal legal system which are recognizable in Canadian law, rendering the Canadian legal framework determinative…
>
> …from the outset of our education, we are immersed in a particular context and point of view. This saturation far transcends our legal training,

---

42 *R. v. Sparrow*, 1990 CanLII 104 (SCC). That case assumed that everyone would agree that salmon conservation was a viable justification for unilaterally abridging Aboriginal rights (the *Sioui* decision about treaty rights came down the same day). Seven years later, in *Delgamuukw v. British Columbia* (1997 CanLII 302 (SCC) at 165), the Supreme Court of Canada announced that "the development of agriculture, forestry, mining, and hydroelectric power, the general economic development of the interior of British Columbia, protection of the environment or endangered species, the building of infrastructure and the settlement of foreign populations to support those aims, are the kinds of objectives that are consistent with this purpose and, in principle, can justify the infringement of aboriginal title." In other words, I have said that anything short of supplying strategic weapons to Kurds in Iraq is a justification for infringing (the word has nothing to do with fringes and everything to do with destruction) on Aboriginal rights. In *Tsilhqot'in Nation v. British Columbia*, 2014 SCC 44 (CanLII), the Supreme Court added that "the broader public goals" that would justify the infringement of Aboriginal rights and title "must further the goal of reconciliation, having regard to both the Aboriginal interest and the broader public objective." It is hard to understand how unilaterally taking people's land and resources furthers reconciliation.

of course: the experience of a cultural experience of a cultural narrative in any form, or on any subject, will be informed—to borrow Julie Cruikshank's framework—by our understandings of place, kinship and ideas about personhood. This is largely an unconscious process. Whether reading a novel or perusing a judgment, our accrued experience sets off a constant series of connective sparks, or internal signals, affirmations, and disruptions, all at a level so deeply ingrained as to take place, most of the time, below the level of awareness.[43]

Twenty-first-century Euro-American lawyers and judges who must weigh the Covenant Chain relationship do so without the scaffolding of language and culture that would enable them to do what their law obliges them to do: to place themselves in the minds of the people who created that relationship, to be able to express what they understood.

To "understand the treaties as the Indians would naturally have understood them," we need to begin with the roots of the legal system in two Haudenosaunee meta-narratives: Creation and the Law of Peace. They provide the lenses through which every transaction within the treaty relationship can be comprehended.

The Law of Peace, *Kayanerenkó:wa*, is based on the three fundamental concepts the Peacemaker enunciated more than five centuries ago. They are often rendered as "peace, power and righteousness." While that translation is catchy, it falls far short on meaning. *Sken:nen* is both peace and health, including mental health. Without one, there is little chance of the other. *Kathstatstensera* is "power," but it is the ability to accomplish things and the force with which to do so. *Kanikonhri:yo* is the "good mind," thinking properly but also functioning well.[44] Together, they create *Kentenron*, compassion. The word describes an act, a practical form of assistance, a love that means doing and not just feeling. *What is the thinking?* The thinking in this way of law is a balanced, thoughtful, responsible

---

43 Lance S.J. Finch, "The Duty to Learn: Taking Account of Indigenous Legal Orders in Practice," *Continuing Legal Education Society of British Columbia* (2012), https://www.cerp.gouv.qc.ca/fileadmin/Fichiers_clients/Documents_deposes_a_la_Commission/P-253.pdf.

44 I am no linguist. My translations are inadequate.

understanding of who we are and how we are to get along with one another as a human family and a family of nations.⁴⁵

Sotsisowah wrote:

> Righteousness means that almost all of us agree that some things are right, correct, positive, which is to say that they may not all agree that some things are obviously right and wrong. But there are some things that they will agree on. So those are the things you start to build on. You have the conversation and your negotiation until you hit the rock hard things. That takes us to the third and final section, which is reason. Reason means that you are going to do the rock hard things. You're not going to settle them, really, but you're going to do the best you can with them. You're going to move them as far forward on as many points as possible. The Iroquois law of peace assumes that you will not achieve peace. You will not achieve a perfect agreement between two warring sides about how the world ought to be in the future. But it also assumes that you can reach enough of it to have something to work on so that you can take the conflict from physical warfare over to a place where, as they used to say, thinking can replace violence.⁴⁶

Haudenosaunee law—unsurprising in a society that did not, and to a great extent still does not, rely on written documents—is to be found in narratives. The Haudenosaunee story of Creation is not just an explanation of how we got here; it is also a guide to how humankind emerges from an ecological collapse and into responsibility as its own agent in the circle of life.⁴⁷ Creation stories are not "just stories." They are laws about

---

45  There is a legend that Princeton history professor Woodrow Wilson fastened upon the Haudenosaunee as the exemplar for the League of Nations when the world emerged from the chaos of the War to End All Wars.
46  Sotsisowah John Mohawk, "What Can We Learn from Native America About War and Peace?: The Progressive Pragmatism of the Iroquois Confederacy," *Lapis Magazine Online*, n.d., http://arnieegel.blogspot.com.
47  Amber Meadow Adams, "Teyotsi'tsiahsonhátye: Meaning and Medicine in the Haudenosaunee (Iroquois) Story of Life's Renewal" (Ph.D. dissertation, Buffalo: State University of New York, 2013).

how people and peoples are to conduct themselves in their biomes[48]—just as the story of the making of the Great Law of Peace is law about how human beings are to conduct their relations with one another and to go about the business of government to maintain peace.[49]

When Jacques Cartier's scruffy "away team" approached Hochelaga in 1534, he was greeted in a ceremony that we can recognize today as the same Woods' Edge that is put through at every Haudenosaunee condolence, as well as at any treaty council. When in 1645, Kiotseaeton, on behalf of the Kanyenkehá:ka, the Mohawks, as the keepers of the Eastern Door of the Haudenosaunee, created a political relationship with the French, he did so as Haudenosaunee today do every year in a day of Midwinter ceremonies: he imparted existence to them, made them family, gave them names.

The written record of treaty relations with European nations begins in the summer of 1645 on the banks of Ken'tarókwen, the St. Lawrence River, at a place downstream from the rock of Tekiatenontarí:kon, a place where three rivers meet.[50] The Kanyenkehá:ka have arrived to meet with the French and their Wendat and Algonquin friends. The Jesuit who described the event to his superiors in France recounted the elaborate pantomime by Kiotseaeton. In those gestures, we can discern many of the elements of Haudenosaunee thought, law, and process about relations

---

48  Euro-American courts, composed of people whose sacred places are generally somewhere in the Middle East, have failed miserably to respect and appreciate the spiritual connection between Indigenous Ppeoples and the power of place. For miserable examples of this, see *Navajo Nation v. US Forestry Service*, 535 F 3$^{rd}$ 1058 (9$^{th}$ Cir. 2008) and *Ktunaxa Nation v. British Columbia* [2017] 2 SCR 386.

49  When I teach Haudenosaunee law in law schools, after confirming that no students in the class can accurately recite three consecutive sections of the Constitution of Canada, I ask them to tell me the story of Goldilocks and the Three Bears. And they can all do so, to the point of confirming that the baby bowl of porridge was "just right," defying the laws of physics. So, I say, as a society, where are you better off putting your fundamental values: in law books not even the lawyers can remember, or in stories everybody knows?

50  Some places become "fire places," places where specific nations come together for council. Albany (the confluence of the Hudson and Mohawk rivers), Fort Stanwix (the portage from the Mohawk River to Lake Ontario), Niagara, Detroit, and Mackinack are examples. Councils would take place from spring to harvest time, and the rivers were the highways of the day.

between peoples,⁵¹ but the council has a culminating moment. Kiotseaeton, "who was high in stature, rose and looked at the Sun, then cast his eyes over the whole Company; he took a collar of porcelain beads in his hand and commenced to harangue in a loud voice…Thereupon he began to sing; his countrymen responded; he walked about that great space as if on the stage of a theatre…"

> The tenth [wampum] was to bind us all very closely together. He took hold of a Frenchman, placed his arm within his, and with his other arm he clasped that of an Alguonquin. Having thus joined himself to them, "Here," he said, "is the knot that binds us inseparably; nothing can part us." This collar was extraordinarily beautiful. "Even if the lightning were to fall upon us, it could not separate us; for, if it cuts off the arm that holds you to us, we will at once seize each other by the other arm." And thereupon he turned around, and caught the Frenchman and the Algonquin by their two other arms, holding them so closely that he seemed unwilling ever to leave them.⁵²

The meaning of Kiotseaeton's actions would be obvious to anyone who attends Midwinter ceremonies in any Haudenosaunee Longhouse today. A two-year-old boy stands shyly beside his uncle, his mother's brother, his closest male relative in his o:tara, his Clan family. The uncle steps forward and, holding hands with the boy, walks past the wood stove, singing his atonwa (what the anthropologists call his "personal chant"), one of the Four Sacred Ceremonies. The people respond by stamping their feet in recognition and acceptance. Then, the uncle announces the child's name and identifies him as belonging to that family. For much of the day of Midwinter set apart for "naming," this happens again and again. As the American ethnologist

---

51 Alexander von Gernet provides an opposing view. In *Newfoundland v. Drew*, 2003 NLSCTD 173, 2003 NLSCTD 105 (CanLII) at para. 168, he testified that "There's often a tendency for the 16th century scholars to try to squeeze out of these documents more than the evidence warrants simply because they are so vague that you can interpret them according to any pet theory that you have." The warning is real: scholars need to back up their conclusions with layers of persuasive evidence.

52 Reuben Gold Thwaites, ed., *The Jesuit Relations and Allied Documents*, Vol. 27, (Cleveland, Burrows Brothers, 1896–1901): 247–305; cited in Francis Jennings et al., *The History and Culture of Iroquois Diplomacy* (Syracuse, NY: Syracuse University Press, 1985), 127–53.

and Episcopal clergyman William Beauchamp put it, "Kiotseaeton had given the French both an identity and a family relationship to the Haudenosaunee. He had transformed them from strangers into relatives."[53]

Across North America, treaty-making is family-making. But the roots of Haudenosaunee law, the making of the Great Peace, are described as the creation of one family in one Longhouse. There would be no more bloodshed, for now everyone was related. All the *Rotiyanehson* were now brothers, equal in statute and respectability. One symbol of this confederation is the Circle Wampum, signifying that the Chiefs of the Confederacy are standing in a circle (the white wampum signifies peace; the two entwined strings around the circumferences the inseparability of the Great Law and the Great Peace); the fifty strings for the fifty Chiefs; their arrangement stretching toward the middle their yearning to come to one mind. Their arms are joined. They hold each other so tightly that even if a tree should fall on them, it would not break their arms apart, would not cut off their brotherhood. Like every other aspect of the law, effort is required to maintain and renew this link. They cannot hold each other loosely. Across the council fire, like families across the hearth fire from each other in Haudenosaunee longhouses, the relatives on each side are there to help one another.

The relationship forged with the French at Three Rivers in 1645 was an extrapolation of the way the law brought the Haudenosaunee nations together in peace. By transforming strangers into relatives, the Haudenosaunee were creating a "landscape of peace."[54] They were spreading the Great White Roots of the Tree of Peace. They were not creating a Haudenosaunee empire, bringing these other nations under Haudenosaunee dominance, but they were bringing them within the law. The event was the beginning of something.[55]

---

53 William Beauchamp, *Civil, Religious and Mourning Councils and Ceremonies of the New York Indians* (New York State Museum Bulletin 113, 1907), reprinted (Albany: Museum of the State of New York, 1975).

54 Matthew Dennis, *Cultivating a Landscape of Peace: Iroquois-European Encounters in Seventeenth Century America* (Ithaca: Cornell University Press, 1993).

55 *Mikisew Cree First Nation v. Canada (Minister of Heritage)* 2005 SCC 69 (CanLII): "Treaty making is an important stage in the long process of reconciliation, but it is only a stage. What occurred at Fort Chipewyan in 1899 was not the complete discharge of the duty arising from the honour of the Crown, but a rededication of it."

Nearly twenty years later, the transaction at Fort Albany in September 1664 was the first *written* treaty between the Crown and the Haudenosaunee.[56] The document contains many of the elements of modern international treaties: a military alliance, a free trade agreement, and provision for dispute resolution. Since it provides for what modern law would call separate personal criminal[57] jurisdiction, it contains discernible elements of the Two Row principles.[58] But it is very much a preliminary agreement between two nations who are still strangers (the English had just taken over from the Dutch, renaming the colony "New York" and the trading fort "Albany" instead of "Orange"). So much so that while the names of the Chiefs reflect several Nations, the recorder evidently believed that west of the Mohawks were only the "Synichs" (Senecas).[59]

In 1677, the governors of New York, Maryland, and Virginia met with the Haudenosaunee at Albany, which had become the formal and permanent place for councils. After several days of negotiations,[60] the Mohawk speaker took the Crown delegates by the arm, walked them up and down by the council fire, singing, and then explained that they had "made an absolute covenant of peace, which we shall bind with a chain," and that "...wee are now Com togither to mak the Covenant...Seing that the Govr. Genll & wee are one, and one hart and one head, for the Covenant that is betwixt ye

---

56 *Mitchell v. MNR*, 1993 CanLII 2957 (FC).
57 What is called "criminal law" in twenty-first-century North America relies on compendiums, Criminal Codes. In the mid-1600s, they did not exist. The written document of 1664 refers instead to "injury," a term derived from the Latin for "a lack of *ius* or justice."
58 Each nation would be responsible to its counterpart for the actions of its citizens. This reflects the Haudenosaunee legal principle that a family is responsible to other families for the conduct of its members. To the newly arrived British in New York, who were heavily outnumbered and at the mercy of the Haudenosaunee, having this kind of leverage was an important advantage.
59 Harmen van den Bogaert had been the first European to record a visit to the Nations west of the Mohawks, in 1638.
60 Standard procedure in councils between Nations would require the first day to be taken up in greeting (the Three Bare Words at the Woods' Edge) and rest. The second day would see the Nation that had requested the council lay out the purpose of the meeting and explain its views. Their brothers across the fire would then take the rest of the second day to consider what they had heard and would respond on the third day. Council would not go past sundown, for our minds get tired, and may be misled in the dark.

Govr: Genll. And us is inviolable yea so strong yt if ye very Thunder should break upon ye Covenant Chain it wold not not break it sunder."[61]

One analysis that is sorely lacking, and that I will not undertake now, is the understanding, in the mid-1600s, of the meaning of "covenant." Its Latin origin, *con venire*, is "coming together," which implies a union greater than a single transaction. By the 1670s, the King James Bible had seen broad publication (it was first published in 1611), and the Lord's covenant with Israel may have been one of the precursors the recorders of the Haudenosaunee-Crown dealings had in mind. While I would not want to become fixated upon the meaning, to the English, of an English word that was, after all, a translation or interpretation from the Kanyenké:ha words used in council, it is remarkable that there has been so little scholarship focused on it. Words have meaning.

If we accept that modern Euro-American courts need to understand and view not just the individual transactions but the entire relationship through the lens of Haudenosaunee law, we are inevitably led to the question of whether there actually were agreements in the seventeenth and eighteenth centuries. We accept that the people on the Haudenosaunee side of the fire understood what they were doing and the legal meaning of what they were saying. How about their counterparts, their brethren across the fire?

One factor that is often overlooked by historians is the low numbers and vulnerability of Europeans in the first century after "first contact."[62]

---

61 Robert Livingston, *The Livingston Indian Records*, ed. Lawrence H. Leder (Gettysburg, PA: The Pennsylvania Historical Association, 1956), 44–45. See also Charles Howard McIlwain and Peter Wraxall, *An Abridgement of the Records of Indian Affairs: Contained in Four Folio Volumes, Transacted in the Colony of New York, from the Year 1678 to the Year 1751* (Palala Press, 2016) – August 15, 1694: "We promise that [the Covenant Chain] shall be kept on our part so Strong & Inviolable that the Thunder itself shall not break it." Thunder and lightning were the most powerful natural forces known to the Haudenosaunee.

62 In Canadian law, "first contact with Europeans" is the date with respect to which an Indigenous peoples must show that a practice was integral to their distinctive society, if they want a court to accept the practice as an existing Aboriginal right today. Oddly, first contact with any other people has no legal impact. For Haudenosaunee, "first contact" has been held to be Samuel de Champlain's attack on the Haudenosaunee in 1609 near what is now called Lake Champlain (*Mitchell v. MNR*, supra.).

The number of colonial troops involved in the fighting before the 1740s was generally under two hundred. Forts like Niagara, Detroit, Cataraqui (Kingston), and Albany had garrisons of not more than a hundred. European populations hugged the coasts.

It was, therefore, not unexpected that the Europeans would accommodate Indigenous practices in meetings. They had little choice. Besides, those practices were functional and, if respected, led to the results the Europeans wanted. For example, the terms of the 1664 agreement at Albany made each side of the fire responsible to the other for any injuries done by their people. This replicated the way the Haudenosaunee resolved crime within their own society, with a family responsible to other families for the actions of its members. To the British, this represented real leverage: rather than seek jurisdiction over an individual who was inaccessible, they could hold an entire nation accountable. The Haudenosaunee were more than stubborn in insisting that their council rules must be followed. Colonial officials soon became accustomed to them, and some became adept.[63]

By the time Warraghyhagey William Johnson settled on the Mohawk River upstream from Albany in 1738, the Covenant Chain relationship had existed for two generations. He became "Captain General" of the Six Nations (and possibly a Mohawk Pine Tree Chief) in 1747, New York's sole Indian commissioner in 1751, and imperial superintendent general of Indian Affairs in 1755. His partner, Konwatsi'tsiaienni Mary Brant, was a Kanyenkehá:ka Clan Mother. With her, he had eight children. He was fluent enough in Mohawk to correct interpreters.[64] That he once led the Cayugas into Onondaga, singing the entire Condolence song, indicates

---

63 The first official encountered by the Haudenosaunee was called by a translation of his name; for his successors, the name became a title to be passed down, like the title of a *Royaner*. Thus, le Sieur de Montmagny, governor of New France, became Yonondi:io, the Great Mountain. William Penn became Onas, the Quill. Arendt van Curler, the Dutch commissary at Albany, gave his name to successive governors of New York ("Corlaer" in most council records), and the title eventually spread to Indian agents in the twentieth century (usually *Kora*), the King in the 1701 Albany Treaty (*Corachkowa*, or Great Curler), and to Canada (Korahne).

64 Marc Miller, the Superintendent General of Indian Affairs, made history in 2018 when he became the first member of the House of Commons to give a speech in Mohawk in the Parliament of Canada. Continuity.

that his depth of fluency in Haudenosaunee culture was impressive by any standards. As imperial superintendent general, he became the hinge between the Indigenous nations and all the northern British colonies. The title passed to his nephew (and son-in-law) Guy and then to his son John Johnson. Control over the British side of the treaty council fire remained in one family for a crucial and continuous seventy-five years until John Johnson's death in 1830 (the last Johnson descendant in the Indian Department was Joseph Brant Clench, one of Sir William's grandsons, who was western superintendent in the 1850s).

Each British colony had its own "Indian commissioners" who were delegated to attend treaty councils. There were dozens of such councils. Many of them involved the repolishing of the Covenant Chain. While the present historical and political perspective of the United States tends to place the beginning of history in 1776,[65] many of the signers of the Declaration of Independence and framers of the United States Constitution had been colonial treaty commissioners dealing with the Haudenosaunee. If the United States Constitution was influenced by Haudenosaunee law, it probably owes that to the long exposure of those "founding fathers" to the principles that governed the relationship, as much as to Tiyanoga Hendrick Peters' admonitions at Albany in 1754 that the colonies would be better off if they formed a confederation of their own.[66]

Family relations and a multi-generational perspective, derived from Haudenosaunee legal principles, are essential to interpreting and implementing the terms of the individual treaty councils that, together, form the record of the relationship symbolized by the Covenant Chain. But these are only two of the underlying principles of the relationship. There are other equally important principles and mechanisms.

The relationship is sometimes fragile. In metaphor, bloodshed is like acid: it eats through the silver chain and must be wiped off immediately. As in other aspects of Haudenosaunee justice, council will spend

---

65 In 2020, President Donald Trump appointed a "1776 Commission" to promote "patriotic education" and "the miracle of American history" and to counteract the 1619 Project, which aimed to educate people in the United States about the legacy of slavery.

66 Benjamin Franklin, a Pennsylvania treaty commissioner, also undertook to print the Crown's treaties with the Haudenosaunee in his Philadelphia press.

proportionately less time fact-finding and more time considering remedies and restoring peace than modern courts do. The metaphor of the Chain emphasizes that anything that shakes it can be felt by the brothers who hold either end of it. Not only do they grasp it firmly, lest it fall from their hands, but they must pay attention to the tremors. In practical terms, this means that where modern contracts have dispute resolution clauses and processes, the Covenant Chain relationship prevents matters from festering into disputes. It provides for *concern* resolution mechanisms.

The open path of peace and communication is a constant symbol. It is a meaningful one. It must be kept free of obstructions, and it must be in constant use. Historic councils are replete with the equivalent of modern "notice provisions." That is, if you are to engage in business about the matters the treaty relationship addresses, there are specific places to do it and specific people to do it with. Thus, when the French attempted to deal directly with the Onondagas, the Mohawks, through whom the business of nations approaching from the east ought to pass, admonished them that one enters the longhouse through the door, not the smoke hole. When he would repolish the Covenant Chain in council, Warraghyhagey William Johnson would often insist that "you believe no news that comes to you from any other quarter than myself, and not listen to bad birds." This echoed the warning to the *Rotiyanehson* in *Kayanerenkó:wa* that they are not to pay attention to the birds twittering in the branches overhead.[67]

In each wampum belt symbolizing the Covenant Chain relationship, there is both affectionate closeness and respectful distance.[68] The men at each end of the belt are not holding hands; they are holding the chain. If the wampum shows a rectangle—a Nation's council fire—at each end, there is a long path of peace and communication between them to be

---

67 Rumour, which travels at speed, generates a weakness among a people who continue to rely on the moccasin telegraph. The Peacemaker could not prevent this, so the law ordains that the Chiefs' skins are to be seven handspans thick so gossip will not penetrate and that they are to ignore the twittering birds. Ignoring Twitter in the second decade of the twenty-first century has taken on a renewed significance.
68 I suggest that the confrontations and "reclamations" of 2013 and 2020 in Caledonia in the Grand River Territory have a great deal to do with the creeping encroachment of Caledonia's housing developments, violating that respectful distance—as did the plans for the Oka municipal golf course in 1990.

kept clear and open.⁶⁹ The concept of a family in which we remain close enough because we love each other, yet distant because we cannot live in constant peace together, owes its origins to the story of Creation, where Teharionwakon and Tawiskaron concluded that they had to live apart. The three rows of white beads that separate the two parallel rows of purple beads in *Tekeni Teyohàte*, the Two Row Wampum, are more often said to represent the respectful separation of the Haudenosaunee canoe and the Crown's sailing ship rather than their determination to travel the River of Life side by side. Many people refer to the Silver Covenant Chain and the Two Row Wampum as distinct but complementary treaties: it is more correct to consider the Two Row concept as an element of the Covenant Chain relationship—and the belt as a depiction of that relationship flowing through time.⁷⁰

The three rows of white beads in Two Row Wampums,⁷¹ or the three links of the Covenant Chain, symbolize the elements that make the

---

69 Euro-American law seeks to assign a single meaning to principles and words. Haudenosaunee law enjoys it when symbols mean more than one thing. In the Hiawatha Belt, the pine tree at the Confederacy's centre, turned upside down, is its heart. The belt with a straight line linking the two council fires can also be seen as the three links of the Covenant Chain, the path becoming the third link, seen from the side.
70 Was there a transaction with the Dutch upstream from Albany in 1613? Almost certainly. Was it the first Two Row Wampum treaty? That is controversial, and I do not intend to go anywhere near it, because it is not necessary to do so. The Two Row idea is much more ancient than the early 1600s and did not emerge as an extension of the Covenant Chain until the 1700s. When Warraghyhagey William Johnson put the sailing ship and the canoe side by side on his personal seal in 1755 (with six unclothed arms and his clothed one grasping a chain as the circumference of the seal), the symbols must already have been as clear to the Haudenosaunee as the other symbols on the seal—the Tree of Peace, the council house, and the smoking pipe.
71 There is not just one Two Row Wampum belt. There are three at the Grand River Territory today and at least one at Onondaga. There are slight differences between them (one has four rows of white beads between the two rows of dark ones, for example). They all mean the same thing: it was not unusual for a nation to reaffirm its commitments by delivering a new wampum with the same message and symbols as one given at an earlier council. There are also several Covenant Chain wampum belts. While the three main "styles" are (1) a man standing holding the Chain at each end; (2) a council fire rectangle at each end, with the broad path of peace between them; and (3) the Two Row, there are also "zigzag," semi-Greco-Roman chains, and several belts with numerous figures holding arms—like the George Washington Belt, with the former colonies linking arms, and the Mohawks and Senecas guarding the doors of the Longhouse, or the belt given at Niagara in 1764 depicting twenty-four men (for the twenty-four nations present) linking arms between Quebec and the present-bearing ship.

relationship work. Haudenosaunee law insists on getting things in the proper order. *Ohenton Karihwatehkwen,* the Words Before All Else, the opening thanksgiving that precedes every council, is a greeting, acknowledgment, and thanks to all the elements that we share the world with. It is delivered in a deliberate order, radiating from the people to the earth to the waters and upward and outward to the things beyond the sky. The twenty Words of the Condolence are a careful, compassionate way of putting the world back together for people whose minds have been cast down by grief and sorrow. To many elements of Haudenosaunee culture and law, there is a set order. The three elements of the Covenant Chain relationship are respect, trust, and friendship—in that order.[72]

Respect comes first. As Deskaheh Harvey Longboat explained to Quebec's representatives during the "Oka Crisis" of 1990, we need to begin with respect, because without it, we cannot sustain a relationship.[73]

Trust is easily eroded and difficult to repair. Two and a half centuries of dubious land transactions have resulted in seething suspicion, resentment, and distrust. As Joagquisho Oren Lyons explained, speaking to an "Indian Law" conference in Washington in 1975, "land is the issue. Land has always been the issue. You don't want anything else to enter into your mind."[74] However, the erosion of trust through land encroachment and theft is nothing new. Warraghyhagey William Johnson wrote in 1761:

> The sentiments of all these nations with regard to us are nearly the same. They entertain a very slender opinion of our faith and sincerity, they are to the last degree jealous of our designs. Those last connected with us, who had been early taught to entertain a strong dislike for us,

---

72 It was Tsiskokon Belanger Brown, an Oneida *Royaner*, who first took the time to explain this to me. Some people add "peace" as a fourth element, but it is more consistent, I believe, to consider peace to be the context for everything else to work. Peace is why the background to the wampum is white.

73 Onondaga Eel Clan *Royaner* Coleman Powless went further. Speaking to an Anishinaabe Grand Council at Bawating (Garden River) in 1981, he explained that self-respect is first because if you do not have that, you have nothing.

74 Joagquisho Oren Lyons, "When You Talk About Client Relationships, You Are Talking About the Future of Nations," in *Rethinking Indian Law*, ed. National Lawyers Guild, Committee on Native American Struggles (New York: National Lawyers Guild, 1982), iv.

are further confirmed in it, as well thro' the representations of our Secret Enemies, as from our own misconduct, whilst those in our alliance, and from their vicinity more liable to labour under many grievances and impositions, grow more and more discontented thro' the want of redress, and alarm the rest in a most sensible manner.[75]

New York colonial courts upheld the fraudulent Canajoharie and Kayadosseras Patents in Mohawk country.[76] Crown courts, the ancestors of the courts in Canada and the United States, "confused the assertion of sovereign authority with doctrines of feudal land title to deny aboriginal peoples any interest at all in their traditional lands or even in activities related to the use of those lands."[77] Three centuries of overtly racist court decisions[78] were supported by equally racist statutes.[79]

The third component of the Covenant Chain relationship is friendship. Not "friendship" as that word is used in colloquial North American

---

[75] Sir William Johnson, *The Papers of Sir William Johnson* (Albany: University of the State of New York, 1921), I:157–58.

[76] While the Royal Proclamation of 1763 was designed to prevent such "Great Frauds and Abuses" for the future, it did nothing to remedy the recent past ones.

[77] Binnie, J. in *Mitchell v. MNR*, 2001 SCC 33 (CanLII) at para. 151.

[78] In Canada, see *R. v. Syliboy*, 1928 CanLII 352 (NS SC), which denied that Mi'kmaq treaties with the Crown have any validity (and which remained law until 1985, when it was explicitly rejected in *R. v. Simon*, 1985 SCC CanLII at 410), and *Sero v. Gault*, 1921 CanLII 451, which denied the validity of Haudenosaunee treaties with the Crown, calling them as absurd as treaties "with the Jews in Duke Street." In the United States, Walter Echo-Hawk's compendium, *In the Courts of the Conqueror: the 10 Worst Indian Law Cases Ever Decided* (Golden, CO: Fulcrum Publishing, 2010) makes for depressing reading.

[79] In Canada, "Indians" could not consume or possess alcohol on reserves or vote until the 1960s. It was illegal for them to take part in traditional ceremonies like the potlatch or Sun Dance until 1951. It was illegal for them to raise money to make claims against the Crown without the Minister's permission (which was never given) until 1951. Beginning in 1869 and ending in 1985, women were stripped of their rights if they married non-Indians. Inconvenient Indian reserves could be taken by the Crown (like the Mi'kmaq reserve in Sydney, Nova Scotia). And on and on.

English today, but the culmination of a relationship of respect and trust: the creation of a family-like bond.[80]

To make this bond work, when nations come together, their meetings would be conducted according to the principles and processes that made Haudenosaunee treaty-making so effective.[81] There are hundreds of examples of Haudenosaunee treaty councils with Crown colonies and their successor federal, provincial, and state governments.[82] The councils did not end in the nineteenth century; they continue today, and will keep continuing (continuity, in Canada, has been identified as a constitutionally protected Aboriginal right). While the 1985 *History and Culture of Iroquois Diplomacy* describes some of the processes and some of the thinking behind them and provides a list of some of the historic "treaties,"[83] it is far from complete and comes at them all from the perspective of white academics examining the documentary history through the lens of their culture and the writing of their own people.

We begin by giving thanks together. It reminds us that we are only human and that, as humans, we carry responsibilities to the natural world and to future generations. As the speaker recites those first words, we voice our agreement. We begin our councils by already agreeing on

---

80 Between the Crown and the four Wabanaki nations, a series of transactions between 1725 and 1779 were entitled Peace and Friendship Treaties. In the Wolastoqey and Peskotomuhkati languages, what happened was *likutawakon*, "making family." But to the Government of Canada, these were about "mere" political friendship and, therefore, without any meaningful content concerning coexistence and sharing of land.
81 Two demonstrations of the importance of process emerge from relations between the Haudenosaunee and the United States in the last years of the eighteenth century. Preparing for the 1786 Treaty of Fort Stanwix, United States delegates were instructed to violate every rule of Haudenosaunee procedure—belittling, interrupting, pointing, refusing wampum. The result was an abusive transaction that was later roundly rejected by the Haudenosaunee. Preparing for the 1794 Treaty of Canandaigua, Timothy Pickering took a two-week intensive course in Haudenosaunee diplomatic procedure from Sagoyewatha Red Jacket. The result was an agreement that has formed the foundation of Haudenosaunee relations with the United States.
82 In a book on the treaties (rather than in this short article), I intend to refer to hundreds of examples of each of the elements of Haudenosaunee council process, linking internal council ways with international ones, and showing the thinking behind each one.
83 In the trial of *Mitchell v. MNR*, the professional (expert) witness Alexander von Gernet announced that a treaty council that was not on the list could not be a treaty council, because the authors intended their work to be authoritative and comprehensive.

some of the things that really matter. Sharing gratitude is the beginning of harmony.

We condole each other. If our brothers are carrying a burden of loss or sorrow, we seek to ease that burden with the most compassionate words. We are not only removing the barriers to effective and open communication. We are sincerely expressing our empathy and affection, as relatives do. We address each other's humanity. As Sotsisowah John Mohawk explained,

> To bring this into contemporary thinking, if you say, "We don't negotiate with terrorists," you have taken away your own power. You have to negotiate with them; they are the people who are trying to kill you! But to negotiate with them, you have to acknowledge that they're human. Acknowledging that they are human means acknowledging that they have failings, but you don't concentrate on the failings. You concentrate on their humanity. You have to address their humanity if you're going to have any hope of stopping the blood feud. Thus, the first meeting, and subsequent meetings, begin with an acknowledgement that people on all sides have suffered loss and that their losses are traumatic ones.[84]

Where the records of "historic" treaty councils often say they "began with the usual ceremonies," what they are omitting to describe (because it was taken for granted) is several hours of careful, caring ritual.[85] Implicit in this process are other principles: by using wampum, we are invoking the supervision of the sacred and the powerful.[86] By doing the ceremonies with care, we are indicating our intention to proceed with due care and

---

84 Sotsisowah John Mohawk, "The Warriors Who Turned to Peace," *Yes! Magazine*, November 2004, https://www.yesmagazine.org/issues/healing-resistance/.
85 William Fenton claimed to have "discovered" that "the 'Condolence business' permeates the protocol of treaty making" (in Jennings, 4). Any Haudenosaunee participant in modern international relations, and any participant in the treaty councils of the past five centuries, would know that already.
86 Wampum is a useful mnemonic device, a means of recording commitments, and reifying principles. Its use recalls the first use of wampum, when the Peacemaker condoled Hayonwatha and raised up his mind again. The strings used to begin a Haudenosaunee internal council symbolize the Nations bringing their minds together, in the spirit of unity, for the purpose of peace. As a "fire," those strings call the attention of the Creator to our work, as our words and thoughts rise like smoke.

attention to everything we are doing. A careful reading of treaty council records will show that both sides made a point of bringing and pointing out what was most sacred to them. For some Indigenous nations, it is the pipe or calumet. Haudenosaunee councils use wampum and *oyenkwa-on:we*, sacred tobacco. The British insisted that what was most sacred to them was their word or the King's word. British officials would say that the red coats of the officers were a symbol of the rising sun, coming up without fail every day. They would assert that the King's word cannot be broken. In Canadian law, there was a long period of wistful court decisions that treaties ought not to have been broken.[87] Only in 2005 with the *Haida Nation* case, did the honour of the Crown emerge again as a sharp tool.

We avoid confrontation in council.[88] Just as modern international diplomacy has its own delicate language, so the language of Haudenosaunee councils (and those of other Indigenous nations) is replete with expressions that avoid causing offence or anger.[89] English does not provide the kind of dubitative or tentative tenses and cases that allow a matter to be suggested rather than insisted upon. Protocol guided skilled speakers in putting matters across the fire in ways that invited the brothers on the opposite side to add to the idea, building toward consensus. Rather than overt disagreement, a reply might more likely be: "We agree, and furthermore we suggest." Rather than the parliamentary process of putting forward a complete bill for the opposition to attack and improve, Haudenosaunee council procedure builds agreement gradually. It takes longer. We have the time.

---

87 *R. v. George*, 1966 CanLII 2 (SCC).
88 Rather than risk lasting damage to harmony, Haudenosaunee councils are sometimes shut down after someone uses sharp words or makes accusations.
89 In the Ohio country councils of 1792, the warriors of the Western Nations were convinced that the Haudenosaunee were making secret deals with the United States and had decided to assassinate the Haudenosaunee Chiefs. When the Shawnees threw the wampum across the fire into the dirt, Farmer's Brother quietly picked it up, put it on his head so it hung down his shoulders, and said, brothers, you have spoken to us too roughly, we are going to withdraw and consider what to do. Egusheway, the Odawa war chief at Detroit, imposed some peace on the council as the Haudenosaunee took the time to allow matters to cool. See *The Correspondence of Lieut. Governor John Graves Simcoe*, Volume 1 (Toronto: Ontario Historical Society, 1923), 224.

We *listen*. Council protocol requires that one side speak at a time. There would be no interruptions. There might be some polite questions afterward, but only to seek clarification of statements. Usually, the hosts would speak on the first day, and the visitors would take the rest of that day to consider their reply, which would be delivered the next morning.[90] The reply would begin with an accurate recitation of each of the points made the day before,[91] usually with each "word" or matter returned with the wampum that had accompanied it.[92] Twenty-first-century "social strategy" and negotiation courses and books[93] insist on "good listening skills." Seventeenth- and eighteenth-century Haudenosaunee council protocol embodies all of them.

We take the time we need. Because we must consider not only the immediate but also the long term, and because the work of council also includes doing the accompanying ceremonies, we say that "it takes as long as it takes." A major council—Montreal in 1701, Niagara in 1764, or Canandaigua in 1794—could take over a month. Since the delegations attending the councils could amount to over a thousand people, the hosts were hard pressed, in terms of food, finance, and accommodation, to

---

90  To reply quickly is an act of disrespect: it tells your interlocutors that their words were not deserving of serious thought.

91  Several factors enhanced the accuracy: the participation of people trained in memorization; the assignment of remembering each part of the council to different individuals; the use of wampum as an aid to memory; the rhythm of the council itself; and a deliberate structure to the agenda.

92  The earliest European depictions of treaty councils show a horizontal pole between two forked uprights, on which the wampum representing the matters that were spoken were hung. Harmen van den Bogaert, the first European to visit Onondaga, in 1634, saw the same pole in the council house where Grand Councils were held. It is the same pole that Hayonwatha was using when he was trying to condole himself, and which the Peacemaker used to set out the strings of the first ceremonial wampum in the first Condolence.

93  Especially the Harvard Negotiation Project's *Getting to Yes: Negotiating Agreement Without Giving In*, by Roger Fisher and William Ury (Penguin Books, 1981 and 2005), which comes closer to Haudenosaunee values in negotiations than the commercial, transactional, positional handbooks.

care for the visitors. But peace, the product of each of those councils, is worth it.⁹⁴

We use our best thinking. *Kanikonhrí:yo* does not just mean "a good mind" as in having positive thoughts. It also means a mind that is functioning optimally. It is one reason why we condole our friends: we want their minds to be working well, without distractions. We want them to be healthy and at peace. We do not meet after dark because we will be tired, and tired minds become impatient or make mistakes.⁹⁵

In councils and meetings, we care for each other. In the old days, visitors would be greeted at the woods' edge and then conducted into town, where they would be fed and given a place to sleep. Business would not begin until the next day when they were rested. Being a good host was an aspect of reciprocity, too.⁹⁶ Today, in every Indigenous community I know,

---

94 One aspect of treaty councils that is often overlooked, partly because it is the role of men to do the speaking, is the work put in by the women to keep the councils going. The role of women in Haudenosaunee councils goes beyond their provision of sustenance and into recognition of their function as landholders, as well as their participation in discussions and decisions, much of which was invisible to European recorders.

95 In 1974, Justice Osler of the Ontario Supreme Court rendered his decision in the first round of the *Isaac v. Davey* case. John Sopinka, the lawyer for the Confederacy Chiefs, rushed to Six Nations with the news. I was present to hear him say, "You can take over now." "No, we can't," they replied. "We are reciting the Great Law, and will finish doing that first." "Then take over tomorrow," he said. "It takes a week more," they answered. "Let's do it tonight," he suggested. "We don't meet after dark," they explained. He threw up his hands. "Call me when you're ready," he said and returned to Toronto.

96 If Warraghyhagey William Johnson's father was, as he sometimes said, a Scot from Glencoe, it explains a great deal about the two generations of Johnson control over the Imperial Indian Department. It explains why the Johnsons were surrounded by faithful Highlanders. Glencoe was the glen where a British army detachment massacred the MacDonalds. Except they were a sub-sept of the MacDonalds—the MacIans, John-sons. The detachment, mainly lowland Campbells, had been billeted at Glencoe for weeks when it turned on its hosts. Today, in the Highlands, one can still see signs in some establishments: "No Campbells." It makes sense that a clan-based people who did not much trust the English would get along so well with another clan-based people of the same bent. See Colin Calloway, *White People, Indians and Highlanders: Tribal People and Colonial Encounters in Scotland and America* (Oxford: Oxford University Press, 2010).

it is a matter of self-respect and pride to feast one's guests.[97] And while nation-states take similar pride in putting on state dinners for visiting dignitaries, Indigenous delegations to Ottawa are left to fend for themselves.[98]

To make the bond of family[99] between peoples work, several other basic Haudenosaunee principles need to be accepted and applied.

Brothers are equals. The Māori legal proverb *kanohi ki te kanohi*, to deal with it eye to eye, may as well have been a Haudenosaunee one. Beginning with the story of Creation, brothers often have different opinions or priorities, but their relationship is such that they maintain conversation, seek to explain their views, and, above all, based on their affection and their equality, work out differences with reason.[100] The Creator Twins did not, ultimately, differ in their objectives or priorities: both wanted to survive.

Reciprocity flows naturally from equality.[101]

Now, this is the big one. *We help each other.*

---

97  As austerity measures, the governments of Canada and Ontario stopped feeding visiting Indigenous delegations. "Due to fiscal constraints, we cannot provide refreshments," wrote one federal negotiator as we headed to Ottawa. I did not fail to treat this as a breach of treaty. Some federal negotiators, ashamed they are fed well in Indigenous communities that can ill afford the hospitality, dig into their own pockets to buy the coffee. Coffee is not a meal.

98  In 2016, the Director-General of Comprehensive Claims, East-Central, explained to me that he could not take me and the Sakom of the Peskotomuhkati out to lunch because "there might be alcohol, and that would violate our guidelines." He was right in the sense that in treaty negotiations, both sides would avoid introducing mind-changers like alcohol because they could injure the negotiations. But he had not bothered to find out that there was little risk of this, for both Sakom Akagi and I are non-drinkers. We concluded it was just a dodge to get out of buying lunch.

99  I use "family" partly because "kinship" has become both anthropological and obsolete in its usage.

100 The Haudenosaunee view that no people are superior to them is not a denial of the possibility of equality.

101 Sometimes, it is necessary to call out a lack of respectful reciprocity. In 1974, at Kahnawake, there were difficulties between the Kanyenkehá:ka and the Québec provincial police. At the first formal meeting, a sergeant appeared on behalf of the police. "I have no authority to negotiate," he told us, "but I am here to listen to what you have to say and report it back to my superiors." The meeting was inconclusive. At the next meeting, two days later, across the table from the sergeant was a twelve-year-old boy. "I have no authority to negotiate, but I am here to listen to what you have to say," he said. At the following meeting, senior police officers were in attendance.

If the Haudenosaunee had not taken this obligation seriously, northeastern North America might have remained a French colony. What is now Canada might have become part of the United States, either after 1783 or after 1812. The Haudenosaunee have consistently assisted the Crown in its wars, both in North America and elsewhere (most conspicuously in the First and Second World Wars, but also in dozens of smaller conflicts, from the Fenian Raid of 1837 to the rapids of the Nile in 1884).[102] We have fulfilled our side of the relationship in blood, maintained Deskaheh Levi General, objecting in Britain to Canada's interference in Haudenosaunee internal sovereignty. We have fulfilled our side of the relationship in land, maintained Haudenosaunee leaders from Canessategon to Tiyanoga to Thayendenegea. As *Kayanerenkó:wa* explains, families across from each other in the hearths in the longhouse are there to help each other; as the Elder Brothers and Younger Brothers in a Haudenosaunee council constantly ask "How can we help you?" so the obligation of ceaseless mutual aid keeps the Covenant Chain relationship alive. That is why, when I was a young lawyer, I found "the old guys" who taught me absolutely unshakable in their conviction that the Crown *owes* us free education, free health care, and housing. I could not find those promises in any treaty—they are implicit in *every* treaty. They are essential to the relationship and are not specified in any isolated transaction. The debt is not one-sided. It is the logical result of the reciprocity in the relationship.

To seek, secure, and maintain peace, we strive to come to one mind. The procedural structures of council promote that by preventing confrontation and ensuring interest-based negotiations in the context of a long-term relationship. Canadian courts are wrong in presuming that a refusal to pay attention to detail is "unsophisticated." Instead, it allows us to reach more general agreement, and to rely upon good will and trust to look after the rest.[103]

---

102 Carl Benn, *Mohawks on the Nile: Natives Among the Canadian Voyageurs in Egypt, 1884–1885* (Toronto: Dundurn Press, 2009).

103 To arrive at consensus in council, we just need to arrive at a place where we agree on principles and mostly on details. North American culture calls that state "okay." I would prefer to believe the word comes from the Choctaw term for when matters have reached consensus, rather than a misspelling in the American Revolution.

Acknowledging our humanity includes recognizing that we will make mistakes. Our brotherhood means we will forgive each other.

We begin as we end: in council, we open by bringing our minds together in gratitude, and we close the council in the same way. I began this paper with the proposition that the relationship between the Haudenosaunee and Canada, and between the Haudenosaunee and the United States, symbolized by the Covenant Chain, emerges from a firm foundation in Haudenosaunee law; that to understand it "as the Indians would naturally have understood it" requires an understanding of that complex legal system, and that the system itself has its roots in the metaphor of family as a source of peace and unity. To work, the system is supported by functional, integral processes and protocols. That concept propels us into a field of Canadian law that remains almost completely undeveloped. The idea that there are "procedural treaty rights" is fifteen years old. No court has carried it beyond a constitutionally protected right to be consulted: "The honour of the Crown infuses every treaty and the performance of every treaty obligation. Treaty 8 therefore gives rise to Mikisew procedural rights (e.g., consultation) as well as substantive rights (e.g., hunting, fishing and trapping rights)."[104] In seventy years, Canadian law has moved from denying that treaties have any effect to protection of subsistence hunting rights from provincial game laws (1951), to protection of subsistence hunting and fishing rights from federal laws (1984), to protection of some rights to practice religious ceremonies (1990), to protection, subject to regulation, of some commercial fisheries (1999), and treaty protection of the right to be consulted (2005).

The Covenant Chain relationship contains other potentially enforceable rights[105]—and they are enforceable by both parties to the relationship as against each other. There is a right to have one's brother nation pay attention to concerns before they chafe into disputes. There is a responsibility

---

104 *Mikisew Cree First Nation v. Canada (Minister of Canadian Heritage)* 2005 3 SCR 358 at para. 57.

105 Mark D. Walter, "Rights and Remedies Within Common Law and Indigenous Legal Traditions: Can the Covenant Chain be Judicially Enforced Today?," in *The Right Relationship: Reimagining the Implementation of Historical Treaties*, eds. John Borrows and Michael Coyle (Toronto: University of Toronto Press, 2017), 187–205. See also *West Moberly First Nations v. British Columbia*, 2020 BCCA 138 (CanLII).

to account for the conduct of one's own people and institutions. There is a duty to help where help is requested or required—within the relationship as a whole, without the need to produce evidence arising from specific transactions. There is a duty to avoid interfering with a brother nation's internal affairs. There is a duty to periodically renew and reaffirm relations, lest commitments be allowed to slip out of memory. What has been missing is the conversations about how these rights and responsibilities can be made realities in today's world. We should not have to go to Canadian courts either to enforce the relationship or to defend it.

Clearing and following the path of peace and communication ought to be a political journey, a conversation between nations. Instead, the Crown waits for claims and "grievances" to be negotiated. It waits for the rights to find their way into Canadian courts, to be litigated according to Canadian rules before Canadian judges.[106] Interpreting the terms of the treaties as the Indians would have understood them, though, means we need to go back to the council fire together to rekindle that brotherhood, for the sun and the moon still exist.

NOTE: *This chapter has taken three years from writing to publication. While most of it remains true, several recent court decisions have changed Canadian law. The Quebec Superior Court decision in R. c. Montour (2023 QCCS 4154) has directly addressed and affirmed many of the aspects of this paper.*

---

106 As mentioned in footnote 41, the United States Supreme Court said in *McGirt v. Oklahoma*, (2020) 591 US at p. 42: "Yes, promises were made, but the price of keeping them has become too great, so now we should just cast a blind eye. We reject that thinking."

# 2

# Learning from the River

CHAPTER FIVE

# Guswenta Space

## An Invitation to Dialogue

*David Newhouse*

---

*Before all words are spoken, we send greetings to all of creation.*
*We give thanks for the rising of the sun and the light and life that it brings.*
*We give thanks for another day of life.*

*We respectfully acknowledge that we are on the treaty and traditional territory of the Michi Saagiig Anishinaabeg. We offer our gratitude to the First Peoples for their care for, and teachings about, our earth and our relations.*
*May we honour those teachings.*

Traditional Haudenosaunee protocol requires that we begin with an act of thanksgiving to remind us of the nature of the universe, its structure and functioning, our roles and responsibilities to all its aspects, and to foster an attitude of humility and respect.

University protocol requires that we also acknowledge the original inhabitants of this land and their descendants who have lived here for millennia and whose ways of life have changed significantly over this time. We are reminded that we are part of a long line of human and nonhuman inhabitants of this land.

We begin.

"Interpret the teachings for the world you find yourself in." This is the advice that Fred Wheatley, an Anishinaabe language teacher at Trent University, gave to students four decades ago when asked about the relevance of traditional teachings by students in a Native Studies class. These words were echoed by Chief Jake Thomas in his Trent classes on Haudenosaunee culture and traditions. These are powerful words, so powerful, in fact, that I placed them at the centre of a complex social phenomenon I called "retraditionalization," one of the central forces shaping modern Indigenous societies.[1] The desire to use ideas, concepts, and theories from our historic intellectual cultures is very strong and one of the defining aspects of modern Indigenous societies. We see this expressed most visibly in the ubiquitous use of the Medicine Circle or Medicine Wheel in areas such as health policy and programming. Another example is the frequent recitation of the seven generations' value in Indigenous decision-making arenas. The use of opening words by Elders at the start of meetings is another good example of this important phenomenon. The emergence of Elders', Women's, and Youth Councils represents a good example of the interpretation of a traditional value about the importance of all three in society. In Haudenosaunee circles, the use of the Good Mind has become more frequent, as has reference to the *Tekani Teioháte Kaswenta*[2] or Two Row Wampum.

In this paper, I want to explore the Guswenta as an ethical space. I believe that it's important to discuss our knowledge and find ways to use our own concepts and ideas to guide our everyday behaviour and professional lives as academics and teachers. This paper is reflective and exploratory, suggesting one possible interpretation of the Guswenta in modern Indigenous society.

I grew up at Six Nations of the Grand River in what I've come to call the Great Law tradition. My family has been in and around the Confederacy and Longhouse for generations. My ancestors have interpreted Haudenosaunee thought, ceremony, and tradition for more than a hundred years. My great-grandfather, Seth Newhouse, my grandfather, John Henhawk, and my father, Murray Henhawk, have been involved in this project; all believed in the importance of Haudenosaunee thought and its continued relevance to our lives. My great-grandfather, living in the late nineteenth century, was concerned about language loss and believed that our knowledge ought to be conveyed to new generations in English. My father, unlike my great-grandfather and grandfather, believed that it ought to be conveyed only in its original language. It is unfortunate that he did not take the opportunity to help his children learn their birth language. All my learning and teaching has taken place in English. My understanding of the concepts I'm going to discuss is bounded by that language as a result.

I am heartened by the emergence of what I call Indigenous Knowledge scholarship within the Western academy. I teach in the Chanie Wenjack School for Indigenous Studies, formerly the Department of Indigenous Studies, formerly Native Studies, at Trent University. Our approach to Indigenous Knowledge scholarship is to include Indigenous Elders as integral parts of our tenured faculty. Hadajigre:ta', Jake Thomas, Cayuga, from Six Nations of the Grand River, was one of the first to be appointed to the university. He taught courses on the Mohawk language as well as Haudenosaunee culture and tradition, bringing aspects of our knowledge to new generations in a new institutional setting. I am pleased to see the emergence of the Deyohahá:ge: Indigenous Knowledge Centre at Grand River and the creation of the formal position of Indigenous Knowledge Guardians. These actions signal that colonization has not removed our knowledge from the intellectual landscape that the Indian Residential School era attempted to create.

I offer these reflections in the spirit of my family and acknowledge the growing visibility of Indigenous intellectual traditions. When I entered the academy three decades ago, Indigenous Knowledge was seen through the anthropological lens of cultural or local knowledge as laid out by Geertz.[3] It is now widely accepted as a legitimate set of knowledges arising from a well-established knowledge system. Indeed, the Social Sciences and Humanities Research Council recognizes Indigenous Knowledge and Indigenous Knowledge Holders as making scholarly contributions to human knowledge.[4] Canada has the only set of national research granting councils in the world that accepts the validity and contribution of Indigenous Knowledge and enables Indigenous Elders to be co-applicants on research proposals.

The Tri-Council Policy Statement on Research Ethics, which sets out the ethical guidelines for all research involving human beings, has been informed by Indigenous leaders and Indigenous ethical values of mutual respect, mutual responsibility, and reciprocity.[5] It would be fair to say that Indigenous research ethical codes such as OCAP® (Ownership, Control, Access, and Possession), USAI (Utility, Self-Voicing, Access, Inter-Relationality), and Mi'kmaw Ethics Watch have been largely informed by the same traditional ethical values. Some have extended the ethical field to include nonhuman beings and the natural world in accordance with Indigenous understandings of creation and the core value of respect.

I frame my reflections as part of the "politics of respect."[6] I see the Guswenta through the lens of ethical space[7] and etuaptmumk: two-eyed seeing.[8] Cree scholar Willie Ermine argues that one needs to create a space for dialogue between two peoples, while Bartlett, Marshall, and Marshall set out the ethics guiding a respectful dialogue.[9] Coleman argues that a politics of respect enables us to suspend our judgement, see things in their context, and escape our cognitive North Atlantic prisons.[10] My goal is not to create or speak truth but to help foster what I call "complex understanding."[11] A complex understanding enables us to create new knowledge by bringing together diverse perspectives and knowledges into conversation and dialogue. Coming to a complex understanding may be akin to the Haudenosaunee idea of "coming to one mind," which requires careful dialogue and listening to the other. It requires us to adopt a mental position of humility.

The Guswenta has been predominately portrayed through the lens of politics and political relationship, symbolized as pictured on page 9 of this book. Its simplicity hides its complexity. Learning to read the Guswenta is not a simple exercise. What I present is one possible reading, blending a North Atlantic and Haudenosaunee English understanding.

Robert Williams in *Linking Arms Together* argues that the Guswenta is emblematic of a common Indigenous political philosophy.[12] The conventional interpretation of the Two Row Wampum is that of two ships sailing on parallel paths down the river of life. The relationship is defined as one of non-interference and conducted in accordance with the three principles of friendship, peace, and forever. Guswenta defines a nation-to-nation relationship between Indigenous and European nations. The Two Row Wampum has emerged as a powerful symbol of Indigenous sovereignty and is used as one of the foundational documents supporting Indigenous governance.

The Guswenta, though, is about more than politics. To see it only through a political lens is to interpret it narrowly and limit its usefulness. The Guswenta is an answer to a broader question: *How do we live well together?* The Guswenta was one answer to that question in a world that was decidedly multi-national and multi-cultural at the height of its use as a form of engagement with the newly arrived Europeans of the seventeenth and eighteenth centuries. Can we interpret and apply the Guswenta to our contemporary lives in a multi-cultural country? To answer that question, we must turn to the story of the founding of the Haudenosaunee Confederacy, the concepts embedded in the Gayanashagowa or The Great Binding Law: the central notions of the Good Mind and Condolence and the story of Sky Woman and the creation of this world. The Guswenta sets out an ethical set of principles about how to live well in a multi-cultural world.

## THE ETHIC OF RESPECT, COOPERATION, COLLABORATION, AND CARETAKING

We start our story in midflight: Sky Woman is falling from the hole in the sky when the animals notice her fall and decide that they have to do something to lessen her fall and provide a place for her to land gently. Birds fly up and create a cushion with their wings to lower her gently; the turtle offers his back; animals dive into the water to seek and bring back earth. After great effort, one of the smallest animals brings back earth, which is placed on the turtle's back and the earth grows. Sky Woman transforms the earth using the plants she grabbed in an effort to keep herself from falling. Her twin children create the world as we know it. They also embody the tension inherent in all human beings: the desire to do good and the potential to do evil. Human beings are given original instructions and are tasked with the caretaking of the world.

Things don't go well; humans fight among themselves, and a messenger arrives with a powerful set of teachings about how to live well together. The Gayanashagowa or The Great Binding Law is built upon two premises: the idea of the Good Mind and Condolence, for the two are linked and that living well together—in other words, creating peace—requires the use of our good minds. Peace is not a static state to be achieved once and for all but a set of actions carried out within an ethical framework of respect, cooperation, collaboration, dialogue, discussion, and debate. Peace requires that we use our rationality to make it. It also requires our continuous effort and an understanding that peace requires health—of our bodies, minds, communities, nations, and the natural environment. Peace means that we need to acknowledge and restrain the worst parts of ourselves and summon our goodness to the task.

I tell my students that the Sky Woman story is a story about cooperating and working together, a story about how animals and humans created the world by working together, a story about knowledge and skill that we bring to various tasks, but overwhelmingly a story about the ethic of cooperation; an ethic that is built into Haudenosaunee culture. We see the same ethic exemplified in the story of the creation of the league and the actions of the Peacemaker and Hiawatha.

## GAYANASHAGOWA, THE GREAT LAW

We tell the story of a time before the founding of the Haudenosaunee league of nations. It was a time of great strife, a world of continual conflict and warfare, a world where brother fought against brother. The Peacemaker was born into this world with a mission to create peace among the various nations who were at war with one another. Together with Hiawatha, he sought to bring nations into a Great Peace by using reason rather than domination and subordination. The journey to the Great Peace, or The Great Binding Law, was an arduous journey of collaboration between the two friends. It was also a journey of perseverance as the idea of a Great Peace was not initially accepted. The Peacemaker and Hiawatha did not force their ideas on the warring nations but helped them to come to peace by respecting each nation's position and power and responding to their questions and tests of integrity. The Great Binding Law was formally presented at the first meeting of the League.

This Great Law is a prescription for living well together, for creating social harmony, and is a theory of human society. It was developed as a direct result of the disharmony that existed among Indigenous nations in the northeast part of North America. It is an elaborate ethical code based upon the idea of society as a longhouse with many families who need to learn how to get along. It is premised upon the idea that human beings desire to get along with one another and that all have a good mind that can be awakened through ceremony. A good mind is one that remembers its original instructions.

## GANIGONHI:OH, THE GOOD MIND

Within the Haudenosaunee, the concept of Ganigonhi:oh, "the Good Mind" illustrates an ethical responsibility to use one's mind in a way that balances reason and passion. At the beginning of his journey to foster the Great Peace, the Peacemaker encountered a young man living in the forest and in a state of deep grief. He had lost his family and found it difficult to continue with his daily life. We would describe his mind as spread out on the ground. The Peacemaker performed a ceremony for him to help him overcome his grief and enable him to return to his daily life.

The Condolence Ceremony, used for the installation of Chiefs, is intended to restore the good mind of leaders so that they may carry out their responsibilities:

> We now do crown you with the sacred emblem of the deer's antlers, the emblem of your chieftainship. You shall now become a mentor of the people of the Five Nations. The thickness of your skin shall be seven spans, which is to say that you shall be proof against anger, offensive actions and criticism. Your heart shall be filled with peace and good will. Your mind shall be filled with a yearning for the welfare of the people of the League. With endless patience you shall carry out your duty and your firmness shall be tempered with tenderness for your people. Neither anger nor fury shall find lodging in your mind. All your words and actions shall be marked with calm deliberation. In all your deliberations in the Council of the League, in your efforts at law-making, in all your official acts,

self-interest shall be cast away. Do not cast over your shoulder behind you the warnings of your nephews and nieces should they chide you for any error or wrong you may do, but return to the Great Law which is right and just. Look and listen for the welfare of the whole people, and have always in view not only the present, but also the coming generations, even those whose faces are yet beneath the surface of the ground—the unborn of the future Nation.[13]

Here, we see a statement of Haudenosaunee ethics: concern for the common good—not just now but for future generations—kindness, patience, perseverance, calmness and intellectual rationality, deliberation, and certainty of purpose.

## THE CONDOLENCE CEREMONY

*I wipe the tears from your eyes so that you may see; I clear the obstruction from your ears so that you may hear; I clear your throats so that you may speak. With these three actions, I restore your good mind so that you may take your place among human beings again.*

The Condolence Ceremony, whose opening "words" or ritual actions I have summarized above, is intended to restore our good minds, to clear the grief of existence from our minds and hearts, and to restore balance to them. It is intended to remind us of our highest ethical value: to use our good minds to act for peace. It reminds us that we are human beings and that all human beings desire peace. It reminds us of our common humanity, subject to all the strengths and fragilities of being human. It connects us one to the other through a common experience of grief. It restores us and strengthens us for the arduous job of creating peace. It sustains us through the darkest of days and reminds us that there can be lightness again. It is a reminder that we can begin again and that we must begin again, over and over again, for all time. It is a ceremony of hope for creation and a hope that peace is possible.

## OHEN:TON KARIHWATEHKWEN, THE THANKSGIVING ADDRESS

The Thanksgiving Address, recited at council, reminds us of the ethical field we live within. We are part of a huge interrelated and interconnected web of beings, human and nonhuman. The Address reminds us to act with kindness and respect towards all living beings, acknowledging them as part of our family. It reminds us of our responsibilities towards them.

When we come to read the Guswenta and interpret it for our twenty-first-century lives, we come with these ethical understandings: that we are part of a huge family, human and nonhuman, living in one house; that we have a set of responsibilities to one another, responsibilities to treat each other with respect and kindness and helpfulness; and that we are expected to cooperate with one another, to work and live together and to use our good minds to always foster peace.

## GUSWENTA SPACE

The Guswenta principles are given physical expression through a wampum: the Two Row Wampum embodies Haudenosaunee ideals about political relationships and how to live well together. It is an ethical statement that is intended to serve as a guide for our actions in a shared world. Each wampum belt is made for a specific situation and serves as an aide-memoire to a particular relationship. Like all ethical codes, it requires interpretation in a specific context.

The wampum belt itself represents the specific landscape of an agreement; the two rows represent the parties to the agreements and the three rows of beads separating the two rows represent the ethical values of the relationship. The space between the two rows is what I call "Guswenta space."

The conventional understanding is that the wampum, taken as a whole, is indicative of a relationship of non-interference: each party pledges not to interfere in the affairs of the other. The Great Binding Law provides for the sovereignty of each nation in the league and pledges non-interference in their internal affairs, so the conventional interpretation is consistent with Haudenosaunee political philosophy. The Great

Binding Law creates a space for structured dialogue, discussion, debate, and decision: a council with its fifty Chiefs and a Firekeeper. Council discussion and Chiefly behaviour were guided by the ideal of the Good Mind. Chiefs were installed through the Condolence Ceremony, which was intended to restore their good minds so that they could discharge their responsibilities honorably and ethically.

The three rows of white beads separating the two purple rows have been given various interpretations of the values that are intended to inform the relationship between the wampum partners: peace, friendship, forever; peace, power, righteousness; friendship, peace, respect; kindness, respect, friendship. The space between the two rows is an ethical space in the sense developed by Cree scholar Willie Ermine: a space of engagement where peoples of diverse societies and backgrounds can engage with each other.[14] Each person enters the space with their own thoughts, feelings, understandings, histories, moralities, cultural imperatives, and knowledge. Each one retains their unique identity upon entering the space. Guswenta space becomes a space of possibility and transformation and a space of learning. Learning occurs through listening, questioning, dialogue, discussion, and debate. The three beads provide the ethical guidelines for what happens in this space. I interpret the three beads as kindness, respect, and honesty: we treat each other with kindness, we respect the diversity we represent, and we speak honestly to each other. We prepare ourselves for entering the space through the opening words of the Condolence Ceremony, which restores our good mind.

Guswenta space is the space where we use our good minds to tackle the question: How do we live well together? What does kindness mean in these circumstances? What does respect mean? What are the truths that need to be spoken? How do we deal with our grief? How do we create peace? What actions foster the peace? What actions deter peace? How do we deal with disagreements? How do we acknowledge and recognize that each of us has different power?

Guswenta space challenges us to always seek peace. It requires us to acknowledge the other as us, to recognize the implications of power and difference, and to learn to listen with humility. It requires us to find ways to cooperate and collaborate instead of fighting and tearing each other apart. We need preparation to enter Guswenta space, a preparation of the intellect and the emotion. The three opening "words" of the Condolence Ceremony, which restores our good mind, provide a way of doing this. Working in the Guswenta space requires patience and perseverance. It also requires a structure of dialogue and discussion. The use of the circle as a structure for discussion serves us well. The ethics of the circle require that we listen before speaking, consider our words carefully, and speak truthfully and with kindness. Guswenta space offers the possibility of living well together.

The Guswenta interpretation project is an important one. It takes an important idea and practice from Haudenosaunee intellectual history, translates it into a contemporary context, and seeks to interpret it so that it remains relevant and useful to contemporary lives. The 2013 Two Row Wampum Renewal Campaign, which sought to polish the four-hundred-year-old Covenant Chain, is an excellent example. Coleman and Hill interpreted the principles of the Guswenta for the creation of research partnerships in Canadian universities.[15] Mercer wonders whether Guswenta principles could be used in the creation of new ethical spaces in our political cultures to bring Indigenous and non-Indigenous Canadians together.[16] Vachon framed the Guswenta as containing principles for intercultural dialogue between Mohawks and nation-states in North America.[17] In Canada, we live in a multicultural society and seek to find ways to live well together. The Thanksgiving Address reminds us that the ethical field is not just other human beings but all aspects of the natural world.

I use the concept of Guswenta space as a frame for creating a dialogic classroom. I begin with an opening designed to help students make the transition from home or other activities and to bring their good minds to the task at hand. I remind students of the ethics of conversation and try to model kindness, respect, and honesty. In my experience, many of those who come to the site of discussion and learning about Indigenous issues are fearful, anxious, and wondering if they will be battered by the experience. Others are wanting a cultural or spiritual experience. All are somewhat concerned about being transformed by their contact, an anxiety about Indigenous people that is built into North American culture as represented by the captivity narratives of the eighteenth and nineteenth centuries. Guswenta space enables us to come into the space, acknowledge who we are, and respect each other. It invites an honest, respectful dialogue and learning. The use of a structural approach to conversation: the circle brings an Indigenous dialogic approach to the site.

As I prepare this paper, I am readying myself to lead a Canadian Studies graduate course. I'm using the idea of Guswenta space as more than just a dialogic classroom space but as a way of speaking about Canada itself: a grand experiment in living between the Two Rows and trying to answer what I've come to call the Guswenta Question: How do we live well together on this land at this time? John Ralston Saul, in *A Fair Country: Telling Truths about Canada*, argues that Canada is composed of three pillars: English, French, and Indigenous; that the Indigenous pillar has been neglected and that it's time to address this. He also argues that Canadian political culture is informed by ideas coming from Indigenous cultures, most notably the idea of fairness, consensus, and power sharing.[18] His more recent book, *The Comeback: How Aboriginals are Reclaiming Power and Influence*, is his attempt to address this.[19] Perhaps we address the neglect by doing the previously unthinkable: conceiving of the new entity developing on this land through Indigenous theories about how to live well together.

I've tried to present the Guswenta as more than a representation of a political relationship. The Guswenta, conceived as an ethical space, creates a site for an important human conversation about how to live together.

I finish my reflection by thanking you for reading. As you return to your work, may you find your families and loved ones well. May they rejoice at your return. May you always use your good mind to foster peace.

Nia:weh.

CHAPTER SIX

# Navigating the Two Row in the Academy

*Vanessa Watts*

---

## INTRODUCTION

At McMaster University, in a room fittingly called "Council Chambers," where room booking information indicates that "Priority is given to University Governance meetings of the Board of Governors and Senate and the committees which report to them directly," hangs a framed replica of the Six Nations Polytechnic (SNP) Partnership Belt (a variation of the Covenant Chain Wampum). The wampum was gifted to McMaster in 2014 by SNP in recognition of a partnership between the two postsecondary institutions, one that is to be grounded in respect. The partnership between SNP and McMaster is anchored in two critical outcomes described by SNP as including increased student success as indicated by student enrolment, retention, graduation, and employment and critically important advances in Indigenous education through the development of culturally appropriate and responsive learning and research opportunities focused on Hodinohso:ni knowledge and languages. The belt, known as the SNP Partnership Belt, visually depicts this relationship as described in the accompanying text:

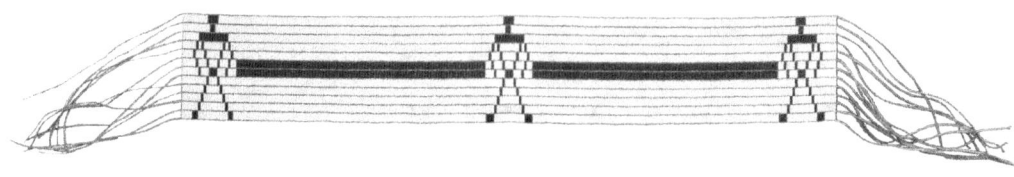

6.1 Six Nations Polytechnic Partnership Belt (Photo credit: Six Nations Polytechnic, 2014)

> In the Six Nations tradition, a Partnership is a relationship of respect, trust and mutual benefit. Each partner will receive a replica of a Covenant Chain wampum belt that features three human figures, one at each end representing SNP and our Post-secondary Partner, with a third figure in the middle representing the learners. This belt codifies the respectful and reciprocal nature of the partnership as it shows the fires of each institute connected by a path of peace, understanding, commitment and cooperation.

The belt hangs on the inside wall of the room, encased in glass, directly above the doorway. It is positioned between painted portraits of university presidents on either side—a symbolically significant placement. It was hung before "Indigenization" became a widespread ambition in Canadian higher education. It gestures towards a form of recognition—that in a space used for top-level university business, where major decisions are made (or where decisions come for formal recognition and endorsement) hangs a visual agreement of mutual aid and respect. On the walls of Council Chambers, then, hang two living reminders: one, in the medium of oil paint, portraits of a genealogy of leaders who have had a turn at the helm of knowledge production and, two, a Haudenosaunee living document representing an agreement between two autonomous groups who can rely on each other in times of need, especially as leaders in distinctive genealogies of knowledge production.

McMaster's land acknowledgement, created by its Indigenous Education Council, reads: "McMaster University recognizes and acknowledges that it is located on the traditional territories of the Mississauga and Haudenosaunee nations, and within the lands protected by the 'Dish with One Spoon' wampum agreement."[1] As has now become common practice in educational institutions, land acknowledgements like these are appended at the end of emails or spoken by rote at the beginning of institutional events—both of which risk normalizing inaction through the symbolic. As part of the *Conversations in Cultural Fluency* video series from SNP, Richard Hill Sr., Tuscarora historian and artist, discusses the Dish with One Spoon agreement in "Ecological Knowledge & the Dish with One Spoon." Hill notes: "Everybody has an equal share to what's inside the dish, but you only take what you need—you don't collect things and hoard them…You always leave something in the dish for other people…You've got to keep the dish clean…Our job as humans is to come in harmony with nature or Creation's intelligence."[2] Relationships with and between other-than-humans are a central concern of Indigenous cosmologies, and, in turn, these relationships are represented in the governance systems and legal orders of our societies. Land is not solely about rights to territory (though it is this, too). Land has local, varied, place-based systems of knowledge production embedded within it, and wampum agreements—such as the SNP Partnership Belt and the Two Row Wampum—provide protocols to maintain these relationships.

The Tékeni Teyohà:te Kaswenta (Two Row Wampum) developed from the first agreements made with European settlers and the Haudenosaunee. It is enlivened by three relational principles, peace, friendship, and respect, that are expressed in the three white rows of wampum that separate the two purple rows of wampum (or the two vessels). This relationship is buoyed by a river where two vessels are traveling. One vessel, a canoe, in which the Haudenosaunee travel, and the other, a ship in which the settlers journey. They may be traveling to the same destination they may not. But they are tethered, in their respective journeys, by these principles and by this river. The Two Row Wampum is grounded by the Covenant Chain wampum, through which, in the principle of friendship, the signatories could call on each other for aid in times of need. The Kaswenta can only flourish if the principles of the Dish with One Spoon Wampum are upheld and adhered to, lest the river be untraversable or dried up. Thus, for the university to take seriously the wampum agreement it literally holds up within its Council Chambers, it must also take seriously the context for that agreement: the principles and sustainability of the Dish.

Relating such land-based worldviews to education, Sami scholar Rauna Kuokkanen's words about the Deatnu (or "Great River" in the Sami language) are fitting: "The river encourages me to develop an epistemology that is grounded in concepts and metaphors derived from Sami cultural practices and circumstances but that also allows me to move into other 'waters.' They allow (and force) me to exist in several different discourses and to recognize their tensions, challenges, and possibilities."[3] However, the Two Row itself *is* a treaty agreement grounded in a particular time and place, complete with implications about specific land, sovereignty, and governance, and anchored by the principles for a relationship with arriving European settlers. In this way, there is a danger in metaphorizing a living agreement into an abstraction dislocated from these very particular conditions. Nonetheless, as Kuokkanen notes, an epistemology that is grounded in place-based Indigenous concepts and agreements not only asserts culturally based articulations of knowledge but teases out how hegemony and power can violate those concepts and agreements. Bearing this in mind, this essay considers how principles of the Two Row (and related living wampum documents) contribute to how we might consider Indigenization efforts in higher education—both with respect to challenges and opportunities. Ways of knowing—or how we come to know (the "river" or "other waters" as Kuokannen writes)—are traversed, on one hand, by knowledge assemblages bound within the university that have neglected, misused, and attempted to steer, on the other hand, Indigenous cultural forms of knowledge.[4] Thinking alongside Two Row Wampum principles, I consider how places of tension might also be iterative and generative since the ship of academic knowledge does not exist in a vacuum.

## INDIANS IN THE ACADEMY

What can we learn from the river and the Dish in higher education? The academy has a long legacy of scholarship centered on the so-called "inherent deficiencies" of Indigenous Peoples and communities—and as such has produced an abundance of scholarship constructing the Indian as a never-ending problem. This dynamic has thus approached Indigenous cultures and peoples as a long-standing research-rich frontier. The academy, therefore, routinely neglected the sophisticated and complex systems of knowledges and governance that exist across diverse Indigenous nations and territories. Today, the university often paints Indigenous knowledges as "newly emerging," despite their having been developed over millennia, or sometimes as a lens by which to view already established Eurocentric conventions of knowledge and modalities. Juxtaposing these histories of cognitive imperialism alongside the Dish with One Spoon leads me to ask: What is *in* the Dish in this broad institutional sense, and what *could* be in the Dish? Answers to these questions constitute a significant disruption to the current postsecondary status quo, which has emerged from an increasing number of Indigenous thinkers gaining entrance into the academy, and national imperatives such as the Truth and Reconciliation Commission (TRC) and its Calls to Action in which higher education is a central focus.

While the TRC Calls to Action have the potential to push the university into reflecting on its ongoing colonial legacies within its walls and beyond, the national imperative of reconciliation continues to be fraught. In the current era of reconciliation, we have witnessed continued assertions of Indigenous sovereignty at Wet'su'weten. Close to home here at Six Nations of the Grand River, the land defence known as 1492 Landback Lane is currently taking place. This 185-year-old unresolved dispute sits at the epicentre of sovereignty and land relations. 1492 Landback Lane was preceded by *Kanohstaton* at Six Nations, a land occupation and defense that took place in 2006 across the road from the current occupation at Landback Lane. *Kanohstaton* intended to halt the development of Douglas Creek Estates on the Haldimand Tract (it was successful), a territory that was part of a larger landbase granted to the Six Nations of the Grand River after the American Revolution. During *Kanohstaton*, there were several encroachments by the Ontario Provincial Police (OPP) over many months, resulting in violence and arrests against Haudenosaunee people. McMaster University was criticized at the time for agreeing to house OPP officers in residence–officers that would be deployed to *Kanohstaton*,[5] a reminder that the university is not innocent and has the ability to change its course, to interfere and interrupt another's path.

The Two Row Wampum may outline peace, friendship, and respect to guide our two vessels, but how can we uphold these principles if the river upon which we journey is unlawfully claimed as private property, filled in, polluted, and developed upon? Reconciliation seems, at the very least, distant in this political moment. Reconciliation at the university, therefore, must be broader and more imaginative than the current political will if it is to be transformative.[6] If the university as an institution relies on national imperatives shaped (and limited) by the state for navigational direction rather than local, place-based ones, reconciliation will only act to universalize and diffuse the parameters for building just relationships based on respect for distinct knowledge traditions. The Tékeni Teyohà:te Kaswenta outlines two distinct pathways characterized by sharing, exchanging but not colliding, and not taking. But what is in the university ship's cargo hold about us? Putting aside for a moment the ostensible successes achieved in spaces of ethical knowledge exchange between Indigenous and non-Indigenous people (which there are), it cannot be ignored that the ship of academia has steered a particular course in hegemonic views about Indigenous peoples.

A key element to continued rationalizations about the benefits of settler colonialism is the notion that Indigenous peoples were not and are not "modern." That is, that European nations were/are more advanced on the spectrum of modernity and, therefore, colonialism was and is ultimately justified. This sort of dynamic produces a "modern-versus-amodern" binary in thinking about Indigenous-settler relations, which continues to infuse the academy. Battiste and Henderson refer to the propping up of this sort of binary as *European diffusionism*: the spread of European peoples and their thought to modernize Indigenous places, and the consequent "benefit" of this diffusion for Indigenous peoples themselves to progress in terms of "creativity, imagination, invention, innovation, rationality, and sense of honor or ethics."[7] In this hallucinated worldview, the ship forges ahead while the canoe lags behind, buoyed by the possibility of "progress" but always in need of updating and uplift. Through assumptions such as these, the imperialist pursuits of Europe in North America simultaneously shaped the ideological underpinning of research agendas.[8] Moreover, the conditions produced by settler colonialism (e.g., land theft, lack of access to healthcare, racist policies) produced the "premodern" conditions that became the basis of the study of Indigenous people. In short, imperialistic attitudes have pathologized Indigenous peoples and communities in academic research.[9]

Elaborating on this point, Shawn Wilson describes five phases of Indigenous-centred research in the academy: 1) the Terra Nullius Phase (1770–1900): research on Indigenous peoples was generated by imperial desires to control land. Wilson documents research during this period as largely concerned with characterizing Indigenous peoples as subhuman, emphasizing that this sort of "scientific" rationale would serve to help normalize the removal of Indigenous peoples from land either by force, legislation, or death. 2) The Traditionalizing Phase (1900–1940): this phase continued the former discourse of Indigenous peoples as subhuman, which rationalized a landscape for research aimed at "civilizing" practices. 3) The Assimilationist Phase (1940–1970): research on Indigenous people transitioned from a focus on physical characteristics to the identification of social and kinship structures. Further, this phase rationalized its operations as aimed at the "preservation" of a vanishing race as well as research dedicated to providing solutions to "Aboriginal problems." Wilson notes that it was during this phase that research on Indigenous people became increasingly popular and profitable for both businesses and academics. 4) The Early Aboriginal Research Phase (1970–1990s): Indigenous researchers began to emerge in this phase, but Wilson points out that Indigenous-focused research continued on a trajectory of welfarist research, with subject matter focusing on linguistics, religion, education, and health. Academics, professionals, and researchers in this phase were seen as the mediators of Indigenous dependency. 5) The Recent Aboriginal Research Phase (1990s–2000s): this phase sees the emergence of Indigenist research, wherein space for more collaborative research begins to take hold.[10]

According to Wilson, we have now entered a potential sixth, "Indigenist Phase," as it is only more recently that Indigenous ways of knowing are being significantly integrated into Indigenous-based research.[11] Further, Indigenous Studies as a discipline is gaining momentum in the academy, as are Indigenous scholars within this field. As a result, the deepening of Indigenist intellectual traditions is taking shape in contemporary academia. Canadian universities have taken up the cause of "reconciliation," in which Indigenization and decolonization are two priorities. In their article, "Indigenization as Academy Inclusion, Reconciliation, and Decolonization: Navigating the Different Visions for Indigenizing the Canadian Academy," Gaudry and Lorenz remark on varied levels of

Indigenization strategies taking place in higher education across Canada and find that Indigenization occurs in three different institutional orientations: 1) Indigenous inclusion, 2) reconciliation Indigenization, and 3) decolonial Indigenization. Decolonial Indigenization is divided into two parts: i) treaty-based decolonial Indigenization and ii) resurgence-based decolonial Indigenization. What can a treaty-based or wampum-based approach teach us about relationships, sustenance, and our future journey in academia?[12] According to Gaudry and Lorenz, a treaty-based decolonial Indigenization is one of the most radical options, requiring substantial systemic change that recognizes, protects, and grants authority to Indigenous scholars, units, and communities over Indigenous Knowledge. They write that it is necessary for the university to understand that "indigenization isn't just a 'pro forma' program, but rather a process built on collaboration, consensus, and meaningful partnership."[13] The Two Row and Dish with One Spoon provide important insights in terms of how we might think about new (based on old) formulations.

## 1. THE TWO ROW AND THE DISH WITH ONE SPOON: CULTURE SHOCK AND CULTURE GARB

Hill and Coleman describe the Two Row Wampum as a basis for attempting to create a dynamic based on an "understanding of the protocols for productive relationships between sovereign and interdependent peoples."[14] Given the impetus to reconciliation within the university since the TRC, there is genuine interest and curiosity about how to create a more just learning and research environment. However, there are also some who hold pre-formed views in these settings. The interest in Indigenization has facilitated genuine curiosity, concern, interest, and collaboration, but it has also provoked a bigger echo chamber for stereotypes and myths to proliferate. Many of us share lived experiences with the research we do, and navigating those stereotypes and myths can be more than a bit tricky. Indigenous faculty and learners can sometimes be viewed as essentialists or guilty of a lack of "distance" from their research subjects, yet they are increasingly looked to as gateways to partnerships with Indigenous communities and organizations. Both of these orientations facilitate a high-stakes situation for Indigenous scholars where engagement opportunities *are* exciting, where it *is time* to have Indigenous voices leading initiatives and partnerships, but when Indigenization is taken up by the university as a politically correct "trend," Indigenous faculty, staff, and learners can then find themselves in positions where accessing these exciting opportunities results in tokenization: we become statistics used to prove institutional morality while behind the scenes we continue to experience overburden and tokenism.

In comments at the Deyohahá:ge: Indigenous Knowledge Centre on the history of the Two Row Wampum, Richard Hill quoted Cayuga Chief, Jacob Thomas: "We will appear the way we did when we first met."[15] Hill explained that the intention of Chief Thomas's words were to emphasize that in traveling down the river of life in distinct yet connected vessels, the Haudenosaunee and the newcomers would continue to wear their distinctive and respective clothing. This image strikes a particular chord in an educational context, wherein Indigenous faculty, administrators, students, and staff operate within the newcomers' sailing ship, with its particular traditions and conventions, whether acknowledged or unacknowledged. Can we bring who we are to bear on such an institution and still retain the garb of our own knowledge traditions? I am reminded of a time during my undergraduate studies when a professor said to me, "keep your culture checked at the door." At the time, I was pretty pissed off (I still am). It is reminiscent of a common experience Indigenous students still encounter in the classroom. As Marie Battiste puts it: "While all of humanity's knowledge bases are drawn similarly from experience, perception, cultural transmission, and experimentation, not all peoples equally value those experiences, nor do they put their faith equally in their perceptions."[16]

Similarly, in Saunders and Hill's work on the education system, they contend that a form of coalition-building between institutions and communities (including community-based knowledge holders) is necessary to achieve excellence with respect to Indigenous pedagogies in the classroom. Neither a "do not enter" sign nor an "add and stir" method will do—cultural knowledge as a form of excellence lies at the basis of coalition-building.[17]

## 2. RELATION-SHIPPING

Indigenous cosmologies refer to the origins of how human beings are intended to relate to the world around us. Cosmologies contain elements such as origin stories, scientific practices, and relationship dynamics that exist between humans and other humans, between humans and other-than-humans, and between other-than-human beings themselves. Cosmologies are often grounded by particular places; that is, Indigenous cosmologies are distinct and vary across the diverse Indigenous territories that exist. Oftentimes, Indigenous origin stories are viewed as creation "myths" rather than historical events by the scientific and social scientific communities.[18] This sort of orientation can devalue or deauthorize Indigenous stories as invalid or illegitimate. To honour the covenant agreement between the Haudenosaunee and McMaster University within the Dish, there must be respect for Indigenous Knowledges. Have we reached a point where our cultural conventions can find a respectful and generative space in university institutions? I don't know. I think in certain contexts where relationships between people rather than institutional agendas guide the destination, this is possible, and it quietly creates generative spaces.

An example of this is the Two Row Research Partnership (TRRP) seminars hosted at Deyohahá:ge: Indigenous Knowledge Centre at SNP since 2015. Richard Hill and Daniel Coleman describe these meetings as an opportunity for community-based researchers at Six Nations and researchers from nearby universities to gather and discuss a Two Row approach to ethical research partnerships.[19] As one of the chapters in this present volume demonstrates, Bonnie Freeman, an Algonquin and Mohawk scholar and member of the TRRP, exemplifies such a Two Row research paradigm through her participation in the Two Row Paddle on the Grand River. Freeman and her research colleague, Trish van Katwyk (who is non-Indigenous), are regular attendees of the annual canoe journey down the Grand River. They write: "The canoe is not only a metaphorical space, it is also a literal space in which both Bonnie and Trish have explored their research relationship, as well as engaged with the community they were working with."[20] This journey creates an ethical space between Indigenous and settler vessels that connects and guides their journeys down the river as well as Bonnie's and Trish's research relationship, a material yet also metaphorical and pedagogical experience. In this ethical space, we can imagine the principles of peace, friendship, and respect (or the white rows of the Two Row Wampum) as guiding the distinct but conjoined relations of their journey: "Guided by the Tekéni Teyohà:ke Kahswénhtake, the canoe that Bonnie and Trish are in becomes an ethical space in which the respect for diversity and the understanding of relationships become an opportunity for growth and learning."[21] Respect for a diversity of knowledges and approaches to these knowledges is acknowledged and enacted. Both scholars are tethered to their respective academic institutions, with each institution having its own set of knowledge histories and presences. But Freeman and van Katwyk embark on a cultural practice, idea, and agreement that is grounded in Haudenosaunee thought, and they find that their knowledges can be maintained yet shift in important ethical ways, can flourish and be diverse—perhaps they appear the way they did when they first met, albeit, fundamentally re-oriented. And so, when these Two Row principles of peace, friendship, and respect are enacted as the basis of relating, two distinct journeys can have a shared experience and even a common destination while maintaining the autonomy of experience and method.

Part of peace, friendship, and respect, however, can also mean one's journey to a destination does not support the other's—it could indeed destroy it. An awareness of irreconcilability can also maintain peace.

## 3. UNPACKING THE VESSELS

Second, when I recall that professor's command during my undergrad years, I think about the settler desire for guilt-free, romanticized consumption of Indigenous cultural representations. For example, Tuscarora scholar, Jolene Rickard reflects on her time as a guest curator at the National Museum of the American Indian, noting that the museum represented the "natural Native," thus erasing the innovation and inventiveness of diverse Indigenous civilizations. She writes: "Museum management refused established museological categories like fine and folk art or anthropological and material culture as organizing principles, which resulted in a confused reception by an audience expecting conventional classification. Instead, multiple Indigenous worldviews were brought forward as cosmological stories but were set in apolitical frames."[22] Indigenous art as myth. Indigenous art as in the past. Rickard's contention that representation of material culture is up for a multitude of interpretive lenses, usually absent of political (and place-based) contexts, is reminiscent of Linda Tuhiwai Smith's description of the "ethnographic gaze of anthropology" and the collection and consequent classification of Indigenous material cultures that both motivates and extends the settler gaze.[23] In this context, perhaps keeping one's culture checked at the door is good advice, lest one's clothing be stolen and donned by another!

This is not to say that disciplines and institutions have not or are not currently engaged in efforts to decolonize. There are hopeful examples of ethical Two Row relation-shipping between those in the academy and Indigenous communities and knowledge. In her recent article in *The Rambling*, for example, Eugenia Zuroski writes about how the Two Row Wampum provides important insights for decolonizing the field of eighteenth-century literary studies: "We're not starting from how things were when the wampum was first made. The ship has wrecked things, and its sailors have a lot of work to do before the vessel can be considered close to seaworthy again—to demonstrate its fitness to proceed respectfully in these waters."[24] In this sense, decolonization might be considered an outcome of reasserting the governing principles of a Two Row relationship: peace, friendship, and respect. In the absence of these principles, the ship Zuroski references is not worthy of engaging with Indigenous knowledge; rather it is destructive towards it.

Finally, I wonder about the stretching and pulling of culture and tradition to fit a sort of prefab. Sioux scholar Vine Deloria Jr. offers a provocation that he hopes his book, *Red Earth, White Lies,* brings to bear on the relationships of the academy, Indigenous scholars, and traditional people. He hopes his book

> will initiate discussions between traditional people and scholars, and that it will provide a basis for the elders to deal with overeducated younger Indians who have uncritically accepted scientific folklore as fact. Nothing is more annoying than listening to an educated Indian parroting what he or she has been told in a lecture and discovering that tribal traditions have

simply been thrown out the window without careful examination. Many non-Indian scholars are ready to accord respect to tribal traditions, but we have to be ready to engage in a free-for-all with them, critiquing their scientific folklore and making them provide the evidence for and basis of their belief.[25]

Here, Deloria points to the consequences of leaving one's culture at the door (and perhaps risk ending up dressing differently than when you came in). Complexities such as those experienced by people who did not grow up with their traditions are not well reflected in Deloria's statement, nor are the potential pressures felt by isolated Indigenous academics who are on their own and do not have a collective Indigenous community to rely on. It also assumes a sort of purism about knowledge whereby Elders are inherently good or better than the young people they have to "deal with."

But I think Deloria raises an important consideration about what gets left behind when culture is stretched too thin or forgotten. Tradition walking in through the door can risk being captured and performed as neo-tradition, abstracted from practice and place. Or not mentioned at all. This scenario animates an ever-present tension: Does Traditional Knowledge belong in and alongside the academy, and can one speak of Indigenous knowledge without being rooted in tradition? This tension has been present for as long as Indigenous thinkers have entered the academy, but it seems even more high stakes now since the emergence of the Indigenization paradigm that is on the agenda across higher education in Canada and alongside important conversations about tradition and purism.

## CONCLUSION: TAKING CARE OF THE CANOE

Daniel Heath Justice questions whether the goal of Indigenizing is appropriate, writing: "Such a goal turns our attention away from lands and cultural traditions and into the inequitable power dynamics of an increasingly corporatized academic world."[26] In other words, Indigenizing the academy focuses our attention on the purple rows of the ship at the expense, perhaps, of our own purple canoe rows. Indeed, if nationally driven "reconciliation" is the discourse by which universities and other public institutions wish to proceed, in the absence of local and culturally informed thinking like that which is embedded in the Two Row, Covenant Chain, and Dish with One Spoon wampums, then Indigenization might be deemed as divisive by these institutions. Perhaps there is too much focus on merging our vessels or anchoring them together. Indigenous ways of knowing, cultural traditions, epistemologies, and ontologies are intimately connected to particular territories and places. The diversity of Indigenous thought across Indigenous nations is emblematic of the diversity of landscapes across Indigenous lands and territories—in other words, such diversity of landscapes promotes a diversity of Indigenous thought and protocol. Yet the legacy of Indigenous-focused scholarship and policy from the Western sailing ship has ignored this diversity (and, in many cases, actively *eroded* it), first by analyzing Indigenous nationhoods and accordant social phenomena using metrics that are absent of Indigenous theorizing, and second by implementing a policy that separates Indigenous peoples from their territories. In this way, the university ship has been off course. Throughout the continued machinations of settler colonialism, Indigenous peoples, and societies have consistently asserted our ways of knowing and thereby enacted resistance to settler colonialism. Our wampum agreements are both present and unrelenting—it is a matter of how we look to them to draw our respective but connected journeys.

In thinking through allyship at a senior administrative level within universities, we need to make room for expertise and leadership approaches deemed "non-traditional" (i.e., not the way the ship usually runs things according to its traditions). Recognizing the service of Indigenous scholars as well as Black scholars and scholars of colour will be crucial in making the ship seaworthy again because *this* is the service work that often leads to institutional transformation. Allyship, therefore, is about relationships, even friendships, and material forms of recognition. In this way, the "consulting" and "service" work of Indigenous academics should be underscored by principles of sharing and replenishing—both material elements of sharing one dish. This is key because it refuses to allow the Dish with One Spoon to be purely symbolic—it requires that the sustenance in the bowl (the resources of knowledge) sustain everyone, but especially those who do the work of maintaining the health and wellness of the bowl for all. Indigenous students, staff, scholars, communities, and organizations can contribute to the transformative work of decolonizing disciplines, making space for Indigenous ideas and fruitful collaborations within the university, but this transformation cannot be achieved meaningfully without material change and exchange (i.e., hiring more Indigenous scholars, material recognition of Indigenous-led research, service work that is recognized and supported materially, and curricular transformation within disciplines that have departmental buy-in). What is in the bowl must be considered within the context of what has been taken out or shut out of the bowl in the past. And what is taken out has to be replenished with "new" (born-from-old) forms of recognition and thinking. In responding to the question of checking one's culture at the door, I wonder, where does culture go when it gets inside? Does it become a performance? Is it used to dress another in one's own clothing? Is it locked in a box or a data set somewhere? Or is it the thing that keeps us as Indigenous peoples who pass through the doors grounded and proud? I think it can become all these things, especially when we operate from the understanding that our cultures are intellectually sophisticated.

CHAPTER SEVEN

# Two Rows of Reconciliation

*Rick Hill*

---

*I have advised my people thus: When you find anything good on the white man's road, pick it up. When you find something that is bad or turns out bad, drop it and leave it alone.*

—SITTING BULL, HUNKPAPA MEDICINE MAN, 1877[1]

A current war cry at land reclamations wonders what happened to the Two Row Wampum treaty. It was supposed to be the foundation of our relationship. But in the 411 years since it was made (assuming the 1613 date is accurate), is it realistic to think that our treaty allies still remember and believe in the Two Row as an agreement to resolve matters with reason instead of violence? It appears not.

It is timely to reflect on what the ideology of the Two Row Wampum relationship means in real terms today. While our oral memory speaks about maintaining the Good Mind in relationships, our protests are usually met with force, violence, and a legal landslide. It has been this way all my life. The fierce protests of the Tuscaroras to defend their land against the Niagara Project in the 1950s, the long protests of the Senecas against the Kinzua Dam during that same era, and the fight of the Kahnawake Mohawks against the St. Lawrence Seaway all resulted in the courts denying the treaties as the law of the land. In these cases, the land we were already holding disappeared under our allies' bulldozers and a tidal wave of water. The Ship always swamped our Canoe.

In the era of the United Nations Declaration on the Rights of Indigenous Peoples (UNDRIP), people seemed to have been lulled into thinking that things have changed and our treaty rights will finally win the day. Yet, there are lingering questions about what this all means for Canada's relationship with the Haudenosaunee. Does the philosophy of the Two Row still offer a way forward? Have things changed so much that the Two Row is no longer valid?

We know that colonization has confused what is in the Haudenosaunee Canoe and what is in the Euro-Canadian Ship. We are in a philosophical and legal dilemma. I want to explore this dilemma from my perspective, but I offer no concrete steps for how to get out of the mess we are in. This is instead a call to put our minds together and raise consciousness about the true nature of that dilemma, as seen through a Two Row Wampum lens.

The Two Row Wampum agreement, in principle, required the culture, laws, and beliefs of the Canoe to stay in the Canoe. Taking them out of the Canoe, separating them from the cultural context of how they were meant to operate, and transporting them in isolation into the Ship, hoping to transform the culture of the Ship, is exactly the thing the agreement tried to prohibit. The call to Indigenize the academies of the Ship seems to violate the original intent of the Two Row Wampum, as our culture, beliefs, and law were to remain in our Canoe. Instead, we Haudenosaunee need to re-Indigenize the Canoe and decolonize some of our own thinking first. We can't have mutual respect for our distinct cultures, beliefs, and laws if what is in our Canoe is no longer distinctive.

As Canoe people, we are not meant to steer the Ship. However, can we sit back and let the Ship continue to create a tidal wave that threatens to sink our Canoe? Maybe we need to have a different kind of alliance to minimize the damage that a rudderless Ship can inflict. For example, Canada's banks continue to invest heavily in fossil fuels. Canada's international trade agenda deals in profiting off fossil fuels, which means more drilling, more pipelines, and more infringement on our rights, much less those of the planet. Can an ancient Two Row ideology change the thinking of Canada's bankers and oil entrepreneurs? If we think that we are safe and isolated in our Canoe, not to be affected by the forthcoming ecological nightmare, we will be gravely surprised.

If we look at the rows of white beads between the wakes of the Ship and the Canoe as a calm space of engagement, we have to be realistic about the nature of our current relationship and the capacity of our allies to rethink their current course. However, the rough waters of today's politics seem to drive our vessels further apart, at least in terms of official, nation-to-nation dialogue. Maybe our governments will never recover their Two Row-ness. Some people from each vessel, however, have taken their responsibility to maintain the principles and are developing a people-to-people Two Row relationship that focuses on individual responsibilities to each other. This might be the only hope for the future of the Two Row.

Is a treaty still valid when one party repeatedly ignores its obligations? During the colonial era, the Dutch, French, and English officials tried to impose their laws, religions, and economies upon the People of the Canoe. The creation of the Indian Act by the Government of Canada was a further violation of Two Row ideology attempting to impose their will upon the People of the Canoe. The British had abandoned the Two Row agreement by the beginning of the nineteenth century, so a generation or two of British subjects grew up not understanding or believing in the premise of the Two Row Wampum. Our deep understanding of the Two Row ended when the last Elder who inherited its message passed away about twenty years ago. A long recitation of the Two Row was recorded and was in the process of being translated when the scholar working on it disappeared, along with the recording and its translations. Unlike the Great Law or *Gaiwiio*, the oral narrative of the Two Row has not been regularly recited within the Haudenosaunee communities.

While it is clear that the Haudenosaunee at Six Nations, Tyendinaga, and Kahnawake tried to remind the new Canadian state of these long-standing obligations, the Canadian Ship had different ideas and chose to ignore the Haudenosaunee. By the time Canada was confederated, government officials had stopped looking at Indigenous nations as real nations. My father was born as a ward to the government, in their eyes, in 1920.

The Two Row crossover intensified when Catholic and Protestant missionaries arrived. The imposition of Ship beliefs still exists in the Ontario Education Act, which defines the duties of teachers in the province "to inculcate by precept and example respect for religion and the principles of Judeo-Christian morality."[2] Given the application of that morality in the past in dealing with Indigenous nations, how will the future be any better? There is no room for Indigenous belief systems in that current paradigm.

In 1790, an Italian visitor, Count Paolo Andreani (1763–1823), travelled through Oneida County and noted the depth of the transformation that had taken place due to colonization:

> The frequent intercourse that this nation has with European colonists, and the religious principles with which they have become accustomed since they embraced Christianity, have influenced greatly their customs; and we can call the Oneida savages half civilized, and although some of them do not profess any religion, nonetheless living together, produced an overall equity.[3]

*Savages half civilized*. That phrase reminded me of what Sir John A. Macdonald, Canada's first prime minister and first superintendent of Indian Affairs, said nearly a century later in 1883: "When the school is on the reserve the child lives with its parents, who are savages, he is surrounded by savages, and though he may learn to read and write, his habits and training and mode of thought are Indian. He is simply a savage who can read and write."[4] The myopic lens of the Ship saw my ancestors as flawed to the core, no matter what clothes they wore, what words they wrote, or what crosses they knelt to. The law, culture, and customs of the Canoe were viewed as backward, savage, heathen, or, at best, the rantings of infidels. A quick reading of letters to the editor of Canadian newspapers of today shows that those attitudes still exist among white Canadians. Many do not want to reconcile because they prefer the *Us-As-Dominant* tradition. No number of commemorations of the Two Row will change their minds.

In the United States, Canada, and Great Britain, the confounding matter called the "Indian Problem" reached its zenith in the mid-nineteenth century. These nation-states looked upon their former Indigenous allies, allies that they once seduced through Covenant Chain and wampum diplomacy, as helpless in the tidal wave of colonization. In many ways, their Covenant Chain concepts overrode the precepts of the Two Row Wampum.

Originally, the Canoe and Ship were tied together, first with a rope and then with an iron chain. The oral narrative of the Two Row includes reference to the Covenant Chain, meaning that the agreed-upon principles would still drive the nature of the relationship. The Dutch concept of a covenant—as a sacred agreement—fit in with the Haudenosaunee concept of a sacred wampum agreement. When the British defeated the Dutch in 1664 and took over the operation of the New York colony, they transformed that iron chain into the Silver Covenant Chain.

In 1677, the British changed that tie to a silver chain and, rather than representing a people-to-people agreement, inserted the Crown as the governing authority over that Chain. Where the original Two Row was an agreement of equals, the Crown became the judge and jury of what would be allowed under the Covenant Chain relation. A new metaphor was added, that of "polishing the chain," which was thought of as a diplomatic metaphor meaning to knock the rust (inattention, transgressions, cheating, violence, death, etc.) off the chain by renewing the intent of the agreement, thereby making the chain shine again and becoming stronger. However, the intent of the Covenant Chain is different for the Two Row. By the "Friendship Belt," the Crown offered to look after our general welfare, provided we did the bidding of the Crown. If we did what was asked, then we were considered faithful allies. Rather than resolving matters together as in the Two Row, the Crown would decide what the resolution should be, and we have petitioned the Crown for justice ever since to no avail.

The treaties tore our people apart. We once believed in the Great Peace and the shared Dish with One Spoon. Divided loyalties, reinforced through the treaty-making process, corrupted our core values. We fought over who would benefit from the fur trade. We turned the great Dish upside down. We gave up jurisdiction over millions of acres of land. The Ship turned into an out-of-control steam roller or harvester that chewed up Indigenous lands from coast to coast. My ancestors resisted this, but today, most of the Haudenosaunee consider their homestead as private property, granted by the Minister of Indigenous Affairs, not owned collectively by their family clan.

We were squeezed into tiny postage stamps on the postcards of our own demise. We let them take our children. Our Canoe became weaker. We could no longer row in unison. We drifted on the River of Life.

By the time my ancestors were looked upon as wards of the government, dependent upon the care provided by Ottawa or Washington, DC, our Canoe was swamped with colonial baggage. It has been overloaded for generations. We developed a taste for what the Ship offered.

The Canadian Ship continues to try to steer our Canoe. The new oarsmen who have invaded our Canoe are the police, judges, child-snatching social workers, drug dealers, and murderers stalking our women and girls. Most of the intelligentsia of the Canoe now are employed in the institutions of the Ship. It is like a brain drain that detours their minds. Our scholars have an increasing voice within the academy, but at what cost? They run the danger of being more concerned about their standing in the academy than helping to resolve the real-life treaty dilemmas of their cousins back in the community. Certainly, this is not true of all Indigenous peoples within the Ship, but trying to keep a foot in the Canoe and a foot in the Ship is a dangerous proposition, as the Two Row tells us. Life on the River of Life has become messy and complicated. Our loyalties have become divided. Our footing is unsure. Many have fallen out of the Canoe and are lost in the dark waters between the Canoe and the Ship. I have felt caught between two worlds all my adult life. There are no lifelines from the Canoe, only a feeling that you get what you deserve. Too many simply watch as more and more Indigenous youth disappear beneath the surface of the water. Perhaps, in re-Indigenizing the Canoe, we need a safety net of compassion and to find more ways to embrace the minds of our scholars in the real needs of their community.

The question we face is how true reconciliation can be possible, given this mixed-up Canoe-Ship matrix. Let's take a look at three possibilities.

## RECONCILIATION WITHIN THE CANOE

In 1798, a year before Handsome Lake had a series of visions that prompted an era of cultural revitalization among the Haudenosaunee, a Mohawk man at Grand River envisioned the return of the white dog sacrifice, a practice that Anglican Mohawk patriarch Joseph Brant had prohibited. The visionary said that the Creator ("The One Who Completed Our Bodies") was upset with the Haudenosaunee, for they had deprived him of his favorite meal—roasted white dog. The Mohawk prophet said the Creator was unhappy with the Senecas because they had discontinued this ceremonial offering. Longhouse people asked Brant if they could revive the practice. Brant's Christian mentality said no, but his rational mentality said otherwise. He realized that this was important to some of the people and that to further ban it would cause unrest and weaken his hold over his own people. So, he said yes.

A dog was sacrificed once again. The news spread to the Oneida Nation, and after a thirty-plus-year lull, a white dog was sacrificed there too. I'm not sure what happened. Some say that people got sick when they ate the roasted dog. Others say that the breed of dog has disappeared. Still, others say that someone had a dream that the practice should be halted again.

No more such dog roams our communities anymore. No roasting of the white dog takes place. No food is offered to the One Above. Yet, if what our ancestors held to be true is still true, what happens when the Creator is denied his favorite meal? Does he get hangry? Does he take it out on us? Is this why our Canoe flounders?

The point is that we must reconcile within our Canoe, with our own past, with our own laws, beliefs, and customs. We no longer have one mind and one heart, nor do we speak with one voice as we were instructed to do by the Peacemaker. We have become a deeply fractured people.

Perhaps by renewing our "treaty" with the Creator, we might gain the spiritual energy and will to transform our negative behaviors and mend broken relationships within our families, clans, and nations. In other words, we can't reconcile with anyone if we do not first unburden our trauma, grief, and sense of loss. We must recover our humanity that was nearly lost through colonization and resulted in what has been labeled ethnostress—the loss of Indigenous joy. In an unhealthy state, we are not trustworthy to ourselves, our families, or others. We are driven by anger, fear, or a sense of helplessness. We have adopted many of the biases that once offended us. Reconciliation requires the recovery of mutual respect, trust, and friendship. Our culture teaches us that this is true.

We have been reciting the narrative of the Great Law of Peace for several years in our communities. We have recovered our wampum belts, and they are providing a road map to our collective recovery. We are restoring our languages as best we can. We are beginning to better understand our Original Instructions, not as the Ten Commandments, but as a way of thinking that connects us to the earth, encourages our thankfulness, and sets our minds to create a peaceful and healthy place for future generations. But it is a long and difficult path ahead.

## RECONCILIATION WITHIN THE SHIP

"Our objective is to continue until there is not a single Indian in Canada that has not been absorbed into the body politic and there is no Indian question, and no Indian Department," testified Duncan Campbell Scott, deputy superintendent of Indian Affairs in Ottawa in 1920.[5]

Ironically, Scott identified a concern that we share. We, too, wish there was no problem with us and no federal department that hangs over our heads like a bloody tomahawk. Of course, Scott had a different purpose in mind: no reserves, no treaties, no land claims, and no need to reconcile.

The Canadian Ship has had to look at its relationship with Indigenous peoples and nations through a series of Royal Commissions. Each time, they wring their hands, shed a few tears, and make a few promises, but the Ship continues on its pre-determined course—the course of destruction of Indigenous realities. Little has changed despite the evidence of the need to change the course of their Ship.

The truth is that the Canadian Ship needs to decolonize before reconciliation can be made real. The biased nature of the worldview within the Ship needs to change. Here is the challenge. How can Canadians keep the inclusive aspects of their culture while letting go of their need to control Indigenous peoples and territories? Canada's economic future depends on the further exploitation of natural resources found on Indigenous lands. To end the prejudice against Indian rights, Canada needs a value change away from colonization and the environmental storm it creates to a more meaningful, spiritual relationship with the land and its inhabitants. Canadians must recover the sacred.

I dare say that they require a spiritual change, as well. Now that hundreds of cases of abuse have been witnessed within the church, within the schools, and within the Boy Scouts, the church system has been revealed as a cover for pedophilia operations. It has produced a culture that allows church officials to abuse children, ask for forgiveness, and then feel exonerated. It is an unending cycle that needs to be broken and prayers of forgiveness to God are not enough. Missionaries from the Ship created mental and emotional terror in the hearts and minds of the People from the Canoe that they targeted for conversion. They said that God would punish the sinner, that he could be a cruel and vengeful God, and that people faced eternal damnation if they did not transform their evil behaviors. It makes you wonder where that kind of God has been in dealing with the sins committed in his name against Indigenous children.

These are not isolated cases. The churches knew what was going on and attempted to cover it up. Despite a few cases in the 1990s that resulted in the conviction of several Christian pedophiles, the Government of Canada has given the molesting priests, staff, and teachers immunity in the final settlement. To receive a payment from the Indian Residential Schools Settlement Agreement, Survivors had to waive their rights to seek justice from those who harmed them. The taxpayers of Canada paid for the sins of the church. This still needs to be reconciled within Canadian society. The churches then refused to pay their court-ordered restitution payments, and again, the government let them go free. The healing is incomplete because those who harmed children, those who covered up the harm, and those who have made excuses for the harm done by their religion have not really made things right. Some have confessed and apologized. However, countless IRS staff have been harmed by what they participated in. They suffer from the trauma they personally committed, witnessed, or pretended did not happen under their watch. Some have passed that inner guilt onto their siblings. They carry unresolved trauma, like many Germans have over the conduct of the Nazis.

If reconciliation is the return to normal relations, a new normal is required. Christian principles such as the Ten Commandments must be made real in relationship to Indigenous peoples. The theft of land needs to be reconciled, not with the payment of money to waive all future Indigenous rights, but the land needs to be given back under the belief that *Thou Shall Not Steal*. The Canadian Ship has to make sure that the ideology that drove and continues to drive racist attitudes is dismantled. It is not about statutes. It is about thinking. Reconciliation requires clear-headed thinking, guilt-free hearts and minds, and humbleness that moves beyond dogma and rhetoric. Canada needs to heal itself.

## RECONCILIATION BETWEEN THE ROWS OF THE WAMPUM BELT

Rowing together along the Grand River is not enough. What does it take to remove the trauma and shame of history from both the descendants of the People of the Ship and the People of the Canoe? Recently, efforts have been made to bring our hearts and minds back in partnership on the water. The 2013 Two Row Wampum Renewal Campaign flotilla retraced the paths of the Ship and the Canoe, with stops along the Hudson River to rekindle peaceful relations, share histories, and project a mutual vision of the future in which the ideology of the Two Row Wampum would guide our conduct towards each other. Locally, Two Row paddling on the Grand River each year aims to create a virtual community of like-minded peoples between Haudenosaunee and our neighbours to reimagine the possibilities of what Good Minds can create—peace and ongoing friendships. It is the start of building personal relationships, but we need transformative relations within both the Ship and the Canoe, as well as transcending relationships between the two vessels.

The transcendence necessary is to overcome hundreds of years of betrayal to the values of the Two Row agreement. Specifically, how do we develop *respect* with a government that has repeatedly treated us with disrespect? Is it possible to have mutual respect for our laws, beliefs, and customs while the land swindles, historical traumas, and lost trust funds create huge waves on the River of Life for our people? How do we push the reset button on our relationship to get back to what it was when the Two Row Wampum was first agreed to? So much has happened since then to make us Onkwehón:we a very suspicious people.

In the subsequent years of colonization, our people have become very angry and distrustful, some say with justification. The centuries of suffering from the power imbalances that resulted after the Dutch were defeated by the British in 1664 have created a state of anomie in which the ethical standards of the past (respect, equality, compassion) were replaced with colonized behaviors—the abnormal became the new normal. It is a mental disease that limits our hearts and minds, and we Haudenosaunee no longer see white or Black people as our brothers and sisters. We no longer believe what the Creator instructed us to do—to treat *everyone* as if they are members of one family. It is also within our family tradition that there are two sides to the longhouse, meaning gender and clan relations. However, the two sides work together to make the society whole. Haudenosaunee social organization provides important functions to each side of the house, in service to the other side of the house. It is our original covenant. Those traditions need to be reconciled with the modern Two Row interpretation of separating humans into different vessels. Perhaps seeing each other as members of one family—as outlined in the Covenant Chain agreement that set the context of the Two Row—might be the only way to recover the Good Mind when we treat everyone with love.

How do we develop *trust* with people who have historically been untrustworthy? We don't believe the government bureaucrats and politicians when they promise green pastures. Racism still gets in the way, as does the old-fashioned feeling of superiority of most of the people in the Ship. Once you have been bitten by a snake, you learn not to put yourself in a vulnerable position, or simply stay away from snakes. We had medicine to help keep snakes away or to treat a snake bite, but we don't have medicine to make people trustworthy. That will only be possible once the People of the Ship decolonize their inherited bias and reconcile with themselves with what they have done, and have transformed their harmful behaviors. They need a Healing Circle among themselves.

How do we develop *friendships* that can weather stormy events without driving the Ship and Canoe further apart? Many of us have real friendships across the divide of the Ship and Canoe. Many have begun the personal healing needed. But our governments are another matter. It might not be possible for the Haudenosaunee and the Government of

Canada to enact a Two Row Wampum relationship. But that should not stop a people-to-people movement of reconciliation and re-empowerment.

How do we make *peace* while our women are still getting murdered or disappeared? How do we make peace when our children are hauled out of their homes at a bigger rate than they were during the residential school era? How do we make peace when land defenders are hauled off by the police and held financially liable for their actions to protect the land? How do we make peace when racist words are flung at our players at sporting events? How can we make peace with a government that denies our nationhood and the right to carry our own passports? Really, how can we make peace at all?

When we say that we are all treaty people, we have to know what vessel we are in and how that vessel can operate to promote respect, trust, friendship, and peace. We all hold part of the Covenant Chain. We all take from the great Dish. However, we must turn to a new era of sharing. We can no longer place Indigenous peoples and lands on the sacrificial altar to Canadian growth. We need a new economic aspect of the Covenant Chain that provides for the long-term sustainability of all people.

Canada is changing. Multiculturalism is producing a Canadian landscape that is increasingly populated by non-Europeans, people with whom we have no treaty. The Two Row Wampum ignores Africa, Asia, the Middle East, and, in fact, most of the rest of the world. Historically, the Two Row focuses on the West because that is who arrived in our lands to develop nation-to-nation relations. By the time other cultures arrived, they had arrived as individuals, not diplomats, to a treaty-making relationship. This does not mean that we could not make such agreements with other nations of the world, but the Two Row agreement represents a critical moment when the possibilities of peaceful coexistence were actually possible. Maybe the Ship represents all whose ancestors were not born of this land. Whereas the Covenant Chain is focused on the Crown of Great Britain, is it fair to ask where the other Crown heads of state reside with the Chain? Where are the non-European governments?

It is time for the Two Row to expand its scope. The Haudenosaunee need to make relations with people beyond the Netherlands, France, and Great Britain. We also must reconcile with the fact that Joseph Brant bought and sold Black slaves. We must atone for that sin if we want a Two

Row relationship with people of color. Considering UNDRIP, we have a moral obligation to seek formal relationships with other Indigenous nations of the world. Can we claim a right that we are not willing to give to others? The Haudenosaunee are attempting to send a lacrosse team to the 2028 Olympics in Los Angeles. The International Olympic Committee recognizes a nation-state as one that is recognized by the United Nations and the international community of nations. We will not be able to field a team for international competition unless more nations recognize our sovereignty as an Indigenous nation. The expanded Two Row might be the avenue to Olympic gold!

Think of many Two Rows that go beyond the Canoe and the Ship—the Canoe and the Native Hawaiian Outrigger; our Canoe and the Haida Canoe; Our Canoe and the Woi Wurrung bark Canoe of the Aborigines of Australia; our Canoe and a dugout Canoe from Cameroon; or our Canoe and the Okinawan sabani. Many vessels, many paths, many wampum belts.

We need to shake our heads to get our eyes unstuck on Western Europe. For the Two Row ideology to be honored, we must honour all peoples of the world. We must build constructive relations with the other Canoes of the world.

My Lakota friend, Arthur Amiotte, said it best (if we reconsider the gender bias) when he wrote in 1971,

> Until we are able to realize what we have picked up and left behind, and until we are able to discriminately practice [Sitting Bull's] words in an enlightened manner by ourselves, we will continue to become more and more of that which has made us less and less of the true men we once were and are still capable of becoming. Perhaps then, and only then, will we be able to emerge as transformed men instead of continuing as a self-pitying, object lesson of man's inhumanity to man.[6]

In the tradition of the Haudenosaunee, we need to greet the people who arrived at the edge of our woods. We need to help them wipe the tears created by the colonization of the lands of people of color. This will allow them to see that we are still here on our land. We need to help them recover their hearing from the dust of war and death in their homelands. This will allow them to hear our words and take them to heart.

We need to refresh their bodies with whatever water Nestle corporation leaves us.[7] This will help them regain their voice to be able to dialogue with us as equals.

Otherwise, the new newcomers will try to recolonize our lands, take our resources, and deny our long-standing case for justice in our homelands. That would be contrary to the spirit and intent of the Two Row Wampum. That would be to the shame of the future generations. Now is the time to decide what we will pick up and what we will lay down as we travel the path of the Canoe.

CHAPTER EIGHT

# Below Decks in the Covenant

## Blackness in the Two Row Tradition

*Phanuel Antwi*

———

In this chapter, I investigate the unacknowledged presence of Black people in the peace-making arrangements between the Six Nations and colonial powers such as the Dutch and the British, which are widely known as the Covenant Chain and the Two Row Wampum agreements. My aim is to ask what prospects for "peace, friendship, and respect" might emerge when we admit that Black people were below decks in the sailing ships of Europeans who were working out protocols with Haudenosaunee canoeists about how to share the river of life on Turtle Island.

In 2006, when the land reclamations at Douglas Creek Estates were unfolding in Caledonia, I had just finished my MA thesis in the Department of English and Cultural Studies at McMaster University on the impacts of police brutality on the lives of Black youths and communities, and I was about to begin my PhD on the avoided presence of Blackness in the social fabric of nineteenth-century Canada. The reach of this territorial conflict, happening twenty-eight kilometres away from campus in the southwestern Ontario rural community beside Six Nations Reserve on the Grand River, was long in both time and space; most immediately, it affected the mood in the city of Hamilton and galvanized activism both on and off campus. Little did I know then that I was bearing witness to a moment that would come to play an important role in how I orient myself to the intellectual work to which I was then apprenticed. The scenes of white settler violence, bolstered by public discourse about Indigenous lawlessness and the militarized presence of police officers living in dormitories on the campus where I was studying and working, resonated with ways that I saw the ideological and repressive regimes in Canada shape how Blackness lives on in Canada.

Two political and intellectual frameworks were guiding how I was, then, thinking about the ways that Canadian public institutions worked to avoid engaging Blackness as part of their self-description. The first framework is what, in academic and activist circles, we call *racial capitalism*. This way of thinking helps us clarify how anti-Black racism has been a fundamental, not incidental, component to the ways we think about capital, value, and labour. Which is to say, anti-Black racism plays a key role in the wealth-making of the territories we call Canada. I put awareness of racial capitalism in direct dialogue with attention to *white-settler colonialism*, which focuses on the structures that emerged from Dutch, British, French, and other European powers establishing colonies in places they claimed to have "discovered," and from this claim, established trade, took lands, and extracted resources. At the same time that they gained possession by dispossessing Indigenous rights, these European empires forced their lifeforms onto the people of the land, assuring themselves that this imposition was good for them. With both interpretive frameworks, I wanted my work on the avoided presence of Blackness in early Canada to think through the genealogies and discontinuities of slavery, settlement, and Indigenous dispossession.

From years of doing this work, I have come to understand that Blackness (in Canada and elsewhere) exists prepositionally; it moves *in* and *out*, *beside* and *between*, *against* and *with* resources and territories.[1] In other words, Blackness exists as a relational dynamic. For me to contend with its hemispheric and transcontinental reach, for example, to grapple with the ways in which its logics entangle Indigenous life and sovereignty, I have to take on the special challenge of questioning why Blackness and Indigeneity often seem to be deployed separately, sometimes even competitively, to explain the legacies of gendered, racialized, and state-sanctioned violence across the Americas. Part of my work, over the years, has been to search for ways to understand the contending colonial and racial regimes of these histories of dispossession alongside and in relation to one another.

And yet, the unfolding of the land reclamation in 2006 made me aware of my sanctioned ignorance, of not knowing my place, hence of not taking up the responsibilities I have to place.[2] It made me want to learn the agreements I have to abide by if I do not want my uninvited presence—and, as a result of their coerced and forced passages, my ancestors' uninvited presence on these lands—to bolster a world of endemic colonial and racial violence that erases the sovereign laws of the place, people, and other-than-human beings I am living among and learning from. Through the anti-colonial activism of my graduate school cohort, which led many of us to learn more about the struggle at Caledonia (we visited the Six Nations Reserve and heard many stories from elders and land protectors), I began to study all sorts of protocols, including the diplomatic traditions of the League such as the Covenant Chain, an agreement that links people of Six Nations to surrounding peoples in a relationship of reciprocity. During that time, I came across the teachings of Cayuga Chief Jake Thomas, through which I learned about the political and legal protocols of the Two Row Wampum agreement that were first made with the Dutch, then the English, and subsequently inherited by Canada. I learned ways that this early treaty agreement negated a hallmark of European colonialism, which involves the ceding of Indigenous sovereignty, a method that European powers used to make unequal treaties with Indigenous peoples and nations to advance their own claims to trade and territory. The more I studied, the more I came to learn that there are instructions in the agreement that offer guidelines on how to live side by side on these lands.

The more I learned about the live dynamism of this treaty, that the agreements in the treaty come with responsibilities, and that we need to revisit these agreements and reactivate their terms, the more my learning began to press against my research and help me perceive the densely complicated interconnections between Black and Indigenous struggles. Which is to say, the more I learned about the Two Row Wampum Belt and the ways that the agreement encoded in it marked relations between Haudenosaunee and European merchants, the more I grappled, and continue to grapple, with ways to understand the place of Blackness in the Covenant Chain-Two Row agreement. In this essay, I follow the work that Rick Hill has done on the "Historic Relationships between African Americans and the Confederacy of the Six Nations."[3] His work has been instructive in my desire to imagine how the Covenant Chain-Two Row agreements made with the Dutch and British, in particular, in the seventeenth and eighteenth centuries, might offer an entry into perceiving the unacknowledged place of Blackness in this treaty agreement and the relations that such imaginings might foster.

Pictographically, the Two Row Wampum Belt is made up of two rows of purple beads set against a background of white beads, symbolizing the purity of the agreement. Jake Thomas's oral narrative helps me understand that the two rows of purple beads signify the paths of two vessels: one is a ship belonging to Europeans, and the other is a birch-bark canoe belonging to the people of the Haudenosaunee Confederacy. In an essay by Rick Hill and Daniel Coleman, Thomas's oral recitation in 1981 to Governor General Edward Schreyer in Rideau Hall contains the popularly known imagery of the Two Row Wampum, where we learn of each vessel containing its own beliefs, culture, and customs:

> "We both have our own authority—strength/power. We have our respective beliefs, from the same Creator. We have our respective laws. We do not have authority over each other or our kind of culture."
>
> The Ongwehowe stated, "The Creator gave us a canoe and you a boat (ship). We will take our vessels to the water and put them in the water, each in their distinctive way. Our people will follow the vessels in the water.
>
> We will place them a certain distance apart, but will line them up so they will always be parallel."
>
> The White man stated, "This is an excellent way to represent our relationship."
>
> The Ongwehowe stated, "Now we have laid our vessels out, parallel to each other, so too it is with our beliefs. My beliefs will be in my canoe, yours will be in your boat. I will also put my laws in my canoe, and you will put your laws in your boat.
>
> Our authority, beliefs, and laws will be dropped into our vessels. That is how people will know it, by the likeness to two paths."[4]

The more I learn about the Covenant Chain-Two Row agreement between Europeans and the League of Six Nations, the more I hear another story within the story of this diplomatic arrangement for peaceful coexistence. As the League of Six Nations was negotiating peace, friendship, and respect with the Dutch and British, another negotiation was happening at the same time on Dutch and British slave vessels: namely, the transatlantic transportation of "uprooted captives-turned-commodities-turned enslaved captives."[5] So, if we keep in mind that the Dutch were participating in the global enslavement enterprise, then we might also hear (or, at least, be willing to listen to me tell) a story that is present by absence within the story of the Covenant Chain-Two Row Wampum. I know the story I want to tell about the treaty raises questions about the relationship that was not overtly under negotiation; however, as with so much Black existence on Turtle Island, Blackness occupies a prepositional existence: we were *in* the ship, *below* decks, *near* the discussions, even though we were not signatories; we were there, but not part of the negotiation.

We can hear what is at the edges of that negotiation by returning to Canesatego's polishing of the wampum agreement in the 1744 speech that is quoted at length in the Introduction to this volume. When he recalls that in the holds of their ships, the Dutch brought "several Goods, such as Awls, Knives, Hatchets, Guns and many other Particulars, which they gave us," and that "they had taught us how to use their Things" and "we were so well pleased with them, that we tied their Ship to the Bushes on the Shore," we know that Black African people were among the "goods" the Dutch and then the British brought with them up the Hudson River. As Rick Hill indicates in his article on African Americans and the Haudenosaunee, one of the things the Europeans brought into the relationship with the Haudenosaunee and other Indigenous people on Turtle Island was the practice of owning enslaved people. "By 1626, the Dutch West India Company had imported [B]lack slaves from Africa for use in the fur trade and building their new colony, New Amsterdam."[6] As a trading company in the seventeenth century, the Dutch West India Company actively traded along the Atlantic coasts of Africa and the Americas, and the Black enslaved people that they captured from Africa worked in the fur trade on the Hudson River, as well as in the Hudson

Bay Company. They learned the language of the Indigenous communities they lived among, becoming translators and intermediaries between the local Indigenous communities and white settlers.[7] All of this is to say that these links between Africans as trade goods in the holds of the ships that arrived in Haudenosaunee territory are not idle speculation. They are directly connected to my own ancestral story. Between the sixteenth and the eighteenth centuries, British and Dutch merchants established trading lodges on the Gold Coast and conducted business with my father's people,[8] the Akan people of the Gold Coast.[9] The abundance of metals along this coastal port, which were the metals from which many of the trade goods were made, explains why gold and captured Akans became key commodities for European commerce.

Given the eighteenth-century Atlantic economy and the fact that Black life was property on European vessels, Canesatego's references to "ship," "iron chains," and "rope," all objects that allude to practices of bondage, prepare me to believe the "several Goods" that the Dutch brought likely included my ancestors, in the hold of the ships.[10] The materials that trace geopolitical intimacy in this context (the ropes and chains necessary for anchoring ships) are also materials for captivity; the ropes and chains used to tie ships to the Haudenosaunee shore came from the holds of ships where they were used to manacle enslaved people below decks. Hence, these materials play a role in helping us visualize the intimately dehumanizing practices that the Dutch and the British used to enslave Black life. In foregrounding the divergent practices that these objects were tasked to perform, I invite us to meditate on the inseparable ways that racial and colonial violence lurks within practices of intimacy. So, please forgive me for using these material objects to raise questions about Black ancestral presence; there is historical spirit in the material of the Covenant Chain Two-Row agreement, making it alive and able to orient us with the knowledge that relations are neither bounded by nor fixed by time, space, and distance.[11] This way of conceptualizing the world, which informs my thinking here, leans on Akan cosmology, which, according to Akan philosopher Kwasi Wiredu, "involves no sharp ontological cleavages such as the Cartesian dichotomy[12] of the material and the [mental/] spiritual. The difference between ordinary material things and those extra-human beings and forces so often called 'spirits' in the literature is the difference between the fully material and the partially material."[13]

My attention to Akan cosmology here is not an attempt to propose a dimensionless project of authenticity; rather, it is my way to foreground the fact that many captured-then-enslaved African people arrived from lands with their own kinship expressions as well as ways of looking at and conceptualizing the world, self, and society. The Akan Kingdoms had their own protocols for contact and combat. When I think about the absence of direct negotiations with my ancestors in the Covenant Chain-Two Row agreement, for example, and about the complex racial calculations and colonial arrangements that converted many of them into Black people in the Americas, I find myself wondering how being in/coming out of degrees of bondage and enslavement impacted the kinds of potential negotiations that Black and Indigenous people were denied in these new lands.

Again, the possibilities I am imagining are not mere speculations. There is the story of Sophia Burthen Pooley and the Mohawk leader Joseph (Thayendanegea) Brant. Brant bought Pooley for an unknown price and resold her for a hundred dollars. She hunted deer with his daughters and sons two kilometres from where I am sitting as I write this. Almost 1,100 words bear the ninety-some-years' weight of this Black woman's life. Born in Fishkill, New York State, to enslaved parents, Oliver and Dinah Burthen, Sophia and her sister were stolen from their parents when she "was seven years old, and brought to [Upper] Canada," an interior colony in British North America (192).[14] Offering her oral history to Benjamin Drew, an American abolitionist from Boston who travelled through Upper Canada in the mid-1850s to interview formerly enslaved people, she says, "My master's sons-in-law, Daniel Outwaters and Simon Knox came into the garden where my sister and I were playing among the currant bushes, tied their handkerchiefs over our mouths, carried us to a vessel, put us in the hold, and sailed up the river."[15] At an auction block in Niagara, Joseph Brant, who was central to the formation of Upper Canada and the alliance that the British made with the Six Nations during the American Revolutionary War, bought Sophia Burthen (who later took the name Pooley when she married Robert Pooley).

Surely, Joseph Brant learned about buying and selling enslaved people from extended stays during his youth on the estate of his sister Mary (Molly) Brant's common-law husband, Sir William Johnson, who served as the first superintendent of Indian Affairs for the Northern Colonies and whose dying words to Joseph Brant, we are told, were, "Joseph, control your people; control your people, for I am going away."[16] He also served as advisor to the King of England, and, as superintendent in 1763, presented and publicized The Royal Proclamation, the document designed to determine both the future of the newly acquired colonies of Quebec, East and West Florida, and Grenada, as well as relations with Indigenous nations. Johnson is known to have purchased and sold Black enslaved people. He is rumoured to have owned over ninety enslaved people in what was gradually becoming the free North when the South was becoming the slave South. In his last will and testament, we see how the possession of Indigenous lands and the economy of slavery and Black labour made his fortune. He bequeathed to his son, Sir John Johnson, "one fourth part of all my slaves" and to his "two daughters, Anne Claus and Mary Johnson, two fourths of my slaves and stock of cattle. The other fourth of my slaves and stock of cattle of every kind, I give and bequeath to the children of Mary Brant, my house keeper, or to the survivors of them."[17]

Brant's ownership of Sophia Burthen, then, was continuous with what he had seen in the Johnson house. Of course, Sophia Burthen was not the only enslaved person Joseph Brant owned: Pooley told Drew that during the time she was with him in Burlington, "Brant had two colored men for slaves: one of them was the father of John Pattern, who lives over yonder, the other called himself Simon Gansevillle." Sophia Burthen Pooley's memory adds weight to the speculation that Brant owned anywhere from twenty to forty Black enslaved people.[18]

Sophia Pooley experienced her sale as a transfer of capital. After living in the Brant household for "twelve or thirteen years," she told Drew that "I was sold by Brant to an Englishman in Ancaster, for one hundred dollars. His name was Samuel Hatt, and I lived with him for seven years."[19] With the 1,200 acres of land granted by the Crown to the Hatt family, Samuel, along with his brother Richard Hatt, established a considerable business enterprise in Dundas, which included two gristmills, a sawmill, a store, a blacksmith shop, a cooper's shop, and a distillery. The

Hatts are now considered founders of that town, in part because they cleared a road from Ancaster to Dundas to gain more customers for their business. This early industrialist, who acquired capital by purchasing enslaved people and whose manufacturing developments went on to shape nearby Hamilton as a thriving manufacturing city, also fought in the War of 1812. He was the head of a militia known as "Hatt's Volunteers," who marched with British General Isaac Brock to help capture Detroit; moreover, he fought in the Battle of Queenston Heights, where Brock was killed, and, in the Battle of Lundy's Lane, where he was wounded. So, when Pooley recalls, "I was seven miles from Stoney Creek at the time of the battle—the cannonade made every thing shake,"[20] she was hearing the cannon fire exchanged at Stoney Creek from the Hatt's home in Ancaster, where she worked as a domestic behind the scenes.

The account Sophia Burthen Pooley gives of Hatt's house is different from those she remembers from Brant's. Recalling memories from her days living with "old Brant," as she names him, her recollections help us parse out the complex domestic relations that can be covered over by terms like *slavery* and *adoption* in the eighteenth and nineteenth centuries. Typically, as a Black enslaved child grew into adulthood, the interaction with their master's children dwindled. Hunting deer at Dundas "at the outlet"—I understand her to mean the water outlet from Dundas Marsh that curved around Burlington Heights and emptied into the bay now known as Hamilton Harbour—with Brant's children, she remembers that they "would let the hounds loose, and when we heard them bark we would run for the canoe—Peggy and Mary, and Katy, Brant's daughters and I. Brant's sons, Joseph and Jacob, would wait on the shore to kill the deer when we fetched him in. I had a tomahawk, and would hit the deer on the head—then the squaws [sic] would take it by the horns and paddle ashore. The boys would bleed and skin the deer and take the meat to the house."[21] The lines between membership in the family and servitude are hard to discern in these memories. The domestic economy they evoke shows how each family member, including Sophia Burthen, had his or her role in carrying out everyday domestic labour.

In fact, she speaks to Brant's parent-like kindness when she recounts Brant's response to a trauma she experienced at the hands of her mistress, Brant's third wife, Catharine (*Adonwentishon*) Croghan, daughter to the Irish-born fur trader and Deputy Indian Agent George Croghan.²² Sophia calls Catherine "a barbarous creature" because, not sparing the rod, she would hit her with anything that came to hand. "I have a scar on my head from a wound she gave me with a hatchet; and this long scar over my eye, is where she cut me with a knife. The skin dropped over my eye; a white woman bound it up. Brant was very angry, when he came home, at what she had done, and punished her as if she had been a child. Said he, 'you know I adopted her as one of the family, and now you are trying to put all the work on her.'"²³

Sophia Burthen Pooley's oral history presents an intriguing complex of possibilities for rethinking the relationship between Black and Indigenous people in the very moment and place where the Six Nations were repolishing the chain of their relationship with the British after the Revolutionary War. Brant had been a major force in getting Sir Frederick Haldimand to arrange for Haudenosaunee allies to move to lands set aside for them six miles on each side of the Grand River in British North America after they had been burnt out of their villages and cornfields in upstate New York by the Sullivan-Clinton Campaign of 1778–79. As Brant's growing dissatisfaction with British paternalism went on to show, troubling the heart of this repolishing, this enactment of the agreement were very different understandings of property, race, family, and adoption, not to mention land. These differences informed the efforts of that moment to enact the principles of "peace, friendship, and respect" that were supposed to guide the two vessels who were preparing to share the river of life in this new location.

Her acculturation to Mohawk societal norms was necessary. Sophia Burthen Pooley says: "I used to talk Indian [Mohawk] better than I could English" but, after being transferred from a Mohawk master to a white master, she had "forgotten some of it—there [being] none to talk it with now."²⁴ This language loss marks Indigenous land losses too, where to this day, Indigenous people connect loss of language with loss of jurisdiction over land and its uses. Recalling the river voyage that brought her through Haudenosaunee country in upstate New York to the auction block in Niagara, Pooley says: "I remember when we came to Genesee,— there were Indian settlements there,— Onondagas, Senecas, and Oneidas. I guess I was the first colored girl brought into Canada."²⁵ In fact, she recalls that "[t]here were hardly any white people in Canada then—nothing here but Indians and wild beasts."[26] Later, she remembers that sometimes, on the hunt with Brant's children, "white people in the neighbourhood" "would come and say 't was their hounds, and they must have the meat," and that "Canada was then filling up with white people. And after Brant went to England, and kissed the queen's hand, he was made a colonel. Then there began to be laws in Canada."[27] Her comments allow us to mark the demographic and legal changes occurring at the time in Upper Canada. Of course, she would be attentive and sensitive to the juridical changes and their impact on her. Earlier in her narration, she says, "I was a grown woman when the first governor of Canada came from England: that was Gov. Simcoe."[28] With Simcoe's arrival, "the white people said I was free, and put me up to running away. He [Hatt] did not stop me—he said he could not take the law into his own hands."[29] After running away, she says, "Then I lived in what is now Waterloo. I married Robert Pooley, a black man. He ran away with a white woman: he is dead."[30] The free Black couple's whole history is conveyed in epigraphic statements, in poetry. Their flight to freedom and family is interrupted by an extra-marital interracial romance, which ends in death.

If we recall, Pooley says that Joseph Brant said to his wife, "You know I adopted her as one of the family, and now you are trying to put all the work on her." Her use of the word *adoption* invites me to think through the Haudenosaunee adoption ceremony, a process whereby outsiders are received into the community, and I wonder what this mark of distinction might offer us in terms of imagining the future relationships between Black people and the Six Nations at the Grand River. Before anyone gets their knickers tangled up, I am keenly aware that adoption does not negate the owning of enslaved people, nor does it justify the difficulty of Black people's presence today on Indigenous lands in Canada. I am equally aware that Brant is a mixed and complex figure in Six Nations history. One temptation is to dismiss him as one more owner of enslaved people in the eighteenth and nineteenth centuries. However, in the interest of linking arms, I want to read through Sophia Pooley's story to see the potential that is in their relationship. I want to read through her generous ways of reading him, by which I mean she did not have to tell the story of him defending her from his own wife's violence. Of course, it's possible to read her defending him as her way to highlight her connections to his celebrity. And yet, her story is a good-minded, balanced story of Brant. She accounted for the complexity of life in his household and did not hide the violence that occurred there. If he was generous in calling her an adoptee rather than a slave, she was generous in the story of living in his house. I think it is important to look through the aperture of this mutual generosity.

Pooley's mention of adoption opens an aperture to possible relationships, not just in the story of her life in Brant's home but also in the relationships signalled in the linked arms of the Covenant Chain agreement. Barbara Alice Mann's entry on "Adoption" in the *Encyclopedia of the Haudenosaunee* suggests that, in the Constitution of the Six Nations, "adoption is one of the legal provisions" that "allows an individual, a group or an entire nation to be taken into the league, either as a full state of the league or as a member of a family, lineage or state."[31] She goes on to point out that "adoptees were often women and children taken during raids on enemy groups and brought back to the home towns of the various war parties."[32] Although, according to Sophia Pooley's account, Brant took her in not by warfare but by purchase, she nonetheless presents her place in Brant's family as a version of adoption, and her story of Brant's anger at his wife over her ill treatment supports the idea that he wanted her to be treated humanely. More than this, he expected she would share the work of the household (whether hunting in Dundas Marsh or domestic work with Catherine) equally. And it is not unreasonable speculation to think of Black servants being adopted in Indigenous homes. We know, for example, from Mrs. Mary Jemison's narrative of her life as an adoptee that some enslaved Africans who escaped from slavery were taken into Seneca homes and families in the same period.[33]

*Seyakhikwatakwénnis ne Tehontatenentshonteronhtáhkwa: Grasping the Chain Again,* Amber Meadow Adams's expert report on the trial of *R v. Montour and White,* has helped me see how elements of adoption ceremony are central to the legal symbols and concepts of the Covenant Chain. Adams tells the story of the speaker for the Kanyen'kehá:ka at Trois-Rivieres, Kiotsaeton, explaining the procedure of the Covenant Chain to the French. She writes, "In 1645, Kiotsaeton puts his arm in the arm of a Frenchman, and says that not even the lightning can part them. This is precisely the form such a bond takes in the [Haudenosaunee] ceremonies of adoption or name-giving."³⁴ Adams explains that "Tehontatenentshonteronhtáhkwa," the sentence which connotes a "treaty relationship," translates into "they (males) have attached their arms (or forearms, or hands together)."³⁵ And that this image of linked arms "grows directly from the ceremonies of naming and adoption. The procedure of making brothers as a 'Covenant Chain' relationship is almost exactly like that of name-giving and adoption."³⁶ She also explains that adoption ceremonies not only "include an agreement between people wishing to become family" but also "a public acknowledgement of the new form the relationship is taking and the responsibilities each party assumes."³⁷ Contained in Sophia Pooley's rhetoric of adoption is a coded message. If we remember that she "used to talk Indian [Mohawk] better than [she] could English," then it is possible she understood the significance of her position as a member of this family, and perhaps this affiliation could explain why she preferred being in Brant's household and why, by contrast, she later runs away from Hatt.

So, given all of the above, what kind of linked arms do we—Haudenosaunee and Black people in Canada—want? And what would it mean for the presence of Blackness to be taken seriously in Haudenosaunee relationship-building today, especially if we are to remember that Black people were likely present there in the ship and the households when the original agreements were signed and when Six Nations was establishing itself in the Grand River? In other words, what would it mean if my ancestors were part of the explicit dialogue? These are not questions I know how to answer. Nonetheless, I will walk you through some of the thinking that my writing this paper has brought me to.

I find myself wanting to know the knowledge that those in the holds of the ship would have brought with them. Because I cannot know what they knew, or even what worldviews informed Pooley, for example, one way to acknowledge the Black people who were unacknowledged in the history of the Covenant Chain-Two Row agreement would be to link arms with them and their "culture, beliefs, and laws"—not the ones that were suppressed below decks and enchained, but the cosmological and historical worldviews they brought with them that resisted and exceeded those bonds. To do so, my inclination has been to reach for Akan cosmologies since historical evidence corroborates the fact that the Dutch and the English were on the shores of Akan land at the same time that they were here on Haudenosaunee shores. I know there is a huge difference among the enslaved people who were captured from the West Coast of Africa and brought to these shores, and I am also aware that other African-descended people will have other values to offer, just like other Indigenous peoples have their own distinctive ones to shape the dialogue. Nonetheless, I reach for the Akan people because they are my father's people, and this familiarity connects me to a knowledge system that I have access to. And I want to use what I have from my vessel, my family, to join this conversation.

If you recall, I began this essay by foregrounding how my knowledge of the Covenant Chain-Two Row agreement emerged through witnessing the struggle and the land reclamation at Douglas Creek Estates at a moment when I was beginning work for my PhD on the avoided presence of Blackness in Canada. What I did not say then was that I was doing this work primarily because I was surprised by the extent to which the scholarship on early Canadian writing did not take Black life into account. Like Sophia Pooley's story, Black people were present everywhere in early Canada, but you would hardly know it from official histories. I became interested in early Black life in Canada, therefore, as a way to learn how acknowledging unacknowledged Black people in early Canada can help me understand the history of my particular placement in this country. In bringing all that I have learned about Blackness and its ligaments across early Canada to bear on my thinking about the Covenant Chain-Two Row agreement, I realize I want to find out more about Akan philosophies and cosmologies to learn what it is that I was separated from as a result of migration, diaspora, and displacement. This is my way of saying that the study I have done on Blackness in early Canada has taken me to finding Black people in Canadian literature and history, but until now, it has not taken me to a study of Akan cosmologies. There is a huge field of study beyond what I know about Akan teachings and philosophies, but for me, it was never a subject of academic study. The things about Akan that I know are from my family, not from the vibrant field of Akan scholarship and cosmologies that exists. I cannot pretend to know it yet as a professional field of scholarship. I can, however, signal what I know based on the transference of knowledge I have picked up from growing up in a household in Canada with an Akan father who uses stories as his way of teaching me. In this sense, my understanding of Akan thinking was passed down to me in a way similar to how Haudenosaunee cosmology was originally passed down from one generation to the next, not in textbooks or academic study, but through family stories. These are the pathways of knowing and perception that offer possible future collaborations between Akan and Haudenosaunee cosmologies.[38]

When Sophia Pooley speaks of being adopted by the Brant family, she opens an aperture for us to ask: What kind of family, what kind of peace, friendship, and respect could emerge from polishing an agreement between Black people and Haudenosaunee people? If we again turn to Sophia Pooley and reread the ending of her biography, it gestures towards two end stories. In one version, we get a story of her flight to freedom, one in which she takes advantage of the law and runs to the Queen's Bush settlement (and we know the land she runs off into is Haudenosaunee territory, and we also know that, too, did not end well).[39] In the other version involving the story of her husband, Robert Pooley, who we know ends up dying, we get a warning story of what happens when one is seduced into the white-settler economy of property and capital, where the flight into the European embrace leads only to death.

With these different ends in mind, what might a different alliance look like? What do we have to do if we want to have a good relationship? Here, the extended notion of family signalled by Pooley's place in the Brant household, of this early Black presence in the Indigenous house, suggests that the possibility for dialogue was real and that it is not simply a speculative desire of mine to imagine backward. It becomes our job to imagine things from now on based on what we know. And it is with this idea of imagining forward that I turn to ideas and understandings rooted in Akan cosmologies to explain why my ancestors' own Indigenous concepts are fully capable of instructing us on Akan modes of meaning construction, make us ready family members with whom Haudenosaunee people can link arms.

The expanded concepts of kinship Sophia Pooley evokes take me to two kin terminologies in Twi, *fiefo*, which translates to residence of a household, and *fie nipa*, members of a lineage. These terms do not come close to encapsulating the many kin relationships that make up an Ashanti household. As my dad reminds me, even though an Ashanti household is a fluid group of people, there are kin terminologies that describe specific affinity, affiliation, descent, and filiation. While this extended understanding of kin relations and membership has a lot to teach us about the social configuration of family, there is another Twi word, *abusua,* that marks Akan matrilineage, a social structure that traces lineage through female lines of descent, which I understand is composed of both living and dead members.[40] This traditional social and political kin structure is emphasized in an Akan expression that I grew up hearing: *oba na owo obarima* (it is a woman who gives birth to a man). As an expression that marks the central and important public roles that women play in the preservation of lineage in order for Akan society to function, the central position that women occupy in governance is further marked by their understanding of land, which is personified by the name of the Goddess who represents the land, *Asasse Yaa. Asasse* means earth or ground, and *Yaa* is a name given to females born on Thursday. In Akan cosmology, Mother Earth is the mother of the universe and grandmother of the ancestors. Whenever libation prayers are poured out for any ceremony, she is often first to be invoked; and likewise, before we can dig a grave to bury a dead person, we pour a libation on and to Her as a way to beg permission to cut open her skin so the body can be returned to Her stomach (which bears the same word as "womb").

Land, then, is not an exclusively human property; it is a legacy that humans have inherited from the spirits of the air and earth. As a result, certain ways of living validly on the land depend upon the respectful approach and ceremonies made to the spirits of earth and air. Libation, this knowing portal that makes regular contact with the spiritual world to mark their interconnection, then, not only connects the spiritual and material worlds, it is also a practice of relationality—of assembly with fellowship and hospitality as well as a respectful reminder of the mutual responsibility and relationship that each world has to the other. These relationships are key to an understanding of land as animated, intelligent, and sacred.

The peace and health of the land, then, are part of peace and health in *abusua.* This connection between kin protocol and relations to land takes me to Haudenosaunee understandings of land-based protocols as expressed in the Covenant Chain-Two Row Wampum agreements. Let us return to Jake Thomas's oration of the Two Row as recorded in Rick Hill's "Oral Memory of the Haudenosaunee" article:

> The whiteman said, "What symbol will you go by?" The Onkwehonweh replied, "When the Creator made Mother Earth, man was created to walk upon the Earth to enjoy all nature's fruits, saying that no one will claim Mother Earth except by rising faces which are to be born. We will go by these symbols: As long as the sun shines upon this earth, as long as the water still flows, and as long as the grass grows green at a certain time of the year, that is how long our agreement will stand. Now we have symbolized this agreement and it shall be binding forever, as long as Mother Earth is still in motion. We have finished and we understand what we have confirmed and this is what our generation should know and learn not to forget."[41]

Matriarchal values of relatedness and interdependence style the ways that *Nyame*/the Creator instructs Akan people to be with the beings of Earth. That the Earth is a Mother in motion structures a responsive relationship that is dynamic rather than a hierarchical relationship structured by domination. In this way, our relationship to creation is future-oriented, suggesting the common understanding of Mother Earth and how humans make agreements of peace, friendship, and respect *so that Mother Earth herself will have peace and a future*. Mother Earth, the land, cannot be "claimed" and is the measure of the time of peace: "as long as the sun shines upon this earth."

Of course, these thoughts are early ones that need further development. They are only gestural, but they indicate what kinds of common understanding the people below decks could bring to a renewed relationship. Rather than assimilating into the arms of racial capitalism (as Robert Pooley did), these formerly unacknowledged treaty partners can seek ways to affirm parallel concepts of kinship and belonging that they have way back in their African and Haudenosaunee cultural ancestry. These are ones that do not try to blend in one vessel but that link arms in learning how to share the river (and the land) for the benefit of the "faces which are to be born."

CHAPTER NINE

# Towards Peace

Living in the Three White Rows of the Two Row

*Sara General*

———

By now, we have no doubt established that the Two Row Wampum Belt, one of the oldest known treaties between Haudenosaunee and settler nations, consists of two rows of purple wampum shells separated on either side and in-between by three rows of white ones. The Two Row has been described as a political protocol outlining the mechanisms for engagement between autonomous yet equal nations.[1] It has also been conceptualized as an Indigenous research methodology by individuals and teams of Indigenous and non-Indigenous scholars across several disciplines[2] and used to frame how Indigenous and Western traditions might view the ethics of research on Haudenosaunee languages.[3] Its imagery is regularly invoked to guide and support relationship-building efforts between Indigenous and non-Indigenous entities.

I have enjoyed hearing and reading about all the different ways community members, educators, linguists, scholars, and others have engaged with the ideas of the Two Row, and I am grateful for the many Elders, Knowledge Keepers, and historians who have shared their understandings about the Two Row with us all. Indeed, having spent so long listening, reading, and learning from others—many of them contributors to this volume—sharing what I've come to know and understand about the Two Row Wampum Belt can feel like a daunting task. How do you say something new or different about such a well and thoughtfully covered area? This is, though, one beauty of the Two Row. Employed as a theoretical framework, there are countless stories across all disciplines it can help tell.

Ultimately, I can only offer what my own journey with the Two Row has been and share how learning about it and how deeply it is connected to other Haudenosaunee oral traditions, including the Story of the Peacemaker and the establishing of the Great Law, has brought greater meaning and focus to my work as a researcher, a storyteller, and an administrator. I'll begin my sharing by expressing immense gratitude for the many mentors I've had, for the land, water, beings, and messengers that have sustained us and allowed for encounter, conversation, and safe travel across Turtle Island and who have, in no uncertain terms, helped grow my understanding of my responsibilities as an Ogwehoweh woman.

At present, I am writing from Six Nations of the Grand River, a First Nations community in what is now known as Southern Ontario, where I was born, raised, and continue to live. I belong to the Mohawk Nation and the Turtle Clan and have for the past eight years worked for Six Nations Polytechnic (SNP), a post-secondary Indigenous institute located within my community. In addition to the roles I've already described, I am a mother, an artist, and a language learner. Over the course of my professional life, I have worked in several capacities for First Nations organizations, primarily in the area of education and, most recently, as the director of the Deyohahá:ge: Indigenous Knowledge Centre at SNP. I attended elementary school first on reserve, then off reserve for several years before taking Indigenous Studies in university. I later completed my doctoral work in educational leadership. While I appreciate the role that formal education has played in my life, a significant portion of my learning about my people's collective history, languages, and intellectual traditions has happened through the time I've spent here at home, whether that was visiting, working, participating in, or attending community events, going to ceremonies, being around family and friends, or reading. I have done a lot of listening and thinking, and even so, I know there is still so much to learn.

I offer this background as a way of engaging in the act of locating myself in the work[4] and to signal that I came to engage with the Two Row through a set of experiences that are probably somewhat unique to my own life, though the teachings about it come from a body of oral traditions, knowledge, and history that have been with the Haudenosaunee people as a whole for a long time.

As I have been writing it, I have also realized that this is an article about the places where we choose to embed our thinking and the lens through which we view the world as we do our work here. As such, my self-location also serves to foreground which knowledge systems have shaped and continue to inform my own. In this chapter, I will be referring to four of what have come to be thought of as the epic historical narratives of Haudenosaunee thought: the Creation Story, The Story of the Fatherless Boy, The Story of the Peacemaker, and The Code of Handsome Lake.[5] Stories are opportunities to learn, and my intent in sharing my own is to explain how the Two Row has come to be a part of my life and work.

## A MESSAGE

Towards the end of 2011, while working for a First Nations organization, I had the opportunity to attend a lodge in a community near the border of Ontario and Manitoba. I was invited to attend as part of the work I was involved in around preparing for a meeting between First Nations across Turtle Island (Canada) and then Prime Minister Stephen Harper that was scheduled to take place at the end of January 2012. The meeting itself was billed as a "Crown-First Nation Gathering," though in truth, it was more of a public relations exercise than a genuine effort to reinvigorate and honour the treaty relationships between First Nations and Britain. Beyond opening remarks offered by then Governor General David Johnston, which invoked references to the Covenant Chain as the "core of the Crown's relationship with its First Nations allies,"[6] the Crown was not, strictly speaking, a direct participant of the gathering. This was one year before a second meeting between Assembly of First Nations (AFN) National Chief Shawn Atleo and Prime Minister Stephen Harper, the events that, in part, spurred the grassroots movement Idle No More.

In the days leading up to the meeting, it became obvious that the agenda would not extend beyond the four or so areas included in a joint action plan that had been formalized between the AFN and Indian and Northern Affairs Canada (INAC) in mid-2011 with only minimal consultation with First Nation communities.[7] And though First Nation leaders across Ontario understood and knew it to be unsatisfactory, they still prepared and came to the meeting to urge action on issues of land, treaty implementation, education, and economic development—while raising other issues pertinent to their home communities. There is much more to say about this meeting, about the nature of representation, the outcomes (or lack thereof), and the efforts and concerns behind the scenes, but those will have to wait for another time. There is a short but nonetheless incisive passage about the meeting in Arthur Manuel and Grand Chief Ronald M. Derrickson's *Unsettling Canada: A National Wake-Up Call* that offers a wide lens into the history of policy efforts that led into the meeting and contextualizes some of the events that occurred in its aftermath.[8] But by the time the meeting was finished, I already knew it was probably the last I'd attend. I had long wanted to turn my focus to language learning, and so I did, starting a conversational class in February and coming to work at SNP a few months later.

Even though I chose a different path, I still believe that efforts to resist the assimilationist agenda common to federal and provincial policy and legislation are important. I appreciate those who have done and continue this challenging work, who raise the alarms about Canada's ongoing attempts to extinguish our land rights through policy processes or legislation, who continue to insist that the Crown honour the treaties, and who urge First Nations leadership to make wise use of the victories in the international arena, in Supreme Court cases, and in Human Rights Tribunals. Having observed the policy relationship between First Nations communities and settler governments firsthand, I can appreciate how many realities and experiences need to be heard and how important strong, rights-and-responsibility-based positioning can be in balancing and grounding policy discussions. I am grateful for everyone who still commits their time to finding a good way forward—including through relationship-building and discussion with settler governments— while resisting policy agendas that will put our rights or our ability to enact and honour our responsibilities in jeopardy. And as I recall my visit to the lodge, I am also grateful for the insights I received while I was there because I believe they were also about the importance of centring

Haudenosaunee ideas, laws, and responsibilities and choosing to ground our actions within them.

My time at the lodge was brief, though the message I heard there has stayed with me for the past ten years. During the writing of this article, I spoke with the Elder who guided the proceedings and asked how to best share what I'd been told, given how the message came about. They encouraged me to do so in a careful, respectful manner, which I will endeavour to do in this chapter by conveying what I heard and describing how it has helped broaden my understanding of the Two Row.

In essence, the message was that the three white rows of wampum in the middle of the Two Row Belt were of paramount importance. I was encouraged to pay close attention to them and understand that when my ancestors made the peace and friendship treaty with settler nations, they knew the settlers were not going to act with honourable intentions. They made the treaty anyway, choosing to do so in a way that would simultaneously assert our sovereignty and make clear how we were going to conduct ourselves on our lands—in peace, friendship, and respect—regardless of who came to share them with us.

Now, I can appreciate that, for some, this might not appear to be much of a revelation. After all, in hindsight, it is obvious that the settler nation's intentions were dishonourable—especially given what we now know about the Doctrine of Discovery and other colonial ideologies and strategies of violence that nations relied upon to impose their jurisdiction. It also seems obvious that our ancestors would make agreements that reaffirmed our positions as sovereign, self-determining Nations, having repeated such a practice in treaty-making with the Dutch, English, and French.[9]

But prior to my visit to the lodge, I had only thought about and seen the Two Row in a few ways—none of which appreciated just how much the Two Row was connected to the Great Law and the oral traditions that preceded it. Rather, I had a generic, surface knowledge, one that had much in common with what Tuscarora historian Rick Hill describes as "the simple summary circulating on the Internet."[10] I had slices of information, a hodgepodge of insights rather than a unified theory, and I had not reckoned deeply with any of them. First, I understood the following: that the Two Row was a belt that conveyed the idea of two vessels, a ship and a canoe, moving alongside one another on the river of life, symbolizing equal but distinct nations and establishing a policy of non-interference.[11] Second, that it was a belt people often used to speak about positive, productive, and well-maintained relationships between Indigenous and non-Indigenous entities. Third, there could be consequences for those who had a foot in both vessels—they could fall in the water between—and those who did find themselves in this situation could only be pulled back out by the Creator.[12]

I still see the Two Row in this manner—as a sacred treaty agreement that does indeed confirm the autonomy of two nations and that can support relationship-building efforts. I will further offer that I have found the cautions it carries to ring true as well, thanks to my overwhelmingly provincial education in the late 1980s and 1990s. While I learned about the nature of mercantilism (twice) and the names of half a dozen "explorers," I honestly cannot recall any reference, accurate or otherwise, to the historical relationships between Indigenous peoples of Turtle Island and the Canadian settler state. As a result, there were points in my life where I felt adrift, disconnected, and certainly without the benefit of any guiding principles that could serve as a touchstone to navigate the rest of the world.

In other words—I lacked a foundation and a lens.

Over time, of course, I was able to learn and fill in the gaps created by my earlier education. This learning was helped in no small part by ceremonies, communal and personal. Ceremony helped to make my mind clearer and my spirit brighter, and opened a pathway for me to follow that made it easier to sustain a peaceful state of being. So, while I had experienced that in-between middle space in the kind of disorienting way that Chief Jake Thomas described, I had also been lifted up in a time of need by the medicinal practices that had been gifted to our people by Creation.

I mention this mostly out of respect for spirit. Spirit is powerful, and it deserves its due, even in articles like this, where there are a lot of citations and references to be made to show that as scholars we read widely and that while our ideas are flexible and capable of growth—they are not carelessly formed. Our spiritual traditions are not carelessly formed either, and while I do not often talk about them in forums like this, sharing what I have is an important part of this story because the message I received came about in a decidedly spiritual manner, and it marked the start of a meaning-making journey as I continued to live, read, learn, and otherwise think about what it meant for the middle rows to be so important. Creation has been a natural and important companion to that journey. In their article about the Two Row Wampum, Hill and Coleman reference the words of Oneida scholar Dr. Bob Antone, writing "that the ceremonial element of the Two Row protocol reminds us that there are three parties present in every sacred agreement: the two human parties (in this case, the Hodinöhsö:ni' and the incoming Europeans) and the Creator and/or Creation. There are two purple (human) rows, but they are embedded in three much larger white (more-than-human) rows of beads."[13] These words offer a reminder of how Creation works through us, alongside us, and on our behalf. We can—and do—reciprocate, lifting one another up, encouraging each other, inviting and welcoming help. Every year, in an uninterrupted cycle of gratitude and ceremony.

I did not always know these things and, therefore, appreciate them a great deal now. Indeed, I am grateful for the many gifts our people have been given. Life. Thought. Medicines. Water. Songs. Seeds. Perhaps especially the stories. Hearing stories about our creation, the origins of our ceremonies, and the other gifts and messages we were given by the Creator has brought an ever-increasing peace to my small corner of the world. It has also made it easier to navigate this larger one, so much so that by the time I started my master's, a year after I began working at SNP, I felt considerably more prepared to navigate my way around the ship that was graduate school.

## RESEARCH

My master's program was an opportunity for me to unpack my learning and working experiences up to that point and to rethink or explore anew how I could support Indigenous education initiatives in my community. I enjoyed the program very much. My doctorate, on the other hand, was quite different, and was without question the most challenging and disorienting academic work I have ever done. It reintroduced me to the tensions that can exist between the ship and the canoe and not necessarily the different ideas that these vessels can have about things like knowledge, research, access, ethics, or intellectual property. I think quite a lot of understanding and openness has emerged regarding how to think about these areas. Rather, it is the roots or colonial legacy of education that has been built so deeply into certain institutional spaces that it is more difficult to dismantle. It is so engrained at times that it is almost difficult to name or point to. And while I think elements of the colonial legacy can creep into all kinds of educational spaces—Indigenous and non-Indigenous—I had been learning in such organic, participatory, experiential processes for such a long time that it was jarring to once again be immersed in the mainstream Western-European education system.

But in truth, these well-known and often discussed tensions were not the issue either. Simply put, I was not at peace in academia. There are many good things happening at universities; shifts and changes are being slowly and diligently made by those working within them. These shifts do not change the fact that research is demanding, requiring long hours of deep work and concentration. I realized midway through my program that I wanted and needed more balance in my academic life. I wanted to learn and practice seed songs with my children. I wanted to garden and do what I could to support the spiritual well-being of myself and my family. I still wanted to learn more languages. But it was hard to learn and make strides in other areas—language in particular—while I was doing my doctorate. There was simply not enough time.

Indeed, time that might have been spent learning new root words and practicing paradigms was spent reading and writing papers about educational leadership, research ethics, epistemologies, ontologies, problems of practice, and research methods. And though I enjoyed most of what I read, it often felt like I was choosing the priorities of the ship over those of the canoe, and it grated me to be back in that position again—especially because I had only myself to blame. After all, no one had forced me to take up doctoral studies, and I was upset with myself on a regular basis for not spending more time writing stories or becoming a better language speaker. I kept going, though, because I believed what I was learning could make me a better support to organizations that I worked for and cared about and because I had a good support system. I also had many role models. Academics from my community and others were doing incredible work—teaching, learning language, practicing ceremony, building relationships within and across institutions, and supporting community. Indigenous Knowledge Guardians continued helping so many people—teaching, sharing their wisdom and time, and deepening our collective knowledge. Their examples made me excited about what a research life could look like after school when I would have time to create and shape my work in ways that brought my interests together in a more natural way. But despite this—despite knowing there was something to look forward to, it was still a stressful four years punctuated with moments of school-related happiness, the greatest of which were those spent reading The Creation Story, The Story of the Fatherless Boy, and The Story of the Peacemaker.

For those of you who are unfamiliar with these stories, I will offer the briefest of summaries. *The Creation Story* tells of Skyworld and the fall of Skywoman, from whom our people are descended. It tells how she participated in the creation of land and gave birth to a daughter who herself gave birth to twin boys, one of whom helped to create humans and sustenance for those humans and who instructed us to give thanks as a daily activity.

*The Story of the Fatherless Boy* tells of a time when our ancestors forgot to be thankful and how the four ceremonies were sent to help them.

*The Story of the Peacemaker* tells of a time when our ancestors were experiencing much war, conflict, and grief and how the Creator sent a messenger who helped establish the Great Law of Peace amongst the five nations, thus forming the Haudenosaunee Confederacy.

My doctoral study utilized an Indigenous research methodology, and I included these stories as a way to explore the concept of collaboration in a Haudenosaunee-specific context. I chose stories that were commonly recognized as playing a significant role in shaping Haudenosaunee thought.[14] I wanted the ideas within these narratives to inform my thinking and writing about my research topic (collaboration in Indigenous language revitalization). In reading them, though, I also came to a greater appreciation of the importance of the three white rows of wampum in the Two Row.

Those who have heard or read these stories will know that peace and thanksgiving are themes that recur across each of them, and there are many examples that show how peace and ga'nigǫhi:yo: (the good mind) were viewed as an ideal or desired state for Ogwehoweh people. For example, J.N.B. Hewitt and Chief John Arthur Gibson's version of the

Creation Story talks of how the Creator provided the first humans with nourishment, support, and encouragement, instructing them to give thanks daily for all that had been provided.[15] Later, when our early ancestors forgot these duties, the Creator sent the four ceremonies to them. And later still, during a time of great conflict, war, and strife, the duty to give thanks became neglected once more. Monture writes, "When the people from the village gathered to hear him speak, the Peacemaker proceeded to outline his message of peace, telling the people that the Creator did not intend human beings to be living in fear and committing violent acts upon one another. He also told them of this plan to unite the nations into a Confederacy built upon the social, spiritual, and political structures of peace, power, and righteousness."[16] The Peacemaker's shared vision reaffirmed the previous messages about the importance of Ogwehoweh people living in peace and practicing gratitude while also establishing a vast spiritual, social, political, and legal network that was invested with and accepted the responsibility to maintain and further peace to this day.

Together, these stories make plain that our peace as Ogwehoweh people had already been disrupted several times throughout our history and also that we had been given the tools to help recover and maintain it. Now, *tools* is perhaps an insufficient word to describe all of the ceremonies, songs, dances, protocols, and speeches that we were given—to say nothing of the learning, the making of objects, as well as the practicing and actual putting through of the ceremonies that occurs. But what I mean to say is that these practices help us maintain peace. Having learned more about them and their purpose, I began to understand that the Two Row was a continuation of these same efforts. While being a sacred agreement in and of itself, it is also a tool that explains who we are and what we are about to others. It reaffirms our commitment to acknowledge and thank Creation and explains that we will continue working towards a shared purpose of peace.

Bonnie Freeman writes,

> For the Haudenosaunee, the Tekeni Teyohha:ke Kahswenhtake (Two Row Wampum) is a strong foundation for our Onkwehonwe beliefs and values, which carries us through generations. By remaining firm in our understanding of and maintaining respect for the teachings of the

Creator, and The Great Law of Peace, we will remain a distinct and resilient people upon our lands. Therefore, Onkwehonwe people are not only seeking peace, quality and justice for their own lives, but also for the earth, the natural environment and all of creation.[17]

It took time for me to reach this understanding that Freeman has articulated so well, but eventually, through listening and reading, I arrived at a similar conclusion. I now see and accept that there exists a collection of instructional ideas within the Two Row that I can utilize within my personal and professional life. For example, I can use it to help me understand and explain the dichotomies that sometimes exist between the canoe and the ship and how differently either might perceive areas like research, ownership, access, or land. Simultaneously, I can appreciate its dialogical nature and how it promotes discourse and knowledge-sharing between those same (and other) entities so that differences might be bridged or shared ideas and sentiments might be explored. From reflection on my personal experiences in education, I can appreciate that it offers a caution, although, like others, I do not think that being in the dreaded middle is a wholly negative or irretrievable thing—especially since I now see those middle rows as a kind of invitation to participate in and honour the Great Law of Peace. To move along the river of life, practicing gratitude all the way.

Not that this is all there is to do. Unfortunately, the Two Row also reminds us of another reality—of how this agreement was not honoured.

## STORYWORK

I formally submitted my dissertation in February 2019. I was starting to see the end of the tunnel, and I was excited to move forward. I dreamed of what I would do when I was finished. I missed writing. I missed art. I missed language. I missed my family. Anyone who has done these large intensive research projects also knows of the sacrifices that are made for them. Those sacrifices look different for each of us, but we all make them.

During this same month, my mother, who had kept a respectful distance from me during nearly four years that I had been labouring over my dissertation, stopped by my house for a visit. She told me during that visit that she had been wondering, as people sometimes do, what happens after we pass away. She said she had been thinking of going somewhere, church perhaps, to ask. I asked her why she hadn't tried coming to Longhouse to learn what our ways had to say. She told me that she didn't speak the language, so she wouldn't be able to understand what they were saying.

I probably don't need to tell you how this made me feel. How deeply I felt its pain. How I smiled at her, nodded understanding, but cried after she left. It wasn't my mother's fault that she didn't understand the language or know that our stories provided insight into the question she was asking. And I realized in that moment that while I could not go back and change that for her, I could share what I knew, little though it may seem. I was, to be honest, somewhat embarrassed with myself for not having offered something like this to her sooner. In any case, I asked my husband if he could help me because he also knew the stories quite well, including Gaihwiyo, an oral tradition telling of the visions of a Seneca Prophet named Handsome Lake, which I had only a cursory understanding of. He said that he would be happy to help.

A few nights later, we attended a family dinner. My parents' house is usually teeming with guests—my siblings, their children, and their grandchildren. Certainly, enough people that telling any kind of story can be a challenge sometimes—especially when we all want to hear what one another has been up to. But that night, it was just me, my parents, my husband, our two children, and my niece. As we finished up dinner, my mother asked the question again.

*What happens when we leave this world?*

I hadn't gone there expecting to talk about it, but I had perhaps thought we would have time to prepare what we were going to say. But there we were, and she was asking, and since I didn't know that another opportunity would present itself, I asked her if she wanted me to tell her what I had learned. And she said yes.

And so, over the course of three hours and several pots of tea—this is the question we tried to answer by sharing what we knew about our stories and oral traditions and what they say about what happens when we die. We started at the earliest beginning we had, telling the story of a young woman and her brother, both born with a kind of magic referred to as *orenda*, in a place called Skyworld, where a great celestial tree stood in the middle, casting its light. How when she was grown, the young woman married the Chief of the Skyworld, came to be with child, and eventually made her way to a world covered in water, where one of her grandchildren would later mold our bodies from clay and breathe us into life.

The versions of the stories I told that night might not have been perfect, but they were told with love to ease the minds and foster a sense of peace for my mother and father, the two people who had opened their lives to me and welcomed my spirit into this world. Ironically, I was mostly able to tell them because of my doctoral work, because I had chosen to read versions of the Creation Story, the Story of the Fatherless Boy, and the Story of the Peacemaker for my research. While it was true that I'd read these texts in search of specific insights and ideas for my dissertation, keeping lists of the references to goodmindedness, descriptions of peaceful states, qualities of leadership, examples, and types of collaboration, I am happy that I was able to retell them when it mattered most.

Much has already been said about the written versions of oral traditions. The relationships between some of the anthropologists and informants who collected oral histories at Six Nations and other Haudenosaunee communities have been explored in Abenaki scholar Margaret Bruchac's exceptional book *Savage Kin: Indigenous Informants and American Anthropologists*.[18] From her work and the work of many other Haudenosaunee scholars, including Susan Hill, Rick Monture, Kevin White, Theresa McCarthy, Rick Hill, and Dawn Martin-Hill, I knew that written versions of these stories had been created during an era of salvage ethnography and that when reading them, I needed to be mindful of the motivations, prejudices, and biases the anthropologist authors may have brought to the page—consciously or unconsciously. I also knew from studying postcolonial theory in both my undergrad and master's program that narrative could be used to further the project of imperialism and to shape the identity of the "other" to better complement the political designs of an unfriendly empire. In short—there are well-known pros and cons to consulting written records.

For my part, I chose to use versions of stories that had been gathered and assembled by late nineteenth and early twentieth-century Tuscarora ethnographer J.N.B. Hewitt. I was drawn to Hewitt's work in part because

I knew that his diligence in documenting language was appreciated by many of my language teachers. I attempted to balance out my reliance on the written record by attending events where the Creation Story was being discussed, by reading other Haudenosaunee scholars who had written about it, and paying heed to the warnings that written versions can subsume or alter the intended meanings of oral stories.[19] Several of the versions I reviewed came from the collection at Deyohahá:ge:, or from the collection of Hewitt materials accessible on the Smithsonian website. I thought often of the spaces where these different versions had come from, where they were still held, and how differently the processes had or had not been for accessing them.

The canoe. The ship.

The night I told my parents about our Creation Story and about the two paths that we encounter on *ohahadihǫh*—the Milky Way—when we pass on, I am not sure which vessel I was drawing from more, but I recognize that it was because of efforts within both that I was able to tell these stories at all. I have written a lot of things and told a lot of stories through various mediums: novels, short stories, poems. But this was the most genuine and heartfelt storytelling I have ever done. I was not there to argue in favour of a particular version or to be a scholar. I was telling stories that help to answer some of our most searching, existential questions for two people I love and respect, who had never had someone sit down and tell it to them before. I was there to share in and spread peace, recover and restore an interrupted line of transmission. It was the kind of storytelling that had all the gravity of a ceremony, and for all the challenge and struggle that accompanied the completion of my doctorate—I can almost believe it was for these three hours alone.

## DEYOHAHÁ:GE:—TWO ROADS

I am a storyteller, a researcher, and an administrator working in support of Indigenous education, language revitalization, and Haudenosaunee knowledges and ways of being. These roles have, at times, felt estranged from one another but are nonetheless connected by me, as well as the hopes, values, and sense of responsibility I bring to each of them. Those values and sense of responsibility have been increasingly informed by reflecting on Haudenosaunee oral traditions, on the ideas they advance about how to live a good life in a good way, and how I can channel and enliven these ideas through my work—such as I am able.

As mentioned in my introduction, I am currently the director of the Deyohahá:ge: Indigenous Knowledge Centre at SNP, an Indigenous institute located in my community, Six Nations of the Grand River. Deyohahá:ge: was started by a group of people: Elders, Indigenous scholars, community members, and university faculty who were champions of Haudenosaunee knowledges and who recognized how "holding these two paths of Western and Hodinǫshǫ:nih knowledges side by side would enable future generations to preserve and regenerate Six Nations ways of knowing and being, as well as build equitable and healthy relationships with Western ways of knowing and being."[20] I view my administrative work as being in support of the vision that was set out by these early founders of the Centre and also as supporting the larger goals and vision of peace that our people have been charged with.

Like many administrative roles, this work also involves developing tools that help Deyohahá:ge: fulfill our community institutional mandate and forward the mission of SNP. My time is, therefore, spent in all kinds of ways: spending time with people, working on projects, and making presentations. Creating reports and policies and sitting on committees. Preparing budgets, attending meetings, and drafting proposals. When my schedule allows, I participate in the many wonderful activities that Deyohahá:ge organizes: lunch-and-learns, beading groups, and field trips. I help to coordinate conferences, symposia, and other special events. I network with representatives of other organizations, both in the community and beyond. Whenever I can, I teach and develop courses or other resources. Lately, I have been spending much of my time reflecting on the Centre's goals and strategic plans, the people and resources that will help us to accomplish them, and honing my own skills so I can be more helpful to this effort. These activities would be familiar to any director, I would think.

And yet, there is much about Deyohahá:ge: that is not like other spaces, Indigenous or institutional. Nor should it be, really. Deyohahá:ge: does not care for and transmit ancestral knowledges and practices in the same way as our Longhouses or the Knowledge Keepers and societies who are responsible for our ceremonies do. Nor is it an archive or a library in the conventional sense. We are somewhat in the middle again, and, as the idea behind the naming of the Centre indicated, there are lessons to be learned from both the canoe and the ship that can help us to do our work and better serve the people of our community. To be more fully what we are.

Everything I have learned about the Two Row thus far, including the message that was shared with me nearly ten years ago, has helped me to see the many possible ways we can move forward together in a good way. Through these years of learning, it has become simpler to see how the Centre can support our community members, deepen our collective knowledge of our history, land, and one another, and build relationships that invite people to join in the work of peacebuilding. Thanks to my colleagues, former colleagues and predecessor, there are many ways that Deyohahá:ge: already supports such activity. The principles of peace, friendship, and respect commonly associated with the Two Row have already been used to good effect, guiding relationship-building efforts with other schools, institutions, museums, colleges, universities, church groups, and community organizations. Indeed, the commitment to peacebuilding through education and knowledge-sharing is one that many institutions have taken part in and one that any institution could be proud to take up. We can and will continue to grow these efforts.

It is also true that we must be mindful of the way that we grow and help our Centre expand in ways that remain consistent with what people love most about its welcoming spirit. While bringing more archival collections to Deyohahá:ge: may mean establishing more protocols, procedures, and systems for our community to access materials—no one wants to create unnecessary bureaucracy. Broadening our research agenda and activities will likewise require new policies and processes, but how can we ensure that we are also creating environments where researchers will feel encouraged, mentored, and valued? In some cases, we may need to review and revisit what an Indigenous archive is, how it is organized, what it contains, and how it is accessed, and prioritize collection growth and accessibility based on our communities' priorities—research and otherwise. It will be a lot of building work on top of the tremendous amount of work that is already ongoing.

And so, when I suggest that the principles of the Two Row shape my administrative practice, this is part of what I am referring to. It is important to me that I stay mindful of the collective teachings of peace and goodmindedness that we as a people share and that these are centred in my asking of the questions specific to my role. How can I honour this vision? How can I honour the peace and well-being of my coworkers and my community? What work needs to be prioritized? What research questions are pressing? What resources does it require, and how can I help acquire them? How do I hear from community—especially those on the Grand River territory who may not think of themselves as scholars but who carry so much valuable knowledge? What kind of opportunities can I create for Indigenous scholars, established and emerging, to come work with us? How can we support and mentor students? How will Haudenosaunee values and principles be reflected in the policies we create, the projects we choose, and the way we present and share information? How do we, as an Indigenous Knowledge Centre, help people become good relatives? What could a new, larger space to one day house the Centre look and feel like? How can others—institutes, museums, archives, schools, and churches—help us with the work we must do? How can they help us further peace?

I like these questions. I like their critical, reflective nature, and I like that they can lead us to ideas, action, and activity. I like answering them with others most of all. With Indigenous Knowledge Guardians, with our community scholars, with the people I work with, and with people who are interested in what Deyohahá:ge: is and does. The way we answer these questions shapes the way I build my work plans, the very practical tools I use to outline what activities I hope to contribute to in the years to come, the events I hope to put on, the stories those events will tell, and the collections we will try to bring home. It is my hope to continue growing the Centre in a way that will encourage those who want to be there to feel safe, welcomed, and surrounded by thoughtful and respectfully curated materials. To give those who have stories to share or questions to pursue a place to do so. To support reflection and meaning-making and storytelling. Just as it has done for me and many others.

## CONCLUSION

As it stands now, there is no part of the Two Row that does not in some way speak to me—even the strings. It is the belt that I first became deeply aware of, and the learning and engagement with it that has since occurred has led me to several others. Since my visit to the lodge, the areas of the belt I think of most often are the three rows of white wampum in the middle. They have come to represent so many things for me: the importance of relationship and the way the space of engagement should feel—peaceful and respectful—whether that engagement is happening with other nations, museums, universities, or family members. They represent commitments that are embedded in the historical narratives of my people. They remind me to value peace, to earn and show respect, and to build friendships with the human and other-than-human beings of this world.

I still have questions. I may never find a document confirming, much less explaining, if and how our ancestors knew that the settlers would not be honourable. But their decision to proceed with treaty-making for the purpose of peace, utilizing principles of fairness and respect to communicate Haudenosaunee sovereignty, an identity that is rooted in thanksgiving and a commitment to the Great Law is, nonetheless, a familiar exercise of power. A similar scenario appears in The Creation Story, when the Creator's attempts to bring forth more creations, including human beings, animals, plants, foods, and medicines, meet with regular opposition and disruption from his brother, Flint. Throughout these disruptions, the Creator maintains a focus on his work, ultimately prevailing over Flint. It is impossible to know for certain if this particular example could have influenced our ancestors in their dealings with settler nations. Whether it did or not, though, there are still lessons I can learn from it—to stay committed to work that helps people, even in the face of opposition or distraction.

In retrospect, I can appreciate why I was guided to view the belt in this way—to see how it is just as much about the tenets of the Great Law and the preceding stories as it is anything else. Now, when I see the Two Row, I see those stories, too. I see a Skyworld under duress and change. I see a woman leaving that world, bringing life and seed to the back of a great turtle. I see an agreement between ourselves and Creation. I see two brothers with very different natures making choices, creating life, sustenance, and conflict here. I see my ancestors struggling with feelings of grief and being gifted with songs, ceremonies, and a path to peace. I see a world alive with spirits helping one another to thrive. And I see myself as part of it all, perhaps not always remembering with perfect clarity why my spirit came here, but knowing what my responsibilities are while I am here on earth—to show appreciation, be and work with the land, give thanks, and help to maintain the peace. We need to uphold our identities as peacemakers and sovereigns, even as we establish respectful relationships with others. This is our lens, after all—the way that we see and move about the world. I hope that I can always be a part of helping to spread and cultivate that peace—even if only within my own family.

Nya:węh.

# 3

# Living on the River

---

CHAPTER TEN

# The Pen Pal Project

## Bridging the Divide with the Teachings of the Two Row Wampum Treaty

*Suzie Miller and Scot Cooper*

---

### BACKGROUND

On February 29, 2006, a small group of women from Six Nations of the Grand River Territory felt compelled to act to stop the construction of a housing development formally called Douglas Creek Estates. Involving approximately twenty people on different days, the occupation of the land was, at first, quiet and peaceful. In the early morning of April 20, 2006, however, the Ontario Provincial Police (OPP) took action against the Haudenosaunee land defenders. Caledonia, then a quiet town of 11,000, erupted into a flashpoint of conflict over long-standing land rights disputes between the Six Nations of the Grand River Territory and the Crown, represented by the Canadian federal government.

This blocked construction site was not the first attempt by Six Nations to seek acknowledgment and restitution of treaty land rights. There were, and continue to be, numerous occasions where Six Nations has attempted not only to have the Canadian government honour and acknowledge their broken treaty promises, but also to get the United Nations to support their concerns over these matters.

This land reclamation was a very distressing time for both communities as conflict overflowed into the streets and was magnified by the media. Images of burning tires, burning bridges, and overturned hydro towers were repeatedly shown by the local television station. These events were the result of years of denial and frustration. When one nation knows its truth and continues to be ignored, they are bound to demand a response. When your community holds treaty rights in high esteem, and yet your community has suffered attempted genocide from the treaty partner, along with attempts to erase your existence, what response is reasonable?

The Neighbouring Communities Project Community Document[1] draws attention to what the conflict, in less than a year, had brought to the people from both communities.

> Members of both communities have endured hardship financially, emotionally, physically, and personally. It has been difficult for the community members to know how to respond, and how to cope with such circumstances…this story of conflict is what is called the "First Story." It involves the tension, hurt, hatred, violence, fear, mistrust, misunderstanding, and prejudice that resulted in the conflicts that ensued. Indeed, the first story serves to separate, segregate and discriminate community against community, neighbour against neighbour, friend against friend, and family member against a family member.[2]

**Scot Cooper**: *As a third-generation Canadian settler of English and Scottish descent, I had never heard of the Two Row Wampum despite my postsecondary university education and fifteen-plus years working within the Haldimand Tract.[3] My participation in the Pen Pal Project was my first introduction to our treaty.*

**Suzie Miller:** *At the time, I was teaching in Six Nations and lived in the town of Caledonia. I am from both sides of the Grand River. My mother was Mohawk Wolf Clan from Six Nations, and my father was from Caledonia. For the past thirty years, I have been deepening my understanding of our Indigenous history in this country we now know as Canada. I did not know this history growing up, my mother did not know it, and my grandmother did not know it either.*

The Two Row Wampum Treaty exists and has been upheld by the Haudenosaunee since its inception in the seventeenth century. Six Nations knows this and always has. Six Nations knows that treaty relationships are the foundation from which all our relations have been built. The treaties define how we are to be living in peace, trust, and friendship, sharing the use of the land. The two purple rows of the Two Row Wampum Treaty represent differing beliefs, perspectives, and ideas of land use and ownership.

The surrounding communities, as well as most Canadians, are (and were) unaware of our treaty relationship. One might ask why that is. Perhaps it is because our education system is written from one perspective—a colonial system built on a hierarchical and linear view vs. Indigenous views and belief systems, which are cyclical and based on natural law. The voice that has been represented through history ("his" story) is the one that is told and understood. I knew that people in Caledonia had little or no knowledge of treaty or land claim issues.

With a deep concern about the children of Six Nations and Caledonia witnessing the images of conflict, I needed to do something. I felt compelled to DO SOMETHING. Throughout history, people have been involved in exchanging letters across continents to connect and build understanding between cultures. I felt the need to connect children from both sides of the Grand River—children who did not necessarily know that there are differences in their lifestyles and histories. Children who did not know they were neighbours to the largest Indigenous population in Canada. Children who witnessed adults behaving in ways that created images of violence, which fostered fear and confusion for so many.

## THE PEN PAL PROJECT

**SM:** Determined to change the imagery and stories that these young people were exposed to, I initiated a Pen Pal Project[4] between my class of Indigenous students from Six Nations and a class of largely non-Indigenous students from Caledonia. This was not an easy exchange to start, as the tension in both communities was still quite prominent. With the support of my principal, I contacted the principal of the school that was adjacent to the reclamation site, and he declined my request. He was too nervous to broach the subject with the teachers. This was understandable, as the school community and the families had experienced quite a bit of trauma from the events that had transpired all around them from April to June. I then approached the school where my children attended (across the river *from the "site"), and the principal there successfully found a teacher who agreed to participate.*

*Throughout the year, via hand-delivered letters, shared art, and sometimes gifts, the students discussed their interests and culture, and they nurtured friendships. At the end of the first year, I thought the children should meet their pen pal in person. The students met face to face at a gathering where they participated in joint fun and educational activities. This "gathering" phase would come to be a highlight of the project where the students could really put the teachings of the Two Row into action.*

*I will share two stories that may give the reader a sense of the negative impact the community conflict had on the children. In September 2007, a teacher from Caledonia contacted me and asked if I could find her a class from Six Nations to pen pal with. (I had asked her the previous year, but she was hesitant to be involved). She relayed a story that had occurred in her Grade 4 class that caused her to reach out. They were working on their spelling words and using them in a sentence. One of the words was "enemy." A student stood up and used the word in the sentence, "People from Six Nations are our enemy." Here is a second story: that same year, in my grade three and four class, one of my students approached me and asked if she could give a letter of apology to one of her classmates. She showed me the letter, which read, "I'm sorry for saying you are from Caledonia." I looked at my student and asked, "Is that the new put-down?" She nodded yes. I wonder what would have happened if we had left the community children to make sense of our conflicts on their own.*

*The Pen Pal Project was born from a desire to promote a sense of understanding between the two communities across the Grand River. It was a gesture, reaching out to the neighbouring community of Caledonia from Six Nations in the spirit of the Two Row and the Covenant Chain of Friendship Wampum Treaty. As a teacher who understood that people were simply unaware of the historical facts in relation to Indigenous populations in Canada, I knew people were responding with fear, frustration, and anger to events that they did not truly understand.*

*Involvement with the Pen Pal Project continued to grow from forty students in 2006–07 to 2,500 in 2016. Local community agencies and businesses sometimes paired up and facilitated activities at the yearly gathering and contributed funding, volunteer support, food, and t-shirts for all the youth and participating adults. It is, and has been, a collective effort,⁵ a magnificent gathering, and to participate has been profound and moving. It is a rich celebration of unity, collective hope, and diversity.*

## CROSS-CULTURAL COMMITTEE

In harmony with the Two Row understanding of traveling the river of life side by side while representing perspectives from the ship and the canoe, a small cross-cultural committee was established in 2008 to assist and guide the planning of the process and yearly events. This committee was composed of community members from Six Nations and Caledonia, including teachers, community organizations, municipal politicians, and provincial Ministry of Education members. The meetings were hosted at Emily C. General School. All voices were honoured. One member once said they had never been involved with a committee where all ideas were considered and discussed. This committee provided a means to stay accountable to each other, promote cultural understanding, and remain within the guidance of the Two Row philosophy. Peace, respect, and friendship were the foundation upon which everyone participated.

**SM:** *One of our favourite ideas had germinated from our early planning meetings. The local OPP inspector and detachment commander who participated on the committee had talked about his nephew, who was a provincial yo-yo champion. The idea of incorporating yo-yos into a joint activity between the students came up over and over throughout the years. It was not until the eighth year, however, that we finally revisited this idea and decided to give yo-yo kits to all the junior-level students (six hundred students). The plan was that they would get their kit, decorate two sides of their yo-yo, and when they met their pen pal, they would exchange one side with each other. They would then have a yo-yo unique to them and their pen pal (See figure 10.1). We were so lucky no one lost an eye during that 2014 gathering at the Caledonia Arena. Remember, kids don't really know how to play with yo-yos!*

## GATHERINGS

After the first year of pen pals meeting in person, it became clear that gatherings like this would remain an important part of the Pen Pal process for students. These gatherings allowed students to come together and participate in safe cross-cultural collective experiences informed by teachings from both sides of the Grand River. The location of the

10.1 Pen pal yo-yos crafted together at the 2014 Pen Pal gathering at the Caledonia Arena. Pen pals exchanged decorated halves of their yo-yo. A yo-yo expert taught the pen pals tricks with their yo-yos. (Source: http://www.penpalproject.ca/gatherings/grades-4-to-6/index.html)

gatherings alternated yearly between on-reserve and significant off-reserve sites. Many non-Indigenous volunteers, let alone students, had never been to the reserve. These visits helped to dismantle stereotypes often perpetuated and sustained in the media. Gatherings became a venue where students could participate jointly in art, song, dance, and fun. The activities at the gatherings were all facilitated by organizations and people from both communities. For example, one year, Ontario Early Years Haldimand-Norfolk and Stoneridge Daycare facilitated the "Old School Games station," where Ganohwkra Sra and Haldimand-Norfolk REACH facilitated beading bracelets and exchanging friendship keepsakes.

The purpose of the Pen Pal Project was to partake in cross-cultural sharing, learning, and experiences of respect. For instance, students shared about their heritage, customs, traditions, celebrations, and ways of life. Sometimes, the experiences were spontaneous, such as during the closing ceremony of the 2009–10 Pen Pal gathering when students, teachers, parents, and adult volunteers spontaneously held hands as Susan Aglukark, a popular Inuit singer, sang her song "O'Siem." Following the gathering, a local teacher noted that her grade one students in Caledonia started to refer to "O'Seim" as the Pen Pal song. They had asked to sing it in class. The teacher printed the lyrics for them, and they wanted to sing it for the whole school.

## COLLECTIVE DOCUMENTS

As part of the Pen Pal Project, we have had a lot of fun and excitement co-creating collective documents. These documents involve pen pals coming together to participate in a collective event that is archived and shared. They can take many forms, such as art, poems, written collections, lists, or photos. They serve not only as an archive of the communities' collective wisdom and knowledge but also as a testament to shared hopes and preferences for the future. In this way, they transcend time by evoking important images of the past, archiving the most present moment (the gathering) while simultaneously proposing what might be possible together for the future.

At the year four gathering (2010), an aerial picture was taken of the six hundred Indigenous and non-Indigenous students ranging in age from six to thirteen who posed shoulder to shoulder along with their adult leaders and volunteers in purple and white t-shirts to create a human replica of the Covenant Chain of Friendship Wampum Treaty (see figure 10.2). This aerial picture was later circulated throughout communities and all participating schools. The activity afforded an opportunity to teach students, teachers, and volunteers about our treaty relationship and for students to participate in making an overhead image celebrating our continued relationship.

Emily C. General Elementary School - O.M. Smith Elementary School - Jamieson Elementary School - I.L. Thomas Elementary School - Caledonia Centennial Public School - River Heights Public School - Oneida Central Public School - St. Patrick's Catholic School - J.L. Michener Public School - Dunnville Central Public School

10.2 Overhead image depicting the Friendship Wampum belt, a treaty pledging friendship and everlasting peace between cultures. Sometimes the Covenant Chain of Friendship needs to be polished. Present in this image are six hundred students and volunteers. (Source: http://www.penpalproject.ca/gatherings/2010.html)

This activity was so well received that it began a yearly Pen Pal t-shirt project to create aerial pictures that represented the teachings the students were learning to circulate the emerging story more widely. Imagine the residual effect of this activity, with six hundred children returning home that afternoon wearing a t-shirt with an image that perhaps they hadn't previously understood, which may have sparked a conversation at the dinner table that night with their family. Parents became more aware of the conversations regarding Caledonia and Six Nations through their children writing letters with their neighbours across the river.

**SM:** *I cannot tell you of the pride I felt after the 2010 gathering. I was following a school bus on my way home, traveling down fourth line, stopping for the flashing lights, and seeing children getting off wearing their t-shirts. Then, driving down my street in Caledonia, seeing children with the same t-shirt. Wow, what a day!*

Over a decade, we created four collective overhead images that reflected the agreed-upon theme/teaching for the Pen Pal year. The second (which included 1,200 pen pals) was of an eastern white pine tree hugging the Earth. The eastern white pine, while being the official Ontario tree, also represents the Tree of Peace. There are videos that document the excitement of the participants.⁶ They solidify the importance of relationship-building. Witnessing these gatherings demonstrates the power of the teachings of the treaty relationship in action.

The third sky art image was created during the June 17, 2013 Pen Pal gathering at Stoney Creek Battlefield House Museum and Park in Ontario, Canada. It is a recreation of the Two Row Wampum Belt (see figure 10.3). This was the seventh such gathering and involved 2,000 First Nations students and their neighbours. This event was particularly meaningful because it was the 200th anniversary of the Battle of Stoney Creek⁷ and the 400th anniversary of the Two Row Wampum Treaty. Again, each student had a t-shirt with an image of the Two Row to share the teachings and spread the story.

These pictures stand as an invitation to consider ways of being with each other, harken back to the rich history of friendship that existed

10.3 The Two Row Wampum Belt Collective Sky Art (2013). Two thousand students and teachers. Photo taken by Daniel Dancer from a helicopter donated by the RCMP. (Source: http://www.penpalproject.ca/gatherings/2013.html)

10.4  This collective document is a replica of the Two Row created from photobooth images of Pen Pals created at the 2015 Pen Pal gatherings at the Iroquois Lacrosse Arena and the Caledonia Arena. (Source: http://www.penpalproject.ca/art/photo-booth-two-row.html)

between the communities, and celebrate the threads of unity in our diversity. They honour treaties and are an expression of a collective preference for friendship and peace.

**SC:** *What I will always remember about the events creating these documents are the smiling faces of the kids and their excitement as they tried to find themselves in these pictures afterward. I believe they have a sense that they are part of something special.*

## SHARING THE STORY

Our shared history with the Two Row creates a thread of connection and guidance on how to be in a relationship. It became important to us early on to circulate and share the story of the pen pals as an example of a more preferred relationship and to extend the teachings to a broader audience.

## THE ROLE OF AUDIENCE

Given this objective, we have actively recruited appropriate audiences. Media, community leaders, law officials, politicians, local artists, Elders, Chiefs, friends, family, and community members around the world experiencing similar struggles have been sought, invited, and courted. They have been recruited to share in our story and bear witness to it. We have had to learn to utilize modern media as a vehicle through which to circulate the telling and retelling within the local communities and in the broader social-political culture. This has meant crafting media releases, a web page that serves as an archive for joint developments and initiatives relevant to the common themes.

We actively continue to recruit politicians and community leaders to share in the ceremonies, the emerging stories, and ongoing developments.

10.5 This picture shows the exchange of friendship bracelets between the Six Nations police chief Glenn Lickers and the inspector of the OPP David McLean during the 2007–2008 Pen Pal gathering. Following the lead of the children, they both decided to make and exchange friendship bracelets crafted in their respective agency colors as a gesture of connection and friendship. Both men proudly displayed their bracelets at meetings later that evening. (Source: http://www.penpalproject.ca/gatherings/2008/index.html)

They are regularly invited to come and witness initiatives and to be part of the foundation for the emerging relationship. At municipal and provincial levels, we have appreciated a good response.

## TRAVELLING ART

What we must remember throughout all of this is that the children are teaching us. One of our most amazing stories has to do with the birth of what was to become the Pen Pal Travelling Art Exhibit. The idea stemmed from a conversation with our students about how our community members were still uncomfortable greeting or making eye contact, even three years after the conflict. Some people from Six Nations still didn't come to Caledonia, or when they did, they felt uncomfortable. There were many people from Caledonia who wanted to reach out and welcome members of Six Nations but did not know how. We thought, perhaps, if we created a lapel pin, something we could wear that says *I want to be your friend, I understand*, it would afford a level of comfort.

**SM:** *I delivered a lesson of peace and friendship with my grade three and four students. We looked at images of our communities and images of peace, and my student's artistic responses were incredibly inspirational.*

This activity grew into a planned art lesson for teachers to deliver to their students prior to our year four gathering. The result was six hundred pieces of art that signified what peace, friendship, and community meant to these students. The overwhelming response from the students inspired the Travelling Art Exhibit curated by Anuva Swift, a retired art teacher from Caledonia. She said, "We needed our community folks to see what the children saw."

Art is often a tool for healing. The youth from both communities created six hundred pieces of art influenced by the teachings of the Two Row Wampum and shared their understanding of peace, respect, friendship, and connection. We selected eighty of those student art pieces to travel as an art exhibit throughout our neighbouring communities and the province. These art pieces shared words of encouragement, local community symbols, and cultural teachings. Phrases such as *Friendship between two*

10.6　This student's image highlights community symbols and cultural teachings with the Hiawatha Belt—a national belt of the Haudenosaunee—and the span bridge—an icon representing Caledonia, placed on two side-by-side turtles representing friendship on Turtle Island (North America). (Credit: Suzie Miller)

10.7　This piece from the Travelling Pen Pal Art Exhibit displays cultural symbols representing the communities coming together on the Grand River in peace. (Source: http://www.penpalproject.ca/art/art-exhibit/index.html)

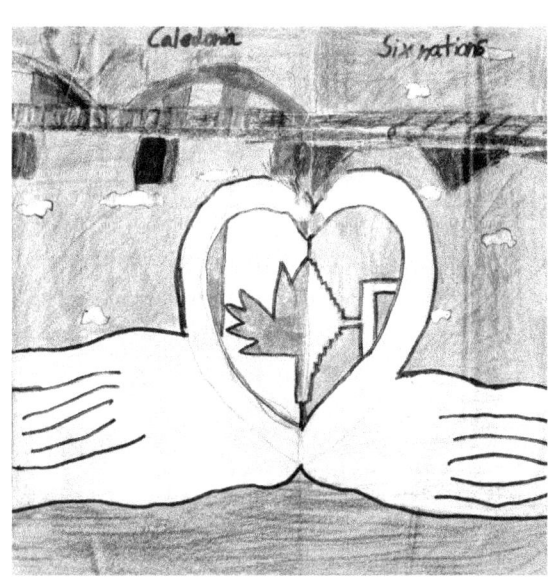

worlds; *We don't hate, we love all the time;* and *On Earth let's be friends, friends not enemies* are poignant, heartwarming, and inspiring examples of the wisdom and knowledge of the youth.

These pieces provide a testament to shared hopes and preferred relations. As such, they provide further retellings of the emerging counter-story to the grand narrative of conflict. They assist moments in time to live on and be shared with a wider audience through exhibitions.

## RESPONSES

As the story of the Pen Pal relationship grew, we sought to share the story and elicit responses from broader communities. The traveling art exhibit provided one such opportunity as visitors were given response cards inviting them to share comments about what drew them to the project and what the project suggests to them about what is possible. Responses were heartwarming.

> Messages of friendship, peace, and cooperation stood out in the images. Stronger and improved relations, based on trust, are possible when these ideas are the foundation of our relationship.

> The artwork made me feel as though new beginnings are truly possible.

> That change IS possible, and with the right teachers teaching the right messages we will come together as one!!

Throughout the years, we have had the opportunity to tell the story of the Pen Pal Project to many groups who have experienced division and isolation. During these presentations, like the traveling art exhibit, we sought responses that were brought back to our home communities as support and further inspiration to continue to work on this relationship.

## RESPONSES FROM INDIA

**SC:** *In 2018, I was invited to Mumbai, India, to share about the Pen Pal Project as part of a broader presentation on narrative community practice. As is our way, I sought responses from the audience to bring back to our home communities of Six Nations and Caledonia.[8] Many responses were inspiring.*

Dear Pen Pals,

First of all, such a big thank you for sharing your journey with us all the way here in India. I wonder if you even thought that your story would touch so many hearts across the globe.

It was so amazing to me to see how you bridged your friendship, and shared your lives, your hopes, your dreams, through letters with each other. Did you imagine that you would grow such beautiful friendships? I think if we also started to share our lives with people we think are 'different' we could also build great relationships.

Perhaps in a country like India where there is so much internal conflict over religion, land, water, resources, race, we could learn to open our hearts to one another.

Perhaps we could be friends with Pakistan one day!

You have given me hope. You have shown me that something beautiful can come out of a small gesture even if I don't know how it is going to be. And so, you have given me the courage to work to open hearts. For that my son T. and I thank you!

Dear Six Nations and Caledonia,

Today I have heard about your pen pal program that has been growing over many years. What started with two classes has truly rippled out to reach further than you might have imagined. I am from Australia and I will share your story with people there who can learn about your Two Row Wampum and the meaning of friendship and may develop their own images of significance...

*These sorts of expressions highlight the vast reach of the teachings of the Two Row Wampum Treaty and how these teachings can shape our relationships for the future.*

## CLOSING

The Pen Pal Project was a local initiative fostering understanding and relationship between Indigenous and non-Indigenous students whose communities were in conflict over land rights. The project spanned ten years (2006–16) and involved thousands of students, teachers, volunteers, and organizations, all finding guidance from the Two Row Wampum agreement.

Fast forward twenty-five years, when the children have grown to adulthood and become our future leaders. Might their understanding of the Two Row Wampum Treaty provide a relationship foundation that assists them in navigating a more just and collaborative future?

**SM:** *I remember teaching about our treaty relationship in classrooms along the Haldimand Tract. The most profound moments I witnessed were the realization that everyone who walks on the grassy earth of Turtle Island (North America) are represented on one of the purple rows. We are obligated to live by this treaty, whether we were present during the time of its inception or not. The fact that we are here obligates us to this promise. The commitment was made, and the living documentation of the Two Row Wampum Belt is the evidence.*

*The Tekeni Teyohàte Kaswentha is tattered, as is our relationship. The Covenant Chain of Friendship Wampum Treaty is related to the Two Row. It is time to polish our chain of friendship, to honour and acknowledge each other in the spirit of peace, trust, and friendship in harmony with the example set by the young pen pals.*

## ONE LASTING IMAGE

10.8 These Pen Pals share in planting an eastern white pine tree together as a symbol of everlasting peace. (Credit: Francie Govan)

CHAPTER ELEVEN

# Deyohahage Gihe gowa'hneh

## Living the Two Row Wampum, On the Grand River

*Ellie Joseph and Jay Bailey*

---

### BIRTH OF TWO ROW ON THE GRAND—ELLIE

In the summer of 2013, paddler friends Ellie Joseph, a member and resident of the Six Nations Reserve, and Jay Bailey, from nearby Simcoe, participated in the Two Row Wampum Renewal Campaign, a sixteen-day paddling journey from Albany to Manhattan, New York, on the Hudson River. This educational and advocacy event marked the four-hundred-year anniversary of the Two Row Wampum Treaty.[1] The purpose of the journey was to polish and renew the chain of friendship established between the Haudenosaunee and the Dutch immigrants in 1613 and later continuing with the French and British.

This was not just a recreational canoeing adventure to be experienced only by the outdoor enthusiast but an actual living re-enactment of the treaty itself. Settlers (allies) literally paddled, bow to stern, alongside the Haudenosaunee. Participants steered their vessels close enough to assist each other when needed, yet far enough apart so as not to interfere with the ways of the other. These two ribbons of vessels, over two hundred in

11.1 Co-founders Jay Bailey (left) and Ellie Joseph (right) sitting on a bench at the Six Nations Haldimand Tract plot, Port Maitland, ON. The bench was donated by Two Row on the Grand Paddle. The picture was taken by an anonymous individual with Ellie Joseph's cellphone, July 28, 2017.

11.2 The Two Row on the Grand flotilla approaching the Cayuga Grand Vista Trail bridge. (Credit: Betsy McBurney, 2019)

number, made their way along, creating a unique alliance. This event had a profound effect on participants and spectators alike. The final day of this historical journey, the very toughest of days on the water, added a three-mile walk, again in two rows, from Pier 96 in Manhattan to the United Nations building, commemorating the International Day of the World's Indigenous Peoples. The cultural teachings, community support, sense of accomplishment, new friendships, and connection to nature were just a few of the gifts from that one-time experience. Both Jay and Ellie felt driven to make a similar event happen on the Grand River.

## THROUGH THE LENS OF ELLIE

Being one of the older female Haudenosaunee paddlers, I truly felt a tremendous connection to my people in a way that I never had before. Here I was on the Two Row Renewal on the Hudson, paddling through my Mohawk homeland territory, where my ancestors fished, hunted, and grew their crops, thriving in their ways of being. I envisioned the longhouses of days gone by, smoke curling upwards into the skies, women working in the fields, babies on their backs, perhaps bringing in armfuls of corn, beans, and squash, preparing for the colder months ahead. I envisioned the men getting ready for the hunt, fashioning tools from flint and bone, and all the while, children playing among the men and women, learning their roles, being mentored and nurtured, all living in a spirit of gratitude, starting each day by giving thanks for all the gifts of our Mother Earth.

I was at home on this river, even though our colourful flotilla of canoes and kayaks paddled past cities with smokestacks churning out black smoke that tainted the horizon, and even though we paddled among the huge barges loaded with garbage, scrap metal, and products that were being shipped all over the world. I was moved, very moved, and I took in this good medicine for my being.

The nature of this event demanded much physical strength. On those days of ideal weather, with the sun shining overhead and the wind at our backs, we chatted with our fellow paddlers, making new friends. On such days, a group of young Haudenosaunee boys could be heard singing their songs, young voices carrying across the peaceful waters of the Hudson. And, of course, there was laughter and splashing to cool each other off.

Or, at a lunch stop, we'd sit and leisurely share our stories of the day's progress, perhaps taking a much-needed stretch and maybe even a brief nap. After each day of the journey, we would pitch our tents for the night and fall asleep easily under the stars, bellies full from a good meal.

But there were many days that certainly were not idyllic. Imagine cold rain and wind in the face for hours, getting soaking wet from the never-ceasing whitecaps that splashed on the bow of the canoe, and, oh, paddling against the tide! Ten strokes forward, two back. Repeat. Keep moving forward. Or at least, try. Imagine having to abort the paddling plan for the remainder of the day because the conditions were such that Coast Guard officials instructed the flotilla to remain onshore. Despite days like these—and there were several—our flotilla of allies and Indigenous paddlers were protected by our ancestors. One only had to gaze up to the grey skies to spot an eagle circling overhead or perhaps watching from its perch onshore, telling us that the universe was unfolding in a good way.

I regarded our final day as our graduation day. We all shared this tremendous sense of accomplishment. Throngs of spectators, media, friends, and families (on land, on water, and even overhead) witnessed our weary group, with our blistered hands, soaking wet clothing, sun-burnt skin, assisting each other out of our vessels, Indigenous and non-Indigenous working together—the Two Row Treaty in action, right there. It was extremely emotional for all of us, a life-changing experience that my Paddle Brother, Jay, and I knew must continue. That Wampum, with its white background and two purple parallel lines, was deeply ingrained within my soul. It truly is a living treaty, and its intent must be shared among all peoples regardless of skin colour, cultural beliefs, or ways of being in maintaining peace, friendship, and respect.

After our return to our respective homes, Jay and I decided that we needed to host a similar event on our own Grand River. We both wanted participants, allies, and community members to experience the physical, emotional, spiritual, and mental treasures that a river can provide.

Groundwork began immediately in late 2013 with two other paddlers we'd met on the Hudson who shared our dreams and aspirations. The river needed to be scoped out for places to camp, support was sought from our Hereditary Chiefs and Council, communities along the river

11.3 From bottom to top: The Two Row Wampum, the Covenant Chain Friendship Wampum, and a wooden bowl with tobacco with everything resting on deer hide. The Wampum is carried by co-founders Ellie Joseph and Jay Bailey during the journey of the Two Row Paddle. Tobacco is shared for prayers and then released to the river. (Credit: Jay Bailey, July 27, 2017)

had to be informed of our intentions, and there were a host of questions to be answered. Participant costs, cultural presentations, a website, canoe and kayak rentals, insurance, meals, ground crew support, and safety on the water and land had to be determined. Finally, in July of 2016, we hosted our Two Row on the Grand, launching in Paris and eight days later ending at Rock Point Provincial Park on Lake Erie, just a short paddle away from our small Six Nations piece of property near the pier in Port Maitland where the Grand River empties into Lake Erie. As the Two Row on the Grand Paddle evolved, a ninth day was added to the itinerary.

That summer brought approximately ninety paddlers to the Grand River. Many joined for the adventure, others for the cultural teachings. Most of our allies on this Grand River journey knew little of Six Nations history other than what they'd been taught from textbooks full of inaccuracies and half-truths, but paddlers were eager to learn. Twenty-five paddlers completed the entire route from Paris to Lake Erie. Unfortunately, my Six Nations community had far fewer participants. Nevertheless, a powerfully dynamic connection developed among all of us, and what is known today as our "Two Row on the Grand Paddle Family" was created out of peace, friendship, and respect.

## THE DAILY ROUTINE FOR THE TWO ROW ON THE GRAND PADDLE—JAY

This annual paddle has grown from seven days, Paris to Port Maitland, to nine days, adding Cambridge to Paris, and in 2022, it became a ten-day paddle, dividing the longest day into two. In 2023, the City of Cambridge opened a closed campground in Churchill Park for us to camp the night before our first day's paddle.

On the morning of the first day, we meet at the launch point with morning snacks and a registration team to welcome everyone. On the subsequent mornings, we leave our tents to have an early breakfast prepared by our ground support crew. Hot water for packets of oatmeal, hot coffee, cold cereal, and bagels with options like cream cheese are available. After breakfast, campers bring tents and baggage to the U-Haul where they are neatly arranged and then loaded by our ground support team as we prepare to paddle.

We start each day's paddle by gathering our vessels, safety kits, water, and snacks and getting ready to launch at the specified hour. Before starting out, a cultural Knowledge Keeper would share the Haudenosaunee Thanksgiving Address. After our minds have been focused on thanks giving for all that we will see and not see on the paddle, Ellie reminds the paddlers about whistle signals, sunscreen, and hydration. Crystal Burning, our Lead Safety Paddler, and I then talk about the logistics for the day's paddle: issues of river, wind, and weather. Together, we help each other position the vessels for launch in steady succession. Once everyone is safely on the water and our sweep, the safety paddler who ensures no one is left behind, gives us the signal, we call, "Paddles up!" When we see that everyone has their paddle up to signal their readiness, we start.

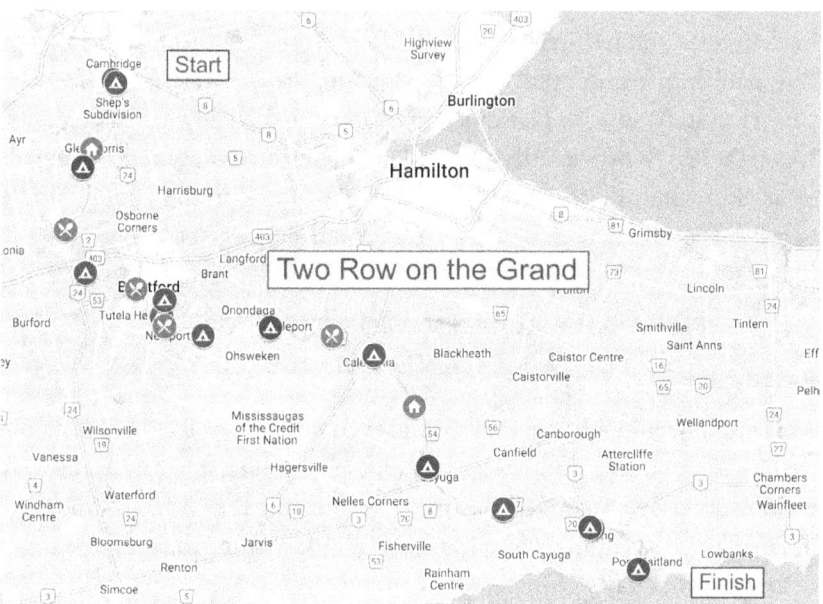

11.4 Two Row on the Grand Canoe Journey on the Grand River, starting at Cambridge to Port Maitland. Map created by Jay Bailey using Google Maps, November 8, 2021, https://www.google.com/maps/d/u/0/edit?mid=1f7mKeHwTzQnio4rnM2X_cmp2BORqjxTw&usp=sharin

As we paddle, where possible, we form up in Two Rows, Ellie leading the Indigenous row and I leading the Ally row, enacting the Two Row Wampum: paddling close enough to help each other when needed but not so close as to interfere with the way the other steers their vessel. Approaching gravel shoals or rapids, we assess the channels available, and one of us takes the lead, with the advice to follow at a safe distance, unless we get stuck! The river itself is a teacher. The current often does not flow directly downriver, and in places, it will carry your vessel in its direction, not yours. Sometimes, a trail of bubbles or reeds trailing on the surface shows you where the current goes. Sometimes, there is little or no indication until you are in it. You learn to be alert and go with the flow to reach your focal point, particularly in faster water. In calm water, negative tension and worry can slip easily into the water and swirl away from you.

Our safety paddlers, spaced out along the length of the group, let us know by walkie-talkie if we are too far ahead of the stragglers. Periodically, we stop anyway for a rest, water break, or salty snack, but sometimes we pause earlier than planned so that our 160 or so paddlers aren't too far apart.

At lunchtime, we meet the ground crew and our caterer at a designated spot where we have a reasonable, pre-arranged takeout, washroom facilities, and room for everyone to eat comfortably. In some places, Ellie arranges for mobile washroom facilities. Likewise, at the end of the day, we meet the ground crew at a reserved camping spot. Tent placement is followed by cultural teachings, followed by supper, which is catered once more by a family from Six Nations. After supper, there is social time, sometimes another teaching or a campfire.

On the last day, we arrive in Port Maitland in time for a late lunch, followed by a Sharing Circle and/or a cultural Closing. Each year, emotional paddlers often share some profound changes in perspective, emotions, life choices, and self-image. Each year, Ellie and I look at each other and, without a word spoken, agree to do this again next year.

## COMMUNITY ENGAGEMENT HAPPENS ON THE RIVER—ELLIE

By our fourth year of hosting the Two Row on the Grand (2019), the trip had become a nine-day paddle from Cambridge to Port Maitland. Jay and I gained tremendous and much-appreciated support from both ally and Six Nations organizations and individuals. My Six Nations community engaged and fully supported this endeavour in many ways. A few landowners eagerly and generously opened their backyards to host our overnight camping spots; volunteers offered their support and assistance not only during the event and the post-paddle duties but also in the year-round planning.

Six Nations Health Services recognizes the importance of land-based healing and has been overwhelmingly supportive, not only financially but also helping with manpower, first aid, and transportation. The Two Row on the Grand Paddle, as a grassroots community initiative, provides an excellent opportunity for nurturing the mental, spiritual, physical, and emotional well-being of the individual, family, and community. As a result of participating in the Two Row on the Grand Paddle, the Six Nations Health Teams, which deliver programs to support mental health, addictions, healthy lifestyles, and youth life promotion programs, offer their clients paddling/training sessions, sponsorship, and support.

Another Six Nations community organization, Ganohkwasra Family Assault Support Services, approached us in 2020 in hopes of learning more about this river journey and discussing what supportive role it could play. Most importantly, they recognized our holistic approach to community well-being and our underlying credo of good minds, good words, and good actions. However, COVID-19 2020 restrictions meant that our typical nine-consecutive-day event could not happen as it did in previous years. The delegates from this organization participated and supported a few of our single-day paddles, taking with them an enthusiasm for future engagement. We look forward to helping mentor healthy and right relationships among our community members.

The Six Nations Economic Development Trust Fund provides an application-based community fund investment available to groups that address community priorities such as the health and well-being of Six Nations community members. The Two Row on the Grand has been successful in garnering financial support from this fund. Because of this grant, we have been able to pay registration fees for community members so that they can attend a family-oriented, drug- and alcohol-free event, develop and maintain healthy relationships with their families and their community, and participate in a unique opportunity to develop healthy connections with neighbouring communities. We all share the river together, honouring the Two Row Wampum.

## COVID-19 AND THE 2020 TWO ROW ON THE GRAND

As co-founders of the Two Row on the Grand Paddle, we had a pandemic to contend with in what was supposed to be our Fifth Year Anniversary on the Grand River. To commemorate this occasion, we had plans to rent a bus to provide Six Nations of the Grand River community, family members, and ally supporters transportation to our final paddling day, where the wampum that we carry (The Two Row Wampum and The Friendship Belt) would have by then reached the mouth of The Grand at Lake Erie. We had

11.5  Paddlers sporting their Two Row masks under the Caledonia Rail Bridge, Caledonia, ON, during the unofficial Two Row 2020 COVID paddle. (Credit: Michelle General, July 21, 2020)

plans to give commemorative t-shirts to participants and plans to provide lunch to our spectators, complete with a Haudenosaunee Social Dance.

Instead, provincial guidelines meant to curb the spread of the COVID-19 virus meant that large groups could not gather, campgrounds were closed, and, for a portion of the paddling season, the Six Nations Reserve had manned safety checkpoints around its borders to lessen the flow of outside traffic into the community. Because of these barriers and obstacles, our Two Row on the Grand could not be held as our regular nine-day paddling and camping event.

To keep the tradition alive, the two co-founders made the decision to paddle the wampum from Cambridge once again to Port Maitland. An itinerary was put together and shared on social media, with an invitation to any interested, self-sufficient participants who would be welcome to join us. There would be no camping, no sharing of meals, and, sadly, no cultural teachings in person. On June 21, 2020, the day of the summer solstice and National Indigenous Peoples Day, our first launch was held at Cambridge, Ontario, with twelve paddlers in accompaniment. A community member opened with The Thanksgiving Address, put tobacco down, and sent prayers up to the Creator. Where physical distancing was difficult, masks were mandatory.

Our summer continued with these "day paddles" from June 21st to late August, and our wampum made their way down the river, launching at Cambridge, Paris, Brantford, Onondaga, Caledonia, Cayuga, and Dunnville. As the day paddles continued, our numbers of participants grew, with a high of thirty-four paddlers who joined in for the final destination to Port Maitland, and for a final time, tobacco was put down, prayers sent up to Creator. What we thought would be a journey of two paddlers turned into a total of fifty-four participants, some old friends from our first four years, and even some new recruits who looked forward to the Two Row on the Grand 2021. Due to the continuance of the COVID-19 pandemic, the wampum was carried in a similar fashion to 2020.

What was missing during this 2020 COVID paddle year? Of course, the catered meals and sitting shoulder to shoulder at mealtimes or assisting each other with tent setup and takedown. However, what was most missed were the cultural teachings, which we simply could not host since the group could not gather in close proximity. Many thanks to The Six Nations Economic Development Trust Fund, which provided financial support to several community Knowledge Keepers so we could create cultural teachings on video instead. These videos have been uploaded to our YouTube channel in a playlist called "TRED Talks, Getting Traction with Reconciliation," and private links are posted in our Facebook Group to bolster the spirits of those in attendance and those who could not attend. We also posted "Trip Clips" from each day's paddle.

## GRATITUDE AND THE
## THANKSGIVING ADDRESS—ELLIE

What is sorely lacking today in this hectic lifestyle of trying to balance career, material gain, fast-paced internet connections, and eyes looking into screens is a close and intimate connection to nature. Sitting for hours at a time working from home in isolation, time constraints, and meeting deadlines can wreak havoc on the soul. We have forgotten to appreciate just what we need to hear from the land. We have forgotten to listen to the Earth, our Mother.

For thousands of years, the Haudenosaunee have spoken the Ohenton Karihwateh'kwen, which is *"the words that come before all else."* These words, uniquely phrased by each speaker, are still recited at the beginning and closing of all ceremonial gatherings today. The Thanksgiving Address, as it is commonly called, is based on the belief that our Mother Earth is not to be taken for granted. Indeed, spiritual expressions of thankfulness and appreciation for all living things must be given. We have been given a role to fulfill, a duty to live in harmony and balance not only with each other but with all of life. When this ceremonial speech is spoken, the hearts and minds of all the people who are gathered align with nature. It is a wholesome way to start and end the day. This recital of words amongst a group, this meditation or prayer, soothes the being. Indeed, it reinforces a tone of gratitude and thankfulness.

Riverside, each morning before launching our vessels on our inaugural Two Row on the Grand, with our paddler community gathered in a circle, the words that come before all else were spoken by one of our community members, first in one of our Six Nations languages, and then interpreted in English. Our minds truly did become one, and our connectedness developed and was strengthened over the days that followed. We learned to offer help if we saw someone struggle, and we learned to ask for help if needed. That gratitude for all was nurtured by the river, the land, the creatures below and above the water, the trees, plants, winds, skies, and our ancestral beings.

While everyone's words were precious to me, there were several from my people that I will never forget: "Never in my life was I treated with more love and respect than I was on this journey." These words were expressed by a community member who struggles with addiction; his role on the journey was that of a safety paddler. Our sweep, who took his job seriously, made sure that no one was left behind. He never tired or complained despite the many times towing a weary paddler to the next stop or sometimes making several portage trips along the way for those who didn't have the strength to continue.

Another of our community members, in his late forties at that time, expressed to this intimate circle of allies and Indigenous paddlers that

11.6 Gathering for one last rest stop before the final push to arrive in Port Maitland. (Credit: Ellie Joseph, August 20, 2020)

he was raised to never trust non-native people and to avoid them where possible. This was a common sentiment among my people who had come from past generations that knew only oppression and mistrust. However, he continued participating in Two Row on the Grand, and he instead developed a new perspective and many wholesome friendships among the ally paddlers. A third paddler, a female in her late teens, shared with the group that she had struggled with anxiety and depression for many years. This Two Row on the Grand event developed and nurtured a close connection to nature within her, and she recognized that this was just what she needed to help her find balance and inner peace. She shed tears during her turn to speak, but her message ended with the most radiant smile.

This close and intimate group setting had set the tone for individuals to share their vulnerabilities, perhaps for the first time for some. After all, these paddlers had sat shoulder to shoulder at the picnic tables during each of our supper hours, paired up to assist one another, to carry kayaks and canoes, or set up and take down tents. They had reached out to help someone up a slippery bank and pointed out to each other the little blessings of lily pads, blue herons, eagles in flight, and egret nests. They had shared sunscreen, rain gear, insect repellent, snacks, flashlights, and, of course, laughter.

It was on this last day when folks said their goodbyes, gave tight hugs, and promised to keep in touch, somehow, that my Paddle Brother Jay and

I just knew without even saying it to each other that this event, this good medicine for allies and Haudenosaunee alike, needed to continue. The Two Row Wampum Treaty was truly in action during this event. Peace, friendship, and respect. Right relationships. Hope for future generations.

## ALLY LEARNING AND HEALING—JAY

We have paddlers who come from as far away as Orillia, Ontario; Zürich, Switzerland; Dubai; and New Zealand. Allies come to learn about past and present experiences of being Indigenous, to experience the culture, to learn from the river, to be present with Indigenous people, and to share the journey as brothers and sisters together in one paddle family.

Allies have shared what it has been like for them on the Two Row on the Grand:

> "This has been a real eye-opener for me. I never realized how deeply the trauma goes."

> "I've been wanting to show my support for Indigenous peoples but never knew how. The teamwork has been a real release for me."

> "I really appreciate the spirituality of the teachings. This is medicine for my spirit."

> "This has been life-changing!"

For me, the opportunity to make a positive difference in the lives of Indigenous and non-Indigenous people, to bring the two closer together, has been the most beneficial effect of the Two Row on the Grand. As a Christian whose national church ran residential schools for the government, each stroke along this river, side by side with Indigenous friends, is both an act of defiance against past and present wrongs and an act of worship. I feel more deeply connected with both creation and Creator through this experience, during which I gladly offer my time and all my capacities for this very fruitful reward.

11.7 Sunset paddle on the Grand River! "Best Day Ever!" (Credit: Ellie Joseph, May 2, 2020)

## THE FUTURE—ELLIE

Even as a very young girl, I cherished the healing gifts of the Grand River, from the immense power she can wield in times of ice breakup and spring floods that rejuvenate the body after a long winter to the comfort and tranquility that she can provide to calm the spirit. I only need to watch the sunrise or experience our Grandmother Moon's beautifully shimmering glow rippling on the water to hear what the land has to say. I must listen. Now, as an older woman approaching my seventh decade in a few short years, I am experiencing a sense of urgency to further develop a deeper connection with nature, with gratitude, with a good mind. I have a strong desire for the right relationships—with myself, my friends and family, my community, and my allies.

My hope is that we can keep Two Row on the Grand Paddle alive and that our youth, Haudenosaunee and ally alike, have the necessary skills and desire to uphold our Two Row Wampum Treaty for the faces yet to come. It will be a much better world.

CHAPTER TWELVE

# The Deep and Rippling Consciousness of Water

## Youth Experiences of Transition with the Two Row on the Grand River Paddle

*Bonnie M. Freeman and Trish van Katwyk*

### INTRODUCTION

Since the release of the Truth and Reconciliation Commission (TRC) Calls to Action in 2015, little has been written about reconciliation initiatives that have been undertaken between Indigenous and non-Indigenous communities, particularly among youth. The focus on youth in this chapter is timely because Indigenous leadership identifies reconciliation as critical to bringing forth truth, acknowledgement, and healing to both Indigenous and non-Indigenous peoples. This chapter explores how six Indigenous and six non-Indigenous youth see and understand the world as they engage in and learn about the Tekéni Teyohà:ke Kahswénhta through their participation in a joint community-based initiative and research project, the *Two Row Canoe Paddle on the Grand River*. The youth involved in this project shared what they have come to understand about themselves while learning an Indigenous view of history and culture, the importance of community building and relationships, and environmental justice.

This chapter provides an opportunity to understand the pathways of both Indigenous and non-Indigenous youth "coming to know again"[1] by connecting to the original teachings and methods of the Haudenosaunee in learning about peace, respect, and friendship through the Tekéni Teyohà:ke Kahswénhta while mutually respecting each other's ways of life.[2] We two authors, Bonnie and Trish, joined the canoe paddle described in Ellie Joseph and Jay Bailey's chapter in this volume in 2015 and, as a result of our initial experience on the river, decided to invite both Indigenous and non-Indigenous youth to participate in a project (2016–19) that focused on bringing together Haudenosaunee community members of Six Nations of the Grand River with neighboring communities and people living along the Grand River as a form of reconciliation.

In this chapter, we provide a reflection on the journey and the needs of both Indigenous and non-Indigenous youth as they move beyond themselves to a place of growth, transformation, and awakening regarding social justice. As Education writer Alun David Morgan puts it, "undertaking an *actual* journey is often seen as an outward expression of, and crucially a catalyst for… an inner [psychological or spiritual] journey."[3] Accordingly, we and the youth found that the body, mind, and the world align through journeying on the river, and the journey became more than arriving at the final destination—it became a process, one which involved the transformation, clarification, and liberation of the journey experience.[4] The land, water, and natural environment connects us to "a conscious cultural act rather than a means to an end,"[5] and the assertion of agency is connected to the past, present, and future for all people.[6]

## THE TWO ROW CANOE PADDLE ON THE GRAND RIVER

As mentioned in Ellie Joseph and Jay Bailey's chapter, the Two Row Canoe Paddle on the Grand River was developed by local Six Nations Haudenosaunee and non-Indigenous community members from Southern Ontario who had taken part in the 2013 Two Row Wampum Renewal Campaign starting on the Hudson River from Albany, New York. This renewal campaign brought over two hundred Indigenous and settler canoe and kayak paddlers together to polish and renew the 1613 Two Row Wampum agreement.[7] The original thirteen-day trip ended in New York City, where the paddlers were welcomed by the Dutch Consul General and Haudenosaunee Knowledge Keepers. The paddlers were presented at the United Nations during International Day of the World's Indigenous Peoples.[8] At the United Nations, the Haudenosaunee shared the importance and foundational principles of the continuing and long-standing agreement between the Haudenosaunee and the settlers/newcomers to North America.[9] The Two Row Renewal journey on the Hudson River inspired two paddlers from Six Nations and Paris, Ontario, to co-found the annual Two Row on the Grand River paddle. Ellie Joseph and Jay Bailey describe how this initiative developed in their contribution to this book.

The Grand River in Southern Ontario is a significant location, central to the Haudenosaunee and the Mississaugas of the Credit. The Haudenosaunee have always maintained their sovereignty and nationhood as Onkwehonwe nations. For their alliance with the Queen of England and the British during the Revolutionary War (1775–1783), the Haldimand Proclamation of 1784 gifted the Mohawk and the Haudenosaunee 950,000 acres of land on either side of the Grand River from the mouth to the source.[10] For the co-founders of the paddle, the Haldimand Tract and the river at its centre signify an important place to bring together the Haudenosaunee and their neighboring communities along the Grand River in peace, respect, and friendship. The first Two Row Paddle on the Grand River began as a one-time initiative in 2015, and now it has become an annual grassroots event.

At the same time, a discussion group between members of Deyohahá:ge:, the Indigenous Knowledge Centre at Six Nations Polytechnic[11] and academics (Indigenous and settlers) at McMaster University began meeting in 2013. The Two Row Research group began to reflect upon and share ideas about how the Tekéni Teyohà:ke Kahswénhta could consider research and scholarly practices within a Haudenosaunee framework.[12] At one of their meetings, a community researcher wondered if the principles of the Tekéni Teyohà:ke Kahswénhta could be put into action as a research paradigm. Bonnie, one of the founders of this discussion group, suggested to the group that she participate in the Two Row Paddle on the Grand as a pilot project to see from a community perspective how the teachings of the Tekéni Teyohà:ke Kahswénhta might be used to bring members from both Haudenosaunee/Indigenous and settler backgrounds together as a form of reconciliation. At this time, Bonnie decided to invite Trish to join her on this pilot research exploration with the 2015 Two Row on the Grand Paddle.[13] After three days of paddling and long discussions about what they learned and experienced, Bonnie and Trish garnered support from the Two Row co-founders and Two Row Research group to apply for an Insight Development SSHRC application, which was successfully funded. This research focused on learning more about the Two Row as a research paradigm, as well as how alliances and reconciliation between Indigenous Peoples and settlers (particularly youth) can be supported by Two Row Wampum teachings.[14]

In 2017, six Indigenous youth and six settler youth were invited to participate in pre-journey discussions and community meals as they engaged in three days of the Two Row on the Grand Paddle. Afterwards, the youth were invited to share their experience of the paddle through interviews and by creating digital stories on what they learned about reconciliation, relationship, and alliance. They were also asked about the ongoing impact of their journey and paddle experience. The next section of this paper highlights the thoughts and stories shared by both Indigenous and settler youth regarding their experience while on the Two Row Canoe Paddle.

### THOUGHTS AND STORIES OF INDIGENOUS YOUTH

Indigenous youth[15] who participated on the paddle described their initial sense of fear and risk as they left their places of comfort—home, family, and friends—to enter into an unfamiliar situation with the Two Row Paddle group and on the river. Most of the fear that Indigenous youth shared was about the physical challenges of paddling long distances, ranging from twelve to twenty-six kilometres per day. However, as the youth became familiar with their canoe or kayak, their fear lessened, and their confidence and joy grew.

Another fear described by youth was their hesitation about being in close proximity with non-Native people, anticipating that they would be judged and stereotyped not only for being "Native" but also for being young. One khe'kén:'a sister[16] shared her sense, prior to the paddle, that she would need to be ready to have her defenses up. She explains that the canoe journey allowed her to reduce her fear and embrace the experience, which provided her with a different outlook not only on the paddle but also on non-Indigenous people:

> I kind of feel like I need my guard up in a sense, but that's related to something completely different. That's just because of the whole missing and murdered thing with Indigenous women. I've had my (partner) tell me you don't need to worry about that because you're not in Saskatchewan or you're not in wherever, but it's like it happens everywhere. So, I had my defense up.
>
> I [realized I] wasn't going to go missing and murdered on the Grand River while I'm on this Two Row journey. I didn't feel like anything was going to happen. It was a good experience and a really good environment. That's what I enjoyed about it. It was nice, and it gave me a different outlook on life. (Khe'kén:'a sister 2)

This Khe'kén:'a sister described the experience where paddlers could re-encounter themselves and were able to step away from the judgement, stress, worry, and fast-paced lifestyle that kept them from deeply connecting to themselves and others. Reassurances from both Indigenous and non-Indigenous adults participating in the paddle provided an environment in which Indigenous youth could reduce their levels of fear, anxiety, and defensiveness. Instead, they shifted to feelings of courage, mutual respect, and a sense of belonging with all the participants in the paddle group. The paddle provided Indigenous youth with an opportunity to step away from their regular lives and to immerse in a different experience that included caring for people, a sense of community, and a connection to the natural world. Another Khe'kén:'a sister shared her thoughts on letting her guard down and her connection with being on the water.

> I love the feeling. I like the feeling, you're out of the rat race. You're out of judgement. You're out...you don't have to worry about your bills for a minute. You're out of the world for a bit, you know, like relief. It was an awakening last year. That's what I was saying about the cultural aspects

about getting to know different kinds of people. It's ok to let my guard down and be myself without feeling judged. It was a good feeling, and I didn't want it to end.

    It's freedom being on the water, being able to be yourself, knowing that everybody accepts everybody without…you know, and it's like family. It didn't change when I saw everybody this year, it's like…give everybody big hugs and [say] 'it's good to see you and glad you're here.' That means a lot, because some people don't get that all the time. (Khe'kén:'a sister 1)

Feeling this connection while on the water and in the natural environment, youth became more aware of and talked about the reciprocity of relationships they had with other paddlers. The paddle enabled youth to work cooperatively with everyone, to witness that cooperation in action, from pulling vessels out of the river, assisting with meals, and sharing snacks between vessels to providing encouragement and support when the paddling became difficult even for some of the adults. For example, one Khe'kén:'a sister talked about how she "really liked how everybody pulled together and they did their own dishes, or they helped do dishes, or they would help people. There were good changes, people coming together like a community." (Khe'kén:'a sister 1)

Indigenous youth reflected on the Good Mind[17] and the principles of the Tekéni Teyohà:ke Kahswénhta, where respect and appreciation of difference were honoured, when they discussed the notion of alliances in considering relationships and close friendships with the community of Indigenous and settler paddlers. One value that youth regularly encountered was humility, which guided an ongoing and open desire to learn from one another and for each paddler to teach and share their knowledge. This Khe'kén:'a sister shares her conversation with a settler adult and remembers the importance of respect from the cultural teachings that were shared during the paddle:

The Historian [on the paddle], we were able to share stories and a little bit of history with each other. He shared most of the history about the colonialists and the Haudenosaunee working together. I also learned that it's not that difficult to be able to work with the other or the alliance. Yeah, I gained some knowledge about it, and it was good to be able to learn from the others. Like I said, what I learned was to put yourself in the other person's shoes so that you are understanding. While that's one of the things from the Great Law and how you should be able to speak well and listen well. It was good to be able to do that and listen to them and get to understand them and then speak out about myself and my family. I think it would have been good too to have more Indigenous people on the paddle because I wasn't sure what to expect. I mean I'm glad that they had the students there, that was good, they seemed to have fun and it was nice to be able to try and teach. I remember when we were teaching those young girls to sing our songs that one night. (Khe'kén:'a sister 2)

Youth also described the value of compassion as part of the Good Mind, where they were able to encounter others with respect, peace, and friendship. The value of compassion also enriched their experience so that a deep and trusting experience of family developed. For some of these youth, the experience of nurturing family was something that they had not experienced within their own biological families. This Khe'kén:'a sister shares how it felt good to be part of such a welcoming kin-like group:

It felt good to be accepted and felt good that nobody judged anybody, everybody had a good attitude. Everybody was happy. I was like, what the hell? How can all of these people get along and act like family? You know, look after each other, everybody helped each other without question and that's major because I've never been a part of anything like that. It changed my outlook on how we get along, Native and non-Native. (Khe'kén:'a sister 1)

The power of alliance and friendship on the river was also significant for Indigenous youth. As they engaged with settler youth, they recognized that the dichotomies and stereotypes imposed by the outside world could disappear, and they could become more connected in the journey and with this paddling community. A Khe'kén:'a sister shared her view on the significance of responsibility and change:

It's our responsibility to change the way we look at each other, because if we don't do it, who's gonna? If people don't see that it's possible to break stereotypes or break, I guess you could say, the bad blood, then how else are we gonna do it? Why not on the water, where everything disappears, and we're all there for the same thing. Like I said freedom, happiness—you want to be happy when you're on the water. (Khe'kén:'a sister 1)

The connection to the water and the natural environment for Indigenous youth plays a significant role. The freedom and feeling of happiness they experienced on the water provided youth with the opportunity to develop responsibility and change. A poem written by one of our Khe'kén:'a sisters describes how the deep connections she felt with the natural world (water, land, and sky), as well with humans and animals, were guided by the values and principles of The Great Law of Peace:

"Animals and people coming together in nature"

The river flows before my eyes
And takes me to the seven skies
Underneath the river of love
To the kayakers above
From the tree of peace
And the tree of love,
The Eagle stands.......
…..still.
Sigh ……… (Khe'kén:'a sister 3)

This Khe'kén:'a sister's poem evokes a sense of empathy as well, describing life from different perspectives, looking at what is before us, looking underneath, looking up, as well as the actions of coming together, "flows and stands still." The poem shows how Indigenous youth involved with the paddle described their experiences as a part of something larger than themselves, a transformation that occurred during the Two Row Paddle that connected them on an emotional and spiritual level to one another and the living world of the river. The final deep sigh in the last line evokes a relationship so that each person who experiences this sigh will connect to a feeling that comes from their own experience of the sigh. For example, as we listened to the Khe'kén:'a sister read this poem, the sigh evoked a sense of more-than-intellectual understanding and a mutual respect that arises from belonging to this natural world. Like the poem, these youth described how the paddle experience transformed them in a way that would endure beyond the paddle and well into their daily lives. The friendships, personal experiences, and stories that each youth shared had an everlasting effect and provided a feeling that would carry through time despite their being apart from one another until the next paddle.

## THOUGHTS AND STORIES OF SETTLER YOUTH

Settler youth who participated on the Two Row Paddle shared stories about the realizations that occurred for them. A significant realization was about how a new, expansive conceptualization of relationship was introduced through the collective river journey and the traditional teachings about the Tekéni Teyohà:ke Kahswénhta with its principles of peace, friendship, and respect. The relationships described included a consideration of how change was experienced in the youth's relationships with themselves as they gained a new sense of competence and independence as well as interdependence. The youth talked about deep connections and personal reflections as they developed new paddling skills while they were immersed in the moment, the river, and the collective. One youth described her experience as she kayaked on her own for the first time:

> It felt even more...like just in the surroundings because you just got your own wave that you are going to move through it. As much as teamwork is important, it is hard sometimes...I think a big focus of the Two Row is the companion sort of thing. Working with others. [When I was kayaking] I felt maybe more like I could actually take in...what the other boats were doing in a different way. And...a lot of the trip was hard for us..., but it was interesting being a single thing on the water. It made me more aware...more present, I think. (Younger sister 1)[18]

There was a sense of interdependence within the group, where self and personal location were experienced within a collectivity.

The river and the natural world became important living beings to engage in relationship, to carefully listen to for guidance, and to show accountability and responsibility. One youth described how emotionally affected she was by a landscape she was looking at with different eyes:

> being connected to the land that we live on, knowing that this is so close to home is incredible, and strange that I didn't quite realize how beautiful and how long the river goes and how different it is, like, along like every turn, every turn….it was just really moving. (Younger sister 1)

As the Indigenous and non-Indigenous youth considered themselves allies, they considered the responsibilities that are inherent in such a relationship. In reflecting upon these responsibilities, the youth referenced the actions that would be their contribution to the alliance, actions that include speaking out about Indigenous rights and oppressive colonial structures, as well as opposing environmental damage and the exploitation of the natural world. One youth considered the actions she could take:

> Definitely having conversations with people who didn't get to experience [the paddle], and teaching them about what I have learned, it's kind of like being able to spread the word about it, so people can come back the next year and experience it for themselves, but if they are not able to, they still have my stories to be able to live vicariously through. I feel like the storytelling is really important for people to have a bit of knowledge and understanding what's going on outside of their education, as if like, for me and for other people who are in my Indigenous Studies class it's kind of what's happening outside of the classroom, there is so much more going on. There are ways to get involved outside of that confining room and those experiences can definitely help shape a worldview, of how you see your environment, and if I am able to share those kinds of experiences with people and have them understand, even in the slightest, and they would be able to change their view on the world as well. (Younger sister 2)

The youth described the extensive unlearning that would need to take place to engage in the relationship described by the Tekéni Teyohà:ke Kahswénhta, framed by the Good Mind. The unlearning occurred as they engaged in collective, interdependent approaches to community and listened to traditional Haudenosaunee teachings that featured the Good Mind, peace, and thanksgiving. One youth told a story about the challenge to his individualized sense of achievement:

> ... my commitment to conquer the challenge of carrying a canoe solo, for which I had been preparing since the night before. [My Indigenous knowledge holder's] voice broke into my localized awareness once again, "Get over here and help the rest of us get to land!" It was at this point that I realized the folly of my personal heroic goal. This portage was for the whole group to get through, not just for me to challenge myself. (Younger brother)

The youth described their realizations about the influence of a colonial mindset. One youth explained: "(E)ven in your process of unlearning, you might have not fully unlearned everything yet...I just know that there are things that are ingrained in us, as much as we might care" (Younger sister 1). The youth described the ways in which the colonial mindset is integrated into many of the systems they have participated in, such as educational systems where colonizer versions of history, knowledge production, and spirituality constricted the possibilities to understand more fully the experiences of Indigenous people. The youth made connections between colonization and neoliberal ideologies by identifying the unlearning that occurred for them as they re-encountered ideas of individualized success, private ownership, human-centrism, and white supremacist views of family, morality, and personal worth. One youth described the impact of the paddle experience on her new mindset with regard to the river:

> It has definitely made me more conscious of the environment around me and how it's not just a simple tree, it's so much more than that. It's a life that is giving me life and how my actions affect that life. It's definitely made me realize that there is a circle and it made me truly be able to see that, and that circle is so prevalent in everyday life. It also made me so much more connected to the water that I live nearby, even though we never really went directly through [my town], it definitely made me

realize that the water here is just as important as any other water and that it needs to be protected, especially with like Nestle coming in and trying to take the water. It definitely makes me think a lot more about the actions of the community and my personal actions. It definitely makes me more aware. (Younger sister 2)

The unlearning was described as a disruption where the hold of a colonial mindset was loosened, and new perceptions and understanding could occur. Two noteworthy disruptions were related to time and knowledge. The youth described a different, nonlinear experience of time where the past, present, and future were contained within and relevant to the moment they had become immersed in while paddling and engaging in dialogue on the river. The youth recognized the criticality of historicizing the present to gain a deeper understanding of how profoundly their day-to-day experience is shaped and distorted by the history of colonialism and the trauma of colonial violence against Indigenous people. In considering a provincial policy on a newly proposed health curriculum, for example, one youth described what it was like to gain a new perspective on the impact of history:

how awful that is and how much that affects, like, generations past me, and it kind of made me think a lot about the seven generations teaching and how one simple decision, Ford [provincial premier] deciding that that is no longer a part of education, and that has all those implications, and how not only was it Sex Ed, it was also [the absence of Indigenous learning and pedagogy], so that affects all the progress that has been made and how that will affect the ongoing teachings, the future generations. (Younger sister 2)

Ideas about knowledge were also disrupted for the youth. They described the powerful learning that came from metaphors that they learned about life, growth, communication, and the feeling of connection. One youth described an expanded self-awareness as she considered the metaphor provided by one of the journey leaders:

I know that there was that one thing said when we were all standing in the circle around the fire pit. The stones, the big stones, the little stones, the pebbles. I was definitely a pebble, even a little sand thing, a little grain of sand, but like in the way, like I didn't necessarily carry a lot of responsibility in a context like that and I just sort of just had to go along with what the leaders did. But I think, there is, like, this support no matter how small or large of a role is played, to be part of the circle and interconnected. It is a pretty powerful thing to take away, um, and that it can manifest further in life, in whatever else I get involved in and to not shy away from doing that. (Younger sister 1)

The knowledge went further than metaphor, and, in fact, the knowledge that the youth were tapping into through metaphor was the knowledge of the natural elements, for example, the rocks and the river. These natural elements provided lessons about communication in a shared vessel. The river was described as the source, and the youth described the insight they gained from the river and the knowledge they could acquire as they became proficient in the language of the river. One youth described one of the lessons she received from the river: "because the lack of communication definitely creates more problems and that's when you get stuck on the bottom of the rocks. It's pretty much the river telling you that you need to work together" (Younger sister 2).

Empathy was identified as a valuable aspect of knowledge. This was a teaching that could be acquired through the Good Mind and the Kahswénhta principles of peace, friendship, and respect. Empathy, as knowledge, equips youth for collective ways of being. A youth talked about how important it was to be on a river whose size and continuity erased the sense of borders and private ownership from one town to another and, in so doing, fostered a sense of empathy:

it definitely creates more empathy I feel, like inside, where you, like, empathy and caring mostly, where you are able to look at someone else on the street who you have never spoken to and realize that their experiences could be the same as your experiences, and it is just a matter of having that connection, as simple as living on the same river. It just means so much more. (Younger sister 2)

The youth also described the knowledge of embodiment. They said they experienced a rich and deep kind of knowledge when they were moving, which activated multiple senses. Embodiment generates a unique knowledge that alters the way time can be experienced by expanding a moment of the past through an embodied memory. One youth described the experience of remembering some of the conversations she had while paddling with others: "I've always been able to remember them and...go back to those moments and be able to almost bathe myself in that moment again and feel as if I am back on the water with all of those people again" (Younger sister 2).

## MEANING-MAKING—ANALYSIS

As Native and settler authors of this article, we decided to enact our Two Row research framework[19] by analyzing interviews with Indigenous and settler youth separately to hear what distinctiveness was identified between the colonized experiences of Indigenous and then settler youths. This decision speaks to another lesson the Tekéni Teyohà:ke Kahswénhta offers that parallels Tuck and Yang's insistence that decolonization cannot be subsumed into a kind of universal metaphor for social justice, collapsing all efforts for equity and human rights into one.[20] Colonization has had a distinct and specific impact not only on Indigenous peoples, but also on all people. However, it is only when the distinctness of colonization is recognized that meaningful solidarities and even commensurations occur. Likewise, Daigle and Ramírez describe a process of bringing together while acknowledging distinctions, different efforts to liberate and disrupt, creating clusters that can form an overall constellation of a socially just and decolonized world.[21] Referring to these as "constellations of co-resistance,"[22] Leanne Betasamosake Simpson insists that the relationality of this work is uppermost. "Constellations exist only in the context of relationship; otherwise, they are just individual stars."[23] The same is true with Kahswénhta, as wampum belts are made of wampum beads woven together with sinew that represents the potential for solidarity, even where difference, tension, and disagreement will surely occur. However, in mutual respect and peaceful coexistence, opportunities for solidarity can exist; such relationality is radical in our current alienating, colonial world.

Our analysis began with the two of us considering the broad summary of what had emerged from all the stories and interviews together. Throughout the stories and interviews, the youth identified family, community, self, the natural environment, and transformation as themes in their learning journey. As a second step to our analysis, we each returned to the stories and interviews that correlated to our Indigenous and settler identities, and we each conducted a closer analysis of what the youth shared. As a third step, we returned together, reading through and discussing one another's analyses. In this final analysis, Bonnie highlighted a difference between the two rows. A discussion and reflection between Bonnie and Trish generated curiosity about this difference. This next section shares our dialogue and considerations about this notion of difference and how it is reflected in the words of the youth and in the teachings of the Tekéni Teyohà:ke Kahswénhta.

## DISCUSSION

**Bonnie:** You can see the subtle shifts happening emotionally for the Indigenous youth, but it is more so happening in the minds of settler youth. The difference is that the Indigenous youth were talking about relationships and emotions, and the settler youth talked more about the ways they think about things—cognitions. For the Haudenosaunee, relationships are so central. The Haudenosaunee Thanksgiving Address is rooted in the Great Law of Peace. It acknowledges all our relationships between ourselves and the natural world with humility and gratitude. The purpose of the Thanksgiving Address is to bring our minds together as one in recognition of the people, the relationship we have to people, and the relationship we have with the natural world.[24] I have heard many Haudenosaunee Knowledge Keepers in the past telling us that the natural world can exist and flourish without humans; however, humans cannot exist without the natural world. Therefore, it is our responsibility to acknowledge and show gratitude for the roles and responsibilities of everything in that natural world. Because of what we've experienced through colonization, most of us have been disengaged from that relationship. We feel it very deeply, which is why trauma, addictions, and violence can become a significant part of our lives. Even though this spark of desire for relationship is deep within us, the pain and fear of historical and contemporary traumas from colonization, racism, and strategies to erase our existence continue to haunt us.[25] The young Indigenous people we listened to spoke of the fear and lack of trust they had for the settlers on the paddle. Once these youth started seeing how the paddle was bringing them back to their ways of knowing and being with the natural environment, they began to open up after seeing people come together and work as a community. Relationships and trust began to be established between young and old, and that's where the transition happened for them. The youth know that when the Two Row Paddle happens again and, despite the time away, the sense of connection and friendship is still there. When they get back together, it will be like no time has elapsed. The small "r" of reconciliation is where really powerful things happen. This process of reconciliation is about being genuine and building trust with one another. This is where relationships are formed and lasting.

**Trish**: In the story that was told by one settler youth, he described his enlightenment, where he was able to shift out of his individualized way of thinking. For him, it was about a decolonization of the mind. This is a significant difference between the stories and interviews of the Indigenous and settler youth. One is not better than the other. It speaks to the question of what the transformations are that need to occur.

**Bonnie:** There are different processes happening for settlers and for Native people. Reconciliation for Indigenous Peoples is about reclaiming their cultural knowledge and understanding to begin healing.[26] The initial understanding of reconciliation from the settler perspective is about making things right. Settlers realize that making things right is a lot harder than they anticipate. They can become overwhelmed with fear, guilt, and shame and look for a structured solution.[27] It is not until they realize that reconciliation is more about the daily interactions and relationships they experience between people—helping with tents, sitting around the fire sharing stories about the day and laughing, eating meals, waking up, paddling, sharing snacks across vessels. Not only have settler youth learned about confidence and independence, but they also learned about interdependence. Paddling the Grand River is not enough for reconciliation; there needs to be a continued commitment and responsibility beyond the paddle and into the daily lives of settler participants.

**Trish:** As I think about the differences, I have to keep reminding myself—my own decolonization process is also of the mind—not to think about the Two Row as a binary.

**Bonnie:** That is right. Many think it is a binary because what stands out are the two purple rows between the white rows of beads. When we share the story about the canoe (Haudenosaunee) and the ship (settlers), it sounds like a binary between the two. The white rows of the Two Row Wampum are about coming together to build and maintain our lives and relationships with peace, respect, and friendship. These three white rows are the ethical foundation of how we are to live and co-exist. We have also referred to the white rows of this relationship in connection to how we are to conduct ourselves according to the Great Law of Peace and its central values of peace, power, and righteousness.[28] The heart and soul of this Wampum and the relationships we have with others is to live peacefully as stated in the Great Law of Peace, the power of respect, and to use our Good Mind and enact (righteousness) according to the principles of the Great Law of Peace which emphasize respect for the land, the natural environment, and the people.[29]

**Trish:** The relationality that is described by the Two Row Wampum is disruptive in terms of the disconnected, human-centric model of relationship (or non-relationship) proffered through the colonizer lens. Commodification shapes so many relationships and transposes a utilitarian, objectifying interaction upon the deep and open "being with" that the Two Row depicts.[30] Within that commodifying culture, the "Other" is established in order to coerce, cheat, and pursue a never-fulfilled accumulation. This paradigm generates an equation in which there is one who deserves and one who does not deserve. "Undeserving" is determined through an assessment of humanity so that all who are assessed as being not fully human are undeserving of knowledge, spirituality, and place. Such a model of relationship (or non-relationship) is an exploitative transaction between humans and all that is deemed not human: "savages," animals, land, water, stars, planets, and beyond. The language of "it" allows exploitation to happen.[31] These de-personalizing categories help with this capacity to commodify.

**Bonnie:** Colonization is an explicit project with outcomes that involve violence, trauma, and a persevering relentlessness that specifically targets Indigenous existence with an ethic of consumption, abolishment, and displacement or replacement. The colonial project thrives with the many tenets of neoliberal ideology: competition in order to create an inequity that can support gains for a select few; accumulation so that the gains of the few can multiply; exploitation so the inequity of the accumulation can flourish; binary so that a moral code of deserving and undeserving can be applied to the inequity that characterizes the consumption of resources and opportunities; private ownership that is justified by a Eurocentric superiority to possess and is fortified by the principles of competition, accumulation, and exploitation.[32] The principles of the Two Row Wampum stand in stark contrast to this. In the Wampum, then, we find the generative disorder that Fanon insisted would be the only way that the decolonization process can occur: "Decolonization, which sets out to change the order of the world, is, obviously, a program of complete disorder."[33]

**Trish:** I think the neoliberal categorization of things imposes definitions, for example, of what a family is, and anyone who steps outside of this category is to be suspected. A narrow definition of family accommodates a utilitarian, coercive, and exclusive relationality. In their interviews and stories, the Indigenous and settler youth talked about family, but in different ways.

**Bonnie:** Remember, one settler storyteller was hesitant about the aspect of the family he was being introduced to. This says a lot! The Indigenous youth were hesitant, fearful, and resistant about family, but then they opened up when they were able to feel a connection. The settler youth did, too, but to some extent, there was some kind of boundary that kind of halted things for the settler youth. Whereas from an Indigenous perspective, even when people are not connected by blood, we are family. You and I, we're sisters, so your daughters are my nieces, and my son would be your nephew.

One life, according to the Two Row, is as important as the other, and all lives are intertwined in a mutual regard. An experience of family is deeply shaped by this intertwined and mutual understanding of all lives. The Two Row Wampum, with its infinite lines, flow of life, parallel and non-interfering depictions, and the way it brings lives together to share an ethics of peace, respect, and friendship, presents another order, thus disordering a colonial world by insisting upon humility, gratitude, embrace of difference, peace, acceptance, friendship, respect, and righteousness.

**Trish:** Another decolonization of the mind process that settler youth described had to do with time. Disorder, disruption, and unsettling also can impact how time is considered. I am thinking about how relevant history became to the present moment and the future for the settler youth as they critiqued the ways they had been misinformed about history in institutions like schools.[34] Historicity is an important concept. It calls for deep awareness and ongoing curiosity about the ways in which the present moment is shaped by both history and possible futures. The settler youth described how difficult it was for them to fully understand the current colonized reality without understanding the ways in which historic colonization has built structures and displaced Indigenous ones through comprehensive measures. The colonized state we currently inhabit, the deep and ongoing colonizing impact of our multitude of institutions, the depth and mundanity of settler privilege and Indigenous trauma are most clear within a historical context. With such an acknowledgement of history, we can comprehend the impact the current moment will have on the future. A decolonized understanding of time is the appreciation of how past, present, and future are collapsed together,[35] profoundly relevant to one another. The rows on the Wampum express a similar decolonized collapse of past, present, and future, where there is no beginning or end to each line: they are there, travelling alongside in an everlasting relationship engaged in a parallel journey on the river of life that is committed to a past, present, and future.

**Bonnie:** The youth who spoke with us and shared their journey and stories told us about the disruption that is possible through a commitment to the Two Row Wampum. The experience on the river and the lessons about the Wampum that the youth shared with us brought enlightenment about the significant unlearning that the process of decolonization requires, as both a meaning-making process and a relational healing process through reclaiming and understanding their cultural knowledge. To decolonize for these youth and for the participants on this paddle is to bring complete disorder to their world.[36] Decolonization is a process of resistance and rupture that will liberate people from the violence of colonization[37] and bring them peace within themselves and with others.

## CONCLUSION

The paddle experience provided a sense of new understanding and perspective, accompanied by a connection to and awareness of the Grand River, a commitment to the grassroots paddle project, and a hopeful attitude about relationships and alliances and about the personal capacity and worth of young people. The transformation or internal shift that the youth described was one that could be sustained through new realizations as well through the active commitment to remaining engaged with this community initiative. Connections between the participants' sense of self and community evolved during the paddle, and this evolution was strong and evident. Both Indigenous and settler youth described an awareness of their identity that became immersed in the context of their paddle family. The youth's connection to a sense of self (in their own purple rows) allowed them to acquire patience and compassion that permitted a deeper awareness (across the white rows of the river) of other people and their surroundings. With patience, youth could step out of their fast-paced lives and develop a deep connection to the land, water, and natural environment. In doing so, the youth realized that it became possible to develop empathy and compassion for the experience of others, to experience respect and acceptance even when there is difference. One Khe'kén:'a/younger sister described one of the teachings she heard during the paddle that really resonated with her: "Everyone is born innocent." She realized that we are not damaged or bad when we are born and that negative experiences in life happen to everyone. For the youth on this paddle, this statement allowed them to recognize a place of innocence for all people, including themselves, and that they can experience the good in life.

# Contributors

**AMBER MEADOW ADAMS** Kanyen'kehaka niyakonhwenstyò:ten nok non:wa wehniseratennyons kahyonhakta ye'teron Tsi Kahontayen. Senha ahsen niwahsen niyohserake tsi nahe, yakoterihwayenhstonhatyehahkwe' ne okarashon'a. Ohna'kenha tsi wa'ehyatonhserayenterha'tahkwa'tsherihsa' (ne:ne kwi eytsya ti tsi niyonkwarihòten) skennenha wetetiyonhkehte' tsi akaonhahahon:we. Onwa yekarakayonhatsha tsi yehyatonnyons ne yokara:se. Tokat nonwa ayeyontatya'tenhawe' n'onhka'ok tsi akaonhahahon:we, tokat ayakowennahnironhke.'

**PHANUEL ANTWI** is a poet, literary cultural critic, and researcher in the field of critical Black studies. He is an associate professor in the Department of English Language and Literatures at the University of British Columbia in Vancouver. In 2022, he was named Canada Research Chair in Black Arts and Epistemologies. He writes, researches, and teaches critical Black studies, settler-colonial studies, Black Atlantic and diaspora studies, Canadianliterature and culture since 1830, critical race, gender, and sexuality studies, and material cultures. He has published articles in *Interventions* and *Studies in Canadian Literature*, and has curated art exhibits at the Vancouver Art Gallery and at the Libby Leshgold Gallery at Emily Carr University. His book, *On Cuddling: Loved to Death in the Racial Embrace*, was published in 2024 by Pluto Press, and he is completing a second book, *Currencies of Blackness: Cheerfulness, Faithfulness, and Politeness in Settler Writing*.

After thirty-five years of teaching French, **JAY BAILEY** has become an authentic voyageur, paddling over four thousand kilometres on the fur trade routes of North America, equipped as in 1800. He has staged over five hundred voyageur events, live and online. He is also a published software designer/programmer and curriculum writer. In 2013, his Paddle Sister, Ellie Joseph, invited him to paddle the Two Row Wampum

Renewal Campaign Paddle on the Hudson River. He, Ellie, and two other participants felt it was important to bring the same teachings and experience to communities along the Grand River. They started the annual Two Row on the Grand in 2016.

**DANIEL COLEMAN** is recently retired from Department of English and Cultural Studies at McMaster University and is an associate professor at Six Nations Polytechnic on the Grand River territory. He is fascinated by the power of narrative arts to generate a sense of place and community, mindfulness, and especially wonder. His books include *Masculine Migrations* (1998), *The Scent of Eucalyptus* (2003), *White Civility* (2006; best book in the Humanities in Canada), *In Bed with the Word* (2009), and *Yardwork: A Biography of an Urban Place* (2017, RBC Taylor Prize finalist) a book about the human and environmental history of his home in Hamilton. He has coedited ten scholarly volumes on topics such as early Canadian culture, Caribbean Canadian writing, masculinities, postcoloniality, race, the retooling of the humanities, and displacement.

**SCOT COOPER** RP (he/him) is a registered psychotherapist and manager at a children's mental health centre in Ontario. Scot is a white settler on the territories of the Anishinaabe, Haudenosaunee, and Attawandaron nations. His people are English and Scottish. Scot teaches brief narrative therapy and community work locally and internationally. In practice since 1998, his experience includes specialization in single-session therapy; narrative practice with children, youth and families; and transforming service pathways making services accessible and responsive.

**BONNIE M. FREEMAN** is an Algonquin/Mohawk from the Six Nations of the Grand River Territory and is currently an associate professor in the School of Social Work and the Department of Indigenous Studies at McMaster University. Her work and research are rooted in her connections with Six Nations and Indigenous communities throughout Canada and the United States. Her participatory research studies use an Indigenous methodological perspective of journeying, with a key goal of understanding how Indigenous Knowledge and connection to land and water contributes to positive health and well-being, as well as looking at reconciliation between Indigenous Peoples, non-Indigenous people, and communities through a canoe journey on the Grand River.

**SARA GENERAL** is Mohawk Nation, Turtle Clan from Six Nations of the Grand River, where she lives with her husband and three children. She is an assistant professor and coordinator of the Indigenous Studies program at United College at the University of Waterloo. Sara is a writer, artist, researcher, and language learner. She is currently studying Kanyen'kéha (Mohawk) at Onkwawenna Kenytohkwa. Sara has worked with several Indigenous organizations including the Six Nations Language Commission, Six Nations Polytechnic, and the Deyohahá:ge Indigenous Knowledge Centre. Through her company Spirit & Intent, she makes books, art, and films that celebrate Haudenosaunee languages, stories, and knowledges. Her research interests include Indigenous language learning, Ogwehoweh language revitalization, Indigenous cultural stories, and Indigenous art.

**TAYLOR LEEAL GIBSON:** My name is Taylor Gibson, Turtle Clan, Cayuga Nation, and I'm from Six Nations of the Grand River. I'm currently the senior researcher at Deyohahá:ge Indigenous Knowledge Centre. I have over ten years of experience working in archives and research and am a lifelong learner of the Gayogo̱hó:nǫ' language. I have a passion for preservation of Hodihnohso:ni documentary history, culture, and languages. When I'm not working, I enjoy spending time with my family.

**RICK HILL** is a citizen of the Beaver Clan of the Tuscarora Nation of the Haudenosaunee at Grand River. A practicing artist, curator, art historian, writer, and public speaker, he currently serves as the Indigenous innovation specialist at Mohawk College in Hamilton, Ontario, and as a cultural advisor to FNTI in the Tyendinaga Mohawk Territory. He holds a master's degree in American Studies from the State University of New York at Buffalo and has held many influential positions over the years, including assistant director for public programs, National Museum of the American Indian, Smithsonian Institution; museum director, Institute of American Indian Arts, Santa Fe, New Mexico; assistant professor, Native American Studies, SUNY Buffalo; senior project coordinator of the Deyohahá:ge:

Indigenous Knowledge Centre at Six Nations Polytechnic in Ohsweken, Ontario. He has been centrally involved with other Haudenosaunee since the 1970s in repatriating wampum from museums and private collections around the world.

**ELLIE JOSEPH** is of the Mohawk Nation, Turtle Clan, born, raised, and still living on the Six Nations Reserve along the bank of the Grand River. She retired from a thirty-seven-year tenure as a classroom teacher at elementary schools in the public school system several years ago, but remains an active volunteer in the education field. After participating in the sixteen-day Two Row Renewal Campaign from Albany to Manhattan, New York, on The Hudson River in 2013, she was one of four participants who established what is now known as Two Row on the Grand. This ten-day paddle excursion from Cambridge to Port Maitland brings the Six Nations Community together with ally participants. Cultural teachings are presented along the way, encouraging healthy relationships and connections to Mother Earth. Functioning as a grassroots volunteer committee, she saw this project's participation more than double in size in its nine years of existence. Plans are already underway for Two Row on the Grand 2025. For more information, please visit www.tworowonthegrandriver.com

**DR. KELSEY LEONARD** is an assistant professor in the Faculty of Environment at the University of Waterloo, where her research focuses on Indigenous water justice and its climatic, territorial, and governance underpinnings. Dr. Leonard seeks to establish Indigenous traditions of water conservation as the foundation for international water policymaking. Dr. Leonard has been instrumental in safeguarding the interests of Indigenous Nations for environmental planning and building Indigenous science and knowledge into new solutions for water governance and sustainable oceans. Dr. Leonard is an enrolled citizen of the Shinnecock Nation.

**OREN LYONS** (b. 1930), artist, painter, professor, lacrosse player, and founder of the Iroquois Nationals lacrosse team, is a member of the Onondaga and Seneca nations of the Iroquois Confederacy and a Faithkeeper of the Turtle Clan of the Onondaga Nation. A world-renowned leader and visionary for peace, justice, and sovereignty, Chief Oren Lyons worked with Indigenous Peoples around the world as well as the United Nations for recognition of Indigenous rights. He has addressed the UN General Assembly and other gatherings of world leaders and is a member of the advisory committee for the UN Environment Program. He has served as a speaker, author, publisher, and board member of the Traditional Circle of Indian Elders and Youth, as well as the Seventh Generation Fund for Indian Development. A prominent member of the UN Global Forum of Spiritual and Parliamentary Leaders and a retired professor emeritus of American Indian Studies, SUNY Buffalo, Lyons is the author of several books and the subject of many documentaries and films. Along with other awards, he is the recipient of the Ellis Island Congressional Medal of Honor, the United Nations NGO World Peace Prize, the Smithsonian's Award for Art and Cultural Achievement, and Sweden's prestigious Friend of the Children Award, along with colleague Nelson Mandela.

**SUZIE MILLER** (BA, BEd, MPed.) is currently a teacher consultant with the Grand Erie District School Board. She is Mohawk Wolf Clan and lives in Caledonia. Suzie is committed to her role of honouring and promoting the teachings of the Two Row Wampum Treaty. Living between the rows is sometimes difficult to balance, but it is a place where peace, trust, and friendship exist. Suzie has confidence in the strength of our treaties and strives to teach and model their intended guiding principles in building and maintaining healthy relationships.

**DAVID NEWHOUSE**, Onondaga from the Six Nations of the Grand River, is a professor of Indigenous Studies as well as in the School of Business, and chair of the Chanie Wenjack School for Indigenous Studies. He is co-chair of the Trent Aboriginal Education Council and also teaches in the Graduate Community Economic Development (CED) Program at Concordia University. In 2016, he received the Trent Award for Education Leadership and Innovation. His research interests focus on the emergence of modern Aboriginal society. He is the founding editor of the CANDO *Journal of Aboriginal Economic Development*, the first peer-reviewed academic journal devoted to Aboriginal economic development issues, and a founding editorial board member of *Aboriginal Policy Studies*, an academic journal focusing on urban Aboriginal issues. He served as a member of the Policy Team on Economics for the Royal Commission on Aboriginal Peoples. He serves as the science officer for the Aboriginal Peoples Health research adjudication committee for the Canadian Institutes of Health Research.

**TRISH VAN KATWYK** is a settler of Dutch descent and lives in Tkaronto. Trish is the director of the School of Social Work, Renison University College, University of Waterloo. Much of her scholarship has been done in partnership with Bonnie Freeman. She engages in community-based, land-based, and arts-based approaches to inquiry to further understand and advocate for well-being across many relations.

**VANESSA WATTS** is Mohawk and Anishinaabe Bear Clan, and a member of Six Nations of the Grand River, where she lives with her husband and two children. She is an associate professor of Indigenous Studies and Sociology at McMaster University and holds the Paul R. MacPherson Chair in Indigenous Studies. Her research examines Indigenist epistemological and ontological interventions on place-based, material knowledge production. Vanessa is particularly interested in Indigenous feminisms, sociology of knowledge, Indigenous governance, and other-than-human relations as forms of Indigenous ways of knowing.

**KAYANESENH PAUL WILLIAMS** is writing about the legal ecosystems in which he journeys. He is doing his best to walk the talk.

# Glossary

*Created by Taylor Gibson*

---

| Name/Phrase/Word | Interpretation/Translation |
|---|---|
| Abusua | Twi word, which marks Akan matrilineage, a social structure that traces lineage through female lines of descent, includes both living and dead members. |
| Adonwentishon | Personal name of Catherine Croghan. The third wife of Mohawk leader Joseph Brant and the daughter of a fur trader and deputy Indian agent George Croghan. |
| Agwalongdongwas | Personal name for Good Peter, prominent Oneida historical figure who acted as spokesmen for the Oneidas during the late eighteenth century. |
| ahsonthennehkha | Mohawk word for the "night time." |
| akwe:kon | Mohawk word for "all" or "everything." |
| Akwesasne | "Where the Partridge Drums." Mohawk community bordering the provinces of Ontario and Quebec in Canada and New York State in the U.S. |

| | |
|---|---|
| Anishinaabek | A First Nations group culturally and linguistically linked to the Great Lakes Region in Canada and the U.S. This group belongs to the Algonquian language family. |
| Anishinaabekwe | Anishinaabemowin for "Anishinaabe woman." |
| Anishinaabemowin | The name for the Anishinaabe language. |
| Anishnaabewin Niwin | Anishinaabemowin for "Four Rising Winds." This is also the name of an Anishinaabe academic journal. |
| anokyen | Mohawk word for "muskrat." |
| Asante | Part of the Akan people, who make up the largest ethnic and linguistic group in Ghana with 45 percent of the population. |
| Asasse Yaa | Akan name of the goddess who represents the land: *Asasse*, "Earth or ground" + *Yaa*, a name given to females born on Thursday. |
| atonwa | Mohawk name for a ceremonial personal chant. |
| Aatsi'tsya'ka:yon (also katsi'tsakayon) | Mohawk word for "Mature Blossom," in Hodihnosohni cosmology Mature Blossom was the woman who fell from the Skyworld and was responsible for bringing life to Turtle Island. |
| Awenha'i | Cayuga name—Mature Flower. Same meaning as above. |
| Yotsi'tsishon | Mohawk Name—Mature Flower. Same meaning as above. |

| | |
|---|---|
| Canajoharie | A kettle stuck on a pole, a prominent Mohawk village in 1738. Today, the present-day location is Canajoharie, New York; it is registered as a National Historic Landmark. |
| Canesatego | Fl. 1742 – d. 6 September 1750. Onondaga Chief. He was the Spokesman at the Treaty of Easton 1742. |
| Cayuga | Anglicized word for a Hodihnohsó:ni' Nation. Meaning "the People of the Swamp" or :"the People of the Great Pipe." |
| Corlaer | Arendt van Curler, the Dutch commissary at Albany, gave his name to successive governors of New York ("Corlaer" in most council records), and the title eventually spread to Indian agents in the twentieth century (usually Kora), the King in the 1701 Albany Treaty (Corachkowa, or Great Curler), and to Canada (Korahne). |
| dah nay to | Hodihnohsó:ni' word for "that is all." Used at the end of speeches made by Hodihnohsó:ni' . |
| Dayodekane | Personal name for Seth Newhouse, author, historian, and Pinetree Chief. |
| debwewin | Anisnaabemowin for "to speak the truth." |
| De'haĕn'hiyawǎ"khon' (also Teharionwakon in Mohawk) | Onondaga Name for "Holder of the Heavens." In the Hodihnohsó:ni' cosmology, this being represents the Good-minded Twin, Creation, and Renewal. |

| | |
|---|---|
| Dene Tha' | "People common to the territory." A First Nation in Northwest Alberta, Canada. They are part of the Athapaskan language family. |
| Deskaheh | "More than Eleven." Traditional Hereditary Chief title of Cayuga Nation, Bear Clan. The titles are passed down to each new successor. The author highlights two men, Harvey Longboat who held the title. The Oka Crisis erupted during his tenure. Another man is Levi General, who travelled to England and Geneva 1922–24, to protest Canada's treatment of Hodihnohsó:ni' and uphold treaty rights. |
| Deyohahá:ge: (or Deyohaha:ge:) | A Cayuga word for "Two Roads or Paths." 1. The Two Row Wampum. The founding agreement between Hodihnohsó:ni' and the Dutch. 2. Indigenous Knowledge Centre, SNP, Ontario, Canada. |
| Deyohahage Gihe gowa'hneh: (or Deyohahage Gihe hgowa'hneh) | A Cayuga word for "two paths, On the Grand River." |
| Deyohninhohhakarawenh | Personal name of King Hendrick (1660–1735), a Mohawk leader who visited Queen Anne in 1710. |
| e'tho | Mohawk word for "and." |
| Egusheway | A prominent Odawa war chief at Detroit 1792. |
| èneken | A Mohawk word for "above." |
| Entiehke:ne | Mohawk word for "the sun." |

# GLOSSARY

| | |
|---|---|
| Etshitewahtsi:' | A Mohawk word for "Our Elder Brother." This refers to the Thanksgiving Address. The Hodihnohsoni address the Sun as "Our Elder Brother." |
| fie nipa | Twi words for "members of a lineage." |
| fiefo | Twi word for "residence of a household." |
| ga'nigǫhi:yo: (also ganigonhi:oh); ka'nikonrí:yo, kanikohnri:io, or ka'nikonrí:yo in Mohawk | A Cayuga word for "Good Mind." |
| Gä•sweñta' (also Guswenta in Seneca; Kaswenta, Kaswentha', Kahswénhta in Mohawk) | A Seneca word for the Belt. In this context, the word references the Two-Row Wampum Belt relationship between Onkwehon:we and settlers. |
| Gae Ho Hwako | A personal name of Norma Jacobs. |
| Gaihwiyo (also Gaiwiio) | An anglicized version of the Hodihnohsó:ni' word for "Good Message." The current Longhouse tradition is centred around the "Good Message" delivered by the Seneca Chief Handsome Lake (1735–1815). |
| Ganohwkra sra | A Cayuga word for "love among us." In the Six Nations community, this is the name for family shelters for escaping domestic violence. |
| gawé:no | Onondaga word for "language." |
| Gayogoho:nǫ' (also Gayogǫhó:nǫ') | Meaning "People of the Swamp or People of the Pipe," also referring to their language. This nation was among the Five Nations who accepted the Peacemaker's message. |

| | |
|---|---|
| Hadajigre:ta' | "Descending-Cloud" name of Cayuga Chief Jacob E. Thomas (1922–98). Highly valued for his ability to speak all Six Nations languages, skilled orator, and craftsman. |
| Haida | A First Nations group living in today's British Columbia, occupied traditional lands called Haida Gwaii, an Archipelago off the coast of BC. |
| hati nahòten | Mohawk phrase for "whichever." |
| Haudenosaunee (also Hodinohsó:ni', Hodinöhsö:ni', Hodinǫshǫ:nih; Rotinonhson:ni in Mohawk) | Anglicized word of Hodihnohsó:ni' meaning "Men who build the house." This is understood as "People of the Longhouse," and incorporates all Six Nations members, Mohawk, Oneida, Onondaga, Cayuga, Seneca, and Tuscarora. |
| Iethi'nihstenha | Mohawk word for "Our Mother." |
| Hayonwatha (also Hiawatha) | "He keeps awake." Anglicized word for the Onondaga Hereditary Chief title. He was deputized to assist the Peacemaker unifying the Hodinhohso:ni. |
| iethihsotha | Mohawk word for "our grandmother." |
| iethsotho:kon | Mohawk word for "our grandfathers." |
| iothonton:ni | Mohawk word for "various grasses." |
| iotsistohkwaronnion | Mohawk word for "the ongoing stars." |
| Joagquisho | Personal name of Oren Lyons, Faithkeeper, activist, orator. |
| ka'nikòn:ra (also ka'nikonrí:yo, ni'nikò:nra) | Mohawk word for "mind." |

| | |
|---|---|
| ka'nikonhriyo'tsera't | Mohawk noun for "trust." |
| ka'shatstenhsera (also kasastensera) | Mohawk word for "unity or power, the capacity to bring into being." |
| Kahnawake | Mohawk for "by the rapids." A place name for the historical and present-day Mohawk community in Quebec, Canada. |
| kahnekaronnion | Mohawk word for "bodies of water." |
| kahrharonnion | Mohawk word for "the various bodies of trees." |
| kala pani | Indo-Aryan languages' term for "dark waters," with reference to the ocean crossing of nineteenth-century indentured workers from South Asia to the Caribbean and Africa. |
| Kaniatarake:ron | Mohawk word for "Lake Ontario." |
| Kanien'kéha (also Kanien'kehá) | Mohawk word for "Mohawk language." |
| Kanien'kehá:ka (also Kanyen'kehaka, Kanyen'keháka Kanyenkehá:ka) | "People of the Flint." This Nation was among the Five Nations to accept the Peacemaker's message. |
| kano:ta | Mohawk word for "plants." |
| kanohi ki te kanohi | The Māori legal proverb "to deal with it eye to eye." |
| Kanohstaton | Mohawk place name for "Protected Place." The location of the former Douglas Creek Estates and land protest held by the Six Nations in Caledonia, Ontario, Canada, 2006. |

| | |
|---|---|
| Kanyèn:keh (also Ganienkeh) | Mohawk place name for Mohawk Territory. |
| karahkwa | Mohawk word for "orb." The use of the word is in reference to the sun. |
| karhákta | Mohawk word for "edge or beside the forest." |
| kati | Mohawk word for "therefore." |
| Kayadosseras | A land patent that was granted by Queen Anne of Great Britain to thirteen subjects in 1701. Present day, Saratoga County, parts of Montgomery, Schenectady, and Fulton Counties. |
| Kayanerehkowa (also Kayanerenhtserakó:wa, Kayanerenko:wa, Kayanerenkó:wa, Gayanashagowa) | Mohawk spelling of "The Great Law of Peace." The name of the epic Hodihnohsó:ni' saga of the formation of the Hodihnohsó:ni' government and political system. |
| Kayanesenh | Personal name of Paul Williams, author, speaker, and Hodihnohsó:ni' lawyer. |
| Ken'tarókwen | Mohawk place name for St. Lawrence River. |
| kentèn:ron (kentenron) | Mohawk word for "compassion." |
| khe'kén:'a | Mohawk word for "sister." |
| Kiotsaeton | Personal name of Mohawk Chief, orator, and diplomat. He is documented as the Mohawk diplomat who adorned himself in wampum when making Peace with the French at Three Rivers in 1645. |
| kontirio | Mohawk word for "wild animals or animals." |

# GLOSSARY

| | |
|---|---|
| Konwatikowa:nen | Mohawk word for "the leader of." This is often used to acknowledge the spiritual leader of the various beings during the opening and closing of the Thanksgiving Adress or Words that Come Before All Else. |
| Konwatsi'tsiaienni | Personal name of Mary Brant. |
| Korahne | Mohawk word for "Canada." Arendt van Curler, the Dutch commissary at Albany, gave his name to successive governors of New York ("Corlaer" in most council records), and the title eventually spread to Indian agents in the twentieth century (usually Kora), the King in the 1701 Albany Treaty (Corachkowa, or Great Curler), and to Canada (Korahne). |
| Likutawakon | In Wolastoqey and Peskotomuhkati languages, "making family." In this context, the author is describing eighteenth-century peace treaties. |
| Mi'kmaq | First Nations group living along the Atlantic coast, near present-day Nova Scotia. They are part of the Algonquian language family. |
| Miigis | Anishinaabemowin for "shells," especially cowrie shells; this has been generalized to refer also to 'wampum' |
| Mikisew | "Golden Eagle" Cree First Nation is in northeastern Alberta and in Northwest Territories, Canada. |
| Mohawk | Anglicized word for a Hodihnohsó:ni' Nation. Meaning the People of the Flint. *See also* Kanien'kehá:ka. |

| | |
|---|---|
| nia:weh (also nyawen or nya:węh in Cayuga) | Mohawk word for "thank you." |
| nigaweño'deñ | Hodihnohsó:ni' ' word for "speech or language." |
| niiohontehsha | Mohawk word for "syrup." |
| niwahsen | Mohawk word for "tenths." This doesn't normally occur alone. In this context, the author added Ahsen Niwahsen to make it thirty. |
| niyohontehsha | Mohawk word for "wild strawberry." |
| Nyame | Akan name for "The Creator." |
| odagahodę:s: | Cayuga word for "always looking back" or in this context "reflecting on our journeys." |
| o:nenhste | Mohawk word for "corn." |
| o:tara | Mohawk word for "clan." |
| Oba na owo obarima | Akan expression: "it is a woman who gives birth to a man." |
| Odadrihonyanisoh | Personal name of Sara General. |
| O'hā'ǎ' | Mohawk word for "Flint." In Hodinhnohso:ni Cosmology, this is one of the names of the Twins born on Turtle Island. This name is given to the Bad-Minded Twin. His body is described in stories as being made of sharp flint points. His birth is responsible for the death of his mother. |
| ohahadihǫh | Cayuga word for "The Starlite Road or Milky Way." |

| | |
|---|---|
| Ohen:ton Karihwatehkwen (also Ohenton Karihwateh'kwen, Ohenton Karihwatehkwen) | Mohawk name for "Words that Come before All Else" The Thanking Address, a traditional protocol when meeting provides acknowledgment to the natural world, through sixteen stanzas or sections. However, this speech can be adjusted. This speech is customarily given before the meeting to open and at the end of the meeting to close. |
| ohsahe:ta | Mohawk word for "beans." |
| Ohsweken, Uswé:gę, Gyęhahsędáhkwa' | "Pouring out Place." The village of Six Nations of the Grand River. |
| ohwahta | Mohawk word for "maple." |
| Onas | Hodihnohsó:ni' name meaning "The Feather (Quill) or Pen." This name was given to William Penn, founder of the state of Pennsylvania, by a visiting delegation of Hodihnohsó:ni'. All governors of Pennsylvania were subsequently addressed as Onas by Hodihnohsó:ni' treaty delegations. |
| Oneida | Anglicized word for a Hodihnohsó:ni' nation that was among the Five Nations to accept the Peacemaker's message. Meaning People of Standing Stone. |
| Ongwehowe (also Ogwehoweh, Onkwehón:we, Onkwehonwe, Onkwehonweh) | Hodihnohsó:ni' word for "Real or Original people." |

| | |
|---|---|
| Onkwa'nikon:ra | Mohawk phrase for "in our minds" is utilized by Hodihnohsó:ni' speakers in traditional speeches such as the Thanksgiving Address, to signal to the audience the importance of remembering and reflecting on the matters being spoken about. |
| onkwe'shon:'a. | Mohawk word for "people." |
| Onodja | Onondaga word for "the Tooth." Referencing the Dogtooth Lily. In J.A. Gibson's version of the Hodihnohsó:ni' Cosmology, this name is used for the tree that brightens the world. |
| Onödowá'ga: (see also Seneca) | "People of the Great Mountain." This also refers to their language. This nation was among the Five Nations to accept the Peacemaker's message. |
| Onoñda'gegá' (also Anglicized as Onondaga) | "People of the Great Hills." This also refers to their language. This nation was among the Five Nations to accept the Peacemaker's message. *See* Seneca. |
| Onʌjotaʔa:ka (also Anglicized as Oneida) | Meaning "People of the Standing Stone," this nation was among the Five Nations that accepted the Peacemaker's message. This also refers to their language. |
| orenda | A term used by Tuscarora Anthropologist John Napoleon Bonaparte Hewitt to describe the Hodihnohsó:ni' philosophy of the power of living beings on Earth |
| oskenon:ton | Mohawk word for "deer." |
| otsi'nehtara'shón:'a | Mohawk word for "wampum beads." |

| | |
|---|---|
| oyen'kwahon:we (also oyenkwaon:we) | Mohawk word for "real smoke or real tobacco." This form of tobacco differs from the commercial tobacco. This tobacco is typically homegrown and is used to carry the words to the Creator. |
| Passmaquoddy/Peskotomuhkati | "The People who Spear Pollock." They are a federally recognized Nation in the U.S.; their traditional lands are the present-day border between New Brunswick and Maine. However, they are seeking recognition for First Nations status in Canada. |
| poquaûhock | "hard clam," or quahog. |
| Ranyahtenhkó:wa | Mohawk word for "The Great Snapping Turtle." |
| Ratironhia'kehro:non | Mohawk term for the "the protecting guardians" |
| ratiwe:ras | Mohawk name for "the thunders." |
| ro'nihstenha | Mohawk word for "his mother." |
| Rotihnahon:tsi | Mohawk name for "people who have dark skin"; Black people. |
| Rotinonhson:ni (see Hodinohso:ni in Cayuga above) | Mohawk name for "Men who build the Longhouse." The word is also understood as "People of the Longhouse." This includes Mohawk, Oneida, Onieda, Tuscarora, Onondaga, Cayuga, and Seneca Nations. |
| Rotiyanehson | Mohawk word for Traditional Hereditary "Chiefs." |

| | |
|---|---|
| Sadakanahtie | Onondaga orator and spokesman, who flourished from 1640–1710. |
| Seneca | Anglicized word for a Hodihnohsó:ni' nation that was among the Five Nations to accept the Peacemaker's message. Meaning the People of the Great Mountain. |
| Seyakhikwatakwénnis ne tehontatenentshonteronhtáhkwa | Mohawk Phrase meaning "grasping the chain again." |
| Shakoyewatha | "Keeper Awake." Name of Seneca warrior, orator, and Chief of the Wolf Clan (1750–1830). |
| Shinnecock | A federally recognized Nation in the United States, whose traditional lands are on Long Island, New York. They are part of the Algonquian language family. |
| Shonkwaia'tishon | Mohawk name for "The Creator." |
| Six Nations | The Six Nations refers to the united peoples of the following Nations: Mohawk, Oneida, Tuscarora, Onondaga, Cayuga, and Seneca. The Six Nations of the Grand River is a reserve in Ontario, Canada. |
| ska'nikòn:ra (also skatne ka'nikòn:ra) | Mohawk phrase for "one mind." This concept is that all parties are in agreement on the subject matter and have become one with the same thought. |
| Skanawati | "Other side of the swamp." Traditional Hereditary Chief title of the Onondaga Nation. |
| Skaniatari:io (also Skanyatarí:yo) | "Handsome Lake." Traditional Hereditary Chief title of the Seneca Nation. Also Lake Ontario. |

# GLOSSARY

| | |
|---|---|
| Skarò·rę? | "People of the Shirt." Originally from North Carolina, the Tuscarora people joined the Hodihnohsó:ni' in 1713 to make the "Sixth" Nation. |
| skén:nen | Mohawk word for "peace or hello." |
| skennenha | Mohawk word for "slowly." |
| Sotsisowah | "Corn Tassel." Personal name of John Mohawk (1945–2006). |
| Taharonhyawakon (De'haĕn'hiyawă"khon' in Onondaga) | Variation of the spelling "Holder of the Heavens." |
| taiethinonhwera:ton | Mohawk word for "we will give thanks" or "we will thank them." |
| Takarihoga | "Between Matters." Traditional Hereditary Chief title of the Mohawk Nation. |
| Tatshitewatenonhwera:ton | Mohawk word for "now we will thank." |
| Tawiskaron | Mohawk word for "Flint." In the Hodihnohsó:ni' cosmology, the name is given to the Bad-Minded Twin. See *O'hā'ă'*. |
| Tehontatenent/ shonteronhtahkwa (also Tehontatenent/ shonteronhtáhkwa) | Mohawk treaty phrase "the thing by which they link arms, linking arms together." From the author, Amber Meadow Adams: "word-paints two people, or groups of people, or wills of people, with the ends of their arms attached to each other's, past and now, perpetually, in an act of sustained connection. Layers of specific action within a matrix of relationships." |

| | |
|---|---|
| teionkhiia:taton | Mohawk word for "protecting." |
| Teionkwakhashion Tsi Niionkwariho:Ten | Mohawk phrase for "we are sharing our matters." This is also the title of a book by Dr. Rick Monture. |
| Teiowerawenrie | Mohawk word for "the winds." |
| Tekarihoken | "Between Matters." Traditional Hereditary Mohawk Chief title. |
| Tekéni Teyohà: ke Kahswénhtake (also Tekéni Teyohà: ke Kahswénhtake, Tekéni Teyohà:ke Kahswénhta, Tekéni Teyohà:ke Kahswénhtake, Tékeni Teyohà:te, Tékeni Teyohà:te Kaswenta, Tekeni Teyohàte, Tekeni Teyohàte Kaswentha, Tekeni Teyohha:ke Kahswenhtake) | Mohawk term for "Two Row Wampum Belt." This wampum belt references the 1612 treaty relationship between the Mohawks and Dutch settlers. |
| Tekiatenontarí:kon | Mohawk place name for "A Place Where Two River's Meet." |
| teyakonhwentsyon:ni | Mohawk word for "other side of the fire." |
| Teyonnityohkwanhakstha | "The thing the people use on an ongoing basis to wrap around themselves." Mohawk name for the Circle Wampum Belt, which represents the fifty Chiefs of the Hodihnohsó:ni'. |
| Thadadahoh | "Entangled." Traditional Hereditary Chief Title of the Onondaga Nation. |
| Thayendenegea | "Bundled sticks." Personal name of Joseph Brant, Mohawk. |

# GLOSSARY

| | |
|---|---|
| Tyendinaga | Mohawk place name for Mohawks of The Bay of Quinte, Mohawk Community, Ontario, Canada. |
| Tionhehkwen. | Mohawk name for "Life Sustainers." |
| Tiyanoga | Personal name of Mohawk leader Hendrick Peters (1680–1755). |
| Tsi niyothahinen ne tehontatenent/ shonteronhtáhkwa | Mohawk phrase for "where the roots touch." |
| Tsilhqot'in | "People of the River." Athabaskan-speaking group that lives in what is now known as British Columbia, Canada. |
| Tsiohwentsia:te | Mohawk word for "Earth." |
| Tsiskokon | Personal name of Belanger Brown, Oneida Chief. |
| tsiyonhwenhtsyàke. | Mohawk word for "the existing Earth." |
| Tuscarora | "The People of the Hemp Shirts." Anglicized form of the Hodihnohsó:ni' nation. This nation was admitted as the Sixth Nation in 1713. Their original homelands are in the present State of North Carolina. See Skarò˙rą́ʔ. |
| Tutelo | A Siouan-speaking group adopted by the Cayugas in the eighteenth century. Their original homelands are in the present state of Virginia. |
| Twi | Short form, abbreviation of "Twi-Fantie," see below. |
| Twi-Fantie | Language of the Akan peoples of the Guinea Coast of West Africa. |

| | |
|---|---|
| wahianiiontha | Mohawk word for "the lowest levels of the hanging fruits." |
| Warraghyhagey (also Warragihage) | "Big Business": personal name given to Sir William Johnson, British Loyalist, superintendent of Indian Affairs during the eighteenth century. |
| wenhni:tare | Mohawk word for "the nighttime orb." |
| Wolastoqiyik | "People of the Bright River." They are also known as Maliseet. Their traditional homelands are bordering the Canadian Provinces of Quebec, New Brunswick, and the State of Maine. |
| Wunnáumwash | Shinnecock language for "speaks the truth." |
| Yakoyaner | Mohawk word for "Clanmother." |
| Yakoyaneshon | Mohawk term for "Clanmothers." The Matriarchal leadership of the Hodihnso:ni. |
| Yethi'nihstenha | Mohawk word for "Mother Earth," derived from Yethi'nihstenha tsi yonhwentsyake ("she is mother to us who is (on/at) the Earth") |
| yonkyats | Mohawk word for "my name is." |
| Yonondi:io | Name of the Governor of New France. "The Great Mountain." |

# Notes

## Introduction

1. Readers will notice two spellings of *People/people* on this page. Following the hard-fought gains of the United Nations Declaration on Indigenous Peoples, we capitalize *Peoples* to refer to self-determining Indigenous Nations as distinct from the vaguer, anthropological terms "populations" or "groups." We use *people,* however, to refer to everyday folks who may find themselves occupying the water between the two vessels of the Indigenous canoe and the settler colonial/European ship. We capitalize *Indigenous* or *Kanien'kehá:ka* or *Mohawk* to signal self-determining national status parallel to *Canadian* or *American*.
2. See Six Nations Polytechnic, "Deyohahá:ge: Indigenous Knowledge Centre 10th Anniversary," *YouTube*, March 24, 2021, video, 31:57, https://www.youtube.com/watch?v=EF05-RFNVTU&t=4s.
3. Gae Ho Hwako, Q *da gaho dẹ:s: Reflecting on Our Journeys* (Montreal: McGill-Queens University Press, 2022).
4. These definitions are from Amber Meadows Adams, *Seyakhikwatakwénnis ne Tehontatenentshonteronhtáhkwa; Grasping the Chain Again* (R. v. Derek White & Hunter Montour, S.C. 505-01-137394-165 and CM-2018-000545), (Expert Report, June 4, 2021): 79.
5. Kayanesenh Paul Williams, "The Chain, Naturally Understood," pages 74–75 in this volume. Following Williams, we capitalize the proper names for wampum, such as the "Two Row Wampum," but we do not capitalize words that translate these wampum agreements into English such as "treaty" or "tradition," since wampum agreements are much more than "laws" or "treaties," serving simultaneously as friendship ceremonies, spiritual commitments, legal-diplomatic agreements, and artistic depictions of significant cultural understanding.
6. *R. vs Montour and White* (505-01-137394-165), November 1st, 2023, "Summary, III Treaty Rights," p. 16.
7. These are Adams' translations; "Where the Roots Touch: tsi niyothahinen ne Tehontatenentshonteronhtáhkwa," page 36 in this volume.
8. Adams, "Where the Roots Touch," pages 36–37 in this volume.
9. Rick Hill, "Linking Arms: The Haudenosaunee Context of the Covenant Chain," in *Mamow Be-Mo-Tay-Tah: Let Us Walk Together*, eds. José Zárate and Norah McMurtry (Toronto: Canadian Ecumenical Anti-Racism Network, 2009), 17.

10 Hill, "Linking Arms," 17–18.
11 Spellings are in Onondaga language from "Iroquoian Cosmology" by John Arthur Gibson (Seneca), who was fluent in Onondaga and transcribed and translated by J.N.B. Hewitt in *Forty-Third Annual Report of The Bureau of American Ethnology to the Secretary of the Smithsonian Institution, 1925–1926*, (Washington: United States Government Printing Office, 1928): 449–819.
12 Rick Hill, "Oral Memory of the Haudenosaunee: Views of the Two Row Wampum," in *Indian Roots of American Democracy,* ed. José Barreiro (Ithaca, NY: Akwe:kon P/Cornell UP, 1992), 155.
13 A sign of how widely known the Two Row has become can be seen in the use of the term *kaswentha*, the word for "wampum" in general, as if it is the name of the *Tékeni Teyohà:te* in particular. Rather, it is a kind of short form—a contraction—that has become widely used. The most extensive discussion of the history of the Covenant Chain-Two Row treaty tradition (445 pages), for example, was written by Kayanesenh Paul Williams and Chief Curtis Nelson for the Royal Commission for Aboriginal Peoples (RCAP 1996). It is entitled *Kahswentha*.
14 Hill, "Oral Memory," 156.
15 Paul Williams and Curtis Nelson, *Kahswentha* (Royal Commission on Aboriginal Peoples, 1995), 432.
16 Hill, "Oral Memory," 155.
17 Hill, 158
18 Hill, 158.
19 Hill, 159.
20 Sara General, "Towards Peace: Living in the Three White Rows of the Two Row," page 184 in this volume.
21 In *Linking Arms Together: American Indian Treaty Visions of Law and Peace* (New York: Routledge, 1999), legal historian Robert A. Williams Jr. writes: "In countless treaties, councils, and negotiations, American Indians insisted upon the relevance of the principles contained in tribal traditions such as the *Gus-Wen-Tah* for ordering the unique and fractious kind of multicultural society that was emerging on the continent. Throughout this period, Europeans secured Indian trade, alliances, and goodwill by adapting themselves to tribal approaches to the problems of achieving law and peace in a multicultural world" (5). In Judge Sophie Bourque's decision that the Covenant Chain is indeed a treaty as recognized in Section 35(1) of the Constitution Act, she was convinced by the Applicant's reference to ten documented treaty council agreements between 1677 and 1760, agreeing that "these treaties formed what is known as the 'Covenant Chain,' a symbol of the alliance between the parties. In the words of the Applicants, the Covenant Chain is a series of treaties that were meant to record military and trade alliances (and, in some cases, neutrality pacts) between the British Crown and the Mohawk nation and other nations of the Iroquois Confederacy, especially in the context of the ongoing colonial rivalry between the French and British Crowns in the

17th and 18th centuries which ultimately culminated in the conquest of New France in 1760" (*R. vs. Monture*, p. 5).

22  See *The Jesuit Relations*, vol. 27, ed. Reuben Thwaites (Cleveland: Burrows Brothers Company, 1898), 247–93.

23  See Cadwallader Colden, *History of the Five Indian Nations*, 1727 (Toronto: Coles Publishing Co., 1968), 149–50.

24  Benjamin Franklin, *Indian Treaties printed by Benjamin Franklin, 1736–1762; Introduction by Carl van Doren and Historical and Bibliographical Notes by Julian P. Boyd* (Philadelphia: The Historical Society of Pennsylvania, 1938), 51–52. Cited in Adams, *Seyakhikwatakwénnis*, 53–54.

25  Williams, "The Chain, Naturally Understood," page 69 in this volume.

26  June 18, 1755. Library and Archives Canada, Record Group 10 (Indian Affairs), Vol. 1822, 35.22. Cited in Adams, *Seyakhikwatakwénnis*, 57.

27  Alan Corbiere, "'Their Own Forms of Which They Take the Most Notice': Diplomatic Metaphors and Symbolism on Wampum Belts," in *Anishnaabewin Niwin: Four Rising Winds*, eds. Alan Ojig Corbiere, Mary Ann Naokwegiig Corbiere, Deborah MacGregor and Crystal Migwans. (M'Chigeeng ON: Ojibway Cultural Foundation, 2013), 61. The two-day commemoration of the 1764 Treaty of Niagara mentioned in the image caption was co-organized by the Association of Iroquois and Allied Indians, the Chiefs of Ontario, and the Six Nations Legacy Consortium. Descendants of the original twenty-four Indigenous "signatory" Nations to the treaty were in attendance along with The Hon. David Zimmer, Ontario Minister of Aboriginal Affairs, Deputy Minister David de Launay, and The Honorable David C. Onley, Lieutenant Governor of Ontario. As part of his address to the assembled Nations commemorating the Treaty of Niagara, Minister Zimmer presented each of the twenty-four nations that gathered 250 years ago with two strings of wampum to evoke the Two Row Wampum relationship.

28  Corbiere, 62.

29  See Marie L'Incarnation's description of Couture's wampum-for-wampum speech on behalf of the French governor, *Word From New France: The Selected Letters of Marie de l'Incarnation*, trans. and ed. Joyce Marshall (Toronto: Oxford University Press, 1967), 147–48.

30  See Adams, *The Covenant Chain in Passamaquoddy Country* (Draft Report for the Passmaquoddy First Nation, February 17, 2006), 9. As one example of Johnson's efforts, see his September 24, 1766 letter of instructions to his new Deputy Superintendent of Indian Affairs for Nova Scotia, Joseph Goreham. Johnson wrote: "We are now at Peace with all nations of Indians, and expect that they will be careful in preserving the Covenant Chain of Friendship on their Parts, to which end you will occasionally meet them to repeat former Treaties, and Engagements. – And you are then to deliver them a large Belt of Wampum in my name willing them to hold fast thereby, and not suffer themselves to be misled, but to cast their Eyes toward the Sun setting where I reside, and hold fast one

end of the Belt as Superintendent of Indian Affairs in the Northern Department" (*Papers of Sir William Johnson*, vol. 7:196; cited in Adams, *The Covenant Chain in Passamaquoddy Country* 49–50).
31. Kelsey Leonard, "*Wunnáumwash*: Wampum Justice," page 59 in this volume.
32. Leonard, page 64 in this volume.
33. David Newhouse, "Guswenta Space: An Invitation to Dialogue," pages 112–13 in this volume.
34. Newhouse, page 120 in this volume.

## Chapter 1: Gä•sweñta' Reflections

1. Julian Taub, "The Iroquois are Not Giving Up," *The Atlantic*, August 17, 2013. https://www.theatlantic.com/national/archive/2013/08/the-iroquois-are-not-giving-up/278787.
2. Taub.
3. Chief Oren Lyons, "Oren Lyons: On the Indigenous View of the World," interview by Leila Conners, *11th Hour Research Tapes,* Sept 16, 2016, https://ratical.org/many_worlds/6Nations/OrenLyons-IndigenousWorldView.html#s24.
4. Hayden King, "The Erasure of Indigenous Thought in Foreign Policy," *Open Canada*, July 13, 2017, https://opencanada.org/erasure-indigenous-thought-foreign-policy/.
5. Alberta Council of Women's Shelters. "Treaty Relations: Spirit, Intent and First Nations Perspectives," in *Stepping into the Circle: A Call to Conversation and Workbook Exploring Indigenous Knowledge*, https://acws.ca/wpcontent/uploads/2020/09/ Stepping_into_the_Circle-M3.pdf.
6. Lyons, "Oren Lyons."
7. Renée Gadoua, "Face Time: Keeping the Faith," *Syracuse New Times*, 2014, https://www.syracusenewtimes.com/keeping-the-faith/2014.
8. Lyons, "Oren Lyons."
9. Lyons, "Oren Lyons."
10. Chief Oren Lyons, "Opening Statement: The Year of the Indigenous Peoples (1993)," transc. Craig Carpenter (speech, United Nations General Assembly Auditorium, United Nations Plaza, New York City, December 10, 1992), https://ratical.org/many_worlds/6Nations/ OLatUNin92.html.
11. "Two Row Wampum: Symbol of Sovereignty; Metaphor for Life," *PBS*, accessed Sept. 7, 2022, http://www.pbs.org/warrior/content/timeline/hero/wampum.html.
12. Lyons, "Oren Lyons."

## Chapter 2: Where the Roots Touch

1 Sotsisowah John C. Mohawk, *John Arthur Gibson and J.N.B. Hewitt's Myth of the Earthgrasper* (Buffalo, NY: Mohawk Publications, 2005), 15.
2 Mohawk, 15.

## Chapter 3: *Wunnáumwash*

1 This term is used throughout the chapter to refer to eastern Atlantic Indigenous Nations of what is currently known as Canada and the United States. These Nations include Abenaki, Penobscot Nation, Passamaquoddy Tribe, Houlton Band of Maliseet Indians, Narragansett Indian Tribe, Mashantucket Pequot Tribal Nation, Wampanoag Tribe of Gay Head (Aquinnah), Aroostook Band of Micmacs, The Mohegan Tribe, Mashpee Wampanoag Tribe, Shinnecock Indian Nation, Pamunkey Indian Tribe, Rappahannock Tribe, Chickahominy Indian Tribe, Chickahominy Indian Tribe – Eastern Division, Upper Mattaponi Indian Tribe, Nansemond Indian Nation, Monacan Indian Nation, Acadia First Nation, Annapolis Valley First Nation, Bear River First Nation, Eskasoni First Nation, Glooscap First Nation, Membertou First Nation, Millbrook First Nation, Paq'tnkek First Nation, Pictou Landing First Nation, Potlotek First Nation, Sipekne'katik First Nation, Wagmatcook First Nation, We'koqma'q First Nation, among others. I also recognize that the word is not Indigenous to our languages but is now part of the lexicon of our contemporary use as an identifier of our connection through language, culture, and history as eastern Indigenous Peoples of Turtle Island.
2 Heather Davis and Zoe Todd, "On the Importance of a Date, or, Decolonizing the Anthropocene," *ACME: An International Journal for Critical Geographies* 16, no. 4 (2017): 776.
3 See Bradly A. Knox, "The Visual Rhetoric of Lady Justice: Understanding Jurisprudence Through 'Metonymic Tokens,'" *Inquiries Journal* 6, no. 05 (2014). http://www.inquiriesjournal.com/articles/896/the-visual-rhetoric-of-lady-justice-understanding-jurisprudence-through-metonymic-tokens.
4 See Roger Williams, *A Key into the Language of America*, 1827 (Project Gutenberg, 2020), https://www.gutenberg.org/files/63701/63701-h/63701-h.htm; Marc Shell, *Wampum and the Origins of American Money* (Champaign, Illinois: University of Illinois Press, 2013).
5 Vanessa Watts, "Indigenous Place-Thought and Agency Amongst Humans and Non Humans (First Woman and Sky Woman Go on a European World Tour!)," *Decolonization: Indigeneity, Education & Society* 2, no. 1 (2013): 30.
6 Early Hodinöhsö:ni' stories about the first uses of wampum indicate that Ayenwatha (a.k.a. "Hiawatha") used cored lengths of sumac or basswood twigs before using shells to make wampum. See John Arthur Gibson, *Concerning*

*the League: The Iroquois League Tradition as Dictated in Onondaga by John Arthur Gibson,* 1912, eds. Hanni Woodbur, Reg Henry, and Harry Webster (Winnipeg, MB: Algonquian and Iroquoian Linguistics, 1992), 133–53.

7. Coastal Resources Management Council, Narragansett Bay Estuary Program, and Save The Bay, "Quahog (Mercenaria Mercenaria)," *University of Rhode Island Environmental Data Center,* 2001, https://www.edc.uri.edu/restoration/html/gallery/invert/quahog.htm.

8. Iain D. Ridgway et al., "New Species Longevity Record for the Northern Quahog (= Hard Clam), Mercenaria Mercenaria," *Journal of Shellfish Research* 30, no. 1 (2011): 35–38.

9. See Coastal Resources Management Council "Quahog"; R. Cool, "Hard Times for Hard Clams," *The Bay Journal* 8, no. 4 (June 1998).

10. See Sandra B. Robinson et al., "Growth Rates for Quahogs (Mercenaria mercenaria) in a Reduced Nitrogen Environment in Narragansett Bay, RI," *Northeastern Naturalist* 27, no. 3 (2020): 534–54.; Christopher J. Gobler and Hannes Baumann, "Hypoxia and Acidification in Ocean Ecosystems: Coupled Dynamics and Effects on Marine Life," *Biology letters* 12, no. 5 (2016): 1–8.; Christopher J. Gobler et al., "Hypoxia and Acidification Have Additive and Synergistic Negative Effects on the Growth, Survival, and Metamorphosis of Early Life Stage Bivalves," *PloS one* 9, no. 1 (2014), https://journals.plos.org/plosone/article?id=10.1371/journal.pone.0083648.; Bradford Burdette, "Mercenaria Mercenaria (Northern Quahog)," *Animal Diversity Web,* 2001, https://animaldiversity.org/accounts/Mercenaria_mercenaria/.

11. See Andrew W. Griffith and Christopher J. Gobler, "Transgenerational Exposure of North Atlantic Bivalves to Ocean Acidification Renders Offspring More Vulnerable to Low pH and Additional Stressors," *Scientific Reports* 7, no. 1 (2017): 1–11.

12. See Kelsey Leonard, "WAMPUM Adaptation Framework: Eastern Coastal Tribal Nations and Sea Level Rise Impacts on Water Security," *Climate and Development* (2021): 1–10.

13. See Joshua Manitowabi, "Wii Niiganabying (Looking Ahead)," *Turtle Island Journal of Indigenous Health* 1, no. 1 (2020): 59–71.; Alan Theodore Ojiig Corbiere, "Anishinaabe Treaty-Making in the 18th-and-19th-Century Northern Great Lakes: From Shared Meanings to Epistemological Chasms" (PhD diss., York University, 2019), https://yorkspace.library.yorku.ca/xmlui/handle/10315/37402.; Leanne Simpson, "Looking After Gdoo-naaganinaa: Precolonial Nishnaabeg Diplomatic and Treaty Relationships," *Wicazo Sa Review* 23, no. 2 (2008): 29–42.; Penelope Myrtle Kelsey, *Reading the Wampum: Essays on Hodinöhsö: ni' Visual Code and Epistemological Recovery* (NY: Syracuse University Press, 2014).

14. Marcus Hendricks, "The History of Wampum - Real Story from Local Massachusetts Native American," interview by Jeffrey Wyman, *YouTube,* Aug. 5, 2019, video, 3:24. https://www.youtube.com/watch?v=90vyScbrXyQ.

15 See Jeffery G. Hewitt, "Certain (Mis) Conceptions: Westphalian Origins, Portraiture and Wampum," in *Routledge Handbook of International Law and the Humanities*, eds. Shane Chalmers and Sundhya Pahuja (New York: Routledge, 2021), 159–72.

16 See Southampton City Council, "Wampum: Stories from the Shells of Native America," *Mayflower 400 Southampton*, 2021, https://mayflower400southampton.co.uk/events-and-workshops/wampum-belt.

17 See Alasdair C. MacIntyre, *Whose Justice? Which Rationality?* (Notre Dame, IN: University of Notre Dame Press, 1988).

18 See John Borrows, *Drawing Out Law: A Spirit's Guide* (Toronto: University of Toronto Press, 2010).; Deborah McGregor, "Mino-Mnaamodzawin: Achieving Indigenous Environmental Justice in Canada," *Environment and Society* 9, no. 1 (2018): 7–24.

19 See John Randolph Lucas, "Justice." *Philosophy* 47, no. 181 (1972): 229–48.

20 However, Indigenous sovereignty and autonomy to dispense justice is not always recognized or supported by settler-colonial states. See John Rawls, *A Theory of Justice: Revised Edition* (Cambridge: Harvard University Press, 1999).; Jeff Corntassel, "Indigenous Storytelling, Truth-Telling, and Community Approaches to Reconciliation," *ESC: English Studies in Canada* 35, no. 1 (2009): 137–59.

21 McGregor, "Mino-Mnaamodzawin," 12.

22 See Williams, *A Key into the Language of America*.

23 James Hammond Trumbull, *Natick Dictionary* (Washington D.C.: Government Printing Office, 1903), https://archive.org/details/natickdictionar02trumgoog.

24 See Corbiere, "Anishinaabe Treaty-Making."

25 Victoria Valerie Weaver, "Wampum as Social Practice" (PhD diss., Pennsylvania State University, 2009).

26 See Rick Hill, "Talking Points on History and Meaning of the Two Row Wampum Belt," *Two Row Wampum Renewal Campaign*, 2013, https://honortheworow.org/wp-content/uploads/2013/03/TwoRowTalkingPoints-Rick-Hill.pdf.; Sarah Duignan, Tina Moffat, and Dawn Martin-Hill, "Using Boundary Objects to Co-Create Community Health and Water Knowledge with Community-Based Medical Anthropology and Indigenous Knowledge," *Engaged Scholar Journal: Community-Engaged Research, Teaching and Learning* 6, no. 1 (2020): 49–76.

27 See Bonnie Freeman and Trish van Katwyk, "Navigating the Waters: Understanding Allied Relationships Through a Tekéni Teyohà: ke Kahswénhtake Two Row Research Paradigm," *Journal of Indigenous Social Development* 9, no. 1 (2020): 60–76.; Susan M. Hill, *The Clay We Are Made Of: Haudenosaunee Land Tenure on the Grand River* (Manitoba: University of Manitoba Press, 2017).; Rick Monture, *We Share our Matters: Two Centuries of Writing and Resistance at Six Nations of the Grand River* (Manitoba: University of Manitoba Press, 2014).

28 Royal Commission on Aboriginal Peoples, "Report of the Royal Commission on Aboriginal Peoples." *Looking Forward, Looking Back* 1 (1996): 97.

29  See Freeman and van Katwyk, "Navigating the Waters"; Hill, "Talking Points on History."
30  See Duignan, Moffat, and Martin-Hill, "Using Boundary Objects."
31  See Kathryn V. Muller, "The Two 'Mystery' Belts of Grand River: A Biography of the Two Row Wampum and the Friendship Belt," *American Indian Quarterly* (2007): 129–64; Beverly Jacobs, "International Law/The Great Law of Peace." (master's thesis, University of Saskatchewan, 2000), https://www.collectionscanada.gc.ca/obj/s4/f2/dsk3/SSU/TC-SSU-07042007083651.pdf.
32  Jessica Hallenbeck, "Returning to the Water to Enact a Treaty Relationship: The Two Row Wampum Renewal Campaign," *Settler Colonial Studies* 5, no. 4 (2015): 351.
33  See James W. Ransom and Kreg T. Ettenger, "'Polishing the Kaswentha': A Haudenosaunee View of Environmental Cooperation," *Environmental Science & Policy* 4, no. 4–5 (2001): 219–28.; Deborah McGregor, "Traditional Ecological Knowledge and the Two-Row Wampum," *Biodiversity* 3, no. 3 (2002): 8–9.
34  Daniel Coleman, "The Two Row Wampum-Covenant Chain Treaty and Trans-Systemic Resilience," in *Glocal Narratives of Resilience*, ed. Ana María Fraile-Marcos (New York: Routledge, 2019), 27.
35  Richard W. Hill Sr. and Daniel Coleman, "The Two Row Wampum-Covenant Chain Tradition as a Guide for Indigenous-University Research Partnerships." *Cultural Studies↔ Critical Methodologies* 19, no. 5 (2019): 344–45.
36  Jacobs, "International Law."
37  See Hallenbeck, "Returning to the Water"; S. Kathleen Barnhill-Dilling, Louie Rivers, and Jason A. Delborne, "Rooted in Recognition: Indigenous Environmental Justice and the Genetically Engineered American Chestnut Tree,"*Society & Natural Resources* 33, no. 1 (2020): 83–100.; Jon Parmenter, "The Meaning of Kaswentha and the Two Row Wampum Belt in Haudenosaunee (Iroquois) History: Can Indigenous Oral Tradition Be Reconciled with the Documentary Record?," *Journal of Early American History* 3, no. 1 (2013): 82–109.; Morten Skumsrud Andersen and Iver B. Neumann, "Practices as Models: A Methodology with an Illustration Concerning Wampum Diplomacy," *Millennium* 40, no. 3 (2012): 457–81.; George S. Snyderman, "The Functions of Wampum." *Proceedings of the American Philosophical Society* 98, no. 6 (1954): 469–94.; Wilbur R. Jacobs, "Wampum: The Protocol of Indian Diplomacy," *The William and Mary Quarterly: A Magazine of Early American History* (1949): 596–604.
38  See Hewitt, "Certain (Mis) Conceptions"; Saleem Ali and Helena Vladich, "Environmental Diplomacy," *The SAGE Handbook of Diplomacy*, eds. Costas M. Constantinou, Pauline Kerr, and Paul Sharp (London: SAGE Publications, 2016): 601–16.
39  John Carlson, "Manoomin is Not Wild Rice: An Anishinaabeg Treaty," *Zeitschrift für Kanada-Studien* 38, no. 1 (2018).

40 See Ali and Vladich, "Environmental Diplomacy"; Vine Deloria and Raymond J. DeMallie, *Documents of American Indian Diplomacy: Treaties, Agreements, and Conventions, 1775–1979*. Vol. 1 (OK: University of Oklahoma Press, 1999).
41 Corbiere, "Anishinaabe Treaty-Making."
42 Jacobs, "Wampum," 596.
43 Shell, *Wampum and the Origins of American Money*.
44 Williams, *A Key into the Language of America*.
45 Watts, "Indigenous Place-Thought," 22.
46 Jacobs, "Wampum," 596.
47 See Daniel F. Harrison, "Change Amid Continuity, Innovation Within Tradition: Wampum Diplomacy at the Treaty of Greenville, 1795," *Ethnohistory* 64, no. 2 (2017): 191–215; Snyderman, "The Functions of Wampum"; Jacobs, "Wampum."
48 See Leonard, "WAMPUM Adaptation Framework"; Griffith and Gobler, "Transgenerational Exposure"; Gobler and Baumann, "Hypoxia and Acidification in Ocean Ecosystems"; Gobler et al., "Hypoxia and Acidification."
49 See Wenona Victor, "Indigenous Justice: Clearing Space and Place for Indigenous Epistemologies" (research paper, National Centre for First Nations Governance, December 2007), https://fngovernance.org/wp-content/uploads/2020/09/wenona_victor.pdf.

## Chapter 5: Guswenta Space

1 David Newhouse, "From the Tribal to the Modern: The Development of Modern Aboriginal Societies," in *Expressions in Canadian Native Studies*, eds. Ron F. Laliberte et al. (Saskatoon: University of Saskatchewan Extension Press, 2000), 395–409.
2 I capitalize the term to signify its importance as a Haudenosaunee cultural concept representing more than the symbol of a political relationship. The full translation of the Two Row Wampum is *Tekani Teiohàte Kaswenta* (in Mohawk). In this article, I use the term Guswenta (spelled with the hard "G" to help English pronunciation) as a short form.
3 Clifford Geertz, *The Interpretation of Cultures* (New York: Basic Books, 1973).
4 Social Science and Humanities Research Council, "Guidelines for the Merit Review of Indigenous Research," *Social Science and Humanities Research Council*, 2018, https://www.sshrc-crsh.gc.ca/funding-financement/merit_review-evaluation_du_merite/ guidelines_research-lignes_directrices_recherche-eng.aspx.
5 Marlene Brant Castellano, "Ethics of Aboriginal Research," *International Journal of Aboriginal Health* 1, no. 1 (2004): 98–114.
6 Daniel Coleman, "Epistemic Justice, CanLit, and the Politics of Respect," *Canadian Literature* 204 (Spring 2010): 124–26.
7 Willie Ermine, "The Ethical Space of Engagement," *Indigenous Law Journal* 6, no. 1 (2007): 193–203.

8   Cheryl Bartlett, Murdena Marshall, and Albert Marshall, "Two-Eyed Seeing and Other Lessons Learned Within a Co-Learning Journey of Bringing Together Indigenous and Mainstream Knowledges and Ways of Knowing," *Journal of Environmental Studies and Sciences* 2, no. 5 (October 2012): 331–40.
9   See Bartlett, Marshall, and Marshall.
10  See Coleman, "Epistemic Justice."
11  David Newhouse, "Debwewin: To Speak the Truth – Nishabek de'bwewin: Telling Our Truths," *Academic Matters: OCUFA's Journal of Higher Education* (Fall 2018): 13–17.
12  Robert Williams, *Linking Arms Together: American Indian Treaty Visions of Law and Peace, 1600–1800* (Philadelphia: Routledge, 1999).
13  Ganienkeh Territory, "Wampum #28," *Kayanerehkowa: The Great Law of Peace*, http://www.ganienkeh.net/thelaw.html.
14  See Ermine. "The Ethical Space of Engagement."
15  Richard W. Hill Sr. and Daniel Coleman, "The Two Row Wampum-Covenant Chain Tradition as a Guide for Indigenous University Research Partnerships," *Cultural Studies ‑Critical Methodologies* 19, no. 5 (2019): 339–59.
16  Tim Mercer, "The Two-Row Wampum: Has This Metaphor for Co-Existence Run its Course?," *Canadian Parliamentary Review* 42, no. 2 (2019), http://www.revparlcan.ca/en/the-two-row-wampum-has-this-metaphor-for-co-existence-run-its-course/.
17  Robert Vachon, "Guswenta or The Intercultural Imperative," *INTERculture International Journal of Intercultural and Transdisciplinary Research* 27, no. 2 (1995): 8–73.
18  John Ralston Saul, *A Fair Country: Telling Truths about Canada* (Toronto: Penguin Canada, 2008).
19  John Ralston Saul, *The Comeback: How Aboriginals Are Reclaiming Power and Influence* (Toronto: Penguin Random House, 2014).

## Chapter 6: Navigating the Two Row in the Academy

1   "Land Acknowledgments: A Guide," *McMaster University Student Success Centre*, 2018, https://healthsci.mcmaster.ca/docs/librariesprovider59/resources/mcmaster-university-land-acknowledgment-guide.pdf?sfvrsn=7318d517_2.
2   Rick Hill, "Ecological Knowledge & the Dish with One Spoon: Conversations in Cultural Fluency #2," *Six Nations Polytechnic*, January 29, 2016, https://www.youtube.com/ watch?v=RL83GvOO_Co.
3   Rauna Kuokkanen, *Reshaping the University: Responsibility, Indigenous Epistemes, and the Logic of the Gift* (Vancouver: UBC Press, 2011), xvi.
4   Kuokkanen.

5. Richard W. Hill Sr. and Daniel Coleman, "The Two Row Wampum-Covenant Chain Tradition as a Guide for Indigenous-University Research Partnerships.," *Cultural Studies – Critical Methodologies*, 19, no. 5 (2019): 342.
6. Vanessa Watts, in Rochelle Coté et al., "Indigenization, Institutions, and Imperatives: Perspectives on Reconciliation from the CSA Decolonization Sub-Committee, *Canadian Review of Sociology*, 58, no. 1 (2021): 105–18.
7. Marie Battiste and James Youngblood Henderson, *Protecting Indigenous Knowledge and Heritage: A Global Challenge* (Vancouver: UBC Press, 2000), 21.
8. Linda Tuhiwai Smith, *Decolonizing Methodologies: Research and Indigenous Peoples* (London: Zed Books Ltd., 2013).
9. Shawn Wilson, *Research is Ceremony: Indigenous Research Methods* (Winnipeg: Fernwood, 2008.
10. Wilson.
11. Wilson.
12. Adam Gaudry and Danielle Lorenz, "Indigenization as Inclusion, Reconciliation, and Decolonization: Navigating the Different Visions for Indigenizing the Canadian Academy," *AlterNative: An International Journal of Indigenous Peoples* 14, no. 3 (2018): 218–27.
13. Gaudry and Lorenz, 224.
14. Hill and Coleman, "The Two Row Wampum," 341.
15. Rick Hill, "Talking Points on History and Meaning of the Two Row Wampum Belt," *Deyohahá:ge: Indigenous Knowledge Centre*, 2013: 6.
16. Marie Battiste, *Decolonizing Education: Nourishing the Learning Spirit* (Vancouver: UBC Press, 2017), 159.
17. Sabrina E. Redwing Saunders and Susan M. Hill, "Native Education and In-Classroom Coalition-Building: Factors and Models in Delivering an Equitous Authentic Education," *Canadian Journal of Education/Revue Canadienne de l'Éducation* 30, no. 4 (2007): 1015–45.
18. Vanessa Watts, "Indigenous Place-Thought & Agency Amongst Humans and Non-Humans (First Woman and Sky Woman go on a European world tour!)," *Decolonization: Indigeneity, Education & Society* 2, no.1 (2013): 20–34.
19. Hill and Coleman, "The Two Row Wampum."
20. Bonnie Freeman and Trish van Katwyk, "Navigating the Waters: Understanding Allied Relationships Through a Tekéni Teyohà: ke Kahswénhtake Two Row Research Paradigm," *Journal of Indigenous Social Development* 9, no. 1 (2020): 62.
21. Freeman and van Katwyk, 72.
22. Jolene Rickard, "Visualizing Sovereignty in the Time of Biometric Sensors," *South Atlantic Quarterly* 110, no. 2 (2011): 466.
23. Smith, *Decolonizing Methodologies*.
24. Eugenia Zuroski, "This Ship We're In." *The Rambling* 9, August 7, 2020, https://the-rambling.com/2020/08/07/issue9-zuroski/.
25. Vine Deloria, *Spirit & Reason: The Vine Deloria, Jr., Reader* (Golden, CO: Fulcrum Publishing, 1999), 120.

26 Daniel Heath Justice, "Seeing (and Reading) Red: Indian Outlaws in the Ivory Tower," in *Indigenizing the Academy: Transforming Scholarship and Empowering Communities*, eds. Devon Abbott Mihesuah and Angela Cavender Wilson (Lincoln, NE: U of Nebraska Press, 2004), 101.

## Chapter 7: Two Rows of Reconciliation

1 Stanley Vestal, *Sitting Bull: Champion of the Sioux: A Biography* (Boston: Houghton Mifflin, 1932).
2 Education Act, R.S.O. 1990, c E.2; https://www.ontario.ca/laws/statute/90e02?-ga=2.114938887.16551180.1602781958-1519290099.1602781958#BK439.
3 Cesare Marino and Karim M. Tiro, *Along the Hudson and Mohawk: The 1790 Journey of Count Paolo Andreani* (Philadelphia: University of Pennsylvania Press, 2006), 59.
4 Official Report of the Debates of the House of Commons, Parliament (5th, 3$^{rd}$ session: 1885), House of Commons, 1886.
5 National Archives of Canada, Record Group 10, vol. 6810, file 470-2-3, vol. 7, 55 (L-3) and 63 (N-3).
6 Arthur Amiotte, *Photographs and Poems by Sioux Children: From the Porcupine Day School, Pine Ridge Indian Reservation, South Dakota* (Washington, Tipi Shop, DC: Indian Arts and Crafts Board, 1971), 7.
7 See https://www.theguardian.com/global/2018/oct/04/ontario-six-nations-nestle-running-water for background on the impact of the Nestle Corporation's removal of 3.6 million litres of water per day at its Aberfoyle water bottling plant while, in the same watershed, 91% of residents on Six Nations of the Grand River do not have clean, running water. Nestle has refused to respond to requests of the Six Nations to reduce the amount of water removed from the aquifer that serves the Haldimand Tract.

## Chapter 8: Below Decks in the Covenant

1 I have developed a fuller discussion of "fugitive prepositions" in the grammar of what I call a Black undercommons in *On Cuddling: Loved to Death in the Racial Embrace* (Pluto Press, 2023).
2 Not knowing my place is not a static position that remains fixed in time. Given time and patience, two matters are underappreciated in the urgency of now: the dynamism of relationships makes not knowing a dynamic place from which to know. With openness, not knowing my place changes over time.
3 Richard W. Hill, Sr., "Rotihnahon:tsi and Rotinonhson:ni: Historic Relationships between African Americans and the Confederacy of the Six Nations," in *in-diVisible: African-Native American Lives in the Americas*, ed. Gabrielle Tayac

(Washington, DC: Smithsonian Institution's National Museum of the American Indian, the National Museum of African American History and Culture, and the Smithsonian Institution Traveling Exhibition Service, 2009), 99–107.

4 Richard W. Hill, Sr. and Daniel Coleman. "The Two Row Wampum-Covenant Chain Tradition as a Guide for Indigenous-Univeristy Research Partnerships." *Cultural Studies and Critical Methodologies* 19, no. 5 (2019): 339–59.

5 Kwasi Konada. *The Akan Diaspora in the Americas* (New York: Oxford University Press, 2010), 3.

6 Hill, Sr., "Rotihnahon:tsi and Rotinonhson:ni," 100. Referencing the Mohawk term *rotihnahon:sti*—"people who have dark skin"—Hill observes that the Haudenosaunee had an ambiguous relationship to Black slavery. On the one hand, he documents an underground railroad knowingly facilitated by Haudenosaunee footpaths through their territories (106), while on the other, some Haudenosaunee themselves took up the practice of owning enslaved people. In 1699, for example, he notes that Rene-Robert Cavelier de La Salle tried to buy enslaved people from the Senecas to serve as guides when he looked for new trading routes. The Senecas asked him to wait until the enslaved people returned from a trip to the Dutch. La Salle reported that there were protocols for captive enslaved people to become free citizens of the Haudenosaunee Nations and that women had the authority to determine this process (Hill 100).

7 See the entry on "Black Fur Traders in Canada," in *The Canadian Encyclopedia* for some background. https://www.thecanadianencyclopedia.ca/en/article/black-fur-traders-in-canada.

8 My father's people are Asante, from Jamasi. The Asantes are part of the Akan people, who make up about 45% of the population of Ghana, making it the largest ethnic and linguistic group in Ghana. Akan is the ethnic name for the Twi-speaking peoples of the Guinea Coast of West Africa. *Twi-Fantie*, our language, some boast, is the lingua franca of Ghana. The Akan comprise many subgroups, with all of them sharing a common pattern of economic, political, social, and religious structures: the Agona, Ahanta, Akuapem, Akwamu, Akyerm, Aowin, Asante, Assin, Bono, Brong, Denkyira, Fante, Kwawu, Nzema, Sehwi, Twifo, and Wassa (see Albert Adu Boahen, *Ghana: Evolution and Change in the Nineteenth and Twentieth Centuries* (London: Longman, 1975)). My father's people, the Asante, have a kingdom and operate/d as an imperial empire; they fought many wars against many European empires.

9 In his essay, "That Event, This Memory: Notes on the Anthropology of African Diasporas in the New World," David Scott asks an important question worth recalling: "What are the varying ways in which Africa and slavery are employed by New World peoples of African descent in the narrative construction of relations among the past, present, and future?" *Diaspora* 1, no. 3 (1991): 261–84.

10 In 1598, a hundred years after the Portuguese, the Dutch arrived on the Gold Coast, following the Dutch-Portuguese war, which went from 1602 to 1650.

11 A great example of this expressive capacity of wampum is provided in Kelsey Leonard's discussion in this volume of *wunnáumwash*, the shell from which wampum is made, which in her Shinnecock nation's language means "truth-teller." "The material shell-beads," she writes, "recall their water-sifting, truth-telling capacities in anyone who takes up wampum in their hands."
12 Cartesian logic reduces life into types of substances: one being a spiritual substance that thinks, is active, and immaterial; the other, matter, is a substance that is extended and inert.
13 Kwasi Wiredu. *Cultural Universals and Particulars—An African Perspective* (Bloomington and Indianapolis: Indiana University Press, 1996), 53.
14 Benjamin Drew. "Sophia Pooley." *A North-Side View of Slavery. The Refugee: or the Narratives of Fugitive Slaves in Canada. Related by Themselves, with an Account of the History and Condition of the Colored Population of Upper Canada* (Boston: John P. Jewett, 1856), 192.
15 Drew, "Sophia Pooley," 192.
16 Peter Bryce. "Sir William Johnson, Bart., The Great Diplomat of the British-French Frontier," *The Quarterly Journal of the New York State Historical Association* 8, no. 4 (October 1927): 352–73.
17 William L. Stone. *The Life and Times of Sir William Johnson, Bart* (Albany: J. Munsell, 1865), http://threerivershms.com/SWJ%20vol2ap8.htm.
18 Daniel G. Hill. *The Freedom-Seekers: Blacks In Early Canada* (Agincourt, Ontario: Book Society of Canada, 1981), 13; "Thayendanegea" in *Dictionary of Canadian Biography Online*, http://www.biographi.ca/en/bio/thayendanegea_5E.html.
19 Drew, "Sophia Pooley," 194.
20 Drew, "Sophia Pooley," 195.
21 Drew, "Sophia Pooley," 192–93.
22 George Corghan assisted Sir William Johnson, and, for his second wife, married the Mohawk woman, Catherine (*Takarihoga*), daughter of Mohawk Chief Nickus Peters. https://www.howold.co/person/george-croghan/biography.
23 Drew, "Sophia Pooley,"194.
24 Drew, "Sophia Pooley," 193.
25 Drew, "Sophia Pooley," 192.
26 Drew, "Sophia Pooley," 192.
27 Drew, "Sophia Pooley," 193.
28 Drew, "Sophia Pooley," 192.
29 Drew, "Sophia Pooley," 193.
30 Drew, "Sophia Pooley," 195.
31 Barbara Alice Mann. "Adoption," in *Encyclopedia of the Haudenosaunee (Iroquois Confederacy)* (Greenwood Press, 2000), 1–7.
32 Alice, "Adoption," 3.
33 John Seaver, editor, *A Narrative of the Life of Mrs. Mary Jemison*. Reprint of 1824 edition (Syracuse University Press, 1990), 59.

34 Adams, Amber Meadow. *Seyakhikwatakwénnis ne Tehontatenentshonteronhtáhkwa; Grasping the Chain Again* (R. v. Derek White & Hunter Montour, S.C. 505-01-137394-165 and CM-2018-000545). Expert Report, June 4, 2021, 57.
35 Adams, *Seyakhikwatakwénnis*, 88.
36 Adams, *Seyakhikwatakwénnis*, 51.
37 Adams, *Seyakhikwatakwénnis*, 22.
38 I have no interest in turning to the nation-state as a way to imagine this relationship. What makes Blackness get out of the ship of state is that when the ship of Canada "adopts" Black people it has not led to affirming our lives. If avoidance is the orientation to Black presence in Canada, to the nation-state, and if a potential dialogue based on the Covenant Chain-Two Row was unrealized and never came into the foreground of that relationship, then we would need a different agreement than one where absence and unacknowledgement is the basis of our presence.
39 For a discussion on how the Black settlers in the Queen's Bush were "surveyed off" the land by the 1840s and '50s, see Geoff Martin's essay, "Slave Days in the Queen's Bush" in *Hamilton Arts & Letters* 13 no. 1 (2020), https://samizdatpress.typepad.com/hal_magazine_issue_thirte/slave-days-in-the-queens-bush-by-geoff-martin-6.html.
40 I have yet to come across a Twi word that corresponds to "family" either in the sense of a nuclear family composed of a couple with their immediate children or in the sense of an extended family defined as an extension of the nuclear family and based on both marriage and descent.
41 Rick Hill, "Oral Memory of the Haudenosaunee: Views of the Two Row Wampum," in *Indian Roots of American Democracy*, ed. José Barreiro (Ithaca, NY: Akwe:kon P/Cornell UP, 1992), 155.

## Chapter 9: Towards Peace

1 Rick Monture, *Teionkwakhashion Tsi Niionkwariho:Ten: We Share Our Matters, Two Centuries of Writing and Resistance at Six Nations of the Grand River* (Winnipeg: University of Manitoba Press, 2014), 14.
2 See Richard W. Hill Sr. and Daniel Coleman, "The Two Row Wampum-Covenant Chain Tradition as a Guide for Indigenous-University Research Partnerships," *Cultural Studies ↔ Critical Methodologies* 19, no. 5 (Oct. 2019): 339–59.; Bonnie Freeman and Trish van Katwyk, "Testing the Waters: Engaging the Tekéni Teyohà:ke Kahswénhtake /Two Row Wampum into a Research Paradigm," *Canadian Journal of Native Education* 41, no. 1 (2019): 146–67.
3 Carrie Dyck and Amos Key, "The Ethics of Research on Gayogoho:nǫ' (Cayuga)" (poster presentation, Annual Meeting of the Linguistic Society of America, Boston, MA, January 4–6, 2013).

4 Kathy Absolon and Cam Willett, "Putting Ourselves Forward: Location in Aboriginal Research," in *Research as Resistance: Critical, Indigenous and Anti-Oppressive Approaches*, eds. Leslie Brown and Susan Strega (Toronto: Canadian Scholars' Press, 2005), 97.
5 See Susan M. Hill, *The Clay We Are Made Of: Haudenosaunee Land Tenure on the Grand River* (Winnipeg: University of Manitoba Press, 2017), 15.; Monture, *Teionkwakhashion Tsi Niionkwariho:Ten*, 15.; Kevin White, "Rousing a Curiosity in Hewitt's Iroquois Cosmologies," *Wicazo Sa Review* 28, no. 2 (2013): 89–90.
6 "Crown-First Nations Gathering." *The Governor General of Canada*, January 24, 2012, www.gg.ca/en/media/news/2012/crown-first-nations-gathering-0.
7 "Canada-First Nations Joint Action Plan." *Assembly of First Nations*, June 9, 2011, www.afn.ca/canada-first-nations-joint-action-plan2. Accessed February 17, 2021.
8 Arthur Manuel and Grand Chief Ronald M. Derrickson. *Unsettling Canada: A National Wake-Up Call* (Toronto: Between the Lines, 2015).
9 Monture, *Teionkwakhashion Tsi Niionkwariho:Ten*, 14.; Hill and Coleman, "The Two Row Wampum," 2.
10 Hill and Coleman, 17.
11 Monture, *Teionkwakhashion Tsi Niionkwariho:Ten*, 14.
12 Jake Thomas, *The Friendship Treaty Belt, the Two Row Wampum Treaty Belt* (Wilsonville, Ontario: Sandpiper Press, 1978), 2.
13 Hill and Coleman, "The Two Row Wampum," 10.
14 Hill, *The Clay We Are Made Of*, 8.; Monture, *Teionkwakhashion Tsi Niionkwariho:Ten*, 13.
15 Monture, 6.
16 Monture, 7.
17 Bonnie Freeman, "The Spirit of Haudenosaunee Youth: The Transformation of Identity and Well-being Through Culture-based Activism" (PhD diss., Wilfrid Laurier University, 2015): 36, https://scholars.wlu.ca/cgi/viewcontent.cgi?article=2789&context=etd.
18 Margaret M. Bruchac, *Savage Kin: Indigenous Informants and American Anthropologists* (Tucson: University of Arizona Press, 2018).
19 Hill, *The Clay We Are Made Of*, 16.; White, "Rousing a Curiosity," 100.
20 Hill and Coleman, "The Two Row Wampum," 3–4.

## Chapter 10: The Pen Pal Project

1 The 2017 Neighbouring Communities Project was a relationship-building initiative between Six Nations and Caledonia. You can read about it at http://www.neighbouringcommunities.net/documents/CDShort.pdf.
2 "Community Document," *Neighbouring Communities Project*, March 2007, 5, www.neighbouringcommunities.net/documents/CDShort.pdf.

3 The territory of the Six Nations was set out in the Haldimand Proclamation of 1784, including six miles deep on each side of the Grand River beginning at Lake Erie and extending to the head of the river.
4 The Pen Pal Project is archived on the website http://www.penpalproject.ca.
5 The Pen Pal Project was made possible by students, teachers, and volunteers from both sides of the river, supported by in-kind donations from local agencies and organizations, along with funding grants through multiple stakeholders.
6 For the 2013 gathering video visit http://www.penpalproject.ca/gatherings/2013.html.
7 The Battle of Stoney Creek featured the alliance between First Nations, mostly Haudenosaunee, and the British in the War of 1812 when invading troops from the United States were defeated. It is known as a turning point in the defence of Upper Canada.
8 To read the complete responses from India visit http://www.penpalproject.ca/information/mumbai-responses.pdf.

## Chapter 11: Deyohahage Gihe gowa'hneh

1 "Epic Canoe Trip," *Two Row Wampum Renewal Campaign*, 2013, http://honorthetworow.org/epic-canoe-trip/.

## Chapter 12: The Deep and Rippling Consciousness of Water

1 See Kathleen E. Absolon, *Kaandossiwin: How We Come to Know* (Winnipeg: Fernwood Publishing, 2011).
2 See Kayanesenh Paul Williams. *Kayanerenko:wa: The Great Law of Peace* (Winnipeg: University of Manitoba Press, 2018).
3 Alun David Morgan, "Journeys into Transformation: Travel to an 'Other' Place as a Vehicle for Transformative Learning," *Journal of Transformative Education* 8, no. 4 (2010): 248.
4 Rebecca Solnit, *Wanderlust: A History of Walking* (New York: Penguin, 2001).
5 Rebecca Solnit, "Finding Time," *Orion Magazine* (2007): 14.
6 See Susie O'Brien, "Survival Strategies for Global Times: The Desert Walk for Biodiversity, Health and Heritage," *Interventions* 9, no. 1 (2007): 83–98.
7 See Brooke Hansen and Jack Rossen, "Activist Anthropology with the Haudenosaunee: Theoretical and Practical Insights from the Two Row Wampum Renewal Campaign," *Anthropology in Action* 24 (2017): 32–44.; Jessica Hallenbeck, "Returning to the Water to Enact a Treaty Relationship: The Two Row Wampum Renewal Campaign," *Settler Colonial Studies*, 5, no. 4 (2015): 350–62.
8 "Hudson River Itinerary and Map," *Two Row Wampum Renewal Campaign*, 2013, http://honorthetworow.org/epic-canoe-trip/itinerary-and-map/.

9 See Hallenbeck, "Returning to the Water."
10 See Susan M. Hill, *The Clay We are Made Of: Haudenosaunee Land Tenure on the Grand River* (Winnipeg: University of Manitoba Press, 2017).
11 See https://www.snpolytechnic.com/indigenous-knowledge-centre.
12 See Richard W. Hill Sr. and Daniel Coleman, "The Two Row Wampum-Covenant Chain Tradition as a Guide for Indigenous-University Research Partnerships," *Cultural Studies↔ Critical Methodologies* 19 (2019): 339–59.
13 See Bonnie Freeman and Trish van Katwyk, "Testing the Waters: Engaging the Tekéni Teyohà: ke Kahswénhtake/Two Row Wampum into a Research Paradigm," *Canadian Journal of Native Education* 41, no. 1 (2019): 146–67.
14 See Freeman and van Katwyk, "Testing the Waters."
15 From a Haudenosaunee perspective, young females and males are not considered adults until they have had a child.
16 A young female in a family is referred to as Khe'kén:'a—younger sister in Kanien'kéha (Mohawk) language.
17 See Richard Simonelli, "Use the Good Mind! An Interview with Freida Jacques." *Winds of Change* 12, no. 2 (1997): 46–49.
18 We refer to the non-Indigenous youth that participated in this study in English as "Younger sister" or "Younger brother" to distinguish them from their Indigenous counterparts, *Khe'kén:'a* (Younger sister), in *Kanien'kéha* (Mohawk) language.
19 See Bonnie Freeman and Trish van Katwyk, "Navigating the Waters: Understanding Allied Relationships through a Tekéni Teyohà: ke Kahswénhtake Two Row Research Paradigm," *Journal of Indigenous Social Development* 9 (2020): 60–76; Freeman and van Katwyk, "Testing the Waters."
20 See Eve Tuck and K. Wayne Yang, "Decolonization is Not a Metaphor," *Decolonization: Indigeneity, Education & Society* 1, no. 1 (2012): 1–40.
21 See Michelle Daigle and Margaret Marietta Ramírez, "Decolonial Geographies," in *Keywords in Radical geography: Antipode at 50*, ed. The Antipode Editorial Collective (Hoboken, NJ: Wiley, 2019), 78–84.
22 Leanne Betasamosake Simpson, *As We Have Always Done: Indigenous Freedom Through Radical Resistance* (Minneapolis: U of Minnesota Press, 2017), 2.
23 Simpson, 215.
24 See Rick Hill, "The Haudenosaunee Thanksgiving Address and Its Relevance for Futures and Learnings," in *Indigenous Futures and Learnings Taking Place*, eds. Ligia (Licho) López López and Gioconda Coello (New York: Routledge, 2020), 157–71.
25 See Taiaiake Alfred and Jeff Corntassel, "Being Indigenous: Resurgences Against Contemporary Colonialism," *Government and Opposition* 40, no. 4 (2005): 597–614.
26 See Jeffrey S. Denis and Kerry A. Bailey, "'You Can't Have Reconciliation Without Justice': How Non-Indigenous Participants in Canada's Truth and Reconciliation Process Understand Their Roles and Goals," in *The Limits of Settler Colonial*

*Reconciliation: Non-Indigenous Peoples and the Responsibility to Engage*, eds. Sarah Maddison, Tom Clark, and Ravi de Costa (Singapore: Springer, 2016), 137–58.

27  See Sarah Maddison, Tom Clark, and Ravi de Costa, *The Limits of Settler Colonial Reconciliation: Non-Indigenous Peoples and the Responsibility to Engage* (Signapore: Springer, 2016).

28  See Taiaiake Alfred, *Peace, Power, Righteousness: An Indigenous Manifesto* (Toronto: University of Toronto Press, 1999).

29  See Alfred; Williams, *Kayanerenko:wa*.

30  See Freeman and van Katwyk, "Testing the Waters"; Freeman and van Katwyk, "Navigating the Waters"; Hill and Coleman, "The Two Row Wampum."

31  See Robin Wall Kimmerer, *Braiding Sweetgrass: Indigenous Wisdom, Scientific Knowledge and the Teachings of Plants* (Minneapolis: Milkweed Editions, 2013).

32  See Alfred and Corntassel, "Being Indigenous"; Marie Battiste, "Reconciling Indigenous Knowledge in Education: Promises, Possibilities, and Imperatives," in *Dissident Knowledge in Higher Education*, eds. Marc Spooner and James McNinch (Regina: University of Regina Press, 2018), 123–48.; Henry Giroux, *Youth in a Suspect Society: Democracy or Disposability?* (London: Palgrave Macmillan, 2009).; Yvonna Lincoln, "A Dangerous Accountability: Neoliberalism's Veer Toward Accountancy in Higher Education," *Dissident Knowledge in Higher Education*, eds. Marc Spooner and James McNinch (Regina: University of Regina Press, 2018), 3–20.

33  Frantz Fanon, *The Wretched of the Earth*, trans. Constance Farrington (New York: Grove Press, 1963), 35.

34  See Denis and Bailey, "'You Can't Have Reconciliation Without Justice.'"

35  See Marina Mugalhães, "Technologies of the Body: a Pecha Kucha Talk by Marina Magalhães" (lecture, LA as Lab Conference, Claremont Graduate University, May 4, 2019), https://vimeo.com/338387303.

36  See Fanon, *The Wretched of the Earth*.

37  See Daigle and Ramírez, "Decolonial Geographies."

# Bibliography

Absolon, Kathleen E. *Kaandossiwin: How We Come to Know*. Winnipeg: Fernwood Publishing, 2011.

Absolon, Kathy and Cam Willett. "Putting Ourselves Forward: Location in Aboriginal Research." In *Research as Resistance: Critical, Indigenous and Anti-oppressive Approaches*, edited by Leslie Brown and Susan Strega, 97–126. Toronto: Canadian Scholars' Press, 2005.

Adams, Amber Meadow. *The Covenant Chain in Passamaquoddy Country*. Draft Report for the Passmaquoddy First Nation, February 17, 2006.

Adams, Amber Meadow. *Seyakhikwatakwénnis ne Tehontatenentshonteronhtáhkwa; Grasping the Chain Again* (R. v. Derek White & Hunter Montour, S.C. 505-01-137394-165 and CM-2018-000545). Expert Report, June 4, 2021.

Adams, Amber Meadow. "Teyotsi'tsiahsonhátye: Meaning and Medicine in the Haudenosaunee (Iroquois) Story of Life's Renewal" Ph.D. diss., State University of New York, 2013.

Alberta Council of Women's Shelters. "Treaty Relations: Spirit, Intent and First Nations Perspectives." In *Stepping into the Circle: A Call to Conversation and Workbook Exploring Indigenous Knowledge*, https://acws.ca/wpcontent/uploads/2020/09/Stepping_into_the_Circle-M3.pdf.

Alfred, Taiaiake. *Peace, Power, Righteousness: An Indigenous Manifesto*. Toronto: University of Toronto Press, 1999.

Alfred, Taiaiake. *Wasase: Indigenous Pathways of Action and Freedom*. Toronto: University of Toronto Press, 2005.

Alfred, Taiaiake and Jeff Corntassel. "Being Indigenous: Resurgences Against Contemporary Colonialism." *Government and Opposition* 40, no. 4 (2005): 597–614.

Ali, Saleem and Helena Vladich. "Environmental Diplomacy." In *The SAGE Handbook of Diplomacy*, edited by Costas M. Constantinou, Pauline Kerr, and Paul Sharp, 601–16. London: SAGE Publications, 2016.

Amiotte, Arthur. *Photographs and Poems by Sioux Children: From the Porcupine Day School, Pine Ridge Indian Reservation, South Dakota*. Washington, Tipi Shop, DC: Indian Arts and Crafts Board, 1971.

Andersen, Morten Skumsrud and Iver B. Neumann. "Practices as Models: A Methodology with an Illustration Concerning Wampum Diplomacy." *Millennium* 40, no. 3 (2012): 457–81.

Antwi, Phanuel. *On Cuddling: Loved to Death in the Racial Embrace*. London: Pluto Press, 2023.

Barnhill-Dilling, S. Kathleen, Louie Rivers, and Jason A. Delborne. "Rooted in Recognition: Indigenous Environmental Justice and the Genetically Engineered American Chestnut Tree." *Society & Natural Resources* 33, no. 1 (2020): 83–100.

Bartlett, Cheryl, Murdena Marshall, and Albert Marshall. "Two-Eyed Seeing and Other Lessons Learned Within a Co-Learning Journey of Bringing Together Indigenous and Mainstream Knowledges and Ways of Knowing." *Journal of Environmental Studies and Sciences* 2, no. 5 (October 2012): 331–40.

Battiste, Marie. *Decolonizing Education: Nourishing the Learning Spirit.* Vancouver: UBC Press, 2017.

Battiste, Marie. "Reconciling Indigenous Knowledge in Education: Promises, Possibilities, and Imperatives." In *Dissident Knowledge in Higher Education*, edited by Marc Spooner and James McNinch, 123–48. Regina: University of Regina Press, 2018.

Battiste, Marie and James (Sa'ke'j) Youngblood Henderson. *Protecting Indigenous Knowledge and Heritage: A Global Challenge.* Vancouver: UBC Press, 2000.

Beauchamp, William. *Civil, Religious and Mourning Councils and Ceremonies of the New York Indians.* New York State Museum Bulletin 113 (1907), reprinted by Albany: Museum of the State of New York, 1975.

Benn, Carl. *Mohawks on the Nile: Natives Among the Canadian Voyageurs in Egypt, 1884–1885.* Toronto: Dundurn Press, 2009.

"Black Fur Traders in Canada," in *The Canadian Encyclopedia.* https://www.thecanadianencyclopedia.ca/en/article/black-fur-traders-in-canada.

Boahen, Albert Adu. *Ghana: Evolution and Change in the Nineteenth and Twentieth Centuries.* London: Longman, 1975.

Borrows, John. *Drawing Out Law: A Spirit's Guide.* Toronto: University of Toronto Press, 2010.

Bruchac, Margaret M. *Savage Kin: Indigenous Informants and American Anthropologists.* Tucson: University of Arizona Press, 2018.

Bryce, Peter. "Sir William Johnson, Bart., The Great Diplomat of the British-French Frontier." *The Quarterly Journal of the New York State Historical Association* 8, no. 4 (October 1927): 352–73.

Burdette, Bradford. "Mercenaria Mercenaria (Northern Quahog)." *Animal Diversity Web*, 2001. https://animaldiversity.org/accounts/Mercenaria_mercenaria/.

Calloway, Colin. *White People, Indians and Highlanders: Tribal People and Colonial Encounters in Scotland and America.* Oxford: Oxford University Press, 2010.

"Canada-First Nations Joint Action Plan." *Assembly of First Nations*, June 9, 2011. www.afn.ca/canada-first-nations-joint-action-plan2.

Carlson, John. "Manoomin is not Wild Rice: An Anishinaabeg Treaty." *Zeitschrift für Kanada-Studien* 38, no. 1 (2018).

Castellano, Marlene Brant. "Ethics of Aboriginal Research." *Journal of Aboriginal Health* (2004): 98–114.

Coastal Resources Management Council, Narragansett Bay Estuary Program, and Save The Bay. "Quahog (Mercenaria mercenaria)." *University of Rhode Island Environmental Data Center*, 2001.

Colden, Cadwallader. *History of the Five Indian Nations*. 1727. Toronto: Coles Publishing Co., 1968.
Coleman, Daniel. "Epistemic Justice, CanLit, and the Politics of Respect." *Canadian Literature* 204 (Spring 2010): 124–26.
Coleman, Daniel. "The Two Row Wampum-Covenant Chain Treaty and Trans-Systemic Resilience." In *Global Narratives of Resilience*, edited by Ana María Fraile-Marcos, 21–38. New York: Routledge, 2019.
"Community Document 2007." *Neighbouring Communities Project*, March 2007. www.neighbouringcommunities.net/documents/CDShort.pdf.
Cool, R. "Hard Times for Hard Clams." *The Bay Journal* 8, no. 4 (June 1998).
Corbiere, Alan Theodore Ojiig. "Anishinaabe Treaty-Making in the 18th-and-19th-Century Northern Great Lakes: From Shared Meanings to Epistemological Chasms." PhD diss., York University, 2019. https://yorkspace.library.yorku.ca/xmlui/handle/10315/37402.
Corbiere, Alan. "'Their Own Forms of Which They Take the Most Notice': Diplomatic Metaphors and Symbolism on Wampum Belts." In *Anishnaabewin Niwin: Four Rising Winds*, edited by Alan Ojiig Corbiere, Mary Ann Naokwegiig Corbiere, Deborah MacGregor, and Crystal Migwans. M'Chigeeng, 47–64. ON: Ojibway Cultural Foundation, 2013.
Corntassel, Jeff. "Indigenous Storytelling, Truth-Telling, and Community Approaches to Reconciliation." *ESC: English Studies in Canada* 35, no. 1 (2009): 137–59.
*Correspondence Respecting Indians Between the Provincial Secretary of State and the Governors of British North America*. Queen's Printer, 1837.
Coté, Rochelle et al. "Indigenization, Institutions, and Imperatives: Perspectives on Reconciliation from the CSA Decolonization Sub-Committee." *Canadian Review of Sociology* 58, no. 1 (2021): 105–18.
"Crown-First Nations Gathering." *The Governor General of Canada*, January 24, 2012, www.gg.ca/en/media/news/2012/crown-first-nations-gathering-0.
Daigle, Michelle and Margaret Marietta Ramírez. "Decolonial Geographies." In *Keywords in Radical Geography: Antipode at 50*, edited by The Antipode Editorial Collective. Hoboken, 78–84. NJ: Wiley, 2019.
Davis, Heather and Zoe Todd. "On the Importance of a Date, or, Decolonizing the Anthropocene" *ACME: An International Journal for Critical Geographies* 16, no. 4 (2017): 761–80.
Deloria, Vine. *Spirit & Reason: The Vine Deloria, Jr., Reader*. Golden, CO: Fulcrum Publishing, 1999.
Deloria, Vine, and Raymond J. DeMallie, eds. *Documents of American Indian Diplomacy: Treaties, Agreements, and Conventions, 1775–1979*. Vol. 1. University of Oklahoma Press, 1999.
Denis, Jeffrey S. and Kerry A. Bailey. "'You Can't Have Reconciliation Without Justice': How Non-Indigenous Participants in Canada's Truth and Reconciliation Process Understand Their Roles and Goals." In *The Limits of Settler Colonial*

*Reconciliation: Non-Indigenous Peoples and the Responsibility to Engage*, edited by Sarah Maddison, Tom Clark, and Ravi de Costa, 137–58. Singapore: Springer, 2016.

Dennis, Matthew. *Cultivating a Landscape of Peace: Iroquois-European Encounters in Seventeenth Century America*. Ithaca: Cornell University Press, 1993.

Drew, Benjamin. "Sophia Pooley." In *A North-Side View of Slavery. The Refugee: Or the Narratives of Fugitive Slaves in Canada. Related by Themselves, with an Account of the History and Condition of the Colored Population of Upper Canada*. Boston: John P. Jewett, 1856.

Duignan, Sarah, Tina Moffat, and Dawn Martin-Hill. "Using Boundary Objects to Co-Create Community Health and Water Knowledge with Community-Based Medical Anthropology and Indigenous Knowledge." *Engaged Scholar Journal: Community-Engaged Research, Teaching and Learning* 6, no. 1 (2020): 49–76.

Dyck, Carrie and Amos Key. "The Ethics of Research on Gayogo̱hó:nǫ' (Cayuga)." Poster presented at the Annual Meeting of the Linguistic Society of America, Boston, MA, January 4–6, 2013.

Echo-Hawk, Walter R. *In the Courts of the Conqueror: The Ten Worst Indian Law Cases Ever Decided*. Golden, CO: Fulcrum Press, 2010.

"Epic Canoe Trip." *Two Row Wampum Renewal Campaign*, 2013. http://honorthetworow.org/epic-canoe-trip/.

Ermine, Willie. "The Ethical Space of Engagement." *Indigenous Law Journal* 6, no. 1 (2007): 193–203.

Fanon, Frantz. *The Wretched of the Earth*. Translated by Constance Farrington. New York: Grove Press, 1963.

Finch, Lance S. J. "The Duty to Learn: Taking Account of Indigenous Legal Orders in Practice." *Continuing Legal Education Society of British Columbia*, 2012. https://www.cerp.gouv.qc.ca/fileadmin/Fichiers_clients/Documents_deposes_a_la_Commission/P-253.pdf.

Fisher, Roger and William Ury. *Getting to Yes: Negotiating Agreement Without Giving In*. New York: Penguin Books: 1981, 2005.

Freeman, Bonnie. "The Spirit of Haudenosaunee Youth: The Transformation of Identity and Well-being Through Culture-based Activism." PhD diss. Wilfred Laurier University, 2015. https://scholars.wlu.ca/cgi/viewcontent.cgi?article=2789&context=etd.

Freeman, Bonnie, and Trish van Katwyk. "Navigating the Waters: Understanding Allied Relationships through a Tekéni Teyohà: ke Kahswénhtake Two Row Research Paradigm." *Journal of Indigenous Social Development* 9, no. 1 (2020): 60–76.

Freeman, Bonnie and Trish van Katwyk. "Testing the Waters: Engaging the Tekéni Teyohà:ke Kahswénhtake /Two Row Wampum into a Research Paradigm." *Canadian Journal of Native Education* 41, no. 1 (2019): 146–167.

Gadoua, Renée. "Face Time: Keeping the Faith." *Syracuse New Times*, 2014. https://www.syracusenewtimes.com/keeping-the-faith/2014.

Gaudry, Adam and Danielle Lorenz. "Indigenization as Inclusion, Reconciliation, and Decolonization: Navigating the Different Visions for Indigenizing the Canadian Academy." *AlterNative: An International Journal of Indigenous Peoples* 14, no. 3 (2018): 218–27.

Geertz, Clifford. *The Interpretation of Cultures*. New York: Basic Books, 1973.

Gibson, John Arthur. "Iroquoian Cosmology: Second Part, with Introduction and Notes." In *Forty-Third Annual Report of The Bureau of American Ethnology to the Secretary of the Smithsonian Institution, 1925-1926*, edited and translated by J. N. B. Hewitt, 449–819. Washington: United States Government Printing Office, 1928.

Gibson, John Arthur. *Concerning the League: The Iroquois League Tradition as Dictated in Onondaga by John Arthur Gibson*. 1912. Newly Edited and Translated by Hanni Woodbury in Collaboration with Reg Henry and Harry Webster on the Basis of A.A. Goldenweiser's Manuscript. Memoir 9. Winnipeg, MB: Algonquian and Iroquoian Linguistics, 1992.

Giroux, Henry. *Youth in a Suspect Society: Democracy or Disposability?* London: Palgrave Macmillan, 2009.

Gobler, Christopher J. and Hannes Baumann. "Hypoxia and Acidification in Ocean Ecosystems: Coupled Dynamics and Effects on Marine Life." *Biology Letters* 12, no. 5 (2016): 1–8.

Gobler, Christopher J., Michael H. Doall, Bradley J. Peterson, Craig S. Young, Flynn DeLaney, Ryan B. Wallace, Stephen J. Tomasetti et al. "Rebuilding a collapsed bivalve population, restoring seagrass meadows, and eradicating harmful algal blooms in a temperate lagoon using spawner sanctuaries." *Frontiers in Marine Science* 9 (2022): 911731.

Graymont, Barbara. *The Iroquois in the American Revolution*. Syracuse, NY: Syracuse University Press, 1972.

Griffith, Andrew W. and Christopher J. Gobler. "Transgenerational Exposure of North Atlantic Bivalves to Ocean Acidification Renders Offspring More Vulnerable to Low pH and Additional Stressors." *Scientific Reports* 7, no. 1 (2017): 1–11.

Hallenbeck, Jessica. "Returning to the Water to Enact a Treaty Relationship: The Two Row Wampum Renewal Campaign." *Settler Colonial Studies* 5, no. 4 (2015): 350–62.

Hansen, Brooke and Jack Rossen. "Theoretical and Practical Insights from the Two Row Wampum Renewal Campaign." *Anthropology in Action* 24, no. 3 (2017): 32–44.

Harrison, Daniel F. "Change Mid Continuity, Innovation Within Tradition: Wampum Diplomacy at the Treaty of Greenville, 1795." *Ethnohistory* 64, no. 2 (2017): 191–215.

Hendricks, Marcus. "The History of Wampum – Real Story from Local Massachusetts Native American." By Jeffrey Wyman. YouTube. August 5, 2019. Video, 3:24. https://www.youtube.com/watch?v=9ovyScbrXyQ.

Hewitt, Jeffery G. "Certain (Mis) Conceptions: Westphalian Origins, Portraiture and Wampum." In *Routledge Handbook of International Law and the Humanities*, edited by Shane Chalmers and Sundhya Pahuja, 159–72. New York: Routledge, 2021.

Hill, Daniel G. *The Freedom-Seekers: Blacks in Early Canada*. Agincourt, Ontario: Book Society of Canada, 1981.

Hill Sr., Rick. "Ecological Knowledge & the Dish with One Spoon: Conversations in Cultural Fluency #2." *Six Nations Polytechnic*. YouTube. January 29, 2016. Video, 33:08. https://www.youtube.com/watch?v=RL83GvOO_Co&t=1s.

Hill, Rick. "The Haudenosaunee Thanksgiving Address and its Relevance for Futures and Learnings." In *Indigenous Futures and Learnings Taking Place*, edited by Ligia (Licho) López López and Gioconda Coello, 157–71. New York: Routledge, 2020.

Hill, Rick. "Linking Arms: The Haudenosaunee Context of the Covenant Chain." In *Mamow Be-Mo-Tay-Tah: Let Us Walk Together*, edited by José Zárate and Norah McMurtry, 17–24. Toronto: Canadian Ecumenical Anti-Racism Network, 2009.

Hill, Richard. "Oral Memory of the Haudenosaunee: Views of the Two Row Wampum." In *Indian Roots of American Democracy*, edited by José Barreiro, 149–59. Ithaca, NY: Akwe:kon Press/Cornell University Press, 1992.

Hill, Sr. Richard W. "Rotihnahon:tsi and Rotinonhson:ni: Historic Relationships between African Americans and the Confederacy of the Six Nations." In *indiVisible: African-Native American Lives in the Americas*, edited by Gabrielle Tayac, 99–107. Washington, DC: Smithsonian Institution's National Museum of the American Indian, the National Museum of African American History and Culture, and the Smithsonian Institution Traveling Exhibition Service, 2009.

Hill, Rick. "Talking Points on History and Meaning of the Two Row Wampum Belt." *Two Row Wampum Renewal Campaign*, 2013. https://honorthetworow.org/wp-content/uploads/2013/03/TwoRowTalkingPoints-Rick-Hill.pdf.

Hill Sr., Richard W., and Daniel Coleman. "The Two Row Wampum-Covenant Chain Tradition as a Guide for Indigenous-University Research Partnerships." *Cultural Studies ↔ Critical Methodologies* 19, no. 5 (2019): 339–59.

Hill, Susan M. *The Clay We are Made Of: Haudenosaunee Land Tenure on the Grand River*. Winnipeg: University of Manitoba Press, 2017.

Hough, Franklin B., ed. *Documents Relating to the History of the Colony of New York*. Albany, 1861.

Jacobs, Beverly. "International Law/The Great Law of Peace." Master's thesis, University of Saskatchewan, 2000. https://www.collectionscanada.gc.ca/obj/s4/f2/dsk3/SSU/TC-SSU-07042007083651.pdf.

Jacobs, Wilbur R. "Wampum: The Protocol of Indian Diplomacy." *The William and Mary Quarterly: A Magazine of Early American History* (1949): 596–604.

Jennings, Francis et al. *The History and Culture of Iroquois Diplomacy*. Syracuse, NY: Syracuse University Press, 1985.

Johnson, William, Sir. *Papers of Sir William Johnson*. Albany: University of the State of New York, 1921–1965.

Johnston, Charles. *The Valley of the Six Nations*. Toronto: Champlain Society, 1964.

Justice, Daniel Heath. "Seeing (and Reading) Red: Indian Outlaws in the Ivory Tower." In *Indigenizing the Academy: Transforming Scholarship and Empowering Communities*, edited by Devon Abbott Mihesuah and Angela Cavender Wilson, 100–23. Lincoln, NE: University of Nebraska Press, 2004.

Kelsey, Penelope Myrtle. *Reading the Wampum: Essays on Hodinöhsö:ni' Visual Code and Epistemological Recovery*. Syracuse, NY: Syracuse University Press, 2014.

Kimmerer, Robin Wall. *Braiding Sweetgrass: Indigenous Wisdom, Scientific Knowledge and the Teachings of Plants*. Minneapolis, MN: Milkweed Editions, 2013.

King, Hayden. "The Erasure of Indigenous Thought in Foreign Policy," *Open Canada*, July 13, 2017, https://opencanada.org/erasure-indigenous-thought-foreign-policy/.

Knox, Bradly A. "The Visual Rhetoric of Lady Justice: Understanding Jurisprudence Through 'Metonymic Tokens.'" *Inquiries Journal* 6, no. 5 (2014).

Konada, Kwasi. *The Akan Diaspora in the Americas*. New York: Oxford University Press, 2010.

Kuokkanen, Rauna. *Reshaping the University: Responsibility, Indigenous Epistemes, and the Logic of the Gift*. Vancouver: UBC Press, 2011.

"Land Acknowledgments: A Guide." *McMaster University Student Success Centre*, 2018, https://healthsci.mcmaster.ca/docs/librariesprovider59/resources/mcmaster-university-land-acknowledgment-guide.pdf?sfvrsn=7318d517_2.

Leonard, Kelsey. "WAMPUM Adaptation Framework: Eastern Coastal Tribal Nations and Sea Level Rise Impacts on Water Security." *Climate and Development* (2021): 1–10.

L'Incarnation, Marie de. *Word From New France: The Selected Letters of Marie de l'Incarnation*. Translated and edited by Joyce Marshall. Toronto: Oxford University Press, 1967.

Lincoln, Yvonna. "A Dangerous Accountability: Neoliberalism's Veer Toward Accountancy in Higher Education." In *Dissident Knowledge in Higher Education*, edited by Marc Spooner and James McNinch, 3–20. Regina: University of Regina Press, 2018.

Livingston, Robert. *The Livingston Indian Records 1666-1723*. Edited by Lawrence H. Leder. Gettysburg, PA: The Pennsylvania Historical Association, 1956.

Lucas, John Randolph. "Justice." *Philosophy* 47, no. 181 (1972): 229–48.

Lyons, Oren. "Land of the Free, Home of the Brave." In *Indian Roots of American Democracy*, edited by José Barreiro, 30–35. Ithaca, NY: Akwe:kon Press/Cornell University Press, 1992.

Lyons, Chief Oren. "Opening Statement: The Year of the Indigenous Peoples (1993)." Speech given at United Nations General Assembly Auditorium. Transcribed by Craig Carpenter. United Nations Plaza, New York City, December 10, 1992. https://ratical.org/many_worlds/6Nations/OLatUNin92.html.

Lyons, Chief Oren. "Oren Lyons: On the Indigenous View of the World." By Leila Conners. *11th Hour Research Tapes,* Sept 16, 2016. https://ratical.org/many_worlds/6Nations/ OrenLyons-IndigenousWorldView.html#s24.

Lyons, Oren. "When You Talk About Client Relationships, You Are Talking About the Future of Nations." In *Rethinking Indian Law.* Edited by National Lawyers Guild, Committee on Native American Struggles, pp. iv–vi. New York: National Lawyers Guild, 1982.

MacIntyre, Alasdair C. *Whose Justice? Which Rationality?* Notre Dame, IN: University of Notre Dame Press, 1988.

Maddison, Sarah, Tom Clark, and Ravi de Costa. *The Limits of Settler Colonial Reconciliation: Non-Indigenous Peoples and the Responsibility to Engage.* Singapore: Springer, 2016.

Manitowabi, Joshua. "Wii Niiganabying (Looking Ahead)." *Turtle Island Journal of Indigenous Health* 1, no. 1 (2020): 59–71.

Mann, Barbara Alice. "Adoption," in *Encyclopedia of the Haudenosaunee (Iroquois Confederacy),* edited by Bruce Elliott Johansen, Barbara Alice Mann, 1–7. Greenwood Press, 2000.

Manuel, Arthur and Grand Chief Ronald M. Derrickson. *Unsettling Canada: A National Wake-Up Call.* Toronto: Between the Lines, 2015.

Marino, Cesare and Karim M. Tiro. *Along the Hudson and Mohawk: The 1790 Journey of Count Paolo Andreani.* Philadelphia: University of Pennsylvania Press, 2006.

Martin, Geoff. "Slave Days in the Queen's Bush" in *Hamilton Arts & Letters* 13 (1), 2020. https://samizdatpress.typepad.com/hal_magazine_issue_thirte/slave-days-in-the-queens-bush-by-geoff-martin-6.html.

McGregor, Deborah. "Mino-Mnaamodzawin: Achieving Indigenous Environmental Justice in Canada." *Environment and Society* 9, no. 1 (2018): 7–24.

McGregor, Deborah. "Traditional Ecological Knowledge and the Two-Row Wampum." *Biodiversity* 3, no. 3 (2002): 8–9.

McIlwain, Charles Howard and Peter Wraxall. *An Abridgement of the Records of Indian Affairs: Contained in Four Folio Volumes, Transacted in the Colony of New York, from the Year 1678 to the Year 1751.* Palala Press, 2016.

Mercer, Tim. "The Two-Row Wampum: Has This Metaphor for Co-Existence Run Its Course?" *Canadian Parliamentary Review* 42, no. 2 (2019). http://www.revparlcan.ca/en/the-two-row-wampum-has-this-metaphor-for-co-existence-run-its-course/.

Mohawk, Sotsisowah John. *Basic Call to Consciousness.* Akwesasne Notes, 1977. Reprinted by Summertown, TN: Book Publishing Co, 2005.

Mohawk, Sotsisowah John. "The Indian Way is a Thinking Tradition." *Northeast Indian Quarterly* 4, no. 4 (Winter 1987): 13–17.

Mohawk, Sotsisowah John C. *John Arthur Gibson and J.N.B. Hewitt's Myth of the Earthgrasper.* Buffalo, NY: Mohawk Publications, 2005.

Mohawk, Sotsisowah John. "The Warriors Who Turned to Peace." *Yes! Magazine,* November 2004. https://www.yesmagazine.org/issues/healing-resistance/.

Mohawk, Sotsisowah John. "What Can We Learn from Native America About War and Peace?: The Progressive Pragmatism of the Iroquois Confederacy." *Lapis Magazine Online*, n.d. http://arnieegel.blogspot.com.

Monture, Rick. *Teionkwakhashion Tsi Niionkwariho:Ten: We Share Our Matters, Two Centuries of Writing and Resistance at Six Nations of the Grand River*. Winnipeg: University of Manitoba Press, 2014.

Morgan, Alun David. "Journeys into Transformation: Travel to an 'Other' Place as a Vehicle for Transformative Learning." *Journal of Transformative Education* 8, no. 4 (2010): 246–68.

Mugalhães, Marina. "Technologies of the Body: a Pecha Kucha Talk by Marina Magalhães." Lecture presented at the LA as Lab Conference, Claremont Graduate University, May 4, 2019. https://vimeo.com/338387303.

Muller, Kathryn V. "The Two 'Mystery' Belts of Grand River: A Biography of the Two Row Wampum and the Friendship Belt." *American Indian Quarterly* (2007): 129–64.

Newhouse, David. "From the Tribal to the Modern: The Development of Modern Aboriginal Societies." In *Expressions in Canadian Native Studies*, edited by Ron F. Laliberte et al., 395–409. Saskatoon: University of Saskatchewan Extension Press, 2000.

Newhouse, David. "Debwewin: To Speak the Truth – Nishabek de'bwewin: Telling Our Truths." *Academic Matters: OCUFA's Journal of Higher Education* (Fall 2018): 13–17.

O'Brien, Susie. "Survival Strategies for Global Times: The Desert Walk for Biodiversity, Health and Heritage." *Interventions* 9, no. 1 (2007): 83–98.

Parmenter, Jon. "The Meaning of Kaswentha and the Two Row Wampum Belt in Haudenosaunee (Iroquois) History: Can Indigenous Oral Tradition be Reconciled with the Documentary Record?" *Journal of Early American History* 3 (2013): 82–109.

Ransom, James W. and Kreg T. Ettenger. "'Polishing the Kaswentha': A Haudenosaunee View of Environmental Cooperation." *Environmental Science & Policy* 4, no. 4–5 (2001): 219–28.

Rawls, John. *A Theory of Justice: Revised Edition*. Cambridge, MA: Harvard University Press, 1999.

Rickard, Jolene. "Visualizing Sovereignty in the Time of Biometric Sensors." *South Atlantic Quarterly* 110, no. 2 (2011): 465–86.

Ridgway, Iain D. et al. "New Species Longevity Record for the Northern Quahog (= Hard Clam), Mercenaria Mercenaria." *Journal of Shellfish Research* 30, no. 1 (2011): 35–38.

Robinson, Sandra B. et al. "Growth Rates for Quahogs (Mercenaria mercenaria) in a Reduced Nitrogen Environment in Narragansett Bay, RI." *Northeastern Naturalist* 27, no. 3 (2020): 534–54.

Royal Commission on Aboriginal Peoples. "Report of the Royal Commission on Aboriginal Peoples." *Looking Forward, Looking Back* 1 (1996).

Saul, John Ralston. *A Fair Country: Telling Truths about Canada*. Toronto: Penguin Canada, 2008.

Saul, John Ralston. *The Comeback: How Aboriginals Are Reclaiming Power and Influence*. Toronto: Penguin Random House, 2014.

Saunders, Sabrina E. Redwing and Susan M. Hill. "Native Education and In-Classroom Coalition-Building: Factors and Models in Delivering an Equitous Authentic Education." *Canadian Journal of Education/Revue Canadienne de l'Éducation* (2007): 1015–45.

Scott, David. "That Event, This Memory: Notes on the Anthropology of African Diasporas in the New World." *Diaspora* 1, no. 3 (1991): 261–84.

Seaver, John, ed. *A Narrative of the Life of Mrs. Mary Jemison*. Reprint of 1824 edition. Syracuse University Press, Syracuse, NY: 1990. 59.

Shannon, Timothy J. *Indians and Colonists at the Crossroads of Empire: the Albany Congress of 1754*. NY: Cornell University Press, 2000.

Shell, Marc. *Wampum and the Origins of American Money*. Champaign, Illinois: University of Illinois Press, 2013.

Simcoe, John Graves. *The Correspondence of Lieut. Governor John Graves Simcoe: With Allied Documents Relating to His Administration of the Government of Upper Canada*. 5 Vols. Collected and edited by Brigadier General E.A. Cruikshank. Toronto: Ontario Historical Society, 1923–31.

Simonelli, Richard. "Use the Good Mind! An Interview with Freida Jacques." *Winds of Change* 12, no. 2 (1997): 46–49.

Simpson, Leanne Betasamosake. *As We Have Always Done: Indigenous Freedom Through Radical Resistance*. Minneapolis, MN: U of Minnesota Press, 2017.

Simpson, Leanne. "Looking After Gdoo-naaganinaa: Precolonial Nishnaabeg Diplomatic and Treaty Relationships." *Wicazo Sa Review* 23, no. 2 (2008): 29–42.

Six Nations Polytechnic. "Deyohahá:ge: Indigenous Knowledge Centre 10th Anniversary." YouTube. March 24, 2021. Video, 31:57. https://www.youtube.com/watch?v=EF05-RFNVTU&t=4s.

Smith, Linda Tuhiwai. *Decolonizing Methodologies: Research and Indigenous Peoples*. London: Zed Books Ltd., 2013.

Snyderman, George S. "The Functions of Wampum." *Proceedings of the American Philosophical Society* 98, no. 6 (1954): 469–94.

Social Science and Humanities Research Council. "Guidelines for the Merit Review of Indigenous Research." *Social Science and Humanities Research Council*, 2018. https://www.sshrc-crsh.gc.ca/funding-financement/merit_review-evaluation_du_merite/guidelines_research-lignes_directrices_recherche-eng.aspx.

Solnit, Rebecca. "Finding Time." *Orion Magazine*, 2007.

Solnit, Rebecca. *Wanderlust: A History of Walking*. New York: Penguin, 2001.

Southampton City Council. "Wampum: Stories from the Shells of Native America." *Mayflower 400 Southampton*, 2021. https://mayflower400southampton.co.uk/events-and-workshops/wampum-belt.

Stone, William L. *The Life and Times of Sir William Johnson, Bart*. Albany: J. Munsell, 1865. http://threerivershms.com/SWJ%20vol2ap8.htm.

Taub, Julian. "The Iroquois are Not Giving Up." *The Atlantic*, August 17, 2013. https://www.theatlantic.com/national/archive/2013/08/the-iroquois-are-not-giving-up/278787.

"Thayendanegea" in *Dictionary of Canadian Biography Online*. http://www.biographi.ca/en/bio/thayendanegea_5E.html.

Thomas, Jake. *The Friendship Treaty Belt, the Two Row Wampum Treaty Belt*. Wilsonville, ON: Sandpiper Press, 1978.

Thwaites, Reuben Gold, ed. *The Jesuit Relations and Allied Documents*. Vol. 27. Cleveland: Burrows Brothers Company, 1898.

Toffler, Alvin. *Future Shock*. New York: Bantam Books, 1970.

Trumbull, James Hammond. *Natick Dictionary*. Washington, D.C.: Government Printing Office, 1903. https://archive.org/details/natickdictionar02trumgoog.

Truth and Reconciliation Commission of Canada. "Canada: Calls to Action." *Truth and Reconciliation Commission of Canada*, 2015. http://trc.ca/assets/pdf/Calls_to_Action_English2.pdf

Tuck, Eve, and K. Wayne Yang. "Decolonization is Not a Metaphor." *Decolonization: Indigeneity, Education & Society* 1, no. 1 (2012): 1–40.

"Two Row Wampum: Symbol of Sovereignty; Metaphor for Life." *PBS*. Accessed Sept. 7, 2022. http://www.pbs.org/warrior/content/timeline/hero/wampum.html.

Vachon, Robert. "Guswenta or The Intercultural Imperative." *INTERculture International Journal of Intercultural and Transdisciplinary Research* 27, no. 2. (1995): 8–73.

Vestal, Stanley. *Sitting Bull: Champion of the Sioux: A Biography*. Boston: Houghton Mifflin, 1932.

Victor, Wenona. "Indigenous Justice: Clearing Space and Place for Indigenous Epistemologies." Research Paper for the National Centre for First Nations Governance, December 2007. https://fngovernance.org/wp-content/uploads/2020/09/wenona_victor.pdf.

Walter, Mark D. "Rights and Remedies Within Common Law and Indigenous Legal Traditions: Can the Covenant Chain be Judicially Enforced Today?" In *The Right Relationship: Reimagining the Implementation of Historical Treaties*, edited by John Borrows and Michael Coyle, 187–205. Toronto: University of Toronto Press, 2017.

Watts, Vanessa. "Indigenous Place-Thought and Agency Amongst Humans and Non Humans (First Woman and Sky Woman Go On a European World Tour!)." *Decolonization: Indigeneity, Education & Society* 2, no. 1 (2013): 20–34.

Weaver, Victoria Valerie. "Wampum as Social Practice." Master's thesis, Pennsylvania State University, 2009.

White, Kevin. "Rousing a Curiosity in Hewitt's Iroquois Cosmologies." *Wicazo Sa Review* 28, no. 2 (2013): 87–111.

Williams, Kayanesenh Paul. *Kayanerenkó:wa: the Great Law of Peace*. Winnipeg, University of Manitoba Press, 2018.

Williams, Paul and Curtis Nelson. *Kahswentha*. Royal Commission on Aboriginal Peoples, 1995.
Williams, Robert. *Linking Arms Together: American Indian Treaty Visions of Law and Peace, 1600–1800*. Philadelphia: Routledge, 1999.
Williams, Roger. *A Key into the Language of America*. 1827. Project Gutenberg, 2020. https://www.gutenberg.org/files/63701/63701-h/63701-h.htm.
Wilson, Shawn. *Research is Ceremony: Indigenous Research Methods*. Winnipeg: Fernwood Publishing, 2008.
Wiredu, Kwasi. *Cultural Universals and Particulars–An African Perspective*. Bloomington and Indianapolis: Indiana University Press, 1996.
Zuroski, Eugenia. "This Ship We're In." *The Rambling* 9, August 7, 2020, https://the-rambling.com/2020/08/07/issue9-zuroski/.

# Index

Absolon, Kathleen E, 280n4, 281n1
Adams, Amber Meadow: arguments in *R. v. Montour and White*, 10–11, 161–62; on Covenant Chain tradition and Creation of Turtle Island, 10–14; on Tehontatenentshonteronhtáhkwa and "linking arms together," 261
adoption, legal provisions of (among Haudenosaunee), 161–62
Aglukark, Susan, 195
Akan people and cosmologies, 155–56, 162–66, 277n8
Akwesasne, 43, 247
Algonkian peoples, use of term, 269n1
allies, allyship, 40, 206: contemporary settler-Indigenous relations as, 34, 80n36, 134, 206, 209–11, 213–14, 218–20, 230; in the Covenant Chain-Two Row treaty tradition, 14, 20, 29, 169; European nations failing obligations as 80, 136–38, 140; Haudenosaunee and British as historic, 10, 13, 159; Indigenous and European, 79n33
Amiotte, Arthur, 148
Anthropocene, 53, 62
anthropology and ethnographic gaze, 132, 179
anti-Black racism, 151
Antone, Bob, 173
Antwi, Phanuel, 16
Assembly of First Nations (AFN), 17, 169
Atleo, Shawn, 169

Atsi'tsya'ka:yon (Sky Woman, Mature Blossom), 11, 13, 36, 39–40, 42, 113–14, 248
Awenha'i, 11, 13, 36, 39–40, 42, 113–14, 248

Bailey, Jay, 17, 25, 209–11, 222–23
Bartlett, Cheryl, 112
Battiste, Marie, 126, 129
Beauchamp, William, 88
Black fur traders in Canada, 154–55, 277n7
Blackness: avoided presence of in Canada and entangled with Indigenous life, 150–52, 162, 279n38
Bomberry, Heather, 6
Bourque, Sophie, 10–11, 266n21
Brant, Joseph (Thayendanegea), 78, 78n31, 103, 263, 278n18; and third wife Catherine Croghan (Adonwentishon), 158–59, 161, 247; bought and sold Black enslaved people, 147; central to formation of Upper Canada, 156; owning/adopting Sophia Burthen Pooley, 156–64; prohibiting white dog sacrifice, 142
Brant, Konwatsi'tsiaienni Mary (Molly), 20, 91, 157, 158, 255
Britain: Indigenous cultures of, 19; parliamentary process of and differences with Haudenosaunee procedure, 99
British Crown: abandoned the Two Row in 1800s, 138; arrival

on Turtle Island, 19; ceding Haudenosaunee heartland after War of Independence, 79–80; increasing paternalism to Haudenosaunee, 159; inserted as governing authority over the Covenant Chain, 82, 99, 140; invited into the longhouse, 48–49; prerogative powers of, 69, 69n6; repolishing the chain after Revolutionary War, 159; treaty diplomacy with Indigenous Nations, 68n4, 150, 266n21. *See also* Canada
Brock, Isaac, 158
Brown, Tsiskokon Belanger, 95n72, 263
Bruchac, Margaret M., 179

Caledonia, 24, 190–203, 215–16; land reclamations in, 93n63, 150, 152, 189, 254
Canada: and Euro-Canadian Ship on the Two Row, 137–38, 140–41; assimilationist agenda of, 170; avoidance of Black presence in, 150–51, 162–63, 279n38; banks and trade agenda regarding fossil fuels, 137; Crown-First Nation Gathering, 169–70, 280n7; and the need to decolonize before reconciliation, 143, 230; infringements on Indigenous life in, 96n79, 232; Joint Parliamentary Committee on Indian Affairs, 81; lack of knowledge about Indigenous history and treaties in, 191; legal cases denying validity of treaties, 96n78; legal shifts in Canadian law, 104; limitations of public education system, 172, 231; and the need to heal itself, 145; neglect of the Indigenous pillar, 120; negotiations on fisheries with Wabanaki Nations, 67n1; prerogative powers of, 69, 69n6; recognized and affirmed treaty rights in 1982 constitution, 72–73; rights-and-responsibilities-based policy discussions of, 170–71. *See also* British Crown
Canajoharie, 20, 96, 249
Canesatego, 18–19, 21, 154–55, 249
Carlson, John, 63
Cartier, Jacques, 13, 86
Chain of Linked Arms, 13
Christian missionaries, 32, 80, 139, 142, 144, 219
climate change, 4, 55, 65
Colden, Cadwallader, 79
Coleman, Daniel, 4, 112, 130, 153, 173
Coleman, Will, 4
colonialism: and capitalist harm of Indigenous and Black kin, 17; as catastrophe on Indigenous people and Nations, 32; and imposition of laws, religions, and economies on People of the Canoe, 138, 141; and mischaracterizations and theft of wampum, 52–53, 58; and misinformation of history of, 239; and neoliberalism, 231, 238; as attack on Indigenous cosmologies, 63; damaged relationships under, 3, 146, 235; dating Anthropocene to, 53; failure to fulfill commitments made in wampum agreements, 62; Haudenosaunee Canoe and Euro-Canadian Ship, confusion between, 137; human-centric model of relationship, 237–38; in higher education, 124–25, 174; justified by European nations represented as more advanced, 126; nation-states continuing, 32; rivalry between British and French crowns, 268–69n21; terra nullius phase of, 127; unlearning, mindset of, 231–32; violence and trauma of, 232, 235–36, 238. *See also* settler colonialism

INDEX   *   299

Condolence Ceremony, 76n26, 86, 91, 95, 100n92, 113–19
Cooper, Scot, 24
Corbiere, Alan Ojiig, 21–22, 63
Covenant Chain Wampum: as a treaty recognized in Constitution Act, 266n21; as evolving and deepening, as perpetual, 74n20, 79–82; as metaphor of family relations, 76, 92, 146; Belt, photograph of, 9; British governors, agreement made with, 89–90; collective responsibility toward, 147; collective sky art recreation of, 195–96; duties/responsibilities of both parties, 104–5; formed by record of treaty councils, 92; expanding the, 21; friendship as third component in, 96–97; invoked by Governor General David Johnston, 169; references to Two Row in, 94–95, 140; setting context for the Two Row Wampum, 123, 146; used by Johnson in Niagara Belt for Treaty of Niagara, 21
Covenant Chain–Two Row Wampum Tradition: and American revolt, 20–21; Blackness in the, 153–54, 162–63; akin to British common law, 22; building trust, friendship, and peace, 4, 8, 23, 95, 97n80, 145–47; shaped by Creation story and Peacemaker, 12–13, 30–31; expectations of treaty partners, 46; extensive discussion of, 266n13; and French resistance, 20–21; historical flow of, 10–11; historic spirit in material objects of (ropes and chains), 155; including non-human relations, 23–24, 26, 30; influence of smallpox, tuberculosis, and firearms on, 14; Johnson's Niagara Belt, 21–22; meanings and confusions of the word covenant in, 90, 140; naming of, 10; ongoing influence of, 3, 5, 7, 24–26, 134, 165; predating arrival of Europeans, 9–10; protocols of the tradition throughout colonial era, 18–21, 96–102; reviving and polishing of, 16; separate boats in, 14–15, 140–41, 153;; teaching of cross/bi-cultural living in the, 16–17, 26, 130–31; white rows in, 17, 30, 94–95, 95n72, 138, 171
Covid-19, 7, 25, 35, 214–16
Croghan, Catharine (Adonwentishon), 91–92, 157, 247
Croghan, George, 159, 247
Curler, Arendt Van, 91n63, 249, 255

Daigle, Michelle, 234
Davis, Heather, 53
de Champlain, Samuel, 13, 14, 90n62
decolonization: and dating Anthropocene to colonialism, 53; and the mind, 236–37, 239–40; as program of complete disorder (Fanon), 238; time and, 239; Two Row thinking on, 15; and the university, 127–28, 132–33
De'haën'hiyawǎ"khon' (He Grasps the Sky with Both Hands, good-minded twin), 13–14, 250. *See also* Taharonhyawakon; Twins, creation story
Deloria, Vine, 132–33
Deyohahá:ge:: *Tékeni Teyohà:te* (Mohawk), 9, 14, 250; two roads or paths (Cayuga), 3–4, 250
Deyohahá:ge: Indigenous Knowledge Centre, 6, 250; future vision of, 111, 180–82, 183; hosting Two Row Research Partnership seminars, 130, 223; learning from both the boat and the canoe, 180–82; naming and logo of, 3–4, 5; researchers and directors

of, 9, 168, 181; Two Row Wampum discussions at, 129, 130
Deyohninhohhakarawenh (King Hendrick), 20, 250
disaster, prophecies of, 32–33
Dish with One Spoon agreement, 123–25, 130, 134, 140, 147; old and new formulations of, 128
Doctrine of Discovery, 171
Douglas Creek Estates (Kanohstaton), 6, 24, 125, 150, 189–90, 254
Drew, Benjamin, 156–57
Dundas, 157–58
Dutch (people): arrival on Turtle Island, 18–19; in Canesatego's 1744 speech, 154; Consul General, welcoming Two Row Renewal paddlers, 222–23; diplomacy with Haudenosaunee, 30, 60, 68n4, 150
Dutch West India Company, 154

eastern white pine, 196–97, 205
Ecological Knowledge, 123
edge of the woods, 86, 89n60, 101, 148
Egusheway, 99n89, 251
English language, limitations and differences in, 99
Ermine, Willie, 112, 118
ethic of cooperation, 114, 130

family: and relations in treaty councils, 91; constituted by treaty-making, 88; continuity of (in Haudenosaunee law), 81; everyone as a member, 146; kinship and, 102n99; mutual help according to *Kayanerenkó:wa*, 103; narrow definitions of, 238; nuclear vs. extended, 75n22; obligations and hard work of, 76n25
Fanon, Frantz, 238
Finch, Lance, 83
first contact, 90n62
Fletcher, Benjamin, 18

Flint (bad-minded twin). See O'hā'ă'; Tawiskaron; Twins, creation story
fossil fuels, 137
France: negotiations with Kiotsaeton at Three Rivers, 18, 22, 161, 255; relations with Haudenosaunee, 86, 88
Freeman, Bonnie M., 4, 25, 130–31, 176–77, 235–40

Gae Ho Hwako (Norma Jacobs), 8, 251
ga'nigǫhi:yo:, 175, 251. See also Good Mind
Gaihwyio (Gaiwiio), 142, 169, 178, 251, 261
Ganohkwasra Family Assault Support Services, 214
Gaudry, Adam, 127–28
Geertz, Clifford, 111
General, Deskaheh Levi, 103, 250
General, Sara (Odadrihonyanisoh), 6, 15, 17, 257
Gibson, Skanyataríːyo John Arthur, 40–41, 175–76, 261, 266n11
Gibson, Taylor, 9
Gobler, Christopher, 54
Good Mind: alternate names and spellings of, 251, 253; and value of compassion, 227; in Covenant Chain agreement, 11; and concept of Ganigonhi:oh, 115–16; between Haudenosaunee and neighbours, 145; Indigenous and settler youth reflecting on, 226, 230–31; power of, 34, 45, 110, 113–18, 146, 175; in relationships, 136, 237. See also ga'nigǫhi:yo:; ka'nikòn:ra; kanikohnri:io; ka'nikonrí:yo, ni'nikò:nra
Grand River: communities across, 3, 7–8, 17, 24, 190–93, 201; cross-cultural experiences along, 193–194; healing gifts of, 220; significance to Haudenosaunee and Mississaugas of

the Credit, 223; teachings from both sides of, 194–95
Grand River paddle. *See* Two Row on the Grand Paddle
Grand River Territory, 93, 94, 159, 183, 223. *See also* Haldimand Tract
grandfather of the treaties, 3, 23. *See also* Two Row Wampum Treaty
Great Binding Law. *See* Great Law of Peace
Great Law of Peace (Great Binding Law), 110–11, 113–18, 140, 168, 237, 254; connected to the Two Row Wampum tradition, 171; recitation of, 138, 143; and sovereignty, 117; values and principles of, 227–28; *See also* Kayanerenkó:wa
Griffith, Andrew W., 54
Guswenta: alternate names for, 251, 273n2; and contemporary living, 117; as a frame for a dialogic classroom, 119–20; as ethical space, 17, 24, 109–20. *See also* Two Row Wampum Belt; kaswentha

*Haida Nation v. British Columbia*, 68
Haldimand Tract, 125, 159, 190, 204, 207, 223, 278n7. *See also* Grand River Territory
Haldimand, Frederick, 78n31, 80n37, 159
Hallenbeck, Jessica, 61
Hamilton, city, 150–51, 158
Handsome Lake, 142, 169, 178, 251, 261
Harper, Stephen, 169
Hatt, Samuel, 157–58, 162
Haudenosaunee: creation story, 13, 43–45, 47–48, 74
Haudenosaunee (Hodihnohsó:ni'): adoption ceremony, 160–61; ambiguous relationship to Black enslavement, 277n6; and Two Row obligations of Canada, 138; ceremony and storytelling, 172; 180; cosmology, 75n24, 164, 169, 179, 257, 258; councils and ceremonies, protocols for, 89n60, 96–102; creation story, 13, 36–41, 85, 113–14, 169, 173–76, 184; diplomacy with Dutch, British, and French, 18–20, 60, 72, 86, 91, 138, 150, 171; Elders, 111, 133, 152; environmental law, 50–51; founding of the League, 114; Knowledge Guardians/Keepers, 7, 175, 181, 183, 216, 223, 235; and lacrosse team to 2028 Olympics, 148; language use in this book, 8–9; laws governing relations with colonial powers, 72; as long-standing British allies, 103; name and social organization of longhouse, 146, 252; principles of peace-making, law, diplomacy, and councils, 3, 10–11, 19–20, 99n88; Rotiyanesonh (Chiefs), 6, 14, 18, 21, 31, 81, 88; sovereignty, 14–15, 70n7, 103, 148, 171, 184, 223; Yakoyaneshon (Clan Mothers), 6, 31, 265
He Grasps the Sky with Both Hands (good-minded twin). *See* De'haĕn'hiyawă"khon'; Taharonhyawakon; Twins, Creation story
Henderson, James Youngblood Sa'ke'j, 126
Hendricks, Marcus, 56
Hewitt, Jeffrey G., 58
Hewitt, J.N.B, 40–41, 51, 175, 179–80, 259
Hiawatha, 114, 253, 271n6
Hiawatha Belt, 94n69, 201
Hill, Karen, 4
Hill, Richard (Rick), 15, 29, 123, 129, 130, 166; on Peacemaker and the Two Row tradition, 12–13, 171, 173; on relations between African Americans and Haudenosaunee, 153, 154; on story of the Peacemaker

in Two Row tradition, 12–13; on the Dish with One Spoon agreement, 123
Hill, Susan M., 129, 179
Hill, Tanis, 6
Honor the Two Row Paddle (New York), 25. *See also* Two Row Wampum Renewal Campaign
Hudson Bay Company, 154

Idle No More, 169
Indian Act, 16, 138
Indian Affairs, 20, 81, 91, 91n64, 139, 143, 157, 267n30
Indian and Northern Affairs Canada, 170
Indian Residential Schools (IRS), 6, 16, 68n3, 111, 147, 219
Indian Residential Schools Settlement Agreement, 144
Indigeneity: and Blackness, 151–52
Indigenization, 122, 124, 127–29, 133–34
Indigenous Knowledge, 4, 54, 112, 124, 130, 134
Indigenous Nations: and land claims, 125; and language revitalization, 175; and legal systems in Canada, 69–70, 70n7; and material culture in museums, 132; and sovereignty, 32, 56, 58, 61, 68n3, 125, 151–52; title and rights, infringement of, 83n42
Indigenous People: and resilience, 58–59; and tokenization, 128–29; assimilation efforts regarding, 127, 170; dispossession of, 151; Elders, 111, 133, 152; in the academy, 141, 174–75; joy, the loss of, 142; struggles interconnected with Black struggles, 152
Indigenous world views: conceptions of justice, 53–54, 59–66, 221–22; cosmologies, 75n24, 130, 155–56, 164–65; origin stories as place-based not "myth," 130; understandings of family, 238–39
Indigenous-based research, 127–28, 130, 167, 175

Jacobs, Beverly, 62
Jacobs, Wilbur R., 63–64
Jamieson, Rebecca, 4
Jemison, Mary, 161
Joagquisho (Oren Lyons), 3, 23, 29, 33, 95, 253
Johnson, Ima, 4
Johnson, William (Warraghyhagey): and the Covenant Chain, 22, 93, 96, 267n30; biographical details, 91–92, 157, 264; clan-based Scottish paternity of, 101n96; dying words to Joseph Brant, 157; fluent in Haudenosaunee culture, 90–91, 93; Niagara Belt and the creation of, 21–22; ship and canoe on personal seal, 94n70; speech to Mohawk leaders, 20–21
Johnston, David, 169
Joseph, Ellie, 17, 24–25, 206–11, 222–23
Justice, Daniel Heath, 133

Kahnawake, 102n101, 136, 138, 253
ka'nikòn:ra, 11–12, 36, 40–45, 51, 101, 253, 261. *See also* Good Mind
ka'nikonrí:yo: 60, 251, 253. *See also* Good Mind
kanikohnri:io, 101, 251, 253. *See also* Good Mind
Kanohstaton (Douglas Creek Estates), 6, 24, 125, 150, 189–90, 254
kaswentha: agreements more than "laws" or "treaties," 265n5; Circle Wampum (Teyonnityohkwanhakstha), 12, 88, 262; false equivalence of wampum as currency/money, 63; harvesting and carving of, 56–59,

61; holding and making the ancient truth-teller, wunnáumwash, 23, 26, 52–66; in Kiotseaeton's 1645 peace diplomacy, 86–87; mischaracterizations and theft of, 52–53, 58–59, 63; names and meanings across Turtle Island, 60; in negotiations between Haudenosaunee and Dutch, British, 18–19; new belt of (2020), 58–59; and use in Niagara Belt, 21–22; and power to hold memory, 62, 278n11; recovering wampum belts, 143; relationality, kinship, and connection with, 55, 234; reviewing the meanings of, 23, 98n86; as the name of the Tékeni Teyohà:te, 265n5; wampum-based approaches in universities, 128. *See also* Two Row Wampum Belt; Guswenta
Kayadosseras, fraudulent land patents in, 96, 254
Kayanerenhtserakó:wa, 38
Kayanerenkó:wa, 13, 82n40, 93, 103; alternate names and spellings of, 254; and treaties with newcomers, 69; as environmental constitutional law, 74n21; as law about relations, 85–86; consensus at core of, 38, 99, 103n103; embodied in Two Row Wampum, 60; making everyone into relatives, 75, 75n24; peace, power, and good mind, principles of, 84; seminal moment as the act of compassion, 76. *See also* Great Law of Peace
Kinzua Dam, protests against, 136
Kiotsaeton (Kiotseaeton), 18, 22, 86–87, 161, 254
Kuokkanen, Rauna, 124

land acknowledgement, 109, 121–22
land protectors, 152

land reclamations in the Haldimand Tract, 6, 24, 125, 150, 152, 163, 189–90, 254
land, conceptions of, 123, 165
language loss and revitalization, 170, 174, 178, 180
Leonard, Kelsey, 23, 278n11
Lickers, Glenn, 199
linked arms: between the Haudenosaunee and British, 18; Haudenosaunee model of, 7, 13, 17; in the Haudenosaunee Longhouse of Nations, 19; evolving story of the linked arms, 21; wampum image of, 21, 161–62. *See also* Covenant Chain Wampum
Longboat, Deskaheh Harvey, 95, 250
Lorenz, Danielle, 127–28
Lyons, Oren (Joagquisho), 3, 23, 29, 33, 95, 252

Macdonald, John A., 139
MacIntyre, Alasdair C., 59
Mann, Barbara Alice, 161
Manuel, Arthur, 170
Maracle, Ken, 22
Marshall, Murdena, 112
Martin-Hill, Dawn, 4, 179, 273n26, 274n30
Mature Blossom, Sky Woman, 11, 13, 36, 39–40, 42, 113–14, 248
McCarthy, Theresa, 179
McGregor, Deborah, 59, 271n18, 271n21, 272n33
McLean, David, 199
McMaster University, 6–7, 130, 150, 223; housing OPP officers, 125, 150–51; partnership agreement with Six Nations Polytechnic, 121–22; partnership in Deyohahá:ge: and TRRP, 4, 130, 223
Mercer, Tim, 119
Mi'kmaw Ethics Watch, 112

Middle Passage, 16, 154
Miller, Marc, 91n64
Miller, Suzie, 24
missionaries (Catholic and Protestant), 32, 80, 139, 142, 144, 219
Mohawk, Sotsisowah John, 72, 75n24, 81, 82n40, 85, 98, 261
Monture, Rick, 4, 176, 179, 262
Morgan, Alun David, 222
Mother Earth: in Akan cosmology, 165–66; in Haudenosaunee cosmology, 75n24; human connections to, 43, 216, 244; in Jake Thomas's oration of the Two Row, 14, 166; injuries to, 33; wampum connecting humans to, 55–56. *See also* Thanksgiving Address
multicultural society, living well together in, 113, 119–20, 147, 266n21
Myers, Mike, 15

narrative community practice, 203
National Museum of the American Indian, 131
Neighbouring Communities Project, 190, 280n1
New France, 20, 91n63, 264, 267n29
Newhouse, David, 17, 24
Newhouse, Dayodekane Seth, 41, 110, 249
Niagara Belt, 22. *See also* Treaty of Niagara
ni'nikò:nra, 43, 253
Norma Jacobs (Gae Ho Hwako), 8, 251

Odadrihonyanisoh (Sara General), 6, 15, 17, 257
O'hā'ă' (Flint, bad-minded twin) 13–14, 257. *See also* Tawiskaron; Twins, creation story
Ohenton Karihwatehkwen, (the Words Before All Else), 95, 97, 217, 257
Oka Crisis, 46, 93n68, 95, 250
Onkwehonwe, 16, 176–77, 223, 257

Ontario Education Act, 139
Ontario Provincial Police (OPP), 125, 189, 193, 199
Ownership, Control, Access, and Possession (OCAP), 112
oyenkwaon:we (sacred tobacco), 39, 99, 210, 215–16, 259

Paolo Andreani, 139
peace, friendship, and respect: between Black and Haudenosaunee people, 150, 151, 154, 164; within ethical framework, 114, 166; Haudenosaunee negotiating with Dutch and British for, 154, 159; along the Grand River, 223; in Pen Pal Travelling Art Exhibit, 200; symbolized by three white rows of wampum, 15, 60, 123; treaties defining how to live in, 191; in treaty after Revolutionary War, 159; negotiations, 171; during the Two Row on the Grand Paddle, 211, 219, 227, 229; and the Two Row Wampum, 123, 125, 131–32, 150, 171, 182, 209, 222, 233
Peacemaker, establishing *Kayanerenkó:wa*, the "Great Law of Peace," 13, 31, 82n40, 114, 168, 175–76
Pen Pal Project: creating collective documents, 195–98; exchange of yo-yos and friendship bracelets in, 193–94, 199; explanation of, 24, 190–92, 283nn4–6; images of, 194, 196–99, 201, 205; Travelling Art Exhibit, 200–202
Penner Commission, 15
People/people, use of capitalization, 267n1
police, 6, 102n101, 141, 147, 150–51, 189. *See also* Ontario Provincial Police
Polishing, act of, 26, 62, 64, 140; and Canestago, 154; the Covenant Chain

and Two Row Wampum, 23, 55, 65, 119, 204, 206, 223; and Pen Pal Project, 24; following Revolutionary War, 159; and wampum (quohog), 6, 23, 55
Pontiac, Chief, 21
Pooley, Robert, 156, 164, 166
Pooley, Sophia Burthen, 156–64

quahog: as alive and polishing the chain, 23–24; as alive, filtering water, polishing the chain, 23–24; as ancient mollusc relative of humans, 52; as first food for Algonkian peoples, 56; filtering and purifying water, 63; misapplied Latin name *(Mercenaria mercenaria)*, 63; photograph of harvest, 57; Poquaûhock or "hard clam," 259. *See also* wampum (kaswentha)
Queen's Bush, 164, 279n39

*R. v. Donald Marshall*, 67n1, 73–74
*R. v. Montour and White*, 10–11, 161
racial capitalism, 16, 151, 166
racism and racial superiority, 146, 238
Ramirez, Margaret Marietta, 234
reciprocity, 101–2, 102nn97–98, 103, 152
reconciliation: and infringement of Aboriginal rights and titles, 83n42; challenges to, 141; definitions of, 68n3; for Indigenous people and for settler people, 236; initiatives between non/Indigenous communities, 189–205, 206–20, 221–24; as locally and culturally informed thinking, 134; as people-to-people movement, 147, 236; and requirement to give land back, 145; between the rows of Two Row wampum belt, 145–49; supported by Two Row Wampum teachings, 142–45, 223–24; treaty-making as important stage in, 88n55; in the university, 126–27; and waiving future Indigenous rights, 145
Residential Schools (IRS), 6, 16, 68n3, 111, 147, 219
respect, politics of, 112
retraditionalization, as central force shaping Indigenous societies, 110
Rickard, Jolene, 131
Royal Commission on Aboriginal Peoples, 266n13, 271n28
Royal Proclamation (1763), 77n29, 78n31, 79n34, 96n76, 157

Sadakanahtie, 18
salvage ethnography and ethnographic gaze, 132, 179
Saul, John Ralston, 120
Saunders, Sabrina E., 129
Schreyer, Edward, 153
Scott, Duncan Campbell, 143
settler colonialism: and harm to Black and Indigenous kin, 17; conditions produced by, 126; as based on Euro-American values, laws, interests, 68, 151; and notion of Indigenous Peoples as not "modern," 126; and pathologization of Indigenous Peoples, 126, 151; as supertanker not sailing vessel, 14; *See also* colonialism; white settler colonialism
Seven Years War (1756–63), 21
Shell, Marc, 63
Shinnecock, 52, 55, 57, 260
Shonkwaia'tishon ("The Creator"), 15–16, 260
Silver Chain, 19, 20, 74n20, 76, 92, 140. *See also* Covenant Chain
Simcoe, John Graves, 160
Simpson, Leanne Betasamosake, 234, 270n13, 282nn22–23
Sitting Bull, 136

Six Nations Economic Development Trust Fund, 214
Six Nations Health Services, 213
Six Nations of the Grand River, 110–11, 168; community organizations at, 213–14; Deyohahá:ge: Indigenous Knowledge Centre at, 4, 181; land reclamations, 24, 93n63, 125, 150, 189, 254; support for the Two Row on the Grand Paddle, 213–14, 222; water issues and water politics, 149, 232, 276n7
Six Nations Polytechnic, 4, 121, 168, 173, 265n2, 274n2
Six Nations Polytechnic Partnership Belt, 121–22
sixties scoop, 16
Sky Woman, Mature Blossom, 11, 13, 36, 39–40, 42, 113–14, 248. *See also* Atsi'tsya'ka:yon
Skye, Hubert, 4
Skye, Lottie, 4
Skyworld, *see also* Sky Woman, 175, 178–79, 184, 248
slavery, institution of, 16, 154–55, 277n6
Smith, Linda Tuhiwai, 132, 275n8, 275n23
St. Lawrence River (Ken'tarókwen), 13, 86, 136, 255
Staats, Linda, 4
Stoney Creek Battlefield House Museum and Park, 197
Story of the Fatherless Boy, 169, 175
Supreme Court of Canada, 70, 72, 73–74, 73n17
Swift, Anuva, 200

Taharonhyawakon, 43–44, 46–50, 94, 261. *See also*: Twins, creation story; De'haĕn'hiyawă"khon' (He Grasps the Sky with Both Hands)
Tawiskaron (Flint, bad-minded twin), 43–44, 46–50, 94, 262. *See also* O'hă'ă'; Twins, creation story

Tehontatenentshonteronhtáhkwa, 9–12, 17, 35–38, 46, 48–51, 161–62, 261. *See also* Covenant Chain Wampum
Tekéni Teyohà: ke Kahswénhta, 14, 131, 221–24, 226, 229–30, 234–35, 262. *See also* Two Row Wampum Belt; Deyohahá:ge:
Tékeni Teyohà:te Kaswenta, 9–10, 14, 51, 110, 123, 126, 262, 266n13. *See also* Deyohahá:ge:
Thanksgiving Address, 31, 75, 95, 109, 117, 119, 211, 215–17, 235; in glossary, 251, 258. *See also* Mother Earth
Thomas, Jacob (Jake), 110–11; Hadajigre:ta' ("Descending Cloud") Cayuga name, 111, 252; Two Row account, 15, 129, 152, 153, 172
Tiyanoga Hendrick Peters ("King Hendrick"), 77–78, 92
Todd, Zoe, 53
transatlantic slave trade, 49, 154
treaties. *See also* wampum justice: "as the Indians would have understood them," 69–71, 104–5; beginning in the cord blood, 49; as centring on relationality over rights, 30, 171; and common phrase, "as long as," 29, 30, 78–79, 166; as defining rights and obligations for both parties, 68n3, 170, 191; as different from rest of Canadian law, 69; as "the hinge between nations," 67; as always inclusive of all life, 30; as ongoing agreements not historical documents, 68, 72–73, 76; and rights, 70n8; as stories, 51; denied as law of the land, 136; Europeans adapting to Indigenous approaches, 266–67n21; governmental efforts to minimize, 67; Mohawk treaty phrase (Tehontatenentshonteronhtahkwa), 262
Treaty of Fort Stanwix (1768 and 1784), 97n81

Treaty of Lancaster (1744), 18
Treaty of Niagara (1764), 21, 79, 94n71, 100, 267n27; and Niagara Belt replica of Covenant Chain Wampum, 21–22
TRED Talks, 216
Tree of Peace, 13, 88, 94n70, 196, 288
Trent University, 110–11
Trumbull, James Hammond, 59
Truth and Reconciliation Commission of Canada (TRC), 68n3, 71n10, 221, 282n26; Calls to Action in higher education, 125, 128; moving beyond "calls to action," 33
Tuck, Eve, 234
Tuscaroras, defending land against Niagara Project, 136
Tuscaroras, joining Haudenosaunee, 13
Twins, creation story, 4, 11, 13, 43–44, 49, 102. See also De'haĕn'hiyawǎ"khon' (He Grasps the Sky with Both Hands); O'hā'ǎ' (Flint), Taharonhyawakon; Tawiskaron
Two Row on the Grand Paddle, 17, 24–25, 145, 206–20, 221–40; Covid-19 adaptations during, 214–16; creation of environmental connections, 230–32; daily routine of, 211–13; expressions of gratitude for, 217–19, 236; images of, 207, 210, 212, 215, 218, 220; Indigenous and settler youth experiences on, 224–34; lessons from the river, 232–33, 240; teaching interdependence, 236, 239
Two Row Research Partnership (TRRP), 6, 7, 130, 223–24
Two Row Wampum Belt, 70n7, 94n71; alternate names, 262, 273n2; between the rows of, 16–17, 117–18, 172; and considerations of the Middle Passage, 15–16, 150; expanding the scope of, 147–48; as foundational treaty, 16–17, 61, 89, 112–13, 123, 136, 167, 206; grandfather of the treaties, 3, 23; grounded by Covenant Chain wampum, 123; imagery of, 167, 171–72, 183, 191, 237; expression of Guswenta/kaswentha in, 24, 26, 117–18; including non-human relations, 177; non-European governments (not) in, 147, 172, 173, 203, 237; as non-binary, 237; as peace-building efforts, 176, 204; photograph of, 9; power imbalances, 141–146; principles of peace, friendship, and respect, 126, 131, 171, 176, 226, 229, 233, 239; as oral narrative, 138, 140, 153; and reconciliation, 223–24; as research methodology or theoretical framework, 167–68, 234; as sacred as story of separation or unity, 15–16, 137–38; and ship of academic knowledge, 124, 126, 134, 174; sky art recreation of, 197; and sovereignty, 112–13, 124; symbolism of three white rows, 15–17, 30, 94–95, 95n72, 138, 171, 173, 184, 237, 240; terms of relationality, 60, 128–29, 151–52, 177, 204, 226, 237; treaty agreement, 124, 134, 172–73, 204; youth engagement in and learning about the, 221. See also Guswenta Space; kaswentha
Two Row Wampum Renewal Campaign, 119, 145, 206–9, 222–23, 241, 271n26, 272n32. See also Honor the Two Row Paddle (New York)
Tyendinaga, 138, 243, 263

United Nations: and Two Row Wampum Renewal Campaign, 208, 223; Declaration on the Rights of Indigenous Peoples (UNDRIP), 137, 148, 265n1; International Day of the World's Indigenous Peoples, 208, 223; Sotsisowah's speech to, 75n24

United States: as Haudenosaunee heartland after War of Independence, 79–80; assumed beginning of history in 1776, 92, 92n65; fraudulent land titles upheld by courts, 96; long exposure of "founding fathers" to Haudenosaunee law, 92, 92n66; relations with Haudenosaunee, 97n81; settler-colonial nation based on Two Row treaty, 61; Trump administration, dealings of, 77
United States Supreme Court, 70, 71, 82
Utility, Self-Voicing, Access, Inter-Relationality (USAI), 112

Vachon, Robert, 119
van Katwyk, Trish, 25, 130, 131, 235–40

Wabanaki Nations/Confederacy, 22, 67n1, 69, 97n80
Wampum justice, 53–54, 59–62, 63–66; distinctions between Westphalian logics and, 63–64

wampum. *See* kaswentha
War of 1812, 103, 158, 281n7
Watts, Vanessa, 15, 53, 63
Wet'su'weten, 125
Wheatley, Fred, 110
white dog sacrifice, 142
White, Kevin, 179
white-settler colonialism, 151, 160, 164. *See also* settler colonialism
Williams, Kayanesenh Paul, 10, 19, 266n13
Williams, Robert, 112, 266n21
Williams, Roger, 59
Wilson, Shawn, 127
Wiredu, Kwasi, 155–56
wunnáumwash ("speaks the truth"), 59, 264, 277n11

Yang, K. Wayne, 234
Yotsi'tsishon, 11, 13, 36, 39–40, 42, 110–11, 113–14, 168, 248

Zuroski, Eugenia, 132

Books in the Indigenous Imaginings series
Published by Wilfrid Laurier University Press

*Deyohahá:ge:: Sharing the River of Life*
Daniel Coleman, Ki'en Debicki, and Bonnie M. Freeman, editors
2025 / xxii + 310 pp. / 978-1-77112-647-2